David Hume's *History of England*

Edited for the Modern Reader

Volume 5, 1603-1649

David Hume's *History of England*

Edited for the Modern Reader

Volume 5, 1603-1649

Edited by William W. Berry

CreateSpace

Editor's Preface

Of all the great philosophers, David Hume is the only one who turned his hand to a large-scale history. That fact in itself might well commend Hume's six-volume *History of England* to us; it did to me.

When I looked into it, I was immediately struck by two things: it is undoubtedly a great work of history, marked by extraordinary power of thought and felicity of expression, but it is also marred throughout, for the contemporary reader, by a massive encrustation of archaic style. Archaic spellings constantly interrupt flow. Archaic punctuation produces at best a constant buzzing irritation, at worst a genuine impediment to understanding. Obsolete renderings of the names of persons and places often make it difficult to tell at a glance who or what is being described and sometimes produce complete bafflement, followed by a long journey through an encyclopedia. Archaic words, completely gone from the language, impel resort to a good, and preferably old, dictionary. Archaic senses of still used words set a more subtle trap for the reader: all the words in a sentence apparently can be read, but the sentence's meaning is not understood. Archaic idioms produce puzzlement; old-fashioned syntax can interfere with understanding and induce fatigue.

I was disquieted after that first look at Hume's *History*. I was then engaged in planning the high school home school reading list of one of my sons, Richard. We both wanted his curriculum to include as many great books, as opposed to routine textbooks, as possible, and we were sorely tempted to include volumes five and six of the Hume as one of the main components of the British history course. But in their original state? I could read them only with difficulty; surely a teenager would find them far more frustrating than illuminating.

I had worked for some years as a book copyeditor, and I knew something of seventeenth-century British history. So in the do-it-yourself spirit that home schooling both requires and inspires (and underestimating by at least an order of magnitude the amount of work involved), I resolved to edit volumes five and six of Hume's *History* to modern standards of style.

As the project proceeded, Richard and I were delighted with the result: a remarkable work was revealed as those encrustations were scraped away. As we discussed Hume's *History* in some detail, it became clear to us that the work had great merit and interest on three different levels.

On the first and most basic level, that of recounting a narrative of events, Hume's strong, genial hand unfailingly shapes a huge and sprawling mass of events into an understandable but never oversimplified narrative. Full mastery of the art of writing is exhibited at all levels, from the smallest anecdote to the largest thematic sweep. His style, at the same time vigorous and elegant, is a constant pleasure. Frequent flashes of wit add to both the fun and the wisdom.

On the second level, Hume, always the philosopher, uses his narrative of English events as an example of how he thinks history should be written, and thus his philosophy of history is embedded in it. That philosophy, consistent with the views set forth in his *Treatise of Human Nature*, gives primacy in human affairs to passions and beliefs, the stuff of the mind. To Hume, great social and political changes occur first in "the minds of men," and only later play out in the great events on the public stage.

Finally, on the third level, the book is so woven through with a view for the patterns of human conduct, so dense with sagacious comments on the ways things work among people, that it is also a great work of social and political philosophy. The narrative history can be seen as a series of case studies of the more explicit statements of social and political philosophy that Hume makes in the *Treatise* and the *Essays Moral and Political*. As just one important example of these, it becomes clear to a reader of the *History* that there is for Hume no one best form of government that can be discovered by reason and established among all people in all times. A good government is one that fits a particular people as they are, and thus conduces toward their happiness. A government that uses abstract philosophy to create a plan of administration, which it then imposes on the people, is likely to lead to general unhappiness, and thus for Hume is a species of bad government. Interestingly, the latter approach—designing plans of government by abstract reasoning—has been followed by almost all Enlightenment-inspired political philosophies. Considering the many failures that have resulted from those plans, there is perhaps significant value for us today in revisiting Hume's quite different, but also Enlightenment-inspired, approach.

Given all this, Hume's *History* cannot be adequately replaced by a routine contemporary retelling of the chronology, and it should not be allowed to die merely because the language Hume used has now gone obsolete.

After we finished our study of Hume's *History*, Richard and I thought that it would be good if we could offer our modernized version to other home schoolers and general readers. Fortunately, the advent of do-it-yourself publishing, utilizing the new technologies of print-on-demand books and e-readers, has enabled us to do just that. We hope you enjoy the result as much as we have.

Notes on the text:

• The goal of this project is not to rewrite Hume but to reveal him. I have striven to edit only style, not substance, and to preserve as much of Hume's style as is consistent with modern standards of readability. Hume has not been fact checked or bowdlerized.

• This volume is not intended as an abridgement of Hume's *History*; it contains the full narrative history of Hume's volume five. However, Hume's footnotes have been omitted, since the modern general reader has little or no interest in knowing precisely where Hume gathered any particular fact or in the details of disputes among historians of Hume's day. A few pieces of narrative material of high interest that appeared in the notes in some editions during Hume's lifetime have been retained and moved into the running text. The last three paragraphs of chapter 49 and the third and fourth to last paragraphs of chapter 59 have been omitted as uninteresting catalogs of officeholders during the reigns of the kings. Also omitted is the "Appendix to the Reign of James I," which is separate from the narrative history and consists of such things as lengthy lists of the prices of goods and Hume's quirky opinions of the relative merits of various writers active during the reign.

• Archaic terms that appear in quotations or are terms of art have been retained; explanations of the meanings of many such terms have been provided in square brackets.

• Topic phrases that were printed in the margins in Hume's editions have been rendered as subheads.

• Dates that were printed in the margins in Hume's editions have been run into the text at appropriate locations. All dates are per Hume.

Thanks are offered to the Liberty Fund and its Online Library of Liberty website, which contains the complete six-volume Hume *History*; their fine edition of volume five, which I consulted frequently during this project, may be found at http://oll.libertyfund.org/index.php?option=com_staticxt&staticfile=show.php%3Ftitle=792&layout=html.

Thanks are offered to the compilers and publishers of the 1913 and 1828 Webster's dictionaries on the website of the ARTFL Project, which were my constant companions during this project and which may be found at http://machaut.uchicago.edu/websters.

Thanks are offered to Google and to Wikipedia for their aid in researching modern renderings of names of seventeenth-century people and places.

Finally, thanks and love to my son Richard, without whom this project would not have been started, and without whose help it could not have been completed.

William W. Berry
July 2013
Norcross, Georgia

CONTENTS

CHAPTER 45
1603 – 1604

*Introduction – James's first transactions – State of
Europe – Rosny's negotiations – Raleigh's conspiracy –
Hampton Court conference – A Parliament –
Peace with Spain*

Introduction

THE Crown of England was never transmitted from father to son with greater tranquility than it passed
from the family of Tudor to that of Stuart. During the whole reign of
Elizabeth, the eyes of men had been employed in search of her successor; and when old age made the prospect of her death more immediate, there appeared none but the king of Scots who could advance any
just claim or pretension to the throne. He was great-grandson of Margaret, elder daughter of Henry VII; and on the failure of the male line,
his hereditary right remained unquestionable. If the religion of Mary,
queen of Scots, and the other prejudices contracted against her had
formed any considerable obstacle to her succession, these objections,
being entirely personal, had no place with regard to her son. Men also
considered that though the title derived from blood had been frequently violated since the Norman Conquest, such licenses had proceeded more from force or intrigue than from any deliberate maxims
of government. The lineal heir had still in the end prevailed; and both
his exclusion and restoration had been commonly attended with such
convulsions as were sufficient to warn all prudent men not lightly to
give way to such irregularities. If the will of Henry VIII, authorized by
act of Parliament, had tacitly excluded the Scottish line, the tyranny
and caprices of that monarch had been so signal that a settlement of

1603

1

this nature, unsupported by any just reason, had no authority with the people. Queen Elizabeth too, with her dying breath, had recognized the undoubted title of her kinsman James; and the whole nation seemed to dispose themselves with joy and pleasure for his reception. Though James had been born and educated amidst a foreign and hostile people, men hoped, from his character of moderation and wisdom, that he would embrace the maxims of an English monarch; and the prudent foresaw greater advantages resulting from a union with Scotland than disadvantages from submitting to a prince of that nation. The alacrity with which the English looked towards the successor had appeared so evident to Elizabeth that, concurring with other causes, it affected her with the deepest melancholy. That wise princess, whose penetration and experience had given her the greatest insight into human affairs, had not yet sufficiently weighed the ingratitude of courtiers and the levity of the people.

James's first transactions

As victory abroad and tranquility at home had attended Elizabeth, she left the nation in such flourishing circumstances that her successor possessed every advantage except that of comparison with her illustrious name when he mounted the throne of England. The king's journey from Edinburgh to London immediately afforded to the inquisitive some circumstances of comparison, which even the natural partiality in favor of their new sovereign could not interpret to his advantage. As he passed along, all ranks of men flocked about him from every quarter, allured by interest or curiosity. Great were the rejoicings and loud and hearty the acclamations which resounded from all sides; and everyone could remember how the affability and popular manners of their queen displayed themselves amidst such concourse and exultation of her subjects. But James, though sociable and familiar with his friends and courtiers, hated the bustle of a mixed multitude; and though far from disliking flattery, yet was he still fonder of tranquility and ease. He issued, therefore, a proclamation forbidding this throng of people on pretense of the scarcity of provisions and other inconveniences which, he said, would necessarily attend it.

He was not, however, unaware of the great flow of affection which appeared in his new subjects; and being himself of an affectionate temper, he seems to have been in haste to make them some return of kindness and good offices. To this motive, probably, we are to ascribe that profusion of titles which was observed in the beginning of his reign; in the six weeks after his entrance into the kingdom, he is computed to have bestowed knighthood on no less than 237 persons. If Elizabeth's frugality of honors—which was as great as that of money—had formerly been complained of, it began now to be valued and esteemed. And everyone perceived that the king, by his lavish and premature conferring of favors, had failed to oblige the persons on whom he bestowed them. Titles of all kinds became so common that they were scarcely marks of distinction; and being distributed without choice or deliberation to persons unknown to the prince, they were regarded more as proofs of pliancy and good nature than of any determined friendship or esteem. A pasquinade [lampoon] was affixed to St. Paul's in which an art in retaining the names of the new nobility—very necessary to assist frail memories—was promised to be taught.

We may presume that the English would have thrown less blame on the king's ease in bestowing favors had these been confined entirely to their own nation and had not been shared out in too unequal proportions to his old subjects. James, who through his whole reign was more guided by temper and inclination than by the rules of political prudence, had brought with him great numbers of his Scottish courtiers, whose impatience and importunity were apt in many particulars to impose on the easy nature of their master and extort favors of which, it is natural to imagine, his English subjects would loudly complain. The Duke of Lennox, the Earl of Mar, Lord Home, Lord Kinloss, Sir George Home, and Secretary Elphinstone were immediately added to the English Privy Council. Sir George Home, whom he created Earl of Dunbar, was his declared favorite as long as that nobleman lived and was one of the wisest and most virtuous, though the least powerful, of all those whom the king ever honored with that distinction. Some time later, Hay was created Viscount Doncaster, then Earl of Carlisle, and got an immense fortune from the Crown, all of which he spent in a splendid and courtly manner. Ramsay obtained the title of Earl of Holderness; and many others, being raised suddenly to the highest elevation, increased by their insolence that envy which naturally attended them as strangers and ancient enemies.

In justice to James, however, it must be acknowledged that he left almost all the chief offices in the hands of Elizabeth's ministers and trusted the conduct of political concerns, both foreign and domestic, to his English subjects. Among these, Secretary Cecil—created successively Lord Essendon, Viscount Cranborne, and Earl of Salisbury—was always regarded as his prime minister and chief counselor. Though the capacity and penetration of this minister were sufficiently known, his favor with the king created surprise on the accession of that monarch. The secret correspondence into which he had entered with James, and which had substantially contributed to the easy reception of that prince in England, laid the foundation of Cecil's credit; and while all his former associates—Sir Walter Raleigh, Lord Grey, and Lord Cobham—were disfavored on account of their animosity against Essex as well as for other reasons, this minister was continued in employment and treated with the greatest confidence and regard.

The capacity of James and his ministers in negotiation was immediately put to trial on the appearance of ambassadors from almost all the princes and states of Europe in order to congratulate him on his accession and to form with him new treaties and alliances. Ministers came from Venice, Denmark, and the Palatinate; Frederick Henry of Nassau, assisted by Oldenbarnevelt, the pensionary of Holland, was ambassador from the States of the United Provinces; Arenberg was sent by Archduke Albert, and Taxis was expected soon from Spain. But he who most excited the attention of the public, both on account of his own merit and that of his master, was the Marquess of Rosny, afterwards Duke of Sully, prime minister and favorite of Henry IV of France.

State of Europe

When the dominions of the house of Austria devolved on Philip II, all Europe was struck with terror lest the power of a family which had been raised by fortune would now be carried to an immeasurable height by the wisdom and conduct of this monarch. But never were apprehensions found in the event to be more groundless. Slow without prudence, ambitious without enterprise, false without deceiving anybody, and refined without any true judgment: such was the character of Philip, and such the character which, during his lifetime and after his death, he impressed on the Spanish councils. Rebellious or depopulated provinces, discontented or indolent inhabitants: such were the spectacles which those dominions, lying in every climate of the globe, presented to Philip III, a weak prince, and to the Duke of Lerma, his weak and odious prime minister. But though military discipline, which still remained, was what alone gave some appearance of life and vigor to that languishing body, yet so great was the terror produced by former power and ambition that the reduction of the house of Austria was the object of men's vows throughout all the states of

Christendom. It was not perceived that the French empire, now united in domestic peace and governed by Henry, the most heroic and most amiable prince that adorns modern history, had become by itself a sufficient counterpoise to the Spanish greatness.

Rosny's negotiations

Perhaps Henry himself did not perceive this when he proposed, by his minister, a league with James, in conjunction with Venice, the United Provinces, and the northern Crowns, in order to attack the Austrian dominions on every side and depress the exorbitant power of that ambitious family. But the genius [character; nature] of the English monarch was not equal to such vast enterprises. The love of peace was his ruling passion; and it was his singular felicity that the conjunctures of the times rendered the same object which was agreeable to him in the highest degree advantageous to his people.

The French ambassador, therefore, was obliged to depart from these extensive designs and to concert with James the means of providing for the safety of the United Provinces. Nor was this object altogether without its difficulties. The king before his accession had entertained scruples with regard to the revolt of the Low Countries; and being commonly open and sincere, he had on many occasions gone so far as to give to the Dutch the appellation of "rebels." But having conversed more fully with English ministers and courtiers, he found their attachment to that republic so strong and their opinion of common interest so established that he was obliged to sacrifice to politics his sense of justice, a quality which, even when erroneous, is respectable as well as rare in a monarch. He therefore agreed with Rosny to support secretly the States General in concert with the king of France, lest their weakness and despair would oblige them to submit to their old Spanish master. The articles of the treaty were few and simple. It was stipulated that the two kings would allow the Dutch to levy forces in their respective dominions and would secretly remit to that republic the sum of 1,400,000 livres a year for the pay of these forces; and that the whole sum would be advanced by the king of France, but that a third of it would be deducted from the debt due by him to Queen Elizabeth. And if the Spaniards attacked either of the princes, they agreed to assist each other, Henry with a force of ten thousand men, James with that of six. This treaty, one of the wisest and most equitable concluded by James during the course of his reign, was more the work of the prince himself than any of his ministers.

Raleigh's conspiracy

Amidst the great tranquility, both foreign and domestic, with which the nation was blessed, nothing could be more surprising than the discovery of a conspiracy to subvert the government and to fix on the throne Arabella Stuart, a near relation of the king's by the family of Lennox and descended equally from Henry VII. Everything remains still mysterious in this conspiracy, and history can give us no clue to unravel it. Watson and Clark, two Catholic priests, were accused of the plot, with Lord Grey, a Puritan, Lord Cobham, a thoughtless man of no fixed principle, and Sir Walter Raleigh, suspected to be of that philosophical sect who were then extremely rare in England and who have since received the appellation of "freethinkers." Together with these were Sir George Brooke, brother to Lord Cobham, Sir Griffin Markham, Mr. Copley, and Sir Edward Parham. What cement could unite men of such discordant principles in so dangerous a combination, what end they proposed or what means proportioned to an undertaking of this nature, has never yet been explained and cannot easily be imagined. It was commonly believed that after the queen's death, Raleigh, Grey, and Cobham had opposed proclaiming the king till conditions could be made with him, and they were upon that account extremely obnoxious to the court and ministry; and the people were apt at first to suspect that the plot was merely a contrivance of Secretary Cecil to get rid of his old confederates, now become his most inveterate enemies. But the confession as well as trial of the criminals put the matter beyond doubt. And though no one could find any marks of a concerted enterprise, it appeared that men of furious and ambitious spirits, meeting frequently together and believing all the world discontented like themselves, had entertained very criminal projects; they had even entered, some of them at least, into a correspondence with Arenberg, the Flemish ambassador, in order to give disturbance to the new settlement.

The two priests and Brooke were executed; Cobham, Grey, and Markham were pardoned after they had laid their heads upon the block. Raleigh too was reprieved, not pardoned; and he remained in confinement many years afterwards.

It appears from Sully's *Memoirs* that Raleigh secretly offered his services to the French ambassador; and we may from that presume that, meeting with a repulse from that quarter, he had recourse for the same unwarrantable purposes to the Flemish minister. Such a conjecture we are now enabled to form; but it must be confessed that on his trial there appeared no proof of this transaction, nor, indeed, any circumstance which could justify his condemnation. He was accused by Cobham alone, in a sudden fit of passion upon hearing that Raleigh, when examined, had pointed out some circumstances by which Cobham's guilt might be known and ascertained. This accusation Cobham afterwards retracted; and soon after, he retracted his retraction. Yet upon the written evidence of this single witness—a man of no honor or understanding, and so contradictory in his testimony; not confronted with Raleigh; not supported by any concurring circumstance—was that great man, contrary to all law and equity, found guilty by the jury. His name was at that time extremely odious in England; and every man was pleased to give sentence against the capital enemy of Essex, the favorite of the people.

Sir Edward Coke, the famous lawyer, then attorney general, managed the cause for the Crown and threw out on Raleigh such gross abuse as may be deemed a great reflection not only on his own memory but even, in some degree, on the manners of the age. "Traitor," "monster," "viper," and "spider of hell" are the terms which he employed against one of the most illustrious men of the kingdom, who was under trial for life and fortune and who defended himself with temper, eloquence, and courage.

Hampton Court conference

The next occupation of the king was entirely in accord with his heart's content. He was employed in dictating | *1604* | magisterially to an assembly of divines concerning points of faith and discipline and in receiving the applauses of these holy men for his superior zeal and learning. The religious disputes between the established church and the Puritans had induced him to call a conference at Hampton Court on January 4, on pretense of finding expedients which might reconcile both parties.

Though the severities of Elizabeth towards the Catholics had much weakened that party, whose genius was opposite to the prevailing spirit of the nation, like severities had had so little influence on the Puritans, who were encouraged by that spirit, that no less than 750 clergymen of that party signed a petition to the king on his accession, and many more seemed willing to adhere to it. They all hoped that James, having received his education in Scotland and having sometimes professed an attachment to the church established there, would at least abate the rigor of the laws enacted in support of the ceremonies and against Puritans, if he did not show more particular grace and encouragement to that sect. But the king's disposition had taken strongly a contrary bias. The more he knew the Puritanical clergy, the less favor he bore to them. He had observed in their Scottish brethren a violent turn towards republicanism and a zealous attachment to civil liberty, principles closely allied to that religious enthusiasm with which they were actuated. He had found that, being mostly persons of low birth and mean education, the same lofty pretensions which attended them in their familiar addresses to their Maker—of whom they believed themselves the particular favorites—induced them to use the utmost freedoms with their earthly sovereign. In the capacities of both monarch and theologian, he had experienced the little complaisance which they were disposed to show him; at the same time, they opposed his commands, disputed his tenets, and—to his face, before the whole people—censured his conduct and behavior. If he had submitted to the indignity of courting their favor, he stored up on that account the stronger resentment against them and was determined to make them feel in their turn the weight of his authority. Though he had often met with resistance and faction and obstinacy in the Scottish nobility, he retained no ill will to that order; rather, he showed them favor and kindness in England beyond what reason and sound policy could well justify. But the ascendance which the Presbyterian clergy had assumed over him was what his monarchical pride could never thoroughly digest.

He dreaded likewise the popularity which attended this order of men in both kingdoms. As useless austerities and self-denial are imagined in many religions to render us acceptable to a benevolent Being who created us solely for happiness, James observed that the rustic severity of these clergymen and of their whole sect had given them, in the eyes of the multitude, the appearance of sanctity and virtue. Strongly inclined himself to mirth and wine and sports of all kinds, he perceived their censure for his manner of life, free and disengaged. And being thus averse from temper as well as policy to the sect of Puritans, he was resolved, if possible, to prevent its further growth in England.

But it was the character of James's councils throughout his whole reign that they were more wise and equitable in their end than prudent and politic in the means. Though justly aware that no part of civil administration required greater care or a nicer judgment than the conduct of religious parties, he had not perceived that in the same proportion as this practical knowledge of theology is requisite, the speculative refinements in it are mean, and even dangerous, in a monarch. By entering zealously into frivolous disputes, James gave them an air of importance and dignity which they could not otherwise have acquired; and being himself enlisted in the quarrel, he could no longer have recourse to contempt and ridicule, the only proper method of appeasing it. The Church of England had not yet abandoned the rigid doctrines of grace and predestination; the Puritans had not yet separated themselves from the established church nor openly renounced episcopacy. Though the spirit of the parties was considerably different, the only apparent subjects of dispute were concerning the cross in baptism, the ring in marriage, the use of the surplice [a white vestment worn by some denominations' clergy], and the bowing at the name of Jesus. These were the mighty questions which were solemnly agitated in the conference at Hampton Court between some bishops and dignified clergymen on the one hand and some leaders of the Puritanical party on the other, the king and his ministers being present.

The Puritans were here so unreasonable as to complain of a partial and unfair management of the dispute; as if the search after truth were in any degree the object of such conferences, and a candid indifference, so rare even among private inquirers in *philosophical* questions, could ever be expected among princes and prelates in a *theological* controversy. The king, it must be confessed, from the beginning of the conference showed the strongest propensity to the established church and frequently inculcated a maxim which, though it has some foundation, is to be received with great limitations: "No bishop, no king." The bishops in their turn were very liberal with their praises towards the royal disputant, and the archbishop of Canterbury said that "undoubtedly his majesty spake by the special assistance of God's spirit." A few alterations in the liturgy were agreed to, and both parties separated with mutual dissatisfaction.

It had frequently been the practice of the Puritans to form certain assemblies, which they called "prophesyings," where alternately, as moved by the spirit, they displayed their pious zeal in prayers and exhortations; and from that social contagion which has so mighty an influence on holy fervors and from the mutual emulation which arose in those trials of religious eloquence, they raised their own enthusiasm and that of their audience to the highest pitch. Such dangerous societies had been suppressed by Elizabeth; and the ministers in this conference moved the king for their revival. But James sharply replied, "If

9

you aim at a Scottish presbytery, it agrees as well with monarchy as God and the devil. There Jack and Tom and Will and Dick shall meet and censure me and my council. Therefore I reiterate my former speech: Le roi s'avisera ['The king will consider of it'; traditional phrase signifying a king's dissent to an act of Parliament]. Stay, I pray, for one seven years, before you demand; and then, if you find me grow pursy [short-winded] and fat, I may perchance hearken unto you. For that government will keep me in breath, and give me work enough." Such were the political considerations which determined the king in his choice among religious parties.

A Parliament

The next assembly in which James displayed his learning and eloquence was one that showed more spirit of liberty than appeared among his bishops and theologians. The Parliament was now ready to assemble, being so long delayed on account of the plague which had broken out in London and raged to such a degree that more than thirty thousand persons are computed to have died of it in a year, though the city contained at that time little more than one hundred fifty thousand inhabitants.

The speech which the king made on opening the Parliament on March 19 fully displayed his character and proved him to have possessed more knowledge and better faculties than prudence or any just sense of decorum and propriety. Though few productions of the age surpassed this performance either in style or matter, it lacked that majestic brevity and reserve which becomes a king in his addresses to the great council of the nation. It contained, however, a remarkable stroke of candor when he confessed his too great pliancy in yielding to the solicitations of suitors, a fault which he promised to correct but which adhered to him and distressed him during the whole course of his reign.

The first business in which the Commons were engaged was of the utmost importance to the preservation of their privileges, and neither temper nor resolution were lacking in their conduct of it.

In the former periods of the English government, the House of Commons was of so small weight in the balance of the constitution that little attention had been given by the Crown, the people, or the house itself to the choice and continuance of the members. It had been usual, after Parliaments were prolonged beyond one session, for the chancellor to exert a discretionary authority of issuing new writs to supply the place of any members whom he judged incapable of attending on account of their employment, their sickness, or other impediment. This practice gave that minister, and consequently the monarch, an unlimited power of modeling at pleasure the representatives of the nation; yet so little jealousy [apprehension; suspicious fear] had it created that the Commons—of their own accord, without any court influence or intrigue, and contrary to some former votes of their own—confirmed it in the twenty-third year of Elizabeth. At that time, though some members whose places had been filled on account of sickness had now recovered their health, appeared in the house, and claimed their seat, such was the authority of the chancellor that merely out of respect to him, his sentence was adhered to, and the new members were continued in their places. Here a most dangerous prerogative was conferred on the Crown; but to show the genius of that age, or rather the channels in which power then ran, the Crown put very little value on this authority, with the result that two days later, the chancellor of his own accord resigned it back to the Commons and gave them power to judge of a particular vacancy in the house. And when the question concerning the chancellor's new writs was again brought on the carpet towards the end of the session, the Commons were so little alarmed at the precedent that though they readmitted some old members whose seats had been vacated on account of slight indispositions, they confirmed the chancellor's sentence in instances where the distemper appeared to have been dangerous and incurable. Nor did they proceed any further in vindication of their privileges than to vote, "That during the sitting of Parliament, there do not, at any time, any writ go out for choosing or returning any member without the warrant of the house." In Elizabeth's reign and the reigns preceding, we may notice, sessions of Parliament were not usually the twelfth part as long as the vacations; and during the latter, the chancellor's power, if he pleased to exert it, was confirmed, or at least left, by this vote as unlimited and unrestrained as ever.

In a subsequent Parliament, the absolute authority of the queen was exerted in a manner still more open, and began for the first time to give alarm to the Commons. New writs having been issued by the chancellor when there was no vacancy, and a controversy arising upon that incident, the queen sent a message to the house informing them that it was impertinent for them to deal in such matters. These questions, she said, belonged only to the chancellor; and she had appointed him to confer with the judges in order to settle all disputes with regard to elections. The Commons had the courage a few days later to vote, "That it was a most perilous precedent, where two knights of a county were duly elected, if any new writ should issue out for a second election without order of the house itself; that the discussing and adjudging of this and such like differences belonged only to the house; and that there should be no message sent to the lord chancellor, not so much as to inquire what he had done in the matter, because it was conceived to be a matter derogatory to the power and privilege of the house." This is the most considerable—and almost only—instance of parliamentary liberty which occurs during the reign of that princess.

Outlaws, whether on account of debts or crimes, had been declared by the judges incapable of enjoying a seat in the house, where they must themselves be lawgivers; but this opinion of the judges had been frequently overruled. I find, however, in the case of Vaughan, who was questioned for an outlawry, that having proved all his debts to have been contracted by suretyship and most of them to have been honestly compounded, he was allowed on account of these favorable circumstances to keep his seat, which plainly supposes that otherwise it would have been vacated on account of the outlawry.

When James summoned this Parliament, he issued a proclamation in which—among many general advices which, like a kind tutor, he bestowed on his people—he strictly enjoined them not to choose any outlaw for their representative. And he added, "If any person take upon him the place of knight, citizen, or burgess, not being duly elected according to the laws and statutes in that behalf provided, and according to the purport, effect, and true meaning of this our proclamation, then every person so offending [is] to be fined or imprisoned for the same." A proclamation here was plainly put on the same footing with a law, and that in so delicate a point as the right of elections: most alarming circumstances, had there not been reason to believe that this measure, being entered into so early in the king's reign, proceeded more from precipitation and mistake than from any serious design of invading the privileges of Parliament.

Sir Francis Goodwin was chosen member for the county of Bucks; and his return, as usual, was made into Chancery. The chancellor, pronouncing him an outlaw, vacated his seat and issued writs for a new election. Sir John Fortescue was chosen in his place by the county; but the first act of the house was to reverse the chancellor's sentence and restore Sir Francis to his seat. At the king's suggestion, the House of Lords desired a conference on the subject; but this request was absolutely refused by the Commons, as the question entirely regarded their own privileges. The Commons, however, agreed to make a remonstrance to the king by the mouth of their speaker, in which the house maintained that though the returns were by form made into Chancery, yet the sole right of judging with regard to elections belonged to the house itself, not to the chancellor. James was not satisfied and ordered a conference between the house and the judges, whose opinion in this case was opposite to that of the Commons. This conference, he said, he commanded as an "absolute" king; an epithet, we are apt to imagine, not very gratifying to English ears, but one to which they had already been somewhat accustomed from the mouth of Elizabeth. He added, "That all their privileges were derived from his grant, and [he] hoped they would not turn them against him," a sentiment which, from her conduct, it is certain Elizabeth had also entertained, and which was the reigning principle of her courtiers and ministers and the spring of all her administration.

The Commons were in some perplexity. Their eyes were now opened, and they saw the consequences of that power which had been assumed by the chancellor and to which their predecessors had in some instances blindly submitted. "By this course," said a member, "the free election of the counties is taken away, and none shall be chosen but such as shall please the king and Council. Let us, therefore, with fortitude, understanding, and sincerity, seek to maintain our privilege. This cannot be construed any contempt in us, but merely a maintenance of our common rights, which our ancestors have left us, and which it is just and fit for us to transmit to our posterity." Another said, "This may be called a quo warranto to seize all our liberties." "A chancellor," added a third, "by this course may call a Parliament consisting of what persons he pleases. Any suggestion, by any person, may be the cause of sending a new writ. It is come to this plain question, whether the Chancery or Parliament ought to have authority."

Notwithstanding this watchful spirit of liberty which now appeared in the Commons, their deference for majesty was so great that they appointed a committee to confer with the judges before the king and Council. There the question of law began to appear in James's eyes a little more doubtful than he had previously imagined it; and in order to extricate himself with some honor, he proposed that both Goodwin and Fortescue be set aside and a writ be issued, by warrant of the house, for a new election. Goodwin gave his consent, and the Commons embraced the expedient, but in such a manner that while they showed their regard for the king, they secured for the future the free possession of their seats and the right which they claimed of judging solely in their own elections and returns.

A power like this—so essential to the exercise of all their other powers, themselves so essential to public liberty—cannot fairly be deemed an encroachment by the Commons, but must be regarded as an inherent privilege, happily rescued from that ambiguity which the negligence of some former Parliaments had thrown upon it.

At the same time, the Commons, in the case of Sir Thomas Shirley, established their power of punishing the persons at whose suit any member was arrested as well as the officers who either arrested or detained him. Their asserting of this privilege admits of the same reflection.

About this period, the minds of men throughout Europe, especially in England, seem to have undergone a general but unperceived revolution. Though letters had been revived in the preceding age, they were chiefly cultivated by those of sedentary professions, nor had they till now begun to spread themselves in any degree among men of the world. Arts, both mechanical and liberal, were every day receiving great improvements. Navigation had extended itself over the whole globe. Traveling was secure and agreeable. And the general system of politics in Europe had become more enlarged and comprehensive.

In consequence of this universal fermentation, the ideas of men enlarged themselves on all sides; and the several constituent parts of the Gothic [medieval] governments, which seem to have lain long inactive, began everywhere to operate and encroach on each other. On the Continent, where the necessity of discipline had begotten standing armies, the princes commonly established an unlimited authority and overpowered the liberties of the people by force or intrigue. In England, the love of freedom, which flourishes extremely in all liberal natures unless checked, acquired new force and was regulated by more enlarged views, suitable to that cultivated understanding which became every day more common among men of birth and education. A familiar acquaintance with the precious remains of antiquity excited in every generous breast a passion for a limited constitution and begat an emulation of those manly virtues which the Greek and Roman authors, by such animating examples as well as passionate expressions, recommend to us. The severe, though popular, government of Elizabeth had confined this rising spirit within very narrow bounds. But when a new and a foreign family, and a prince less dreaded and less beloved, succeeded to the throne, symptoms immediately appeared of a more free and independent genius in the nation.

Happily, this prince possessed neither sufficient capacity to perceive the alteration nor sufficient art and vigor to check it in its early advances. Jealous of regal because conscious of little personal authority, he had established within his own mind a speculative system of absolute government which few of his subjects, he believed, and none but traitors and rebels, would scruple to admit. On whichever side he cast his eye, everything concurred to encourage his prejudices. When he compared himself with the other hereditary sovereigns of Europe, he imagined that as he bore the same rank, he was entitled to equal prerogatives, not considering the innovations lately introduced by them and the military force by which their authority was supported. In England, that almost unlimited power which had been exercised for more than a century, especially during the late reign, he ascribed solely to royal birth and title, not to the prudence and spirit of the monarchs nor to the conjunctures of the times. Even the opposition which he had struggled with in Scotland encouraged him still further in his favorite notions, for there he saw that the same resistance which opposed regal authority violated all law and order and made way either for the ravages of a barbarous nobility or for the more intolerable insolence of seditious preachers. In his own person, therefore, he thought all legal power to be centered by a hereditary and a divine right. And this opinion might have proved dangerous, if not fatal, to liberty had not the firmness of the persuasion and its seeming evidence induced him to trust solely to his right without making the smallest provision, either of force or politics, to support it.

Such were the opposite dispositions of Parliament and prince at the commencement of the Scottish line; dispositions just beginning to exist and to appear in the Parliament, but thoroughly established and openly avowed on the part of the prince.

The spirit and judgment of the House of Commons appeared not only in defense of their own privileges but also in their endeavor, though at this time in vain, to free trade from those shackles which the high-exerted prerogative—and in this respect, even the ill-judged tyranny—of Elizabeth had imposed upon it.

James had already of his own accord called in and annulled all the numerous patents for monopolies which had been granted by his predecessor and which extremely fettered every species of domestic industry. But the exclusive companies—another species of monopoly, by which almost all foreign trade, except that to France, was brought into the hands of a few rapacious engrossers [wholesalers who corner a market and resell at a raised price]—still remained, and all prospect of future improvement in commerce was forever sacrificed to a little temporary advantage of the sovereign. These companies, though arbitrarily erected, had carried their privileges so far that almost all the commerce of England was centered in London; and it appears that the customs of that port amounted to £110,000 a year, while those of all the kingdom beside yielded only £17,000. Indeed, the whole trade of London was confined to about two hundred citizens, who were easily enabled, by combining among themselves, to fix whatever price they pleased both to the exports and imports of the nation. The committee appointed to consider this enormous grievance—one of the greatest which we read of in English history—insisted on it as a fact well known and avowed (however contrary to present received opinion) that shipping and seamen had gradually decayed during all the preceding reign. And though nothing is more common, even during the most flourishing periods, than complaints of the decay of trade, yet this is a consequence which might naturally result from such arbitrary establishments at a time when the commerce of all the other nations of Europe except Scotland enjoyed full liberty and indulgence.

While the Commons were thus attempting to give liberty to the trading part of the nation, they also endeavored to free the landed property from the burden of wardships [Crown revenue from the estates of minors] and to remove those remains of the feudal tenures under which the nation still labored. A just regard was shown to the Crown in the conduct of this affair; nor was the remedy sought for considered as a matter of right, but merely of grace and favor. The profit which the king reaped both from wards and from respite of homage [payments in lieu of formally swearing vassalage] was estimated, and it was intended to compound [settle a claim] for these prerogatives by a secure and independent revenue. But after some debates in the house and some conferences with the Lords, the affair was found to contain more difficulties than could easily be surmounted at that time, and it was not then brought to any conclusion.

The same fate attended an attempt of a like nature to free the nation from the burden of purveyance [prerogative of the Crown to requisition goods and services]. This prerogative had been much abused by the purveyors, and the Commons showed some intention to offer the king £50,000 a year for the abolition of it.

Another affair of the utmost consequence was brought before the Parliament, in which the Commons showed a greater spirit of independence than any true judgment of national interest. The union of the two kingdoms was zealously, and even impatiently, urged by the king. He justly regarded it as the singular felicity of his reign that he had terminated the bloody animosities of these hostile nations and had reduced the whole island under one government, enjoying tranquility within itself and security from all foreign invasions. He hoped that while his subjects of both kingdoms reflected on past disasters, they would—besides regarding his person as infinitely precious—entertain the strongest desire of securing themselves against the return of like calamities by a thorough union of laws, Parliaments, and privileges. He considered not that this very reflection operated as yet in a contrary manner on men's prejudices and kept alive that mutual hatred between the nations which had been carried to the greatest extremities and required time to allay. The more urgent the king appeared in promoting so useful a measure, the more backward was the English Parliament in concurring with him, as they ascribed his excessive zeal to that partiality in favor of his ancient subjects of which they thought that they had reason to complain on other occasions. Their complaisance for the king, therefore, carried them no further than to appoint forty-four English to meet with thirty-one Scottish commissioners in order to deliberate concerning the terms of a union, but without any power of making advances towards the establishment of it.

The same spirit of independence, and perhaps not better judgment, appeared in the House of Commons when the question of supply [money provided by the Parliament to the monarch] was brought before them by some members attached to the court. In vain was it urged that though the king received a supply which had been voted to Elizabeth and which had not been collected before her death, yet he found it burdened with a debt contracted by the queen equal to the full amount of it; that peace was not yet thoroughly concluded with Spain, and that Ireland was continually expensive to him; that on his journey from Scotland amidst such a concourse of people, and on that too of the queen and royal family, he had expended considerable sums; and that as the courtiers had looked for greater liberalities from the prince on his accession and had imposed on his generous nature, so the prince in his turn would expect at the beginning some mark of duty and attachment from his people and some consideration of his necessities. No impression was made on the House of Commons by these topics, and the majority appeared fully determined to refuse all supply. The burden of government at that time lay surprisingly light upon the people; and that very reason, which to us at this distance may seem a motive of generosity, was the real cause why the Parliament was on all occasions so remarkably frugal and reserved. They were not as yet accustomed to open their purses in so liberal a manner as their successors in order to supply the wants of their sovereign; and the smallest demand, however requisite, appeared in their eyes unreasonable and exorbitant. The Commons seem also to have been desirous of reducing the Crown to still further necessities by their refusing a bill sent down to them by the Lords for entailing [settling property inalienably on a line of descendants] the Crown lands forever on the king's heirs and successors. The dissipation made by Elizabeth had probably taught James the necessity of this law and shown the Commons the advantage of refusing it.

In order to cover a disappointment with regard to supply which might bear a bad construction both at home and abroad, James sent a message to the house in which he stated that he desired no supply; he was very forward in refusing what was never offered him. Soon after, on July 7, he prorogued the Parliament, not without revealing in his speech visible marks of dissatisfaction. Even so early in his reign, he saw reason to make public complaints of the restless and encroaching spirit of the Puritanical party and of the malevolence with which they endeavored to inspire the Commons. Nor were his complaints without foundation or the Puritans without influence; for the Commons, now finding themselves free from the arbitrary government of Elizabeth, made application for a conference with the Lords and presented a petition to the king, the purport of both of which was to procure, in favor of the Puritans, a relaxation of the ecclesiastical laws. The use of the surplice and of the cross in baptism was there chiefly complained of; but the remedy seems to have been expected solely from the king's dispensing power [prerogative to suspend the operation of a law]. In the papers which contain this application and petition, we may also see proofs of the violent animosity of the Commons against the Catholics, together with the intolerant spirit of that assembly.

Peace with Spain

This summer the peace with Spain was finally concluded and was signed by the Spanish ministers at London on August 18. In the conferences previous to this treaty, the nations were found to have so few claims on each other that except for the support given by England to the Low Country provinces, the war might appear to have been continued more on account of personal animosity between Philip and Elizabeth than any opposition of political interests between their subjects. Some articles in the treaty which seemed prejudicial to the Dutch commonwealth were never executed by the king; and as the Spaniards made no complaints on that head, it appeared that by secret agreement, the king had expressly reserved the power of sending assistance to the Hollanders. The Constable of Castile came into England to ratify the peace, the Earl of Hertford was sent by England into the Low Countries for the same purpose, and the Earl of Nottingham, high admiral, went into Spain. The train of the latter was numerous and splendid; and the Spaniards, it is said, were extremely surprised when they beheld the blooming countenances and graceful appearance of the English, whom their bigotry, inflamed by the priests, had represented as so many monsters and infernal demons.

Though England was perfectly secure by means of its naval force during the latter years of the Spanish war, James showed an impatience to put an end to hostilities; and soon after his accession, before any terms of peace were concerted or even proposed by Spain, he recalled all the letters of marque which had been granted by Queen Elizabeth. Archduke Albert had made some advances of a like nature, which invited the king to take this friendly step. But it is remarkable that in James's proclamation for that purpose, he plainly supposed that as he himself had always lived in amity with Spain while king of Scotland, peace was attached to his person, and that merely by his accession to the Crown of England, without any articles of treaty or agreement, he had ended the war between the kingdoms. This ignorance of the law of nations may appear surprising in a prince who was thirty-six years of age and who had reigned from his infancy if we did not consider that a king of Scotland who lived in close friendship with England had few transactions to manage with foreign princes and had little opportunity of acquiring experience. Unhappily for James, his timidity, his prejudices, his indolence, his love of amusement—particularly of hunting, to which he was much addicted—always prevented him from making any progress in the knowledge or practice of foreign politics, and soon diminished that regard which all the neighboring nations had paid to England during the reign of his predecessor.

CHAPTER 46
1604 – 1612

*Gunpowder conspiracy – A Parliament – Truce between
Spain and the United Provinces – A Parliament – Death of
the French king – Arminianism – State of Ireland*

Gunpowder conspiracy

WE are now to relate an event—one of the most memorable that
history has conveyed to posterity—containing at once a singular
proof both of the strength and weakness of the human mind, its wid-
est departure from morals and most steady attachment to religious
prejudices. It is the "gunpowder treason" of which I speak, a fact as
certain as it appears incredible.

The Roman Catholics had expected great favor and indulgence on
the accession of James, both as he was descended from Mary, queen of
Scots, whose life they believed to have been sacrificed to their cause,
and as he himself in his early youth was imagined to have shown some
partiality towards them, which nothing, they thought, but interest and
necessity had since restrained. It is claimed that he had even entered
into positive pledges to tolerate their religion as soon as he would
mount the throne of England; either their credulity had interpreted in
this sense some obliging expressions of the king's or he had employed
such an artifice in order to render them favorable to his title. Very
soon they discovered their mistake; and they were both surprised and
enraged to find James on all occasions express his intention of strictly
executing the laws enacted against them and of persevering in all the
rigorous measures of Elizabeth. Sir Robert Catesby, a gentleman of
many talents and of an ancient family, first thought of a most extraordinary method of revenge; and he opened his intention to Sir Thomas

Percy, a descendant of the illustrious house of Northumberland. In one of their conversations with regard to the distressed condition of the Catholics, Percy broke into a sally of passion and mentioned assassinating the king. Catesby took the opportunity of revealing to him a nobler and more extensive plan of treason, which not only included a sure execution of vengeance but also afforded some hopes of restoring the Catholic religion in England. In vain, said he, would you put an end to the king's life: he has children who would succeed both to his crown and to his maxims of government. In vain would you extinguish the whole royal family: the nobility, the gentry, the Parliament are all infected with the same heresy and could raise to the throne another prince and another family, who, besides their hatred to our religion, would be animated with revenge for the tragic death of their predecessors. To serve any good purpose, we must destroy at one blow the king, the royal family, the Lords, the Commons, and bury all our enemies in one common ruin. Happily, they are all assembled on the first meeting of the Parliament and afford us the opportunity of glorious and useful vengeance. Great preparations will not be requisite. A few of us, combining, may run a mine below the hall in which they meet, and choosing the very moment when the king harangues [addresses] both houses, consign over to destruction these determined foes to all piety and religion. Meanwhile, we ourselves—standing aloof, safe and unsuspected—shall triumph in being the instruments of divine wrath and shall behold with pleasure those sacrilegious walls, in which were passed the edicts for proscribing our church and butchering her children, tossed into a thousand fragments, while their impious inhabitants—meditating, perhaps, still new persecutions against us—pass from flames above to flames below, there forever to endure the torments due to their offenses.

Percy was charmed with this project of Catesby; and they agreed to communicate the matter to a few more, and among the rest to Thomas Wintour, whom they sent over to Flanders in quest of Guy Fawkes, an officer in the Spanish service with whose zeal and courage they were all thoroughly acquainted. When they enlisted any new conspirator, they always, in order to bind him to secrecy, employed the communion, the most sacred rite of their religion, together with an oath. And it is remarkable that no one of these pious devotees ever entertained the least compunction with regard to the cruel massacre which they projected of whatever was great and eminent in the nation. Some of them were startled only by the reflection that many Catholics necessarily would be present as spectators or attendants on the king or as having seats in the House of Peers. But Oswald Tesimond, a Jesuit priest, and Henry Garnet, superior of that order in England, removed these scruples and showed them how the interests of religion required that the innocent should here be sacrificed with the guilty.

All this passed in the spring and summer of the year 1604, when the conspirators also hired, in Percy's name, a house adjoining to that in which the Parliament was to assemble. Towards the end of that year, they began their operations. That they might be less interrupted and give less suspicion to the neighborhood, they carried in stores of provisions with them and never desisted from their labor. Obstinate in their purpose and confirmed by passion, by principle, and by mutual exhortation, they little feared death in comparison with a disappointment; and having provided arms together with the instruments of their labor, they resolved to perish there in case of a discovery. Their perseverance advanced the work, and they soon pierced the wall, though three yards in thickness; but on

1605

approaching the other side, they were somewhat startled at hearing a noise which they knew not how to account for. Upon inquiry, they found that it came from the vault below the House of Lords, that a magazine of coals had been kept there, and that as the coals were selling off, the vault would be let to the highest bidder. The opportunity was immediately seized, the place hired by Percy, thirty-six barrels of powder lodged in it, the whole covered up with fagots and billets, the doors of the cellar boldly flung open, and everybody admitted as if it contained nothing dangerous.

Confident of success, they now began to look forward and to plan the remaining part of their project. The king, the queen, and Prince Henry were all expected to be present at the opening of Parliament. The sovereign's second son, Charles, would be absent by reason of his tender age; and it was resolved that Percy would seize or assassinate him. The princess Elizabeth, a child likewise, was kept at Lord Harrington's house in Warwickshire; and Sir Everard Digby, Ambrose Rookwood, and John Grant, being let into the conspiracy, agreed to assemble their friends on pretense of a hunting match, seize that princess, and immediately proclaim her queen. So transported were they with rage against their adversaries and so charmed with the prospect of revenge that they forgot all care of their own safety; trusting to the general confusion which necessarily would result from so unexpected a blow, they failed to foresee that the fury of the people, now unrestrained by any authority, would have turned against them and would probably have satiated itself by a universal massacre of the Catholics.

The day so long wished for, on which the Parliament was appointed to assemble, now approached. The dreadful secret, though communicated to more than twenty persons, had been religiously kept during the space of nearly a year and a half. No remorse, no pity, no fear of punishment, no hope of reward had as yet induced any one conspirator either to abandon the enterprise or make a disclosure of it. The holy fury had extinguished in their breast every other motive; and at last it was an indiscretion proceeding chiefly from these very bigoted prejudices and partialities which saved the nation.

Ten days before the meeting of Parliament, Lord Monteagle, a Catholic, son to Lord Morley, received the following letter, which had been delivered to his servant by an unknown hand: "My Lord, Out of the love I bear to some of your friends, I have a care of your preservation. Therefore I would advise you, as you tender [value] your life, to devise some excuse to shift off your attendance at this parliament. For God and man have concurred to punish the wickedness of this time. And think not slightly of this advertisement; but retire yourself into your country, where you may expect the event in safety. For, though there be no appearance of any stir, yet, I say, they will receive a terrible blow, this parliament, and yet they shall not see who hurts them. This counsel is not to be contemned, because it may do you good, and can do you no harm: For the danger is past, as soon as you have burned the letter. And I hope God will give you the grace to make good use of it, unto whose holy protection I commend you."

Monteagle knew not what to make of this letter; and though inclined to think it a foolish attempt to frighten and ridicule him, he judged it safest to carry it to Lord Salisbury, secretary of state. Though Salisbury too was inclined to pay little attention to it, he thought it proper to lay it before the king, who came to town a few days later. To the king it appeared not so light a matter; and from the serious, ardent style of the letter, he conjectured that it implied something dangerous and important. A "terrible blow," and yet the authors concealed; a danger so sudden and yet so great: these circumstances seemed all to denote some contrivance by gunpowder; and it was thought advisable to inspect all the vaults below the Houses of Parliament. This care belonged to the Earl of Suffolk, lord chamberlain, who purposely delayed the search till the day before the meeting of Parliament. He observed those great piles of wood and fagots which lay in the vault under the upper house; and he cast his eye upon Fawkes, who stood in a dark corner and passed himself for Percy's servant. That daring and determined courage which so much distinguished this conspirator, even among those heroes in villainy, was fully painted in his countenance and was not passed unnoticed by the chamberlain. Such a quantity of fuel, for the use of one who lived so little in town as Percy, also appeared a little extraordinary; and upon considering all circumstances, it was resolved that a more thorough inspection should be made. About midnight, Sir Thomas Knyvet, a justice of peace, was sent with proper attendants; and finding Fawkes, who had just finished all his preparations, before the door of the vault, he immediately seized him, and turning over the fagots, discovered the powder. The matches and everything proper for setting fire to the train were taken in Fawkes's pocket; he, finding his guilt now apparent and seeing no refuge but in boldness and despair, expressed the utmost regret that he had lost the opportunity of firing the powder at once and of sweetening his own death by that of his enemies. He displayed the same intrepid firmness, mixed even with scorn and disdain, before the Privy Council, refusing to reveal his accomplices and showing no concern but for the failure of the enterprise. This obstinacy lasted two or three days; but being confined to the Tower, left to reflect on his guilt and danger, and the rack being just shown to him, his courage—fatigued with so long an effort and unsupported by hope or society—at last failed him, and he made a full disclosure of all the conspirators.

Catesby, Percy, and the other criminals who were in London, though they had heard of the alarm taken at a letter sent to Monteagle, though they had heard of the chamberlain's search, yet were resolved to persist to the utmost and never abandon their hopes of success. But at last, hearing that Fawkes was arrested, they hurried down to Warwickshire, where Sir Everard Digby, thinking himself assured that success had attended his confederates, was already in arms in order to seize the princess Elizabeth. She had escaped into Coventry; and they were obliged to put themselves on their defense against the country, who were raised from all quarters and armed by the sheriff. The conspirators, never exceeding eighty persons with all their attendants and being surrounded on every side, could no longer entertain hopes either of prevailing or escaping. Therefore, having confessed themselves and received absolution, they boldly prepared for death and resolved to sell their lives as dearly as possible to the assailants.

But even this miserable consolation was denied them. Some of their powder took fire and disabled them for defense. The people rushed in upon them. Percy and Catesby were killed by one shot. Digby, Rookwood, Wintour, and others, being taken prisoners, were tried, confessed their guilt, and died by the hands of the executioner, as did Garnet. Notwithstanding this horrid crime, the bigoted Catholics were so devoted to Garnet that they fancied miracles to be wrought by his blood; and in Spain he was regarded as a martyr.

No desperate fortune of the conspirators had urged them to this enterprise, nor had any former profligacy of their lives prepared them for so great a crime. Before that audacious attempt, their conduct seems in general to be liable to no reproach. Catesby's character had entitled him to such regard that Rookwood and Digby were seduced by their implicit trust in his judgment; and they declared that from the motive alone of friendship to him, they were ready on any occasion to have sacrificed their lives. Digby himself was as highly esteemed and beloved as any man in England; and he had been particularly honored with the good opinion of Queen Elizabeth. It was bigoted zeal alone—the most absurd of prejudices masked with reason, the most criminal of passions covered with the appearance of duty—which seduced them into measures that were fatal to themselves and had so nearly proved fatal to their country.

The Lords Mordaunt and Stourton, two Catholics, were fined—the former £10,000, the latter £4,000—by the Star Chamber because their absence from Parliament had begotten a suspicion of their being acquainted with the conspiracy. The Earl of Northumberland was fined £30,000 and detained several years prisoner in the Tower because, not to mention other grounds of suspicion, he had admitted Percy into the number of gentlemen pensioners without his taking the requisite oaths.

The king, in his speech to the Parliament, observed that though religion had engaged the conspirators in so criminal an attempt, yet ought we not to involve all the Roman Catholics in the same guilt or suppose them equally disposed to commit such enormous barbarities. Many holy men, he said, and our ancestors among the rest, had been seduced to concur with that church in her scholastic doctrines, who yet had never admitted her seditious principles concerning the pope's power of dethroning kings or sanctifying assassination. The wrath of heaven is denounced against crimes, but innocent error may obtain its favor; and nothing can be more hateful than the uncharitableness of the Puritans, who condemn alike to eternal torments even the most inoffensive partisans of popery. For his part, he added, that conspiracy, however atrocious, should never alter in the least his plan of government: while with one hand he punished guilt, with the other he would still support and protect innocence. After this speech, he prorogued the Parliament till January 22.

The moderation—and I may say magnanimity—of the king immediately after so narrow an escape from a most detestable conspiracy was in no way agreeable to his subjects. Their animosity against popery had risen to a great pitch even before this provocation; and it would perhaps have been more prudent in James to have conformed himself to it by a little dissimulation. His theological learning, confirmed by disputation, had happily fixed his judgment in the Protestant faith; yet his heart was a little biased by the allurements of Rome, and he would have been well pleased if the making of some advances could have effected a union with that ancient Mother Church. He strove to abate the acrimony of his own subjects against the religion of their fathers; he became himself the object of their dissidence and aversion. Whatever measures he embraced—in Scotland, to introduce prelacy; in England, to enforce the authority of the established church and support its rites and ceremonies—were interpreted as so many steps towards popery and were represented by the Puritans as symptoms of idolatry and superstition [veneration for objects; scrupulous rigor as to rites and symbols]. Ignorant of the consequences or unwilling to sacrifice his inclination—which he called his conscience—to politics, he persevered in the same measures and gave trust and preferment almost indifferently to his Catholic and Protestant subjects. And finding his person as well as his title less obnoxious to the church of Rome than those of Elizabeth, he gradually abated the rigor of those laws which had been enacted against that church and which were so acceptable to his bigoted subjects. But the effects of these dispositions on both sides remained largely unperceived till towards the conclusion of his reign.

A Parliament

At this time, James seems to have possessed the affections even of his English subjects, and in a tolerable degree

1606

their esteem and regard. Previously their complaints were chiefly leveled against his too great constancy in his early friendships, a quality which, had it been attended with more economy, the wise would have excused and the candid would even perhaps have applauded. His faculties (which were not despicable) and his learning (which was great), being highly extolled by his courtiers and university men and not yet tried in the management of any delicate affairs (for which he was unfit), raised a high idea of him in the world. Nor was it always through flattery or insincerity that he received the title of the second Solomon. A report suddenly spread about this time that he had been assassinated visibly struck a great consternation into all orders of men. The Commons in this session also abated somewhat of their excessive frugality and granted him an aid, payable in four years, of three subsidies and six fifteenths [fixed amounts of money], which Sir Francis Bacon said in the house might amount to about £400,000; and for once, the king and Parliament parted in friendship and good humor. The hatred which the Catholics so visibly bore him gave him at this time an additional value in the eyes of his people. The only considerable point in which the Commons incurred his displeasure was by demonstrating their constant good will to the Puritans, in whose favor they desired a conference with the Lords, which was rejected.

The chief affair transacted next session was the intended union of the two kingdoms. Nothing could exceed the king's passion and zeal for this noble enterprise but the Parliament's prejudice and reluctance against it. There remain two excellent speeches in favor of the union which it would not be improper to compare together: that of the king and that of Sir Francis Bacon. Those who affect in everything such an extreme contempt for James will be surprised to find that his discourse, both for good reasoning and elegant composition, approaches very near that of a man who was undoubtedly at that time one of the greatest geniuses in Europe. A few trivial indiscretions and indecorums may be said to characterize the address of the monarch and mark it for his own. And in general, so open and avowed a declaration in favor of a measure while he had taken no care, by any precaution or intrigue, to ensure success may safely be pronounced an indiscretion. But the art of managing Parliaments by private influence or cabal, being found previously of little use or necessity, had not as yet become a part of English politics. In the common course of affairs, government could be conducted without the assistance of Parliament; and when their concurrence became necessary to the measures of the Crown, it was, generally speaking, except in times of great faction and discontent, obtained without much difficulty.

The king's influence seems to have rendered the Scottish Parliament cordial in all the steps which they took towards the union.

Though the advantages which Scotland might hope for from that measure were more considerable, yet its objections too were more striking and obvious. The benefit which must have resulted to England, by accession of both strength and security, was not despicable; and as the English were by far the greater nation and possessed the seat of government, the objections either from the point of honor or from jealousy [suspicious caution or fear] could not reasonably have any place among them. The English Parliament indeed seem to have been swayed merely by the vulgar motive of national antipathy. And they persisted so obstinately in their prejudices that all the efforts for a thorough union and incorporation ended only in the abolition of the hostile laws formerly enacted between the kingdoms.

Some precipitate steps which the king had taken soon after his accession in order to promote his favorite project had been here observed to do more injury than service. From his own authority, he had assumed the title of king of Great Britain and had quartered the arms of Scotland with those of England in all coins, flags, and ensigns. He had also engaged the judges to make a declaration that all those who would be born in either kingdom after the union of the Crowns were, for that reason alone, naturalized in both. This was a nice question, and according to the ideas of those times, susceptible of subtle reasoning on both sides. The king was the same; the Parliaments were different. To render the people the same, therefore, we must suppose that the sovereign authority resided chiefly in the prince, and that these popular assemblies were instituted to assist with money and advice rather than endowed with any controlling or active powers in the government. "It is evident," said Bacon in his pleadings on this subject, "that all other commonwealths, monarchies only excepted, do subsist by a law precedent. For where authority is divided amongst many officers, and they not perpetual, but annual or temporary, and not to receive their authority but by election, and certain persons to have voices only in that election, and the like; these are busy and curious frames, which of necessity do presuppose a law precedent, written or unwritten, to guide and direct them. But in monarchies, especially hereditary, that is, when several families or lineages of people do submit themselves to one line, imperial or royal, the submission is more natural and simple; which afterwards, by law subsequent, is perfected, and made more formal; but that is grounded upon nature." It would seem from this reasoning that the idea of a *hereditary, limited* monarchy, though implicitly supposed in many public transactions, had scarcely ever as yet been expressly formed by any English lawyer or politician.

Except the obstinacy of the Parliament with regard to the union and an attempt on the king's ecclesiastical jurisdiction, most of their measures during this session were sufficiently respectful and obliging, though they still reveal a vigilant spirit and a careful attention towards national liberty. The votes also of the Commons show that the house contained a mixture of Puritans who had acquired great authority among them and who, together with religious prejudices, were continually suggesting ideas more suitable to a popular than a monarchical form of government. The natural appetite for rule made the Commons lend a willing ear to every doctrine which tended to augment their own power and influence.

A petition was moved in the lower house for a more rigorous execution of the laws against popish recusants [those who refused to attend services of the Church of England, as was required by law] and an abatement towards Protestant clergymen who scrupled to observe the ceremonies. Both these points were equally unacceptable to the king; and he sent orders to the house to proceed no further in that matter. The Commons were inclined at first to consider these orders as a breach of privilege; but they soon acquiesced when told that this measure of the king's was supported by many precedents during the reign of Elizabeth. Had they been always disposed to make the precedents of that reign the rule of their conduct, they needed never have had any quarrel with any of their monarchs.

The complaints of Spanish depredations were very loud among the English merchants. The lower house sent a message to the Lords on June 5 desiring a conference with them regarding their presenting a joint petition to the king on the subject. The Lords took some time to deliberate on this message because, they said, the matter was "weighty" and "rare." It probably occurred to them at first that the Parliament's interposing in affairs of state would appear unusual and extraordinary. And to show that in this sentiment they were not guided by court influence, they agreed, after they had deliberated, to the conference.

The House of Commons began now to feel themselves of such importance that on the motion of Sir Edwin Sandys, a member of great authority, they entered for the first time an order for the regular keeping of their journals. When all business was finished, the king prorogued the Parliament.

About this time there was an insurrection of the country people in

Northamptonshire headed by one Reynolds, a man of low condition. They went about destroying enclosures but carefully avoided committing any other outrage. This insurrection was easily suppressed; and though great lenity was used towards the rioters, yet some of the ringleaders were punished. The chief cause of that trivial commotion seems to have been far from trivial itself. The practice still continued in England of disusing tillage and throwing the land into enclosures for the sake of pasture. By this means, the kingdom was depopulated, or at least prevented from increasing so much in people as might have been expected from the daily increase of industry and commerce.

Truce between Spain and the United Provinces

The next year presents us with nothing memorable; but in the spring of the subsequent, after a long negotiation, that war which for nearly half a century had been carried on with such fury between Spain and the States of the

| 1608 |
| 1609 |

United Provinces was concluded by a truce of twelve years. Never had a contest seemed at first more unequal; never was a contest finished with more honor to the weaker party. On the side of Spain were numbers, riches, authority, discipline; on the side of the rebellious provinces were found the attachment to liberty and the enthusiasm of religion. The republic maintained its armies by its naval enterprises; and joining peaceful industry to military valor, it was enabled by its own force to support itself and gradually rely less on those neighboring princes who, from jealousy to Spain, were at first prompted to encourage its revolt. Long had the pride of the Spanish monarchy prevailed over its interest and prevented it from hearkening to any terms of accommodation with its rebellious subjects. But finding all intercourse cut off between its provinces by the maritime force of the States, it at last agreed to treat with them as a free people and solemnly to renounce all claim and pretension to their sovereignty.

This chief point being gained, the treaty was easily brought to a conclusion, on March 30, under the joint mediation and guaranty of France and England. All exterior appearances of honor were paid equally to both those Crowns; but very different were the sentiments which the parties—as well as all Europe—entertained of the princes who wore them. Frugality [careful management; judicious use of all things of value] and vigor, the chief circumstances which procure regard among foreign nations, shone out as conspicuously in Henry as they were deficient in James. To a contempt of the English monarch,

Henry seems to have added a considerable degree of jealousy [mistrust] and aversion, which were sentiments altogether without foundation. James was just and fair in all transactions with his allies, but it appears from the memoirs of those times that each side deemed him partial towards their adversary and fancied that he had entered into secret measures against them. So little equity have men in their judgments of their own affairs; and so dangerous is that entire neutrality affected by the king of England!

A Parliament

The little concern which James took in foreign affairs renders the domestic occurrences, particularly those of Parliament, the most interesting of his reign. A new session was held this spring; the king full of hopes of receiving supply, the Commons, of circumscribing his prerogative. The Earl of Salisbury, now created treasurer on the death of the Earl of Dorset, laid open the king's necessities, first to the Peers, then to a committee of the lower house. He insisted on the unavoidable expense incurred in supporting the navy and in suppressing a late insurrection in Ireland. He mentioned three numerous courts which the king was obliged to maintain, for himself, for the queen, and for the Prince of Wales. He observed that Queen Elizabeth, though a single woman, had received very large supplies in the years preceding her death, which were the only ones expensive to her. And he remarked that during her reign, she had alienated many of the Crown lands, an expedient which, though it supplied her present necessities without laying burdens on her people, extremely multiplied the necessities of her successor. From all these causes, he thought it in no way strange that the king's income would fall short by so great a sum as £81,000 of his stated and regular expense, without mentioning contingencies, which ought always to be appraised a fourth of the yearly charges. And as the Crown was now necessarily burdened with a great and urgent debt of £300,000, he inferred from that the absolute necessity of an immediate and large supply from the people. To all these reasons, which James likewise urged in a speech addressed to both houses on March 21, the Commons remained inexorable. But not to shock the king with an absolute refusal, they granted him one subsidy and one fifteenth, which would scarcely amount to £100,000. And James received the mortification of revealing in vain all his wants and of begging aid of subjects who had no reasonable indulgence or consideration for him.

Among the many causes of disgust and quarrel which now daily and unavoidably multiplied between prince and Parliament, this article of money is to be regarded as not the least considerable. After the discovery and conquest of the West Indies, gold and silver became every day more plentiful in England as well as in the rest of Europe, and the price of all commodities and provisions rose to a height beyond what had been known since the decline of the Roman Empire. As the revenue of the Crown rose not in proportion, the prince was gradually reduced to poverty amidst the general riches of his subjects and required additional funds in order to support the same magnificence and force which had been maintained by former monarchs. But while money thus flowed into England, we may observe that at the same time—and probably from that very cause—arts and industry of all kinds received a mighty increase, and elegance in every enjoyment of life became better known and more cultivated among all ranks of people. The king's servants, both civil and military, his courtiers, and his ministers demanded more ample supplies from the impoverished prince and were not contented with the same simplicity of living which had satisfied their ancestors. The prince himself began to regard an increase of pomp and splendor as requisite to support the dignity of his rank and to preserve the same superiority above his subjects which his predecessors had enjoyed. It was natural too for him to desire some equality and proportion to the other sovereigns of Europe; and as they had universally enlarged their revenue and multiplied their taxes, the king of England deemed it reasonable that his subjects, who were generally as rich as theirs, should bear with patience some additional burdens and impositions.

Unhappily for the king, those very riches, with the increasing knowledge of the age, bred opposite sentiments in his subjects, and begetting a spirit of freedom and independence, disposed them to pay little regard either to the entreaties or menaces of their sovereign. As long as the barons possessed their former immense property and extensive jurisdictions, they were, at every disgust, apt to endanger the monarch and throw the whole government into confusion [disorder; tumult]. But this confusion often in its turn proved favorable to the monarch and made the nation again submit to him in order to reestablish justice and tranquility. After the power of alienations and the increase of commerce had thrown the balance of property into the hands of the Commons, the situation of affairs and the dispositions of men became susceptible of a more regular plan of liberty; and the laws were not supported singly by the authority of the sovereign. In that interval after the decline of the peers and before the people had yet experienced their own force, the monarchs assumed an exorbitant power and had almost annihilated the constitution under the weight of their prerogative; but as soon as the Commons recovered from their lethargy, they seem to have been astonished at the danger and were resolved to secure liberty by firmer barriers than their ancestors had previously provided for it.

Had James possessed a very rigid frugality, he might have warded off this crisis somewhat longer; and waiting patiently for a favorable opportunity to increase and fix his revenue, he might have secured the extensive authority transmitted to him. On the other hand, had the Commons been inclined to act with more generosity and kindness towards their prince, they might probably have turned his necessities to good account and bribed him to depart peaceably from the more dangerous articles of his prerogative. But he was a foreigner and ignorant of the arts of popularity; they were soured by religious prejudices and tenacious of their money. And in this situation, it is no wonder that during this whole reign we scarcely find an interval of mutual confidence and friendship between prince and Parliament.

The king, by his prerogative alone, had some years before altered the rates of the customs and had established higher impositions on several kinds of merchandise. This exercise of power will naturally appear arbitrary and illegal to us; yet according to the principles and practices of that time, it might admit of some defense. The duties of tonnage [imposed on each "tun" (cask) of imported wine] and poundage [imposed on other imported and exported goods by weight] were at first granted to the Crown by a vote of Parliament and for a limited time; and as the grant frequently expired and was renewed, there could not then arise any doubt concerning the origin of the king's right to levy these duties; and this imposition, like all others, was plainly derived from the voluntary consent of the people. But as Henry V and all the succeeding sovereigns had the revenue conferred on them for life, the prince, so long in possession of these duties, began gradually to consider them as his own proper right and inheritance and regarded the vote of Parliament as a mere formality, which expressed the acquiescence of the people in his prerogative rather than bestowed any new gift or revenue upon him.

The Parliament, when it first granted poundage to the Crown, had fixed no particular rates; the imposition was given as a shilling in a pound, or 5 percent, on all commodities. It was left to the king him-self and the Privy Council, aided by the advice of such merchants as they should think proper to consult, to fix the value of goods and thereby the rates of the customs. And as that value had been settled before the discovery of the West Indies, it had become much inferior to the prices which almost all commodities bore in every market in Europe; and consequently, the customs on many goods, though sup-posed to be 5 percent, was in reality much inferior. The king, there-fore, was naturally led to think that rates which were now plainly false ought to be corrected; that a valuation of commodities fixed by one act of the Privy Council might be amended by another; that if his right to poundage were inherent in the Crown, he should also possess of his own accord the right of correcting its inequalities; and that if this duty were granted by the people, he should at least support the spirit of the law by fixing a new and a more just valuation of all com-modities. But besides this reasoning, which seems plausible if not sol-id, the king was supported in that act of power by direct precedents, some in the reign of Mary, some in the beginning of Elizabeth. Both these princesses had altered the rates of commodities without consent of Parliament; and as their impositions had all along been submitted to without a murmur and still continued to be levied, the king had no reason to think that a further exertion of the same authority would give any occasion of complaint. That less umbrage might be taken, he was moderate in the new rates which he established; the customs dur-ing his whole reign rose only from £127,000 a year to £190,000, though in addition to the increase of the rates there was a noticeable increase of commerce and industry during that period. In addition, every commodity which might serve to the subsistence of the people or might be considered as a material of manufactures was exempted from the new impositions of James. But all this caution could not pre-vent the complaints of the Commons. A spirit of liberty had now tak-en possession of the house. The leading members, men of an inde-pendent spirit and large views, began to regulate their opinions more by the future consequences which they foresaw than by the former precedents which were set before them; and they less aspired to main-tain the ancient constitution than to establish a new one, a freer and a better one. In their remonstrances to the king on this occasion, they observed it to be a general opinion, "That the reasons of that practice might be extended much further, even to the utter ruin of the ancient liberty of the kingdom, and the subjects' right of property in their lands and goods." Though expressly forbidden by the king to touch his prerogative, they passed a bill abolishing these impositions, which was rejected by the House of Lords.

In another address to the king, they objected to the practice of borrowing upon privy seals and desired that the subjects should not be forced to lend money to his majesty or give a reason for their refusal. Some murmurs likewise were thrown out in the house against a new monopoly of the license of wines. It must be confessed that forced loans and monopolies were established on many precedents both ancient and recent, though diametrically opposite to all the principles of a free government.

The house likewise displayed some discontent against the king's proclamations. James told them, "That though he well knew, by the constitution and policy of the kingdom, that proclamations were not of equal force with laws, yet he thought it a duty incumbent on him, and a power inseparably annexed to the Crown, to restrain and prevent such mischiefs and inconveniences as he saw growing on the state, against which no certain law was extant and which might tend to the great detriment of the subject, if there would be no remedy provided till the meeting of a Parliament. And this prerogative," he added, "our progenitors have, in all times, used and enjoyed." The intervals between sessions, we may observe, were frequently so long as to render it necessary for a prince to interpose by his prerogative. The legality of this exertion was established by uniform and undisputed practice; it was even acknowledged by lawyers, who made, however, this difference between laws and proclamations: that the authority of the former was perpetual, but that of the latter expired with the sovereign who emitted them. But what was the authority which could bind the subject yet be different from, and inferior to, the authority of laws? The matter seems inexplicable by any maxims of reason or politics; and in this instance, as in many others, it is easy to see how inaccurate the English constitution was before the Parliament was enabled, by continued acquisitions or encroachments, to establish it on fixed principles of liberty.

Upon the settlement of the Reformation, that extensive branch of power which regards ecclesiastical matters, being then without an owner, seemed to belong to the first occupant; and Henry VIII failed not to seize it immediately and to exert it, even to the utmost degree of tyranny. The possession of it was continued with Edward and recovered by Elizabeth; and that ambitious princess was so remarkably jealous of this flower of her crown that she severely reprimanded the Parliament if they ever presumed to intermeddle in these matters; and they were so overawed by her authority as to submit and to ask pardon on these occasions. But James's Parliaments were much less obsequious. They ventured to lift up their eyes and to consider this prerogative. There they saw a large province of government possessed by the king alone and scarcely ever communicated with the Parliament. They perceived that this province admitted not of any exact boundary or circumscription. In former ages, they had felt that the Roman pontiff was gradually making advances to usurp the whole civil power under pretense of religion. They dreaded still more dangerous consequences from the claims of their own sovereign, who resided among them and who possessed such unlimited authority in many other respects. Therefore, they deemed it absolutely necessary to circumscribe this branch of prerogative; and accordingly, in the preceding session, they passed a bill against the establishment of any ecclesiastical canons without consent of Parliament. But the House of Lords, as is usual, defended the barriers of the throne and rejected the bill.

In this session, the Commons, after passing anew the same bill, made remonstrances against the proceedings of the High Commission Court. It required no great penetration to see the extreme danger to liberty arising in a regal government from such large discretionary powers as were exercised by that court. But James refused compliance with the application of the Commons. He probably considered that besides the diminution of his authority, many inconveniences must necessarily result from the abolishing of all discretionary power in every magistrate; and that the laws, were they ever so carefully framed and digested, could not possibly provide against every contingency, much less where they had not as yet attained a sufficient degree of accuracy and refinement.

But the business which chiefly occupied the Commons during this session was the abolition of wardships and purveyance, prerogatives which had been more or less touched on every session during the whole reign of James. In this affair, the Commons employed the proper means which might entitle them to success. They offered the king a settled revenue as an equivalent for the powers which he would part with; and the king was willing to hearken to terms. After much dispute, he agreed to give up these prerogatives for £200,000 a year, which they agreed to confer upon him. And nothing remained towards closing the bargain but that the Commons would determine the funds by which this sum would be levied. This session was too far advanced to bring so difficult a matter to a full conclusion; and though the Parliament met again towards the end of the year and resumed the question, they were never able to terminate an affair upon which they seemed so intent. The journals of that session are lost; and as the historians of this reign are very negligent in relating parliamentary affairs, the importance of which they were not sufficiently apprised, we know not exactly the reason of this failure. It only appears that the king was extremely dissatisfied with the conduct of the Parliament, and soon after dissolved it. This was his first Parliament, and it sat nearly seven years.

Amidst all these attacks—some more violent, some less so—on royal prerogative, the king displayed as openly as ever all his exalted notions of monarchy and the authority of princes. Even in a speech to the Parliament where he begged for supply, and where he should naturally have used every art to ingratiate himself with that assembly, he expressed himself in these terms: "I conclude, then, the point touching the power of kings with this axiom of divinity, that as to dispute *what God may do* is blasphemy; but *what God wills*, that divines may lawfully and do ordinarily dispute and discuss. So is it sedition in subjects to dispute what a king may do in the height of his power. But just kings will ever be willing to declare what they will do, if they will not incur the curse of God. I will not be content that my power be disputed upon; but I shall ever be willing to make the reason appear of my doings, and rule my actions according to my laws." Notwithstanding the great extent of prerogative in that age, these expressions would probably give some offense. But we may observe that as the king's despotism was more speculative than practical, so the independence of the Commons was at this time the reverse; and though strongly supported by their present situation as well as disposition, it was too new and recent to be as yet founded on systematic principles and opinions.

Death of the French king

This year was distinguished by a memorable event which gave great alarm and concern in England: the murder of Henry IV by the dagger of the fanatical Catholic Ravaillac on May 3. With Henry's death, the glory of the French monarchy suffered an eclipse for some years; and as that kingdom fell under an administration weak and bigoted, factious and disorderly, the Austrian greatness began anew to appear formidable to Europe. In England, the antipathy to the Catholics revived a little upon this tragic event; and some of the laws which had formerly been enacted in order to keep these religionists in awe began now to be executed with greater rigor and severity.

Arminianism

Though James's timidity and indolence fixed him during most of his reign in a very prudent inattention to foreign affairs, there happened this year an event in Europe of such mighty consequence as to rouse him from his lethargy and summon up all his zeal and enterprise. A professor of divinity named Conrad Vorstius, the disciple of Jacobus Arminius, was called from a German to a Dutch university; and as he differed from his Britannic majesty in some nice questions concerning the intimate essence and secret decrees of God, he was considered as a dangerous rival in scholastic fame and was at last obliged to yield to the legions of that royal doctor, whose syllogisms he might have refuted or eluded. If vigor was lacking in other incidents of James's reign, here he behaved even with haughtiness and insolence; after several remonstrances, the Dutch States were obliged to deprive Vorstius of his chair and to banish him from their dominions. The king carried no further his animosity against that professor, though he had very charitably hinted to the States, "That as to the burning of Vorstius for his blasphemies and atheism, he left them to their own Christian wisdom, but surely never heretic better deserved the flames." It is to be remarked that at this period, all over Europe except in Holland alone, the practice of burning heretics still prevailed, even in Protestant countries; and instances were not lacking in England during the reign of James.

1611

State of Ireland

To consider James in a more advantageous light, we must take a view of him as the legislator of Ireland; and most of the institutions which he had framed for civilizing that kingdom being finished about this period, it may not here be improper to give some account of them. He frequently boasted of the management of Ireland as his masterpiece; and it will appear upon inquiry that his vanity in this particular was not altogether without foundation.

1612

After the subjection of Ireland by Elizabeth, the more difficult task still remained: to civilize the inhabitants, to reconcile them to laws and industry, and to render their subjection durable and useful to the Crown of England. James proceeded in this work by a steady, regular, and well-concerted plan; and in the space of 9 years, according to Sir John Davis, he made greater advances towards the reformation of that kingdom than had been made in the 440 years which had elapsed since the conquest was first attempted.

It was previously necessary to abolish the Irish customs which supplied the place of laws and which were shaped to keep that people forever in a state of barbarism and disorder.

By the "Brehon" law, or custom, every crime, however enormous, was punished not with death but by a monetary penalty which was levied upon the criminal. Murder itself, as among all the ancient barbarous nations, was atoned for in this manner. Each man, according to his rank, had a different rate, or value, affixed to him; if anyone were willing to pay it, he needed not fear assassinating his enemy. This rate was called his "eric." When Sir William Fitzwilliam, being lord deputy, told Maguire that he was to send a sheriff into Fermanagh, which a little before had been made a county and subjected to the English law, Maguire replied, "Your sheriff shall be welcome to me; but let me know beforehand his eric, or the price of his head, that if my people cut it off, I may levy the money upon the county." As for oppression, extortion, and other trespasses, so little were they regarded that no penalty was affixed to them and no redress for such offenses could ever be obtained.

The customs of "gavelkind" and "tanistry" were attended with the same absurdity in the distribution of property. By the custom of gavelkind, the land was divided among all the males of the sept, or family, both bastard and legitimate. If any of the sept died after a partition was made, his portion was not shared out among his sons, but the chieftain at his discretion made a new partition of all the lands belonging to that sept and gave everyone his share. As no man, by reason of this custom, enjoyed the fixed property of any land, it would have been so much lost labor to build, to plant, to enclose, to cultivate, to improve.

The chieftains and the tanists [heirs apparent], though drawn from the principal families, were not hereditary but were established by election—or more properly speaking, by force and violence. Their authority was almost absolute; and notwithstanding that certain lands were assigned to the office, its chief profit resulted from exactions, dues, and assessments, for which there was no fixed law and which were levied at pleasure. From this arose that common byword among the Irish, "That they dwelt westward of the law which dwelt beyond the river of the Barrow," meaning the country where the English inhabited, and which extended not twenty miles beyond Dublin.

After James abolished these Irish customs and substituted English law in their place, he took all the natives under his protection, declared them free citizens, and proceeded to govern them by a regular administration, military at well as civil.

A small army was maintained, its discipline inspected, and its pay transmitted from England in order to keep the soldiers from preying upon the country, as had been usual in former reigns. When O'Doherty raised an insurrection, a reinforcement was sent over, and the flames of that rebellion were immediately extinguished.

All minds being first quieted by a general indemnity, circuits were established, justice administered, oppression banished, and crimes and disorders of every kind severely punished. As the Irish had been universally engaged in the rebellion against Elizabeth, a resignation of all the rights which had been formerly granted them to separate jurisdictions was rigorously exacted; and no authority but that of the king and the law was permitted throughout the kingdom.

A resignation of all private estates was even required; and when they were restored, the proprietors received them under such conditions as might prevent for the future all tyranny and oppression over the common people. The value of the dues which the nobles usually claimed from their vassals was estimated at a fixed sum, and all further arbitrary exactions were prohibited under severe penalties.

The whole province of Ulster having fallen to the Crown by the attainder of rebels, a company was established in London for planting new colonies in that fertile country. The property was divided into moderate shares, the largest not exceeding two thousand acres; tenants were brought over from England and Scotland; the Irish were removed from the hills and fastnesses and settled in the open country; husbandry and the arts were taught them, a fixed habitation secured, plunder and robbery punished. And by these means, Ulster, from being the most wild and disorderly province of all Ireland, soon became the best cultivated and most civilized.

Such were the arts by which James introduced humanity and justice among a people who had always been buried in the most profound barbarism. Noble cares! Ones much superior to the vain and criminal glory of conquests, but requiring ages of perseverance and attention to perfect what had been so happily begun.

A laudable act of justice was about this time executed in England upon Lord Sanquhar, a Scottish nobleman, who had been guilty of the base assassination of Turner, a fencing master. The English people, who were generally dissatisfied with the Scots, were enraged at this crime, equally mean and atrocious; but James appeased them by preferring the severity of law to the intercession of the friends and family of the criminal.

CHAPTER 47

1612 – 1617

*Death of Prince Henry – Marriage of the princess Elizabeth
with the elector palatine – Rise of Somerset – His
marriage – Overbury poisoned – A Parliament – Fall of
Somerset – Rise of Buckingham – Cautionary towns
delivered – Affairs of Scotland*

Death of Prince Henry

THIS year the sudden death of Henry, Prince of Wales, on November 6 diffused a universal grief throughout the nation. Though youth and royal birth—both of them strong allurements—prepossess men mightily in favor of the early age of princes, it is with particular fondness that historians mention Henry; and in every respect, his merit seems to have been extraordinary. He had not reached his eighteenth year, and he already possessed more dignity in his behavior and commanded more respect than his father, with all his age, learning, and experience. Neither his high fortune nor his youth had seduced him into any irregular pleasures; business and ambition seem to have been his sole passion. His inclinations as well as exercises were martial. The French ambassador, taking leave of him and asking his commands for France, found him employed in the exercise of the pike: "Tell your king," said he, "in what occupation you left me engaged." He had conceived great affection and esteem for the brave Sir Walter Raleigh. It was his saying, "Sure no king but my father would keep such a bird in a cage." He seems, indeed, to have nourished too violent a contempt for the king on account of the latter's pedantry and pusillanimity, and by that means struck in with the restless and martial spirit of the English nation. Had he lived, he probably would have promoted the glory, but perhaps not the felicity, of his people. The unhappy prepossession which men commonly entertain in favor of ambition, courage, enterprise, and other warlike virtues engages generous natures, who always love fame, into such pursuits as destroy their own peace and that of the rest of mankind.

Violent reports were propagated that Henry had been carried off by poison; but the physicians, on opening his body, found no symptoms to confirm such an opinion. The bold and criminal malignity of men's tongues and pens spared not even the king on the occasion. But that prince's character seems to have failed in the extreme of affability and humanity rather than in that of cruelty and violence. His indulgence to Henry was great—he gave him a large and independent settlement even in so early youth—and perhaps imprudent.

Marriage of the princess Elizabeth with the elector palatine

The marriage of the princess Elizabeth with Frederick, elector palatine, was finished on February 14, some time | *1613* |
after the death of the prince, and served to dissipate the grief which arose on that melancholy event. But this marriage, though celebrated with great joy and festivity, proved itself an unhappy event to the king as well as to his son-in-law, and had ill consequences on the reputation and fortunes of both. The elector, trusting to so great an alliance, engaged in enterprises beyond his strength; and the king, not being able to support him in his distress, lost entirely, in the end of his life, what remained of the affections and esteem of his own subjects.

Rise of Somerset

Except during sessions of Parliament, the history of this reign may more properly be called the history of the court than that of the nation. An interesting object had for some years engaged the attention of the court. It was a favorite, and one beloved by James with so profuse and unlimited an affection as left no room for any rival or competitor. About the end of the year 1609, Robert Carr, a youth of twenty years of age and of a good family in Scotland, arrived in London after having passed some time in his travels. All his natural accomplishments consisted in good looks, all his acquired abilities in an easy air and graceful demeanor. He had letters of recommendation to his countryman Lord Hay; and that nobleman no sooner cast his eye upon him than he discovered talents sufficient to entitle him immediately to make a great figure in the government. Apprised of the king's passion for youth, beauty, and exterior appearance, he studied how matters might be so managed that this new object would make the strongest impression upon him. Without mentioning Carr at court, Hay assigned him the office, at a match of tilting, of presenting to the king his buckler and device, with the hope that he would attract the attention of the monarch. Fortune proved favorable to his design by an incident which bore at first a contrary aspect. When Carr was advancing to execute his office, his unruly horse flung him and broke his leg in the king's presence. James approached him with pity and concern. Love and affection arose on the sight of his beauty and tender years; and the prince immediately ordered him to be lodged in the palace and to be carefully attended. James himself paid him a visit in his chamber after the tilting, and he frequently returned during Carr's confinement. The ignorance and simplicity of the boy finished the conquest begun by his exterior graces and accomplishments. Other princes have been fond of choosing their favorites from among the lower ranks of their subjects, and have reposed themselves on them with the more unreserved confidence and affection because the object has been beholden to their bounty for every honor and acquisition. James was desirous that his favorite would also derive from him all his sense, experience, and knowledge. Highly conceited of his own wisdom, he pleased himself with the fancy that this raw youth, by his lessons and instructions, would soon be equal to his sagest ministers and be initiated into all the profound mysteries of government on which he set so high a value. And as this kind of creation was more perfectly his own work than any other, he seems to have indulged an unlimited fondness for his minion, beyond even that which he bore to his own children. He soon knighted him, created him Viscount Rochester, gave him the garter, brought him into the Privy Council, and though at first without assigning him any particular office, bestowed on him the supreme direction of all his business and political concerns. Riches were heaped upon the needy favorite in an amount thought suitable to his rapid advancement in confidence and honor; and while Salisbury and all the wisest ministers could scarcely find expedients sufficient to keep in motion the overburdened machine of government, James, with unsparing hand, loaded with treasures this insignificant and useless pageant.

It is said that the king found his pupil so ill educated as to be ignorant even of the lowest rudiments of the Latin tongue, and that the monarch, laying aside the scepter, took the birch into his royal hand and instructed him in the principles of grammar. Affairs of state would be introduced during the intervals of this noble occupation; and the stripling, by the ascendance which he had acquired, was now enabled to repay on political what he had received in grammatical instruction. Such scenes and such incidents are the more ridiculous, though the less odious, as the passion of James seems not to have contained in it anything criminal or scandalous. History charges herself willingly with a relation of the great crimes, and still more with that of the great virtues, of mankind; but she appears to fall from her dignity when necessitated to dwell on such frivolous events and ignoble personages.

The favorite was not at first so intoxicated with advancement as to be unaware of his own ignorance and inexperience. He had recourse to the assistance and advice of a friend, and he was more fortunate in his choice than is usual with such pampered minions. In Sir Thomas Overbury, he met with a judicious and sincere counselor who, building all hopes of his own preferment on that of the young favorite, endeavored to instill into him the principles of prudence and discretion. By zealously serving everybody, Carr was taught to abate the envy which might attend his sudden elevation. By showing a preference for the English, he learned to escape the prejudices which prevailed against his country. And so long as he was content to be ruled by Overbury's friendly counsels, he enjoyed what is rare: the highest favor of the prince without being hated by the people.

To complete the measure of courtly happiness, nothing was lacking but a kind mistress; and where high fortune concurred with all the graces of youth and beauty, this circumstance could not be difficult to attain. But it was here that the favorite met with that rock on which all his fortunes were wrecked and which plunged him forever into an abyss of infamy, guilt, and misery.

No sooner had James mounted the throne of England than he remembered his friendship for the unfortunate families of Howard and Devereux, who had suffered for their attachment to the cause of Mary and to his own. Having restored young Essex to his blood and dignity and conferred the titles of Earl of Suffolk and Earl of Northampton on two brothers of the house of Norfolk, he sought the further pleasure of uniting these families by the marriage of the Earl of Essex with Lady Frances Howard, daughter of the Earl of Suffolk. She was only thirteen, he fourteen years of age; and it was thought proper, till both would attain the age of puberty, that he should go abroad and pass some time in his travels. He returned into England after four years' absence and was pleased to find his countess in the full luster of beauty and possessed of the love and admiration of the whole court. But when the earl approached and claimed the privileges of a husband, he met with nothing but symptoms of aversion and disgust, and a flat refusal of any further familiarities. He applied to her parents, who constrained her to attend him into the country and to partake of his bed. But nothing could overcome her rigid sullenness and obstinacy, and she still rose from his side without having shared the nuptial pleasures. Disgusted with reiterated denials, he at last gave up the pursuit, and separating himself from her, from then on abandoned her conduct to her own will and discretion.

Such coldness and aversion in Lady Essex arose not without an attachment to another object. The favorite had opened his addresses, and he had been too successful in making impression on the tender heart of the young countess. She imagined that she never could be deemed Essex's wife so long as she refused his embraces, and that a separation and divorce might still open the way for a new marriage with her beloved Rochester. Though their passion was so violent and their opportunities of intercourse so frequent that they had already indulged themselves in all the gratifications of love, they still lamented their unhappy fate while the union between them was not entire and indissoluble. And the lover as well as his mistress was impatient till their mutual ardor would be crowned by marriage.

So momentous an affair could not be concluded without consulting Overbury, with whom Rochester was accustomed to share all his secrets. As long as that faithful friend had considered his patron's attachment to the Countess of Essex merely as an affair of gallantry, he had favored its progress; and it was partly owing to the ingenious and passionate letters which he dictated that Rochester had met with such success in his addresses. Like an experienced courtier, he thought that a conquest of this nature would throw a luster on the young favorite and would tend still further to endear him to James, who was charmed to hear of the amours of his court and listened with attention to every tale of gallantry. But great was Overbury's alarm when Rochester mentioned his design of marrying the countess, and he used every method to dissuade his friend from so foolish an attempt. He represented how odious, how difficult an enterprise it would be to procure her a divorce from her husband; how dangerous, how shameful to take into his own bed a profligate woman who, being married to a young nobleman of the first rank, had not scrupled to prostitute her character and to bestow favors on the object of a capricious and momentary passion. And in the zeal of friendship, he went so far as to threaten Rochester that he would separate himself forever from him if he could so far forget his honor and his interest as to prosecute the intended marriage.

Rochester had the weakness to reveal this conversation to the Countess of Essex. When her rage and fury broke out against Overbury, he also had the weakness to enter into her vindictive projects and to swear vengeance against his friend for the worst token which he could receive of his faithful friendship. Some contrivance was necessary for the execution of their purpose. Rochester addressed himself to the king; and after complaining that his own indulgence to Overbury had begotten in the latter a degree of arrogance which was extremely disagreeable, he procured a commission for Overbury's embassy to Russia, which he represented as a retreat both profitable and honorable for his friend. When consulted by Overbury, he warmly dissuaded him from accepting this offer and took on himself the office of satisfying the king if he would be displeased in any way with the refusal. To the king again, he exaggerated the insolence of Overbury's conduct, and on April 21, obtained a warrant for committing him to the Tower. James intended this as a slight punishment for Overbury's disobedience, but the lieutenant of the Tower was a creature of Rochester's and had lately been put into the office for this very purpose. He confined Overbury so strictly that the unhappy prisoner was barred from the sight even of his nearest relations, and no communication of any kind was allowed with him during the nearly six months which he lived in prison.

His marriage

This obstacle being removed, the lovers pursued their purpose; and the king himself, forgetting the dignity of his rank and his friendship for the family of Essex, entered zealously into the project of procuring the countess a divorce from her husband. Essex also embraced the opportunity of separating himself from a bad woman by whom he was hated; and he was willing to favor their success by any honorable expedient. The pretense for a divorce was his incapacity to fulfill the conjugal duties; and he confessed that with regard to the countess, he was conscious of such an infirmity, though he was not aware of it with regard to any other woman. In her place too, it is said, a young virgin was substituted under a mask to undergo a legal inspection by a jury of matrons. After such a trial, seconded by court influence and supported by the ridiculous opinion of fascination, or witchcraft, the sentence of divorce was pronounced between the Earl of Essex and his countess. And to crown the scene, the king, solicitous lest the lady would lose any rank by her new marriage, bestowed on his minion the title of Earl of Somerset.

Overbury poisoned

Notwithstanding this success, the Countess of Somerset was not satisfied till she could further satiate her revenge on Overbury; and she engaged her husband and her uncle, the Earl of Northampton, in the atrocious design of taking him off secretly by poison. Fruitless attempts were reiterated by weak poisons; but at last, on September 16, they gave him one so sudden and violent that the symptoms were apparent to everyone who approached him. His interment was hurried on with the greatest precipitation; and though a strong suspicion immediately prevailed in the public, the full proof of the crime was not brought to light till some years later.

The fatal catastrophe of Overbury increased or begot the suspicion that the Prince of Wales had been carried off by poison given him by Somerset. Men failed to consider that the contrary inference was much more just. If Somerset was so great a novice in this detestable art that a man who was his prisoner and attended by none but his emissaries during the course of five months could not be dispatched but in so bungling a manner, how could it be imagined that a young prince living in his own court and surrounded by his own friends and domestics could be exposed to Somerset's attempts and be taken off by so subtle a poison—if such a one exist—as could elude the skill of the most experienced physicians?

A Parliament

The ablest minister that James ever possessed, the Earl of Salisbury, had died in 1612. The Earl of Suffolk, a man of

1614

slender capacity, had succeeded him in his office; and it was now his task to supply from an exhausted Treasury the lavish expenditure of James and of his young favorite. The title of baronet, invented by Salisbury, was sold; and two hundred patents of that species of knighthood were disposed of for so many thousand pounds. Each rank of nobility also had its price affixed to it: privy seals were circulated to the amount of £200,000, benevolences [forced "gifts"] were exacted to the amount of £52,000, and some monopolies of no great value were erected. But all these expedients proved insufficient to supply the king's necessities, even though he began to enter into some schemes for retrenching his expenses. However small the hopes of success, a new Parliament must be summoned, and this dangerous expedient—for such it had now become—once more be put to trial.

When the Commons were assembled on April 5, they displayed an extraordinary alarm on account of a rumor which was spread abroad concerning "undertakers" [those who undertake, or engage in, a project]. It was reported that several persons attached to the king had entered into a confederacy; having laid a regular plan for the new elections, they had distributed their influence all over England and had undertaken to secure a majority for the court. So ignorant were the Commons that they did not know this incident to be the first infallible symptom of any regular or established liberty. Had they been contented to follow the maxims of their predecessors—who, as the Earl of Salisbury said to the last Parliament, never but thrice in six hundred years refused a supply—they needed not dread that the Crown would ever interest itself in their elections. Formerly, the kings even insisted that none of their household be elected members; and though the charter was later declared void, Henry VI, from his great favor to the city of York, conferred the singular privilege on its citizens that they would be exempted from this trouble. It is well known that in ancient times, it was requisite for the counties and boroughs to pay fees to their representatives, as a seat in the house was considered a burden, attended neither with honor nor profit. About this time, a seat began to be regarded as an honor, and the country gentlemen contended for it, though the practice of levying wages for the Parliament men was not altogether discontinued. It was not till long after, when liberty was thoroughly established and popular assemblies entered into every branch of public business, that the members began to join profit to honor, and the Crown found it necessary to distribute among them all the considerable offices of the kingdom.

So little skill or so small means had the courtiers in James's reign for managing elections that this House of Commons showed rather a stronger spirit of liberty than the foregoing; and instead of entering upon the business of supply as urged by the king, who made them several liberal offers of grace, they immediately resumed the subject which had been opened in the last Parliament and disputed his majesty's power of levying new customs and impositions by the mere authority of his prerogative. It is remarkable that in their debates on this subject, the courtiers frequently pleaded as a precedent the example of all the other hereditary monarchs in Europe, and particularly mentioned the kings of France and Spain; nor was this reasoning received by the house either with surprise or indignation. The members of the opposite party contented themselves either with denying the justness of the inference or disputing the truth of the observation. And a patriot member in particular, Sir Roger Owen, even in arguing against the impositions, frankly allowed that the king of England was endowed with as ample a power and prerogative as any prince in Christendom. The nations on the Continent, we may observe, enjoyed still in that age some small remains of liberty, and the English were possessed of little more.

The Commons applied to the Lords for a conference with regard to the new impositions. A speech of Neile, bishop of Lincoln, reflecting on the lower house begat some altercation with the Peers; and on June 6, the king seized the opportunity of dissolving immediately, with great indignation, a Parliament which had shown so firm a resolution of retrenching his prerogative without communicating in return the smallest supply to his necessities. He carried his resentment so far as even to throw into prison some of the members who had been the most forward in their opposition to his measures. In vain did he plead, in excuse for this violence, the example of Elizabeth and other monarchs of the lines of Tudor and Plantagenet. The people and the Parliament could acquiesce in none of these precedents, however ancient and frequent, without abandoning forever all their liberties and privileges. And were the authority of such precedents admitted, the utmost that could be inferred is that the constitution of England was at that time an inconsistent fabric, whose jarring and discordant parts must soon destroy each other, and from the dissolution of the old, beget some new form of civil government more uniform and consistent.

In the public and avowed conduct of the king and the House of Commons throughout this whole reign, there appears sufficient cause of quarrel and mutual disgust; yet we are not to imagine that this was the sole foundation of that jealousy which prevailed between them. During debates in the house, it often happened that a particular member, more ardent and zealous than the rest, would display the highest sentiments of liberty, which the Commons contented themselves to hear with silence and seeming approbation; and the king, informed of these harangues, concluded the whole house to be infected with the same principles and to be engaged in a combination against his prerogative. On the other hand, the king, though he valued himself extremely on his kingcraft and perhaps was not altogether incapable of dissimulation, seems to have been very little endowed with the gift of secrecy, but openly—at his table, in all companies—inculcated those monarchical tenets which he had so strongly imbibed. Before a numerous audience, he had expressed himself with great disparagement of the common law of England and had given the preference in the strongest terms to the civil law; and for this indiscretion he found himself obliged to apologize in a speech to the former Parliament.

As a specimen of his usual liberty of talk, we may mention a story, though it passed some time later, which we meet with in the life of Waller and which that poet frequently repeated. When Waller was young, he had the curiosity to go to court; and he stood in the circle and saw James dine, where among other company there sat at table two bishops, Neile and Andrews. The king proposed aloud this question: Whether he might not take his subjects' money when he needed it without all this formality of Parliament? Neile replied, "God forbid you should not; for you are the breath of our nostrils." Andrews declined answering and said he was not skilled in parliamentary cases. But upon the king's urging him and saying he would admit of no evasion, the bishop replied pleasantly, "Why, then, I think your majesty may lawfully take my brother Neile's money, for he offers it."

Fall of Somerset

The favorite had till now escaped the inquiry of justice; but he had not escaped that still voice which can make itself be heard amidst all the hurry and flattery of a court and astonishes the criminal with a just representation of his most secret enormities. Conscious of the murder of his friend, Somerset received small consolation from the enjoyments of love or the utmost kindness and indulgence of his sovereign. The graces of his youth gradually disappeared, the gaiety of his manners was obscured, his politeness and obliging behavior were changed into sullenness and silence. And the king, whose affections had been engaged by these superficial accomplishments, began to estrange himself from a man who no longer contributed to his amusement.

The sagacious courtiers observed the first symptoms of this disgust.

Somerset's enemies seized the opportunity and offered a new minion to the king. George Villiers, a youth of twenty-one, younger brother of a good family, returned at this time from his travels and was observed to have the advantages of a handsome person, genteel air, and fashionable apparel. At a comedy, he was purposely placed full in James's eye and immediately engaged the attention, and in the same instant the affections, of that monarch. Ashamed of his sudden attachment, the king endeavored but in vain to conceal the partiality which he felt for the handsome stranger; and he employed all his profound politics to fix him in his service without seeming to desire it. He declared his resolution not to confer any office on him unless entreated by the queen; and he pretended that it would only be in complaisance to her choice that he would agree to admit him near his person. The queen was immediately applied to; but she, well knowing the extreme to which the king carried these attachments, refused at first to lend her support to this new passion. It was not till entreated by Abbot, archbishop of Canterbury—a decent prelate, and one much prejudiced against Somerset—that she would condescend to oblige her husband by asking this favor of him. And the king, thinking now that all appearances were fully saved, no longer constrained his affection, but immediately bestowed the office of cupbearer on young Villiers.

The whole court was thrown into parties between the two minions; while some endeavored to advance the rising fortunes of Villiers, others deemed it safer to adhere to the established credit of Somerset. The king himself, divided between inclination and decorum, increased the doubt and ambiguity of the courtiers; and the stern jealousy of the old favorite, who refused every advance of friendship from his rival, begat perpetual quarrels between their several partisans. But the disclosure of Somerset's guilt in the murder of Overbury at last decided the controversy and exposed him to the ruin and infamy which he so well merited.

An apothecary's apprentice who had been employed in making up the poisons, having retired to Flushing, began to talk very freely of the whole secret; and the affair at last came to the ears of Trumbull, the king's envoy in the Low Countries. By his means, Sir Ralph Winwood, secretary of state, was informed; and he immediately carried the intelligence to James. The king, alarmed and astonished to find such enormous guilt in a man whom he had admitted into his bosom, sent for Sir Edward Coke, chief justice, and earnestly recommended to him the most rigorous and unbiased scrutiny. This injunction was executed with great industry and severity. The whole labyrinth of guilt was carefully unraveled. The lesser criminals—Sir Gervase Helwys, lieutenant of the Tower, Franklin, Weston, and Mrs. Turner—were first tried and condemned. Somerset and his countess were afterwards found guilty. Northampton's death, a little before, had saved him from a like fate.

It may not be unworthy of remark that Coke, in the trial of Mrs. Turner, told her that she was guilty of the seven deadly sins: she was a whore, a bawd, a sorcerer, a witch, a papist, a felon, and a murderer. And what may more surprise us, Bacon, then attorney general, took care to observe that poisoning was a popish trick. Such were the bigoted prejudices which prevailed: poisoning was not by itself sufficiently odious if it were not represented as a branch of popery. Stow tells us that when the king came to Newcastle on his first entry into England, he gave liberty to all the prisoners except those who were confined for treason, murder, and "papistry." When one considers these circumstances, that furious bigotry of the Catholics which broke out in the gunpowder conspiracy appears the less surprising.

All the accomplices in Overbury's murder received the punishment due to their crime; but the king bestowed a pardon on the principals, Somerset and the countess. It must be confessed that James's fortitude would have been highly laudable had he persisted in his first intention of consigning over to severe justice all the criminals. But let us still beware of blaming him too harshly if, on the approach of the fatal hour, he scrupled to deliver into the hands of the executioner persons whom he had once favored with his most tender affections. To soften the rigor of their fate after some years' imprisonment, he restored them to their liberty and conferred on them a pension, with which they retired and languished out old age in infamy and obscurity. Their guilty loves were turned into the most deadly hatred, and they passed many years together in the same house without any intercourse or correspondence with each other.

Several historians, in relating these events, have insisted much on the dissimulation of James's behavior when he delivered Somerset into the hands of the chief justice, on the insolent menaces of that criminal, on his peremptory refusal to stand a trial, and on the extreme anxiety of the king during the whole progress of this affair. Allowing all these circumstances to be true—some are suspicious, if not palpably false—the great remains of tenderness which James still felt for Somerset may perhaps be sufficient to account for them. That favorite was high spirited and resolute to perish rather than live under the infamy to which he was exposed. James was aware that the pardoning of so great a criminal, which was by itself odious, would become still more unpopular if his obstinate and stubborn behavior on his trial would augment the public hatred against him. At least, the unreserved confidence in which the king had indulged his favorite for several years might have rendered Somerset master of so many secrets that it is impossible without further light to assign the particular reason of that superiority which, it is said, he appeared so much to assume.

Rise of Buckingham

The fall of Somerset and his banishment from court opened the way for Villiers to mount up at once to the full height of favor, of honors, and of riches. Had James's passion been governed by common rules of prudence, the office of cupbearer alone would have attached Villiers to his person and might well have contented one of his age and family; nor would anyone who was not cynically austere have much censured the singularity of the king's choice in his friends and favorites. But such advancement was far inferior to the fortune which he intended for his minion. In the course of a few years, he created him Viscount Villiers, Earl, Marquess, and Duke of Buckingham, knight of the garter, master of the horse, chief justice in eyre, warden of the Cinque Ports, master of the King's Bench office, steward of Westminster, constable of Windsor, and lord high admiral of England. His mother obtained the title of Countess of Buckingham, his brother was created Viscount Purbeck, and a numerous train of needy relations were all pushed up into credit and authority. And thus the fond prince, while he meant to play the tutor to his favorite and to train him up in the rules of prudence and politics, took an infallible method to render him forever rash, precipitate, and insolent by loading him with premature and exorbitant honors.

Cautionary towns delivered

A young minion to gratify with pleasure and a necessitous family to supply with riches were enterprises too great for the empty Exchequer of James. In order to obtain a little money, the cautionary towns had to be delivered up to the Dutch, a measure which has been severely blamed by almost all historians. I may venture to affirm that it has been censured much beyond its real weight and importance.

1616

When Queen Elizabeth advanced money for the support of the infant Dutch republic, her purpose was to secure herself against the power and ambition of Spain; but she still reserved the prospect of reimbursement, and she got consigned into her hands the three important fortresses of Flushing, the Brill, and Rammekens as security for the money due to her. Indulgent to the necessitous condition of the States, she agreed that the debt would bear no interest; and she stipulated that if ever England would make a separate peace with Spain, she would pay the troops which garrisoned those fortresses.

After the truce was concluded between Spain and the United Provinces, the States made an agreement with the king that the debt, which then amounted to £800,000, would be discharged by yearly payments of £40,000; and as five years had elapsed, the debt was now reduced to £600,000; and in fifteen years more, if the truce were renewed, it would be finally extinguished. But of this sum, £26,000 a year were expended on the pay of the garrisons; only the remainder accrued to the king. And the States, weighing these circumstances, thought that they made James a very advantageous offer when they expressed their willingness, on the surrender of the cautionary towns, to pay him immediately £250,000 and to incorporate the English garrisons in their army. It occurred also to the king that even the payment of the £40,000 a year was precarious and depended on the accident that the truce would be renewed between Spain and the republic; if war broke out, the maintenance of the garrisons lay upon England alone, a burden very useless and too heavy for the slender revenues of that kingdom. That even during the truce, the Dutch, straitened by other expenses, were far from being regular in their payments, and the garrisons were at present in danger of mutinying for want of subsistence. That the annual sum of £14,000—the whole saving on the Dutch payments—amounted in fifteen years to no more than £210,000, whereas £250,000 was offered immediately, a larger sum; and if money be computed at 10 percent, the current interest was more than double the sum to which England was entitled. That if James waited till the whole debt was discharged, the troops which composed the garrisons would remain a burden upon him and could not be disbanded without receiving some consideration for their past services. That the cautionary towns were only a temporary restraint upon the Hollanders; in the present state of affairs, the conjunction of interest between England and the republic was so intimate as to render all other ties superfluous, and no reasonable measures for mutual support would be lacking from the Dutch, even though freed from the dependence of these garrisons. That the exchequer of the republic was at present very low, with the result that they found it difficult, now that the aids of France were withdrawn, to maintain themselves in that posture of defense which was requisite during the truce with Spain. And that the Spaniards were perpetually insisting with the king on the restitution of these towns as belonging to their Crown, and no cordial alliance could ever be made with that nation while they remained in the hands of the English. These reasons, together with his urgent wants, induced the king to accept the Dutch offer; on June 6, he evacuated the cautionary towns, which held the States in a degree of subjection and which an ambitious and enterprising prince would have regarded as his most valuable possessions. This is the date of the full liberty of the Dutch commonwealth.

Affairs of Scotland

When the Crown of England devolved on James, it might have been foreseen by the Scottish nation that the inde-

1617

pendence of their kingdom—the object for which their ancestors had shed so much blood—would now be lost; and that if both states persevered in maintaining separate laws and Parliaments, the weaker would more sharply feel the subjection than if it had been totally subdued by force of arms. But these views did not generally occur. The glory of having given a sovereign to their powerful enemy, the advantages of present peace and tranquility, the riches acquired from the munificence of their master: these considerations secured their dutiful obedience to a prince who daily gave such evident proofs of his friendship and partiality towards them. Never had the authority of any king who resided among them been so firmly established as was that of James even when absent; and as the administration previously had been conducted with great order and tranquility, there had happened no occurrence to draw our attention there. But this summer the king was resolved to pay a visit to his native country in order to renew his ancient friendships and connections and to introduce that change of ecclesiastical discipline and government on which he was extremely intent. The three chief points of this kind which James proposed to accomplish by his journey to Scotland were the enlarging of episcopal authority, the establishing of a few ceremonies in public worship, and the fixing of a superiority in the civil above the ecclesiastical jurisdiction.

But it is an observation suggested by all history—and by none more than by that of James and his successor—that the religious spirit, when it mingles with faction, contains in it something supernatural and unaccountable; and that in its operations upon society, effects correspond less to their known causes than is found in any other circumstance of government. This is a reflection which may afford both a source of blame against those sovereigns who lightly innovate in so dangerous an article and of defense of those who, when they engage in such an enterprise, are disappointed of the expected result and fail in their undertakings.

When the Scottish nation was first seized with that zeal for reformation which, though it caused such disturbance during the time, has proved so salutary in the consequences, the preachers, assuming a rank little inferior to the prophetic or apostolic, disdained all subjection to the spiritual rulers of the church, by whom their innovations were punished and opposed. The revenues of the dignified clergy, no longer considered as sacred, were either appropriated by the present possessors or seized by the more powerful barons; and what remained after mighty dilapidations [neglectful or intentional impairing of church property by an incumbent] was by act of Parliament annexed to the Crown. The prelates and abbots maintained their temporal jurisdictions and their seats in Parliament, however; and though laymen were sometimes endowed with ecclesiastical titles, the church, notwithstanding its frequent protestations to the contrary, was still supposed to be represented by those spiritual lords in the states of the kingdom. After many struggles, James, while king of Scotland but not yet of England, had acquired sufficient influence over the Scottish clergy to extort from them an acknowledgment, though attended with many precautions, of the parliamentary jurisdiction of bishops, in order to secure themselves against the spiritual encroachments of that order. After his accession to the throne of England, he engaged them, though still with great reluctance on their part, to advance a step further and to receive the bishops as perpetual presidents, or moderators, in their ecclesiastical synods, reiterating their protestations against all spiritual jurisdiction of the prelates and all controlling power over the presbyters. And by such gradual innovations, the king flattered himself that he would quietly introduce episcopal authority. But as his final design was fully seen from the beginning, every new advance gave fresh occasion of discontent, aggravating instead of softening the abhorrence entertained against the prelacy.

What rendered the king's aim more apparent were the endeavors which he used at the same time to introduce into Scotland some of the ceremonies of the Church of England; the rest, it was easily foreseen, would soon follow. The fire of devotion, excited by novelty and inflamed by opposition, had so possessed the minds of the Scottish reformers that all rites and ornaments, and even order of worship, were disdainfully rejected as useless burdens, retarding the imagination in its rapturous ecstasies and cramping the operations of that divine Spirit by which they supposed themselves to be animated. A mode of worship, the simplest and most naked imaginable, was established, one that borrowed nothing from the senses but reposed itself entirely on the contemplation of that divine Essence which reveals itself to the understanding only. This species of devotion—so worthy of the Supreme Being but so little suitable to human frailty—was observed to occasion great disturbances in the breast, and in many respects to confound all rational principles of conduct and behavior. The mind—straining for these extraordinary raptures, reaching them by short glances, sinking again under its own weakness, rejecting all exterior aid of pomp and ceremony—was so occupied in this inward life that it fled from every intercourse of society and from every cheerful amusement which could soften or humanize the character. It was obvious to all discerning eyes, and had not escaped the king's, that by the prevalence of fanaticism, a gloomy and sullen disposition established itself among the people, a spirit obstinate and dangerous, independent and disorderly, animated equally with a contempt of authority and a hatred to every other mode of religion, particularly to the Catholic. In order to mellow these humors, James endeavored to infuse a small tincture of ceremony into the national worship and to introduce such rites as might in some degree occupy the mind and please the senses without departing too far from that simplicity by which the Reformation was distinguished. The finer arts too, though still rude in those northern kingdoms, were employed to adorn the churches; and the king's chapel, in which an organ was erected and some pictures and statues displayed, was proposed as a model to the rest of the nation. But music was grating to the prejudiced ears of the Scottish clergy, sculpture and painting appeared instruments of idolatry, the surplice was a rag of popery, and every motion or gesture prescribed by the liturgy was a step towards that spiritual Babylon so much the object of their horror and aversion. Everything was deemed impious but their own mystical comments on the Scriptures, which they idolized, and whose Eastern prophetic style they employed in every common occurrence.

It will not be necessary to give a particular account of the ceremonies which the king was so intent to establish. Such institutions are esteemed for a time either too divine to have proceeded from any other being than the supreme Creator of the universe or too diabolical to have been derived from any but an infernal demon. But no sooner is the mode of the controversy past than they are universally discovered to be of so little importance as scarcely to be mentioned with decency amidst the ordinary course of human transactions. It suffices here to remark that the rites introduced by James regarded the kneeling at the sacrament, private communion, private baptism, confirmation of children, and the observance of Christmas and other festivals. The acts establishing these ceremonies were afterwards known by the name of the Articles of Perth, from the place where they were ratified by the General Assembly of the Church of Scotland.

James could never hope to establish his aim of a conformity of discipline and worship between the Churches of England and Scotland but by first procuring an acknowledgment of his own authority in all spiritual causes; and nothing could have been more contrary to the practice as well as principles of the Presbyterian clergy. The ecclesiastical courts possessed the power of pronouncing excommunication; and that sentence, besides the spiritual consequences supposed to follow from it, was attended with immediate effects of the most important nature. The person excommunicated was shunned by everyone as profane and impious. His whole estate during his lifetime, and all his movables forever, were forfeited to the Crown. Nor were the procedures required before pronouncing this sentence formal or regular in proportion to the weight of it. Any ecclesiastical court, however inferior, sometimes claimed the power, in a summary manner—without accuser, without summons, without trial—to proclaim excommunication for any cause and against any person, even though he lived not within the bounds of their jurisdiction. And by this means, the whole tyranny of the Inquisition, though without its order, was introduced into the kingdom.

But the clergy were not content with the unlimited jurisdiction which they exercised in ecclesiastical matters. They assumed a censorial power over every part of administration; and in all their sermons, and even prayers, they mingled politics with religion and inculcated the most seditious and most turbulent principles. Black, minister of

St. Andrews, went so far in a sermon as to pronounce all kings the devil's children; he gave the queen of England the appellation of "atheist"; he said that the treachery of the king's heart was now fully discovered [uncovered; revealed]; and in his prayers for the queen he used these words: "We must pray for her for the fashion's sake, but we have no cause: she will never do us any good." When summoned before the Privy Council, he refused to answer to a civil court for anything delivered from the pulpit, even though the crime of which he was accused was of a civil nature. The church adopted his cause. They raised a sedition in Edinburgh. The king was in the hands of the enraged populace for a time, and it was not without courage as well as dexterity that he was able to extricate himself. A few days later, a minister preaching in the principal church of that capital said that the king had been possessed with a devil; and that one devil being expelled, seven worse had entered in his place. To which he added that the subjects might lawfully rise and take the sword out of his hand. Scarcely even during the darkest night of papal superstition are there found such instances of priestly encroachments as the annals of Scotland present to us during that period.

By these extravagant stretches of power and by the patient conduct of James, the church began to lose ground even before the king's accession to the throne of England. But no sooner had that event taken place than he made the Scottish clergy aware that he had become the sovereign of a great kingdom, which he governed with great authority. Though formerly he would have thought himself happy to have made a fair partition with them of the civil and ecclesiastical authority, he was now resolved to exert a supreme jurisdiction in church as well as state and to put an end to their seditious practices. A General Assembly had been summoned at Aberdeen; but on account of his journey to London, he prorogued it to the year following. Some of the clergy, disavowing his ecclesiastical supremacy, met at the time first appointed notwithstanding his prohibition. He threw them into prison. Such of them as submitted and acknowledged their error were pardoned. The rest, six in number, were brought to their trial and condemned for high treason; the king gave them their lives but banished them from the kingdom.

The General Assembly was afterwards induced to acknowledge the king's authority in summoning ecclesiastical courts and to submit to the jurisdiction and visitation of the bishops. Even their favorite sentence of excommunication was declared invalid unless confirmed by the ordinary [a cleric, such as a bishop, with ordinary jurisdiction over a specified territory]. The king recommended to the inferior courts the members whom they should elect to this Assembly, and everything was conducted in it with little appearance of choice and liberty.

By his own prerogative likewise, which he seems to have stretched on this occasion, the king erected a Court of High Commission in imitation of that which was established in England. The bishops and a few of the clergy who had been summoned willingly acknowledged this court, and it proceeded immediately upon business as if its authority had been grounded on the full consent of the whole legislature.

But James reserved the final blow for the time when he would himself pay a visit to Scotland. On June 13, he proposed to the Parliament, which was then assembled, that they should enact that "whatever his majesty should determine in the external government of the church, with the consent of the archbishops, bishops, and a competent number of the ministry, should have the force of law." What number should be deemed competent was not determined, and their nomination was left entirely to the king, so that his ecclesiastical authority, had this bill passed, would have been established in its full extent. Some of the clergy protested. They feared, they said, that the purity of their church would, by means of this new authority, be polluted with all the rites and liturgy of the Church of England. James, dreading clamor and opposition, dropped the bill, which had already passed the Lords of Articles, and asserted that the inherent prerogative of the Crown contained more power than was recognized by it. Some time later, he called a meeting of the bishops and thirty-six of the most eminent clergy at St. Andrews. On July 10, he there declared his resolution of exerting his prerogative and of establishing by his own authority the few ceremonies which he had recommended to them. They entreated him rather to summon a General Assembly and to gain their assent. Accordingly, an Assembly was summoned to meet on November 25 ensuing.

Yet this Assembly, which met after the king's departure from Scotland, eluded all his applications; and it was not till the subsequent year that he was able to procure a vote for receiving his ceremonies. And through every step in this affair, in the Parliament as well as in all the General Assemblies, the nation betrayed the utmost reluctance to all these innovations; nothing but James's importunity and authority had extorted a seeming consent, which was belied by the inward sentiments of all ranks of people. Even the few over whom religious prejudices were not predominant thought national honor sacrificed by a servile imitation of the modes of worship practiced in England. And every prudent man agreed in condemning the measures of the king, who by an ill-timed zeal for insignificant ceremonies had betrayed, though in an opposite manner, equal narrowness of mind with the persons whom he treated with such contempt. It was judged that if these dangerous humors of the Scots had not been irritated by opposition and had been allowed peaceably to evaporate, they would at last have subsided within the limits of law and civil authority; and that as all fanatical religions naturally circumscribe to very narrow bounds the numbers and riches of the ecclesiastics, no sooner is their first fire spent than they lose their credit over the people and leave them under the natural and beneficent influence of their civil and moral obligations.

At the same time that James shocked in so violent a manner the religious principles of his Scottish subjects, he acted in opposition to those of his English ones. He had observed in his progress through England that a Judaic observance of the Sunday, chiefly by means of the Puritans, was every day gaining ground throughout the kingdom, and that the people, under color of religion and contrary to former practice, were barred from those sports and recreations which contributed both to their health and their amusement. Festivals which in other nations and ages were partly dedicated to public worship, partly to mirth and society, were here totally appropriated to the offices of religion and served to nourish those sullen and gloomy contemplations to which the people were of their own accord so unfortunately subject. The king imagined that it would be easy to infuse cheerfulness into this dark spirit of devotion. He issued a proclamation to allow and encourage all kinds of lawful games and exercises after divine service; and by his authority, he endeavored to give sanction to a practice which his subjects regarded as the utmost instance of profaneness and impiety.

CHAPTER 48
1618 – 1621

*Sir Walter Raleigh's expedition – His execution –
Insurrections in Bohemia – Loss of the Palatinate –
Negotiations with Spain – Parties – A Parliament – Fall of
Bacon – Rupture between the king and the Commons –
Protestation of the Commons*

Sir Walter Raleigh's expedition

AT the time when Sir Walter Raleigh was first con-
fined in the Tower, his violent and haughty temper | 1618 |
had rendered him the most unpopular man in England; and his condemnation was chiefly owing to that public odium under which he labored. During the thirteen years' imprisonment which he suffered,
the sentiments of the nation were much changed with regard to him.
Men had leisure to reflect on the hardship, not to say injustice, of his
sentence; they pitied his active and enterprising spirit, which languished in the rigors of confinement; they were struck with the extensive genius of the man, who, being educated amidst naval and military
enterprises, had surpassed in the pursuits of literature even those of
the most reclusive and sedentary lives; and they admired his unbroken
magnanimity, which at his age and under his circumstances could engage him to undertake and execute so great a work as his *History of the
World*. To increase these favorable dispositions, on which he built the
hopes of recovering his liberty, he spread the report of a gold mine
which he had discovered in Guiana [now Guayana, a region of Vene-
zuela], and which was sufficient, according to his representation, not
only to enrich all the adventurers but also to afford immense treasures
to the nation. The king gave little credit to these mighty promises,

both because he believed that no such mine as the one described was anywhere in nature and because he considered Raleigh as a man of desperate fortunes whose business it was, by any means, to procure his freedom and to reinstate himself in credit and authority. Thinking that Raleigh had already undergone sufficient punishment, however, the king released him from the Tower; and when Raleigh's boasts of the gold mine had induced multitudes to engage with him, the king gave them permission to try the adventure; and at their desire, he conferred on Raleigh authority over his fellow adventurers. Though strongly solicited, the king still refused to grant Raleigh a pardon, which the latter deemed a natural consequence when he was entrusted with power and command. But James declared himself still distrustful of Raleigh's intentions; and he meant, he said, to reserve the former sentence as a check upon his future behavior.

Raleigh well knew that it was far from the king's purpose to invade any of the Spanish settlements. Therefore, he firmly denied that Spain had planted any colonies on that part of the coast where his mine lay. When Gondomar, the Spanish ambassador, alarmed at Raleigh's preparations, carried complaints to the king, Raleigh still protested the innocence of his intentions; and James assured Gondomar that Raleigh dared not form any hostile attempt, because he would pay with his head for so audacious an enterprise. The minister, however, concluding that twelve armed vessels were not fitted out without some purpose of invasion, conveyed the intelligence to the court of Madrid, who immediately gave orders for arming and fortifying all their settlements, particularly those along the coast of Guiana.

When the courage and avarice of the Spaniards and Portuguese had discovered so many new worlds, they were resolved to show themselves superior to the barbarous heathens whom they invaded not only in arts and arms but also in the justice of the quarrel. They applied to Alexander VI, who then filled the papal chair; and he generously bestowed on the Spaniards the whole western part of the globe and on the Portuguese the whole eastern. The more scrupulous Protestants, who did not acknowledge the authority of the Roman pontiff, established the first discovery as the foundation of *their* title; and if a pirate or sea adventurer of their nation had but erected a stick or a stone on the coast as a memorial of his taking possession, they concluded the whole continent to belong to them and thought themselves entitled to expel or exterminate as usurpers the ancient possessors and inhabitants. It was in this manner that Sir Walter Raleigh, about twenty-three years before, had acquired to the Crown of England a claim to the continent of Guiana, a region as large as half of Europe; and though he had immediately left the coast, yet he professed that the English title to the whole remained certain and indefeasible. But it had happened in the meantime that the Spaniards, not knowing or not acknowledging this imaginary claim, had taken possession of a part of Guiana, had formed a settlement on the River Orinoco, had built a little town called St. Thomas, and were there working some mines of small value.

To this place Raleigh directly bent his course; and remaining himself at the mouth of the river with five of the largest ships, he sent up the rest to St. Thomas under the command of his son and of Captain Keymis, a person entirely devoted to him. The Spaniards, who had expected this invasion, fired on the English at their landing, repulsed them, and pursued them into the town. Young Raleigh, to encourage his men, called out, "That this was the true mine, and none but fools looked for any other"; and advancing upon the Spaniards, he received a shot, of which he immediately expired. This did not dismay Keymis and the others. They carried on the attack and got possession of the town, which they afterwards reduced to ashes, and found in it nothing of value.

Raleigh did not claim that he had himself seen the mine which he had engaged so many people to go in quest of. It was Keymis, he said, who had formerly discovered it and had brought him that lump of ore which promised such immense treasures. Yet Keymis, who confessed that he was within two hours' march of the place, refused on the most absurd pretenses to take any effectual step towards finding it; and he returned immediately to Raleigh with the melancholy news of his son's death and the ill success of the enterprise. Sensitive to reproach and dreading punishment for his behavior, Keymis, in despair, retired into his cabin and put an end to his own life.

The other adventurers now concluded that they had been deceived by Raleigh; that he never had known of any such mine as he pretended to go in search of; that his intention had always been to plunder St. Thomas, and having encouraged his company by the spoils of that place, to have proceeded from there to the invasion of the other Spanish settlements; that he expected to repair his ruined fortunes by such daring enterprises; and that he trusted to the money he would acquire for making his peace with England, or if that intention failed him, that he purposed to retire into some other country where his riches would secure his retreat.

The small acquisitions gained by the sack of St. Thomas discouraged Raleigh's companions from entering into these designs, though there were many circumstances in the treaty and late transactions between the nations which might have invited them to engage in such a piratical war against the Spaniards.

When England made peace with Spain, the example of Henry IV at the treaty [negotiations] of Vervins was imitated: the French king, finding a difficulty in adjusting all questions with regard to the Indian trade, had agreed to pass over that article in total silence. The Spaniards, having all along published severe edicts against the intercourse of any European nation with their colonies, interpreted this silence in their own favor and considered it as a tacit acquiescence of England in the established laws of Spain. The English, on the contrary, claimed that as they had never been excluded by any treaty from commerce with any part of the king of Spain's dominions, it was still as lawful for them to trade with his settlements in either Indies as with his European territories. In consequence of this ambiguity, many adventurers from England sailed to the Spanish Indies and met with severe punishment when caught, as they often stole from the inhabitants, or when superior in power, forced a trade with them, and resisted— indeed, sometimes plundered—the Spanish governors. It was agreed to bury in total oblivion violences of this nature, which had been carried to a great height on both sides, because of the difficulty which was found in remedying them upon any fixed principles.

But as there appeared a great difference between private adventurers in single ships and a fleet acting under a royal commission, Raleigh's companions thought it safest to return immediately to England and carry him along with them to answer for his conduct. It appears that he employed many artifices, first to engage them to attack the Spanish settlements, then failing of that, to make his escape into France. But all these proving unsuccessful, he was delivered into the king's hands and strictly examined, along with his fellow adventurers, before the Privy Council. The Council, upon inquiry, found no difficulty in pronouncing that the former suspicions with regard to Raleigh's intentions had been well grounded; that he had abused the king in the representations which he had made of his projected adventure; that contrary to his instructions, he had acted in an offensive and hostile manner against his majesty's allies; and that he had willfully burned and destroyed a town belonging to the king of Spain. He might have been tried either by common law for this act of violence and piracy or by martial law for breach of orders; but it was an established principle among lawyers that as he lay under an actual attainder for high treason, he could not be brought to a new trial for any other crime. To satisfy, therefore, the court of Spain, which raised the loudest complaints against him, the king made use of that power which he had purposely reserved in his own hands and signed the warrant for Raleigh's execution upon his former sentence.

Perhaps the king ought to have granted Raleigh a pardon for his old treason and to have tried him anew for his new offenses. His punishment in that case would not only have been just but also conducted in a just and unexceptionable manner. But we are told that a ridiculous opinion at that time prevailed in the nation (and it is plainly supposed by Sir Walter in his defense) that by treaty, war was allowed with the Spaniards in the Indies though peace was made in Europe. While that notion held sway, no jury would have found Raleigh guilty. So if the king had not punished him upon the old sentence, the Spaniards would have had a just cause of complaint against the king sufficient to have produced a war, or at least to have destroyed all cordiality between the nations.

His execution

Raleigh, finding his fate inevitable, collected all his courage; and though he had formerly made use of many mean artifices—such as feigning madness, sickness, and a variety of diseases—in order to protract his examination and procure his escape, he now resolved to act his part with bravery and resolution. "'Tis a sharp remedy," he said, "but a sure one for all ills," when, on October 29, he felt the edge of the axe by which he was to be beheaded. His harangue to the people was calm and eloquent; and he endeavored to revenge himself and to load his enemies with the public hatred by strong asseverations of facts which, to say the least, may be considered very doubtful. With the utmost indifference, he laid his head upon the block and received the fatal blow. And in his death there appeared the same great but ill-regulated mind which during his life had displayed itself in all his conduct and behavior.

No measure of James's reign was attended with more public dissatisfaction than the punishment of Sir Walter Raleigh. To execute a sentence which was originally so hard, which had been so long suspended, and which seemed to have been tacitly pardoned by conferring on him a new trust and commission was deemed an instance of cruelty and injustice. To sacrifice to a concealed enemy of England the life of the only man in the nation who had a high reputation for valor and military experience was regarded as meanness and indiscretion. And the intimate connections which the king was now entering into with Spain, being universally distasteful, rendered this proof of his complaisance still more odious and unpopular.

James had entertained an opinion, which was peculiar to himself and which had been adopted by none of his predecessors, that any alliance below that of a great king was unworthy of a Prince of Wales; and he never would allow any princess but a daughter of France or Spain to be mentioned as a match for his son. This instance of pride—which really implies meanness, as if he could receive honor from any alliance—was so well known that Spain had founded on it the hopes of governing this monarch, so little celebrated for politics or prudence, in the most important transactions. During the life of James's son Henry, the king of Spain had dropped some hints of bestowing on that prince his eldest daughter, whom he afterwards disposed of in marriage to the young king of France, Louis XIII. At that time, the designs of the Spaniards were to engage James into a neutrality with regard to the succession of Cleves, which was disputed between the Protestant and popish line. But the bait did not then take; and James, in consequence of his alliance with the Dutch and with Henry IV of France, marched four thousand men under the command of Sir Edward Cecil, who joined these two powers and put the Marquess of Brandenburg and the Palatine of Neuburg in possession of Cleves.

Gondomar was at this time the Spanish ambassador in England, a man whose flattery was the more artful because covered with the appearance of frankness and sincerity, whose politics were the more dangerous because disguised under the mask of mirth and pleasantry. He now made offer of the second daughter of Spain to Prince Charles. That he might render the temptation irresistible to the necessitous monarch, he gave hopes of an immense fortune which would attend the princess. The court of Spain, though determined to contract no alliance with a heretic, entered into negotiations with James, which they artfully protracted; and amidst every disappointment, they still redoubled his hopes of success. The transactions in Germany, so important to the Austrian greatness, became every day a new motive for this duplicity of conduct.

Insurrections in Bohemia

In that great revolution of manners which happened during the sixteenth and the seventeenth centuries, the only nations who had the honorable, though often melancholy, advantage of making an effort for their expiring privileges were those who were animated, together with the principles of civil liberty, with a zeal for religious parties and opinions. Besides the irresistible force of standing armies, the European princes possessed this advantage: that they were descended from the ancient royal families; that they continued the same designations of magistrates and the same appearance of civil government; and by tightening all the forms of legal administration, they could gradually impose the yoke on their unguarded subjects. Even the German nations, who formerly broke the Roman chains and restored liberty to mankind, now lost their own liberty and saw with grief the absolute authority of their princes firmly established among them. In their circumstances, nothing but a pious zeal, which disregards all motives of human prudence, could have made them entertain hopes of preserving any longer those privileges which their ancestors had transmitted to them through so many ages.

As the house of Austria, throughout all its extensive dominions, had always made religion the pretense for its usurpations, it now met with resistance from a like principle. The Catholic religion, as usual, had ranged itself on the side of monarchy; the Protestant, on that of liberty. The states of Bohemia, having taken arms against the emperor Matthias, continued their revolt against his successor, Ferdinand II, and claimed the observance of all the edicts enacted in favor of the new religion together with the restoration of their ancient laws and constitution. The neighboring principalities—Silesia, Moravia, Lusatia, Austria, even the kingdom of Hungary—took part in the quarrel; and throughout all these populous and martial provinces, the spirit of discord and civil war had universally diffused itself.

Ferdinand II, who possessed more vigor and greater abilities, though not more lenity and moderation, than | *1619* | are usual with the Austrian princes, strongly armed himself for the recovery of his authority. Besides employing the assistance of his subjects who professed the ancient religion, he engaged on his side a powerful alliance of the neighboring potentates. All the Catholic princes of the empire had embraced his defense, as had even Saxony, the most powerful of the Protestant. Poland had declared itself in his favor. And above all, the Spanish monarch, deeming his own interest closely connected with that of the younger branch of his family, prepared powerful succors from Italy and from the Low Countries; and he also advanced large sums for the support of Ferdinand and of the Catholic religion.

The states of Bohemia, alarmed at these mighty preparations, began also to solicit foreign assistance; and together with that support which they obtained from the Evangelical Union in Germany, they endeavored to establish connections with greater princes. They cast their eyes on Frederick, elector palatine. They considered that besides commanding no despicable force of his own, he was son-in-law to the king of England and nephew to Prince Maurice, whose authority had become almost absolute in the United Provinces. They hoped that these princes, moved by the connections of blood as well as by the tie of their common religion, would interest themselves in all the fortunes of Frederick and would promote his greatness. Therefore, they made him a tender of their crown, which they considered as elective. The young palatine, stimulated by ambition, without consulting either James or Maurice, whose opposition he foresaw, immediately accepted the offer and marched all his forces into Bohemia in support of his new subjects.

The news of these events no sooner reached England than the whole kingdom was on fire to engage in the quarrel. Scarcely was the ardor greater than that with which all the states of Europe in former ages flew to rescue the Holy Land from the dominion of infidels. The nation was as yet sincerely attached to the blood of their monarchs, and they considered their connection with the palatine, who had married a daughter of England, as very close and intimate. And when they heard of Catholics carrying on wars and persecutions against Protestants, they thought their own interest deeply concerned and regarded their neutrality as a base desertion of the cause of God and of his holy religion. In such a quarrel, they would gladly have marched to the opposite extremity of Europe, have plunged themselves into a chaos of German politics, and have expended all the blood and treasure of the nation by maintaining a contest with the whole house of Austria at the very time and in the very place in which it was the most potent, and almost irresistible.

But besides James's temper being too little enterprising for such vast undertakings, he was restrained by another motive which had a mighty influence over him: he refused to patronize the revolt of subjects against their sovereign. From the very first, he denied to his son-in-law the title of king of Bohemia. He forbade him to be prayed for in the churches under that appellation. And though he confessed that he had in no way examined the pretensions, privileges, and constitution of the rebellious states, so exalted was his idea of the rights of kings that he concluded subjects must always be in the wrong when they stood in opposition to those who had acquired or assumed that majestic title. Thus even in measures founded on true politics, James intermixed so many narrow prejudices that diminished his authority and exposed him to the imputation of weakness and of error.

Loss of the Palatinate

Meanwhile, affairs everywhere hastened to a crisis. Ferdinand levied a great force under the command of the Duke of Bavaria and the Count of Bucquoy and advanced upon his

1620

enemy in Bohemia. In the Low Countries, Spinola collected a veteran army of thirty thousand men. When Edmonds, James's resident at Brussels, made remonstrances to the Archduke Albert, he was answered that the orders for this armament [armed force] had been transmitted to Spinola from Madrid and that he alone knew the secret destination of it. Spinola then told the minister that his orders were still sealed, but if Edmonds would accompany him in his march to Coblenz, he would there open them and give him full satisfaction. It was easier to see his intentions than to prevent their success. Almost at one time it was known in England that Frederick, being defeated in the great and decisive Battle of Prague, had fled with his family into Holland and that Spinola had invaded the Palatinate, and meeting with no resistance except from some princes of the Union and from one English regiment of two thousand four hundred men commanded by the brave Sir Horace Vere, had soon reduced the greater part of that principality.

The murmurs and complaints against the king's neutrality and inactive disposition were now high. The happiness and tranquility of their own country became distasteful to the English when they reflected on the grievances and distresses of their Protestant brethren in Germany. They failed to consider that their interposition in the wars of the Continent, though agreeable to religious zeal, could not at that time be justified by any sound maxims of politics. That however exorbitant the Austrian greatness, the danger was still too distant to give any just alarm to England. That mighty resistance would yet be made by so many potent and warlike princes and states in Germany before they would yield their neck to the yoke. That France, now engaged to contract a double alliance with the Austrian family, must necessarily be soon roused from its lethargy and oppose the progress of so hated a rival. That in the further advance of conquests, even the interests of the two branches of that ambitious family must interfere and beget mutual jealousy and opposition. That a land war carried on at such a distance would waste the blood and treasure of the English nation without any hopes of success. That a sea war indeed might be both safe and successful against Spain but would not affect the enemy in such vital parts as to make them stop their career of success in Germany and abandon all their acquisitions. And that the prospect of recovering the Palatinate being at present desperate, the affair was reduced to the simple question of whether peace and commerce with Spain or the uncertain hopes of plunder and of conquest in the Indies were preferable, a question which at the beginning of the king's reign had already been decided, and perhaps with reason, in favor of the former advantages.

Negotiations with Spain

James might have defended his pacific measures by such plausible arguments; but these, though the chief motives which swayed him, seem not to have been the only ones. He had entertained the notion that as his own justice and moderation had shone out so conspicuously throughout all these transactions, the whole house of Austria, though not awed by the power of England, would from mere respect to his virtue willingly submit themselves to so equitable an arbitration. He flattered himself that after he had formed an intimate connection with the Spanish monarch by means of his son's marriage, the restitution of the Palatinate might be procured solely from the motive of friendship and personal attachment. He failed to perceive that the more his inactive virtue was extolled, the greater disregard it was exposed to. He was not aware that the Spanish match was itself attended with such difficulties that all his art of negotiation would scarcely be able to surmount them; nor that this match, even if achieved, could not in good policy be depended on as the means of procuring such extraordinary advantages. His unwarlike disposition, increased by age, fixed him still more firmly in his errors and constrained him to seek the restoration of his son-in-law by remonstrances and entreaties, by arguments and embassies, rather than by blood and violence. And the same defect of courage which held him in awe of foreign nations

made him likewise afraid of shocking the prejudices of his own subjects and kept him from openly avowing the measures which he was
determined to pursue. Or perhaps he hoped to turn these prejudices
to account and by their means engage his people to furnish him with
supplies, of which their excessive frugality had previously made them
so sparing and reserved.

He first tried the expedient of a benevolence, or free gift, from individuals, claiming that the urgency of the case would not admit of
leisure for any other measure. But the jealousy of liberty was now
roused, and the nation regarded these pretended benevolences as real
extortions, contrary to law and dangerous to freedom, however authorized by ancient precedent. A Parliament was found to be the only
resource which could furnish any large supplies; and accordingly, writs were issued for summoning that great
council of the nation.

1621

Parties

This Parliament is remarkable for being the epoch in which were first
regularly formed the parties of court and country, though without acquiring these appellations; parties which have ever since continued
and which, while they often threaten the total dissolution of the government, are the real causes of its permanent life and vigor. In the ancient feudal constitution of which the English partook with other European nations, there was a mixture not of authority and liberty—
which we have since enjoyed in England and which now persist uniformly together—but of authority and anarchy, which perpetually col-
lided with each other and which took place alternately, according as
circumstances were more or less favorable to either of them. A Parliament composed of barbarians summoned from their fields and forests,
uninstructed by study, conversation, or travel, ignorant of their own
laws and history and unacquainted with the situation of all foreign nations; a Parliament called precariously by the king and dissolved at his
pleasure, sitting a few days, debating a few points prepared for them,
and whose members were impatient to return to their own castles,
where alone they were great, and to the chase, which was their favorite
amusement: such a Parliament was very little fitted to enter into a discussion of all the questions of government and to share in a regular
manner the legal administration. The name, the authority of the king
alone appeared in the common course of government; in extraordinary emergencies, he assumed with still better reason the sole direc-

tion; the imperfect and unformed laws left in everything a latitude of interpretation; and when the ends pursued by the monarch were in general agreeable to his subjects, little scruple or concern was entertained with regard to the regularity of the means. During the reign of an able, fortunate, or popular prince, no member of either house, much less of the lower, dared think of entering into a formed party in opposition to the court, since the dissolution of the Parliament must in a few days leave him unprotected to the vengeance of his sovereign and to those stretches of prerogative which were then so easily made to punish an obnoxious subject. During an unpopular and weak reign, the current commonly ran so strong against the monarch that none dared enlist themselves in the court party; or if the prince was able to engage any considerable barons on his side, the question was decided with arms in the field, not by debates or arguments in a senate or assembly. And upon the whole, the chief circumstance which during ancient times retained the prince in any legal form of administration was that the sword, by the nature of the feudal tenures, remained still in the hands of his subjects; and this irregular and dangerous check had much more influence than the regular and methodical limits of the laws and constitution. As the nation could not be compelled, it was necessary that every public measure of consequence, particularly that of levying new taxes, should seem to be adopted by common consent and approbation.

The monarchs of the house of Tudor had been able—partly by the vigor of their administration, partly by the concurrence of favorable circumstances—to establish a more regular system of government; but they drew the constitution so near to despotism that the authority of the Parliament was diminished extremely. The House of Lords became in a great degree the organ of royal will and pleasure; opposition would have been regarded as a species of rebellion. And even religion, the most dangerous article in which innovations could be introduced, had admitted in the course of a few years four several alterations from the authority alone of the sovereign. The Parliament was not then the road to honor and preferment; the talents of popular intrigue and eloquence were uncultivated and unknown; and though that assembly still preserved authority and retained the privilege of making laws and bestowing public money, the members did not acquire upon that account, either with prince or people, much more weight and consideration. The king was accustomed to assume of his own accord what powers were necessary for conducting the machine of government. His own revenues supplied him with money sufficient for his ordinary expenses. And when extraordinary emergencies occurred, the prince did not need to solicit votes in Parliament either for making laws or imposing taxes, both of which had now become requisite for public interest and preservation.

The security of individuals, so necessary to the liberty of popular councils, was totally unknown in that age. And as no despotic princes—scarcely even the Eastern tyrants—rule entirely without the concurrence of some assemblies which supply both advice and authority, little but a mercenary force seems then to have been lacking towards the establishment of a simple monarchy in England. The militia, though more favorable to regal authority than the feudal institutions, was much inferior in this respect to disciplined armies; and if it did not preserve liberty to the people, it preserved at least the power, if ever the inclination would arise, of recovering it.

But so low at that time ran the inclination towards liberty that Elizabeth, the last of that arbitrary line, herself no less arbitrary, was yet the most renowned and most popular of all the sovereigns that had filled the throne of England. It was natural for James to take the government as he found it and to pursue her measures, which he heard so much applauded; nor did his penetration extend so far as to discover that neither his circumstances nor his character could support so extensive an authority. His narrow revenues and little frugality began now to render him dependent on his people even in the ordinary course of administration. Their increasing knowledge showed to them that advantage which they had obtained and made them aware of the inestimable value of civil liberty. And as he possessed too little dignity to command respect and too much good nature to impress fear, a new spirit revealed itself every day in the Parliament; and a party watchful of a free constitution was regularly formed in the House of Commons.

But notwithstanding these advantages acquired to liberty, so extensive was royal authority, and so firmly established in all its parts, that it is probable the patriots of that age would have despaired of ever resisting it had they not been stimulated by religious motives, which inspire a courage insurmountable by any human obstacle.

The same alliance which has always prevailed between kingly power and ecclesiastical authority was now fully established in England; and while the prince assisted the clergy in suppressing schismatics and innovators, the clergy in return inculcated the doctrine of an unreserved submission and obedience to the civil magistrate. The genius of the Church of England, so kindly to monarchy, forwarded the confederacy: its submission to episcopal jurisdiction; its attachment to ceremonies, to order, and to a decent pomp and splendor of worship; and in a word, its affinity to the tame superstition [excessive concern for rites, ceremonies, and objects] of the Catholics rather than to the wild fanaticism of the Puritans.

On the other hand, the Puritans' opposition to the established church and the persecutions under which they labored were sufficient to throw them into the country party and to beget political principles little favorable to the high pretensions of the sovereign. The spirit too of enthusiasm, bold, daring, and uncontrolled, strongly disposed their minds to adopt republican tenets and inclined them to arrogate in their actions and conduct the same liberty which they assumed in their rapturous flights and ecstasies. Ever since the first origin of that sect, through the whole reign of Elizabeth as well as of James, Puritanical principles had been understood in a double sense, and expressed the opinions favorable both to political and to ecclesiastical liberty. And as the court, in order to discredit all parliamentary opposition, affixed the appellation of "Puritans" to its antagonists, the religious Puritans willingly adopted this idea, which was so advantageous to them and which confounded their cause with that of the patriots, or country party. Thus were the civil and ecclesiastical factions regularly formed; and the humor of the nation during that age running strongly towards fanatical extravagancies, the spirit of civil liberty gradually revived from its lethargy, and by means of its religious associate, from which it reaped more advantage than honor, it secretly enlarged its dominion over the greater part of the kingdom.

A Parliament

In this Parliament, assembled on June 16, there appeared at first nothing but duty and submission on the part of the Commons; and they seemed determined to sacrifice everything in order to maintain a good correspondence with their prince. They would allow no mention to be made of the new customs or impositions, which had been so eagerly disputed in the former Parliament. The imprisonment of the members of that Parliament was here complained of by some, but that grievance was buried in oblivion by the authority of the graver and more prudent part of the house. And being informed that the king had remitted several considerable sums to the palatine, the Commons unanimously voted him two subsidies; and that too at the very beginning of the session, contrary to the maxims frequently adopted by their predecessors.

They then proceeded, but in a very temperate manner, to the examination of grievances. They found that patents had been granted to Sir Giles Mompesson and Sir Francis Michell for licensing inns and alehouses, that great sums of money had been exacted under pretext of these licenses, and that such innkeepers as presumed to continue their business without satisfying the rapacity of the patentees had been severely punished by fine, imprisonment, and vexatious prosecutions.

The same persons had also procured a patent, which they shared with Sir Edward Villiers, brother to Buckingham, for the sole making of gold and silver thread and lace, and they had obtained very extraordinary powers for preventing any rivalry in these manufactures: they were armed with authority to search for all goods which might interfere with their patent, and even to punish, at their own will and discretion, the makers, importers, and venders of such commodities. Many had grievously suffered by this exorbitant jurisdiction, and the lace which had been manufactured by the patentees was universally found to be adulterated, being composed more of copper than of the precious metals.

These grievances the Commons represented to the king; and they met with a very gracious and very cordial reception. He seemed even thankful for the information given him and declared himself ashamed that such abuses, unknowingly to him, had crept into his administration. "I assure you," said he, "had I before heard these things complained of, I would have done the office of a just king, and out of Parliament have punished them, as severely, and peradventure more, than you now intend to do." A sentence was passed for the punishment of Michell and Mompesson. It was executed on the former. The latter broke prison and escaped. Villiers was at that time sent purposely on a foreign employment; and his guilt being less enormous—or less apparent—than that of the others, he was the more easily protected by the credit of his brother, Buckingham.

Fall of Bacon

Encouraged by this success, the Commons carried their scrutiny, and still with a respectful hand, into other abuses of importance. The great seal was at that time in the hands of the celebrated Francis Bacon, created Viscount St. Alban, a man universally admired for the greatness of his genius and beloved for the courteousness and humanity of his behavior. He was the great ornament of his age and nation; and nothing was lacking to render him the ornament of human nature itself but that strength of mind which might check his intemperate desire of preferment (which could add nothing to his dignity) and restrain his profuse inclination to expense (which could be requisite neither for his honor nor entertainment). His lack of economy and his indulgence to servants had involved him in necessities; and to supply his prodigality, he had been tempted to take bribes, called "presents," and that in a very open manner, from suitors in Chancery. It appears that it had been usual for previous chancellors to take presents; and it is claimed that Bacon, who followed the same dangerous practice, had still in the seat of justice preserved the integrity of a judge and had given just decrees against those very persons from whom he had received the wages of iniquity. Complaints rose the louder on that account; they at last reached the House of Commons, who sent up an impeachment against him to the Peers. The chancellor, conscious of guilt, sought to avert the vengeance of his judges and endeavored by a general avowal to escape the shame of a stricter inquiry. The Lords insisted on a particular confession of all his corruptions. He acknowledged twenty-eight articles and was sentenced to pay a fine of £40,000, to be imprisoned in the Tower during the king's pleasure, to be forever incapable of any office, place, or employment, and never again to sit in Parliament or come within the verge of the court.

This dreadful sentence—dreadful to a man of nice sensibility to honor—he survived five years. Being soon released from the Tower, his genius, yet unbroken, supported itself amidst involved circumstances and a depressed spirit, and it shone out in literary productions which have made his guilt or weaknesses be forgotten or overlooked by posterity. In consideration of his great merit, the king abated his fine as well as all the other parts of his sentence, conferred on him a large pension of £1,800 a year, and employed every expedient to alleviate the weight of his age and misfortunes. And that great philosopher at last acknowledged with regret that he had too long neglected the true ambition of a fine genius, and by plunging into business and affairs, which require much less capacity but greater firmness of mind than the pursuits of learning, had exposed himself to such grievous calamities.

Rupture between the king and the Commons

The Commons had entertained the idea that they were the great patrons of the people and that the redress of all grievances must proceed from them; and to this principle they were chiefly beholden for the regard and consideration of the public. In the execution of this office, they now kept their ears open to complaints of every kind; and they carried their researches into many grievances which, though of no great importance, could not be touched on without perceptibly affecting the king and his ministers. The prerogative seemed every moment to be invaded; the king's authority in every article was disputed; and James, who was willing to correct the abuses of his power, would not submit to have his power itself questioned and denied. After the house, therefore, had sat nearly six months and had as yet brought no considerable business to a full conclusion, the king resolved to interrupt their proceedings under pretense of the advanced season; and he sent them word that he was determined to adjourn them soon till next winter. The Commons made application to the Lords and desired them to join in a petition for delaying the adjournment; this was refused by the upper house. The king regarded this project of a joint petition as an attempt to force him from his measures. He thanked the Peers for their refusal to concur in it and told them that if it were their desire, he would delay the adjournment, but would not do so at the request of the lower house alone. And thus in these great national affairs, the same peevishness which in private altercations often raises a quarrel from the smallest beginnings produced a mutual coldness and disgust between the king and the Commons.

During the recess of Parliament, the king used every measure to render himself popular with the nation and to appease the rising ill humor of their representatives. Previously, he had voluntarily invited the Parliament to circumscribe his own prerogative by abrogating for the future his power of granting monopolies. He now recalled all the patents of that kind and redressed every article of grievance, to the number of thirty-seven, which had ever been complained of in the House of Commons. But he failed to gain the end which he proposed. The disgust which had appeared at parting could not so suddenly be dispelled. He had likewise been so imprudent as to commit to prison Sir Edwin Sandys without any known cause besides his activity and vigor in discharging his duty as member of Parliament. And above all, the transactions in Germany were sufficient, when joined to the king's cautions, negotiations, and delays, to inflame that jealousy of honor and religion which prevailed throughout the nation. This summer, the ban of the empire had been published against the elector palatine, and the execution of it was committed to the Duke of Bavaria. The Upper Palatinate was soon conquered by that prince, and measures were taken in the empire for bestowing on him the electoral dignity of which the palatine was then despoiled. Frederick now lived with his numerous family in poverty and distress either in Holland or at Sedan with his uncle, the Duke of Bouillon. And throughout all the new conquests—in both the Palatinates as well as in Bohemia, Austria, and Lusatia—the progress of the Austrian arms was attended with rigors and severities exercised against the professors of the reformed religion.

Upon their assembling on November 14, the zeal of the Commons immediately moved them to take all these transactions into consideration. They framed a remonstrance which they intended to carry to the king. They represented that the enormous growth of the Austrian power threatened the liberties of Europe; that the progress of the Catholic religion in England bred the most melancholy apprehensions lest it would again acquire an ascendant in the kingdom; that the indulgence of his majesty towards the professors of that religion had encouraged their insolence and temerity; that the uncontrolled conquests made by the Austrian family in Germany raised mighty expectations in the English papists; but above all, that the prospect of the Spanish match elevated them so far as to hope for an entire toleration, if not the final reestablishment, of their religion. The Commons, therefore, entreated his majesty that he would immediately undertake the defense of the Palatinate and maintain it by force of arms; that he would turn his sword against Spain, whose armies and treasures were the chief support of the Catholic interest in Europe; that he would enter into no negotiation for the marriage of his son but with a Protestant princess; that the children of popish recusants should be taken from their parents and be committed to the care of Protestant teachers and schoolmasters; and that the fines and confiscations to which the Catholics were by law liable should be levied with the utmost severity.

By this bold step, unprecedented in England for many years and scarcely ever heard of in peaceable times, the Commons attacked at the same time all the king's favorite maxims of government: his cautious and pacific measures, his lenity towards the Romish religion, and his attachment to the Spanish alliance, from which he promised himself such mighty advantages. But what most disgusted him was their seeming invasion of his prerogative and their laying claim, under color of advice, to direct his conduct in such points as had always been acknowledged to belong solely to the management and direction of the sovereign. He was at that time absent at Newmarket; but as soon as he heard of the intended remonstrance of the Commons, he wrote a letter to the speaker in which he sharply rebuked the house for openly debating matters far above their reach and capacity, and he strictly forbade them to meddle with anything that regarded his government or deep matters of state, and especially not to touch on his son's marriage with the daughter of Spain nor to attack the honor of that king or any other of his friends and confederates. In order to intimidate them the more, he mentioned the imprisonment of Sir Edwin Sandys; and though he denied that the confinement of that member had been owing to any offense committed in the house, he plainly told them that he thought himself fully entitled to punish every misdemeanor in Parliament during its sitting as well as after its dissolution, and that he intended from then on to chastise any man whose insolent behavior there would supply occasion of offense.

This violent letter—in which the king, though he here imitated former precedents, may be thought not to have acted altogether on the defensive—had the effect which might naturally have been expected from it: the Commons were inflamed, not terrified. Secure of their own popularity and of the bent of the nation towards a war with the Catholics abroad and the persecution of popery at home, they little dreaded the menaces of a prince who was unsupported by military force and whose gentle temper would by itself so soon disarm his severity. In a new remonstrance, therefore, they still insisted on their former remonstrance and advice, and they maintained, though in respectful terms, that they were entitled to interpose with their counsel in all matters of government; that to possess entire freedom of speech in their debates on public business was their ancient and undoubted right and an inheritance transmitted to them from their ancestors; and that if any member abused this liberty, it belonged solely to the house, who were witnesses of his offense, to inflict a proper censure upon him.

So vigorous an answer was in no way calculated to appease the king. It is said that when he was notified of the approach of the committee who were to present it, he ordered twelve chairs to be brought, for there were that many kings coming. His answer was prompt and sharp. He told the house that their remonstrance was more like a denunciation of war than an address of dutiful subjects; that their pretension to inquire into all state affairs without exception was such a "plenipotence" [plenitude of power] as none of their ancestors, even during the reign of the weakest princes, had ever pretended to; that public transactions depended on a complication of views and intelligence with which they were entirely unacquainted; that they could not better show their wisdom as well as duty than by keeping within their proper sphere; and that in any business which depended on his prerogative, they had no title to interpose with their advice except when he was pleased to desire it. And he concluded with these memorable words: "And though we cannot allow of your style in mentioning your ancient and undoubted right and inheritance, but would rather have wished that you had said that your privileges were derived from the grace and permission of our ancestors and us (for the most of them grew from precedents, which shows rather a toleration than inheritance); yet we are pleased to give you our royal assurance that as long as you contain yourselves within the limits of your duty, we will be as careful to maintain and preserve your lawful liberties and privileges as ever any of our predecessors were, nay, as to preserve our own royal prerogative."

Protestation of the Commons

This open pretension of the king's naturally gave great alarm to the House of Commons. They saw their title to every privilege, if not plainly denied, yet considered at least as precarious. It might be forfeited by abuse, and they had already abused it. They thought proper, therefore, immediately to oppose pretension to pretension. On December 18, they framed a protestation in which they repeated all their former claims for freedom of speech and an unbounded authority to interpose with their advice and counsel. And they asserted, "That the liberties, franchises, privileges, and jurisdictions of Parliament are the ancient and undoubted birthright and inheritance of the subjects of England."

The king, informed of these increasing heats and jealousies [mistrusts] in the house, hurried to London. He sent immediately for the journals of the Commons; and with his own hand, before the Council, he tore out this protestation and ordered his reasons to be inserted in the council book. He was doubly displeased, he said, with the protestation of the lower house, on account of the manner of framing it as well as of the matter which it contained. It was tumultuously voted, at a late hour, and in a thin house; and it was expressed in such general and ambiguous terms as might serve for a foundation to the most enormous claims and to the most unwarrantable usurpations upon his prerogative.

The meeting of the house might have proved dangerous after so violent a breach. It was no longer possible to finish any business while men were in such a temper. The king, therefore, prorogued the Parliament, and soon after dissolved it by proclamation, in which he also made a justification to the public for his whole conduct.

The leading members of the house, Sir Edward Coke and Sir Robert Phelips, were committed to the Tower, and John Selden, John Pym, and William Mallory to other prisons. As a lighter punishment, Sir Dudley Digges, Sir Thomas Crewe, Sir Nathaniel Rich, and Sir James Perrot, joined in commission with others, were sent to Ireland in order to execute some business. The king at that time enjoyed, or at least exercised, the prerogative of employing any man, even without his consent, in any branch of public service.

Sir John Savile, a powerful man in the House of Commons and a zealous opponent of the court, was made comptroller of the household, a privy counselor, and a baron soon after. This event is memorable as being perhaps the first instance in the whole history of England of any king's advancing a man on account of parliamentary influence and of opposition to his measures. However irregular this practice, it will be regarded by political reasoners as one of the earliest and most infallible symptoms of a regular, established liberty.

The king having thus, with so rash and indiscreet a hand, torn off that sacred veil which had previously covered the English constitution and which threw an obscurity upon it so advantageous to royal prerogative, every man began to indulge himself in political reasonings and inquiries; and the same factions which commenced in Parliament were propagated throughout the nation. In vain did James, by reiterated proclamations, forbid the discoursing of state affairs. Such proclamations, if they had any effect, served rather to inflame the curiosity of the public. And in every company or society, the late transactions became the subject of argument and debate.

All history, said the partisans of the court, as well as the history of England, justify the king's position with regard to the origin of popular privileges; and every reasonable man must allow that as monarchy is the simplest form of government, it must first have occurred to rude and uninstructed mankind. The other complicated and artificial additions were the successive invention of sovereigns and legislators; or if they were imposed on the prince by seditious subjects, their origin must appear on that very account still more precarious and unfavorable. In England, the authority of the king in all the exterior forms of government and in the common style of law appears totally absolute and sovereign; nor does the real spirit of the constitution, as it has always revealed itself in practice, fall much short of these appearances. The Parliament is created by his will; by his will it is dissolved. It is his will alone, though at the desire of both houses, which gives authority to laws. To all foreign nations, the majesty of the monarch seems to merit sole attention and regard. And no subject who has exposed himself to royal indignation can hope to live with safety in the kingdom; nor can he even leave it, according to law, without the consent of his master. If a magistrate environed with such power and splendor would consider his authority as sacred and regard himself as the anointed of heaven, his pretensions may bear a very favorable construction. Or allowing them to be merely pious frauds, we need not be surprised that the same stratagem which was practiced by Minos, Numa, and the most celebrated legislators of antiquity would now, in these restless and inquisitive times, be employed by the king of England. Subjects assembled in Parliament are not raised above the quality of subjects; the same humble respect and deference is still due to their prince. Though he indulges them in the privilege of laying before him their domestic grievances, with which they are supposed to be best acquainted, this does not warrant their bold intrusion into every province of government. And to all judicious examiners it must appear, "That the lines of duty are as much transgressed by a more independent and less respectful exercise of acknowledged powers as by the usurpation of such as are new and unusual."

The lovers of liberty throughout the nation reasoned after a different manner. It is in vain, said they, that the king, in order to represent the privileges of Parliament as dependent and precarious, traces up the English government to its first origin. Prescription and the practice of so many ages must, long before this time, have given a sanction to these assemblies, even though they had been derived from an origin no more dignified than that which he assigns them. If the written records of the English nation, as asserted, represent Parliaments to have arisen from the consent of monarchs, the principles of human nature, when we trace government a step higher, must show us that monarchs themselves owe all their authority to the voluntary submission of the people. But in fact, no age can be shown when the English government was altogether an unmixed monarchy. And if the privileges of the nation have at any period been overpowered by violent irruptions of foreign force or domestic usurpation, the generous spirit of the people has always seized the first opportunity of reestablishing the ancient government and constitution. Though royal authority may be represented as sacred and supreme in the style of the laws and in the usual forms of administration, whatever is essential to the exercise of sovereign and legislative power must still be regarded as equally divine and inviolable. Or if any distinction be made in this respect, the preference is surely due to those national councils, by whose interposition the exorbitances of tyrannical power are restrained and that sacred liberty—which heroic spirits in all ages have deemed more precious than life itself—is preserved. Nor is it sufficient to say that the mild and equitable administration of James affords little occasion, or no occasion, of complaint. However moderate the exercise of his prerogative, however exact his observance of the laws and constitution, "If he founds his authority on arbitrary and dangerous principles, it is requisite to watch him with the same care and to oppose him with the same vigor as if he had indulged himself in all the excesses of cruelty and tyranny."

Amidst these disputes, the wise and moderate in the nation endeavored to preserve as much as possible an equitable neutrality between the opposite parties; and the more they reflected on the course of public affairs, the greater difficulty they found in fixing just sentiments with regard to them. On the one hand, they regarded the very rise of parties as a happy indication of the establishment of liberty; nor could they ever expect to enjoy in a mixed government so invaluable a blessing without suffering that inconvenience which in such governments has always attended it. But when they considered, on the other hand, the necessary aims and pursuits of both parties, they were struck with apprehension of the consequences and could discover no feasible plan of accommodation between them. From long practice, the Crown was now possessed of so exorbitant a prerogative that it was not sufficient for liberty to remain on the defensive or endeavor to secure the little ground which was left her. It had become necessary to carry on an offensive war and to circumscribe within more narrow, as well as more exact, bounds the authority of the sovereign. Upon such provocation, it could not but happen that the prince, however just and moderate, would endeavor to repress his opponents; and as he stood upon the very brink of arbitrary power, it was to be feared that he would hastily and unknowingly pass those limits which were not precisely marked by the constitution. The turbulent government of England, ever fluctuating between privilege and prerogative, would afford a variety of precedents which might be pleaded on both sides. In such delicate questions, the people must be divided. The arms of the state were still in their hands. A civil war must ensue; a civil war where no party, or both parties, would justly bear the blame, and where the good and virtuous would scarcely know what vows to form, were it not that liberty, so necessary to the perfection of human society, would be sufficient to bias their affections towards the side of its defenders.

CHAPTER 49
1622 – 1625

*Negotiations with regard to the marriage and the
Palatinate – Character of Buckingham – Prince's
journey to Spain – Marriage treaty broken –
A Parliament – Return of Bristol – Rupture with Spain –
Treaty with France – Mansfeld's expedition –
Death of the king – His character*

Negotiations with regard to the marriage and the Palatinate

To wrest the Palatinate from the hands of the emperor and the Duke of Bavaria must always have been re-

| 1622 |

garded as a difficult task for the power of England conducted by so unwarlike a prince as James; it was plainly impossible while the breach persisted between him and the Commons. The king's negotiations, therefore, even if they had been managed with the greatest dexterity, now of necessity carried less weight with those conquerors; and it was easy for them to elude all his applications. When Lord Digby, James's ambassador to the emperor, had desired a cessation of hostilities, he was referred to the Duke of Bavaria, who commanded the Austrian armies. That duke told him that it was entirely superfluous to form any treaty for that purpose. "Hostilities are already ceased," said he, "and I doubt not but I shall be able to prevent their revival by keeping firm possession of the Palatinate till a final agreement shall be concluded between the contending parties." Notwithstanding this insult, James endeavored to resume with the emperor a treaty of accommodation; and he opened the negotiations at Brussels under the mediation of Archduke Albert, and after his death, which happened about this time, under that of the infanta. When the conferences were entered upon, it was found that the powers of these princes to settle the controversy were not sufficient or satisfactory. Schwarzenberg, the imperial minister, was expected at London, and it was hoped that he would bring more ample authority; but his commission referred entirely to the negotiation at Brussels. It was not difficult for the king to perceive that his applications were neglected by the emperor; but as he had no choice of any other expedient, and it seemed the interest of his son-in-law to keep alive his pretensions, he was still content to follow Ferdinand through all his shifts and evasions. Nor was he entirely discouraged even when the Imperial Diet at Regensburg—by the influence, or rather authority, of the emperor, though contrary to the protestation of Saxony and of all the Protestant princes and cities—had transferred the electoral dignity from the palatine to the Duke of Bavaria.

Meanwhile, the efforts made by Frederick for the recovery of his dominions were vigorous. Three armies were levied in Germany by his authority under three commanders: Christian, Duke of Brunswick, the prince of Baden-Durlach, and the Count of Mansfeld. The first two generals were defeated by the Count of Tilly and the imperialists; the third, though much inferior in force to his enemies, still maintained the war, but with no equal supplies of money either from the palatine or the king of England. It was chiefly by pillage and free quarters in the Palatinate that he subsisted his army. As the Austrians were regularly paid, they were kept in more exact discipline; and James justly became apprehensive lest so unequal a contest, besides ravaging the palatine's hereditary dominions, would end in the total alienation of the people's affections from their ancient sovereign, by whom they were plundered, and in an attachment to their new masters, by whom they were protected. He persuaded, therefore, his son-in-law to disarm under color of duty and submission to the emperor. And accordingly, Mansfeld was dismissed from the palatine's service; and that famous general withdrew his army into the Low Countries and there received a commission from the States of the United Provinces.

To show how little account was made of James's negotiations abroad, there is a pleasantry mentioned by all historians, which shall have place here for that reason. In a farce acted at Brussels, a courier was introduced carrying the doleful news that the Palatinate would soon be wrested from the house of Austria, so powerful were the succors which were hastening to the relief of the despoiled elector from all quarters: the king of Denmark had agreed to contribute to his assistance a hundred thousand pickled herrings; the Dutch, a hundred thousand butter boxes; and the king of England, a hundred thousand ambassadors. On other occasions, James was painted with a scabbard but without a sword, or with a sword which nobody could draw, though several were pulling at it.

It was not from his negotiations with the emperor or the Duke of Bavaria that James expected any success in his project of restoring the palatine. His eyes were entirely turned towards Spain; and if he could effect his son's marriage with the infanta, he did not doubt that after so intimate a conjunction, this other point could easily be obtained. The negotiations of that court being commonly dilatory, it was not easy for a prince of so little penetration in business to distinguish whether the difficulties which occurred were real or affected; and he was surprised, after negotiating five years on so simple a demand, that he was not more advanced than at the beginning. A dispensation from Rome was requisite for the marriage of the infanta with a Protestant prince; and the king of Spain, having undertaken to procure that dispensation, had thereby acquired the means of retarding or forwarding the marriage at his pleasure, and at the same time of concealing entirely his artifices from the court of England.

In order to remove all obstacles, James dispatched Digby, soon after created Earl of Bristol, as his ambassador to Philip IV, who had lately succeeded his father in the Crown of Spain. James secretly employed Gage as his agent at Rome; and finding that the difference of religion was the principal, if not the sole, difficulty which retarded the marriage, he resolved to soften that objection as much as possible. He issued public orders for discharging all popish recusants who were imprisoned; and it was daily feared that he would forbid for the future the execution of the penal laws enacted against them. For this step, so opposite to the rigid spirit of his subjects, he took care to apologize; and he even endeavored to ascribe it to his great zeal for the reformed religion. He had been making applications, he said, to all foreign princes for some indulgence to the distressed Protestants; and he was continually answered by objections derived from the severity of the English laws against Catholics. It might, indeed, have occurred to him that if the extremity of religious zeal were ever to abate among Christian sects, one of them must begin; and nothing would be more honorable for England than to have led the way in sentiments so wise and moderate.

Not only the religious Puritans murmured at this tolerating measure of the king; the lovers of civil liberty too were alarmed at so important an exertion of prerogative. But among other dangerous articles of authority, the kings of England were at that time possessed of the dispensing power, or at least were in the constant practice of exercising it. Besides, though the royal prerogative in civil matters was then extensive, the princes during some late reigns had been accustomed to assume a still greater one in ecclesiastical matters. And the king failed not to represent the toleration of Catholics as a measure entirely of that nature.

By James's concession in favor of the Catholics, he attained his end. The same religious motives which previously had rendered the court of Madrid insincere in all the steps taken with regard to the marriage were now the chief cause of promoting it. By its means, it was there hoped the English Catholics would for the future enjoy ease and indulgence, and the infanta would be the happy instrument of procuring to the church some tranquility after the many severe persecutions which it had previously undergone. The Earl of Bristol, a minister of vigilance and penetration, who had formerly opposed all alliance with Catholics, was now fully convinced of the sincerity of Spain; and he was ready to congratulate the king on the entire completion of his purposes and projects. A daughter of Spain, whom he represented as extremely accomplished, would soon, he said, arrive in England and bring with her an immense fortune of two million pieces of eight, or £600,000; a sum four times greater than Spain had ever before given with any princess, and almost equal to all the money which the Parliament, during the whole course of this reign, had till now granted to the king. But what was of more importance to James's honor and happiness, Bristol considered this match as an infallible omen of the palatine's restoration; Philip, he thought, would never have bestowed his sister and so large a fortune under the prospect of entering the next day into a war with England. So exact was his intelligence that the most secret counsels of the Spaniards, he boasted, had never escaped him; and he found that they had all along considered the marriage of the infanta and the restitution of the Palatinate as measures closely connected or altogether inseparable. However little was James's character fitted to extort so vast a concession, however improper the measures which he had pursued for attaining that end, the ambassador could not withstand the plain evidence of facts by which Philip now demonstrated his sincerity. Perhaps too, like a wise man, he considered that reasons of state, which are supposed solely to influence the councils of monarchs, are not always the motives which there predominate; that the milder inducements of gratitude, honor, friendship, and generosity are frequently able, among princes as well as private persons, to counterbalance these selfish considerations; that the justice and moderation of James, his reliance on Spain, and his confidence in its friendship had been so conspicuous in all these transactions that he had at last obtained the cordial alliance of that nation, so celebrated for honor and fidelity. Or if politics must still be supposed the ruling motive of all public measures, the maritime power of England was so considerable and the Spanish dominions so divided that the council of Philip might well have been induced to think that a sincere friendship with the masters of the sea could not be purchased by too great concessions. And as James during so many years had been allured and seduced by hopes and protestations, his people enraged by delays and disappointments, it would probably occur that there was now no middle place left between the most inveterate hatred and the most intimate alliance between the nations. Not to mention that as a new spirit began about this time to animate the councils of France, the friendship of England became every day more necessary to the greatness and security of the Spanish monarch.

All measures, therefore, being agreed on between the parties, nothing was lacking but the dispensation from Rome, which might be considered as a mere formality. But as the king, justified by success, now exulted in his pacific counsels and boasted of his superior sagacity and penetration, all these flattering prospects were blasted by the temerity of a man whom he had fondly exalted from a private condition to be the bane of himself, of his family, and of his people.

Character of Buckingham

Ever since the fall of Somerset, Buckingham had governed with an uncontrolled sway both the court and nation; and could James's eyes have been opened, he now had full opportunity of observing how unfit his favorite was for the high station to which he had been raised. Some accomplishments of a courtier he possessed; of every talent of a minister he was utterly destitute. Headlong in his passions and incapable equally of prudence and of dissimulation; sincere from violence rather than candor; expensive from extravagance more than generosity; a warm friend, a furious enemy, but without any choice of discernment in either: with these qualities, he had early and quickly mounted to the highest rank, and he partook of both the insolence which attends a fortune newly acquired and the impetuosity which belongs to persons born in high stations and unacquainted with opposition.

Among those who had experienced the arrogance of this overgrown favorite, the Prince of Wales himself had

not been entirely spared; and a great coldness, if not an enmity, had for that reason taken place between them. Buckingham, desirous of an opportunity which might connect him with the prince and overcome his aversion, and at the same time envious of the great credit acquired by Bristol in the Spanish negotiation, conceived of a single expedient by which he might gratify both these inclinations. He represented to Charles that persons of the prince's exalted station were particularly unfortunate in their marriage, the chief circumstance of life, and commonly received into their arms a bride unknown to them, to whom they were unknown, not endeared by sympathy, not obliged by service, wooed by treaties alone, by negotiations, by political interests. That however accomplished the infanta, she must still consider herself as a melancholy victim of state, and could not but think with aversion of that day when she was to enter the bed of a stranger, and passing into a foreign country and a new family, bid adieu forever to her father's house and to her native land. That it was in the prince's power to soften all these rigors and lay such an obligation on her as would attach the most indifferent temper and warm the coldest affections. That a journey by him to Madrid would be an unexpected gallantry which would equal all the fictions of Spanish romance, and suiting the amorous and enterprising character of that nation, must immediately introduce him to the princess in the agreeable form of a devoted lover and daring adventurer. That the negotiations with regard to the Palatinate, which had till now languished in the hands of ministers, would quickly be terminated by so illustrious an agent, seconded by the mediation and entreaties of the grateful infanta. That Spanish generosity, moved by that unexampled trust and confidence, would make concessions beyond what could be expected from political interests and considerations. And that he would quickly return to the king with the glory of having reestablished the unhappy palatine by the same enterprise which procured him the affections and the person of the Spanish princess.

The mind of the young prince, replete with candor, was inflamed by these generous and romantic ideas suggested by Buckingham. He agreed to make application to the king for his approbation. They chose the moment of his kindest and most jovial humor; and more by the fervor of their expression than by the force of their reasons, they obtained a hasty and unguarded consent to their undertaking. And having gained his promise to keep their purpose secret, they left him in order to make preparations for the journey.

No sooner was the king alone than his temper, more cautious than sanguine, suggested very different views of the matter and represented every difficulty and danger which could occur. He reflected that however the world might pardon this sally of youth in the prince, they would never forgive himself, who at his years and after his experience could entrust his only son—the heir of his crown, the prop of his age— to the discretion of foreigners without so much as providing the frail security of a safe-conduct in his favor. That if the Spanish monarch were sincere in his professions, a few months must finish the treaty of marriage and bring the infanta into England; if he were not sincere, the folly of committing the prince into his hands was still more egregious. That Philip, when possessed of so invaluable a security, might well rise in his demands and impose harder conditions of treaty. And that the temerity of the enterprise was so apparent that a good result, however prosperous, could not justify it, and a disastrous one would render himself infamous to his people and ridiculous to all posterity.

Tormented with these reflections, he informed the prince and Buckingham, as soon as they returned for their dispatches, of all the reasons which had influenced him to change his resolution, and he begged them to desist from so foolish an adventure. The prince received the disappointment with sorrowful submission and silent tears; Buckingham presumed to speak in an imperious tone, which he had always experienced to be victorious over his too easy master. He told the king that nobody in the future would believe anything he said when he retracted so soon the promise so solemnly given; that he plainly discerned this change of resolution to proceed from another breach of his word in communicating the matter to some rascal, who had furnished him with those pitiful reasons which he had alleged, and he doubted not but he would hereafter know who his counselor had been; and that if he receded from what he had promised, it would be such a disappointment to the prince, who had now set his heart upon the journey after his majesty's approbation, that he could never forget it nor forgive any man who had been the cause of it.

The king, with great fervor, fortified by many oaths, made his defense by denying that he had communicated the matter to any; and finding himself assailed by the boisterous importunities of Bucking-ham as, well as by the warm entreaties of his son—whose applications on previous occasions had been always dutiful, never zealous—he again had the weakness to assent to their purposed journey. It was agreed that only Sir Francis Cottington, the prince's secretary, and Endymion Porter, gentleman of his bedchamber, would accompany them; and the former being at that time in the antechamber, he was immediately called in by the king's orders.

James told Cottington that he had always been an honest man; and therefore, he was now to trust him in an affair of the highest im-portance, which he was not, upon his life, to disclose to any man whatever. "Cottington," he added, "here is Baby Charles and Steenie," (these ridiculous appellations he usually gave to the prince and Buck-ingham) "who have a great mind to go post into Spain and fetch home the infanta. They will have but two more in their company and have chosen you for one. What think you of the journey?" Sir Francis, who was a prudent man and had resided some years in Spain as the king's agent, was struck with all the obvious objections to such an enterprise and did not scruple to declare them. The king threw himself upon his bed and cried, "I told you this before," and fell into a new passion and new lamentations, complaining that he was undone and would lose Baby Charles.

The prince showed by his countenance that he was extremely dis-satisfied with Cottington's discourse; but Buckingham broke into an open passion against him. The king, he told him, asked him only of the journey and of the manner of traveling, particulars of which he might be a competent judge, having gone the road so often by post; but that he, without being called to it, had the presumption to give his advice upon matters of state and against his master, which he would repent as long as he lived. A thousand other reproaches he added, which put the poor king into a new agony in behalf of a servant who, he foresaw, would suffer for answering him honestly. Upon which he said with some emotion, "Nay, by God, Steenie, you are much to blame for using him so. He answered me directly to the question which I asked him, and very honestly and wisely; and yet you know he said no more than I told you before he was called in." However, after all this passion on both sides, James renewed his consent, and proper directions were given for the journey. Nor was he now at any loss to discover that the whole intrigue was originally contrived by Bucking-ham as well as pursued violently by his spirit and impetuosity.

These circumstances, which so well characterize the persons, seem to have been related by Cottington to Lord Clarendon, from whom they are here transcribed; though minute, they are not undeserving of a place in history.

Prince's journey to Spain

The prince and Buckingham, with their two attendants and Sir Richard Graham, master of horse to Buckingham, passed disguised and undiscovered through France. They even ventured into a court ball at Paris, where Charles saw the princess Henrietta, whom he later married and who was at that time in the bloom of youth and beauty. On March 7, eleven days after their departure from London, they arrived at Madrid and surprised everybody by a step so unusual among great princes. The Spanish monarch immediately paid Charles a visit, expressed the utmost gratitude for the confidence reposed in him, and made warm protestations of a correspondent confidence and friendship. By the most studied civilities, he showed the respect which he bore to his royal guest. He gave him a golden key which opened all his apartments, so that the prince might have access to him at all hours without any introduction. He took the left hand of him on every occasion, except in the apartments assigned to Charles; for there, he said, the prince was at home. Charles was introduced into the palace with the same pomp and ceremony that attended the kings of Spain on their coronation. The council received public orders to obey him as the king himself. Olivares too, though a grandee of Spain who had the right of being covered before his own king, would not put on his hat in the prince's presence. All the prisons of Spain were thrown open, and all the prisoners received their freedom as if the most honorable and fortunate event had happened to the monarchy. Every sumptuary law with regard to apparel was suspended during Charles's residence in Spain. The infanta, however, was only shown to her lover in public, the Spanish ideas of decency being so strict as not to allow of any further intercourse till the arrival of the dispensation.

The point of honor was carried so far by that generous people that no attempt was made, on account of the advantage which they had acquired, of imposing any harder conditions of treaty. Their pious zeal only prompted them on one occasion to desire more concessions in the religious articles; but upon the opposition of Bristol, accompanied with some reproaches, they immediately desisted. The pope, however, hearing of the prince's arrival in Madrid, tacked some new clauses to the dispensation; and it became necessary to transmit the articles to London, so that the king might ratify them. This treaty, which was made public, consisted of several articles chiefly regarding the exercise of the Catholic religion by the infanta and her household. Nothing could reasonably be found fault with except one article, in which the king promised that the children would be educated by the princess till ten years of age. This condition could not have been insisted on but with a view of seasoning their minds with Catholic principles; and though so tender an age seemed a sufficient security against theological prejudices, yet the same reason which made the pope insert that article should have induced the king to reject it.

Besides the public treaty, there were separate articles privately sworn to by the king in which he promised to suspend the penal laws enacted against Catholics, to procure a repeal of them in Parliament, and to grant a toleration for the exercise of the Catholic religion in private houses. Great murmurs, we may believe, would have arisen against these articles had they been made known to the public, since we find it to have been imputed as an enormous crime to the prince that having received about this time a very civil letter from the pope, he was induced to return a very civil answer.

Meanwhile, Gregory XV, who granted the dispensation, died; and Urban VIII was chosen in his place. Upon this event, the nuncio refused to deliver the dispensation till it would be renewed by Urban; and that crafty pontiff delayed sending a new dispensation in hopes that some expedient might be fallen upon to effect the prince's conversion during his residence in Spain. The king of England as well as the prince became impatient. On the first hint, Charles obtained permission to return; and Philip graced his departure with all the circumstances of elaborate civility and respect which had attended his reception. He even erected a pillar on the spot where they took leave of each other as a monument of mutual friendship; and the prince, having sworn to the observance of all the articles, entered on his journey and embarked on board the English fleet at Santander.

The character of Charles, composed of decency, reserve, modesty, and sobriety, virtues so agreeable to the manners of the Spaniards; the unparalleled confidence which he had reposed in their nation; the romantic gallantry which he had practiced towards the princess: all these circumstances, joined to his youth and advantageous figure, had endeared him to the whole court of Madrid and had impressed the most favorable ideas of him. But in the same proportion that the prince was beloved and esteemed, Buckingham was despised and hated. His behavior, composed of English familiarity and French vivacity, his sallies of passion, his indecent freedoms with the prince, his dissolute pleasures, his arrogant, impetuous temper, which he neither could nor cared to disguise: qualities like these could, most of them, be esteemed nowhere, but to the Spaniards were the objects of particular aversion. They could not conceal their surprise that such a youth could intrude into a negotiation now conducted to a conclusion by so accomplished a minister as Bristol and could assume to himself all the merit of it. They lamented the lot of the infanta, who must be approached by a man whose temerity seemed to respect no laws, divine or human. And when they observed that he had the imprudence to insult the Count-Duke of Olivares, their prime minister, everyone who was ambitious of paying court to the Spanish became desirous of showing a contempt for the English favorite.

Buckingham told Olivares that his own attachment to the Spanish nation and to the king of Spain was extreme, that he would contribute to every measure which could cement the friendship between England and them, and that his particular ambition would be to facilitate the prince's marriage with the infanta. But, he added with a sincerity equally insolent and indiscreet, "With regard to you, sir, in particular, you must not consider me as your friend, but must ever expect from me all possible enmity and opposition." The count-duke replied with a becoming dignity that he very willingly accepted what was proffered him; and on these terms the favorites parted.

Buckingham, aware how odious he had become to the Spaniards and dreading the influence which that nation would naturally acquire after the arrival of the infanta, resolved to employ all his credit to prevent the marriage. By what arguments he could engage the prince to offer such an insult to the Spanish nation, from whom he had met with such generous treatment; by what colors he could disguise the ingratitude and imprudence of such a measure: these are totally unknown to us. We may only conjecture that the many unavoidable causes of delay which had so long prevented the arrival of the dispensation had afforded to Buckingham a pretense for throwing on the Spaniards the imputation of insincerity in the whole treaty. It also appears that his impetuous and domineering character had acquired what it ever after maintained, a total ascendance over the gentle and modest temper of Charles. When the prince left Madrid, he was firmly determined, notwithstanding all his professions, to break off the treaty with Spain.

It is not likely that Buckingham prevailed so easily with James to abandon a project which had been the object of all his wishes for so many years, and which he had now unexpectedly conducted to a happy conclusion. A rupture with Spain and the loss of two million pieces of eight were prospects little agreeable to this pacific and indigent monarch. But finding his only son bent against a match which had always been opposed by his people and his Parliament, he yielded to difficulties which he had not courage or strength of mind sufficient to overcome. The prince and Buckingham, therefore, on their arrival at London, assumed entirely the direction of the negotiation; and it was their business to seek for pretenses by which they could give a color to their intended breach of treaty.

Marriage treaty broken

Though the restitution of the Palatinate had always been considered by James as a natural or necessary consequence of the Spanish alliance, he had always forbidden his ministers to insist on it as a preliminary article to the conclusion of the marriage treaty. He considered that this principality was now in the hands of the emperor and the Duke of Bavaria, and that it was no longer in the king of Spain's power, by a single stroke of his pen, to restore it to its ancient master. The strict alliance of Spain with these princes would engage Philip, he thought, to soften so disagreeable a demand by every art of negotiation; and many articles must of necessity be adjusted before such an important point could be effected. It was sufficient, in James's opinion, if the sincerity of the Spanish court could for the present be ascertained; dreading further delays of the marriage so long wished for, he was resolved to trust the palatine's full restoration to the determination of future counsels and deliberations.

This whole system of negotiation Buckingham now reversed, and he overturned every supposition upon which the treaty had previously been conducted. After many fruitless artifices were employed to delay or prevent the espousals, Bristol received positive orders not to deliver the proxy which had been left in his hands or to finish the marriage till security was given for the full restitution of the Palatinate. Philip understood this language. He had been acquainted with the disgust received by Buckingham; and deeming him a man capable of sacrificing to his own ungovernable passions the greatest interests of his master and of his country, he had expected that the unbounded credit of that favorite would be employed to embroil the two nations. Determined, however, to throw the blame of the rupture entirely on the English, Philip delivered into Bristol's hand a written promise by which he bound himself to procure the restoration of the Palatinate either by persuasion or by every other possible means. When he found that this concession gave no satisfaction, he ordered the infanta to lay aside the title of Princess of Wales, which she bore after the arrival of the dispensation from Rome, and to drop the study of the English language. And thinking that such rash counsels as now governed the court of England would not stop at the breach of the marriage treaty, he ordered preparations for war immediately to be made throughout all his dominions.

Thus James, having by means inexplicable from the ordinary rules of politics conducted to so near an honorable conclusion the marriage of his son and the restoration of his son-in-law, failed at last of his purpose by means equally unaccountable.

But though the expedients already used by Buckingham were sufficiently inglorious both for himself and for the nation, it was necessary for him, before he could fully effect his purpose, to employ artifices still more dishonorable.

A Parliament

The king, having broken with Spain, was obliged to concert new measures. Without the assistance of Parliament, *1624* no effectual step of any kind could be taken. The benevolence which during the interval had been rigorously exacted for recovering the Palatinate, though levied for so popular an end, had procured to the king less money than ill will from his subjects. Whatever discouragements, therefore, he might receive from his disagreements with former Parliaments, there was a necessity of summoning once more this assembly; and it might be hoped that as the Spanish alliance which gave such umbrage had been abandoned, the Commons would now be better satisfied with the king's administration. In his speech to the houses on February 29, James dropped some hints of his cause of complaint against Spain; and he graciously consented to ask the advice of Parliament, which he had always before rejected, with regard to the conduct of so important an affair as his son's marriage. Buckingham delivered to a committee of Lords and Commons a long narrative, which he claimed to be true and complete, of every step taken in the negotiations with Philip. But partly by the suppression of some facts, partly by the false coloring laid on others, this narrative was calculated entirely to mislead the Parliament and to throw on the court of Spain the reproach of artifice and insincerity. He said that after many years' negotiation, the king had found himself no nearer to his purpose, and that Bristol had never brought the treaty beyond general professions and declarations. That the prince, doubting the good intentions of Spain, resolved at last to take a journey to Madrid and put the matter to the utmost trial. That he there found such artificial dealing as made him conclude that all the steps taken towards the marriage had been false and deceitful. That the restitution of the Palatinate, which had always been regarded by the king as an essential preliminary, was not seriously intended by Spain. And that after enduring much bad usage, the prince was obliged to return to England without any hopes either of obtaining the infanta or of restoring the elector palatine.

This narrative deserves great blame, considering the importance of the occasion and the solemnity of that assembly to which it was delivered. Yet it was vouched for as true by the Prince of Wales, who was present; and the king himself indirectly lent it his authority by telling the Parliament that it was by his orders that Buckingham laid the whole affair before them. It is difficult fully to excuse the conduct of these princes. It is in vain to plead the youth and inexperience of Charles, unless his inexperience and youth, as is probable if not certain, really led him into error and made him swallow all the falsities of Buckingham. And though the king was here hurried from his own measures by the impetuosity of others, nothing should have induced him to prostitute his character and seem to vouch for the impostures, or at least false colorings, of his favorite, of which he had so good reason to entertain a suspicion.

Buckingham's narrative, however artfully disguised, contained more contradictory circumstances than were sufficient to open the eyes of all reasonable men; but it concurred so well with the passions and prejudices of the Parliament that no scruple was made of immediately adopting it. Charmed with having obtained at length the opportunity, so long wished for, of going to war with papists, they little thought of future consequences; rather, they immediately advised the king to break off both treaties [negotiations] with Spain, that which regarded the marriage as well as that for the restitution of the Palatinate. The people, ever greedy of war till they suffer by it, displayed their triumph at these violent measures by public bonfires and rejoicings and by insults on the Spanish ministers. Buckingham was now the favorite of the public and of the Parliament. Sir Edward Coke, in the House of Commons, called him the savior of the nation. Every place resounded with his praises. And he himself, intoxicated by a popularity which he enjoyed so briefly and which he so ill deserved, violated all duty to his indulgent master and entered into cabals with the Puritanical members, who had always opposed the royal authority. He even encouraged schemes for abolishing the order of bishops and selling the dean and chapter lands in order to defray the expenses of a Spanish war. And the king, though he still entertained projects for temporizing and for forming an accommodation with Spain, was so borne down by the torrent of popular prejudices, conducted and increased by Buckingham, that he was at last obliged in a speech to Parliament to declare in favor of hostile measures if they would engage to support him. Doubts of their sincerity in this respect—doubts which were shown to be well grounded in the event—had probably been one cause of his former pacific and dilatory measures.

In his speech on this occasion, the king began with lamenting his own unhappiness that having so long valued his epithet of the pacific monarch, he would now in his old age be obliged to exchange the blessings of peace for the inevitable calamities of war. He represented to them the immense and continued expense requisite for military armaments; and besides supplies from time to time as they would become necessary, he demanded a vote of six subsidies and twelve fifteenths as a proper stock before the commencement of hostilities. He told them of his intolerable debts, chiefly contracted by the sums remitted to the palatine. But he added that he did not insist on any supply for his own relief, and that it was sufficient for him if the honor and security of the public were provided for. To remove all suspicion, he—who had always strenuously maintained his prerogative, and who had even extended it into some points considered doubtful—now made an imprudent concession, the consequences of which might have proved fatal to royal authority. He voluntarily offered that the money voted would be paid to a committee of Parliament and would be issued by them without being entrusted to his management. The Commons willingly accepted this concession, so unusual in an English monarch; they voted him only three subsidies and three fifteenths; and they took no notice of his complaints about his own wants and necessities.

Advantage was also taken of the present good agreement between the king and Parliament in order to pass the bill against monopolies, which had formerly been encouraged by the king but which had failed by the rupture between him and the last House of Commons. This bill was conceived in such terms as to render it merely declaratory, and all monopolies were condemned as contrary to law and to the known liberties of the people. It was there supposed that every subject of England had entire power to dispose of his own actions, provided he did no injury to any of his fellow subjects, and that no prerogative of the king, no power of any magistrate, nothing but the authority alone of laws could restrain that unlimited freedom. The full prosecution of this noble principle into all its natural consequences has at last, through many contests, produced that singular and happy government which we enjoy at present.

The House of Commons also corroborated by a new precedent the important power of impeachment, which two years before they had exercised in the case of Chancellor Bacon and which had lain dormant for nearly two centuries, except when it served as an instrument of royal vengeance. The Earl of Middlesex had been raised by Buckingham's influence from the rank of a London merchant to be treasurer of England, and by his energy and adroitness seemed not unworthy of that preferment. But as he incurred the displeasure of his patron by scrupling or refusing some demands of money during the prince's residence in Spain, that favorite vowed revenge and employed all his credit among the Commons to procure an impeachment of the treasurer. The king was extremely dissatisfied with this measure and prophesied to the prince and duke that they would live to have their fill of parliamentary prosecutions. In a speech to the Parliament, he endeavored to apologize for Middlesex and to soften the accusation against him. The charge, however, was still maintained by the Commons; and the treasurer was found guilty by the Peers, though the misdemeanors proved against him were neither numerous nor important. The accepting of two presents of £500 apiece for passing two patents was the article of greatest weight. His sentence was to be fined £50,000 for the king's use and to suffer all the other penalties formerly inflicted upon Bacon. The fine was later abated by the prince when he mounted the throne.

This session, an address craving the severe execution of the laws against Catholics was also made, which the king found very disagreeable. His answer was gracious and accommodating, though he declared against persecution as being an improper measure for the suppression of any religion, in accord with the received maxim, "That the blood of the martyrs was the seed of the church." He also condemned an entire indulgence of the Catholics; and he seemed to represent a middle course as the most humane and most politic. He even went so far as to affirm with an oath that he never had entertained any thoughts of granting a toleration to these religionists. The liberty of exercising their worship in private houses, which he had secretly agreed to in the Spanish treaty, did not appear to him deserving that name; and it was probably by means of this explication that he thought he had saved his honor. And as Buckingham in his narrative confessed that the king had agreed to a temporary suspension of the penal laws against the Catholics, which he distinguished from a "toleration"—a term at that time extremely odious—James naturally deemed his meaning to be sufficiently explained and did not fear any reproach of falsehood or duplicity on account of this asseveration. After all these transactions, the Parliament was prorogued on May 29 by the king, who let fall some hints, though in gentle terms, of the opinion which he entertained of their unkindness in not supplying his necessities.

James, unable to resist so strong a combination as that of his people, his Parliament, his son, and his favorite, had been compelled to embrace measures for which, from temper as well as judgment, he had always entertained a most settled aversion. Though he dissembled his resentment, he began to estrange himself from Buckingham, to whom he ascribed all those violent counsels, and whom he considered as the author both of the prince's journey to Spain and of the breach of the marriage treaty. He impatiently longed for the arrival of Bristol; and it was by the assistance of that minister, whose wisdom he respected and whose views he approved, that he hoped in time to extricate himself from his present difficulties.

Return of Bristol

During the prince's abode in Spain, Bristol, an able negotiator, had always opposed, though unsuccessfully, his own wise and well-tempered counsels to the impetuous measures suggested by Buckingham. After Charles's departure, he still, upon the first appearance of a change of resolution, interposed his advice and strenuously insisted on the sincerity of the Spaniards in the conduct of the treaty as well as the advantages which England must reap from the completion of it. Enraged to find his successful labors rendered abortive by the levities and caprices of an insolent minion, he would understand no hints;

nothing but express orders from his master could engage him to make that demand which, he was aware, must put a final end to the treaty. He was not, therefore, surprised to hear that Buckingham had declared himself his open enemy and on all occasions had thrown out many violent reflections against him.

Nothing could have been of greater consequence to Buckingham than to keep Bristol at a distance both from the king and the Parliament, lest the power of truth, reinforced by so well informed a speaker, would open scenes which were but suspected by the former and of which the latter had as yet entertained no manner of jealousy [suspicion]. He applied, therefore, to James, whose weakness—disguised to himself under the appearance of finesse and dissimulation—had now become absolutely incurable. A warrant for sending Bristol to the Tower was issued immediately upon his arrival in England; and though he was soon released from confinement, yet orders were carried to him from the king to retire to his country seat and to abstain from all attendance in Parliament. He obeyed, but loudly demanded an opportunity of justifying himself and of laying his whole conduct before his master. On all occasions, he protested his innocence and threw on his enemy the blame of every miscarriage. Buckingham, and at his instigation the prince, declared that they would be reconciled to Bristol if he would but acknowledge his errors and ill conduct. But the spirited nobleman, jealous of his honor, refused to buy favor at so high a price. James had the equity to say that the insisting on that condition was a strain of unexampled tyranny. But Buckingham did not scruple to assert, with his usual presumption, that neither the king, the prince, nor himself were as yet satisfied of Bristol's innocence.

While the attachment of Charles to Buckingham and the timidity—or the shame of changing his favorite—of James kept the whole court in awe, the Spanish ambassador, Hinojosa, endeavored to open the king's eyes and to cure his fears by instilling greater fears into him. He privately slipped into James's hand a paper and gave him a signal to read it alone. He there told him that the king of England was as much a prisoner at London as ever Francis I was at Madrid; that the prince and Buckingham had conspired together and had the whole court at their devotion; that cabals among the popular leaders in Parliament were carrying on to the extreme prejudice of his authority; that the project was to confine James to some of his hunting seats and to commit the whole administration to Charles; and that it was necessary for James, by one vigorous effort, to vindicate his authority and to punish those who had so long and so much abused his friendship and beneficence.

What credit James gave to this representation does not appear. He only showed some faint symptoms, which he instantly retracted, of dissatisfaction with Buckingham. All his public measures and all the alliances into which he entered were founded on the system of enmity to the Austrian family and of war to be carried on for the recovery of the Palatinate.

Rupture with Spain

The States of the United Provinces were at this time governed by Maurice; and that aspiring prince, aware that his credit would languish during peace, had renewed the war with the Spanish monarchy on the expiration of the twelve years' truce. His great capacity in the military art would have compensated for the inferiority of his forces had not the Spanish armies been commanded by Spinola, a general equally renowned for conduct and more celebrated for enterprise and energy. In such a situation, nothing could be more welcome to the republic than the prospect of a rupture between James and the Catholic king; and they flattered themselves, as much from the natural union of interests between them and England as from the influence of the present conjuncture, that powerful succors would soon march to their relief. Accordingly, an army of six thousand men was levied in England and sent over to Holland, commanded by four young noblemen—Essex, Oxford, Southampton, and Willoughby—who were ambitious of distinguishing themselves in so popular a cause and of acquiring military experience under so renowned a captain as Maurice.

Treaty with France

It might reasonably have been expected that as religious zeal had made the recovery of the Palatinate appear a point of such vast importance in England, the same effect must have been produced in France by the force merely of political interests and considerations. While that principality remained in the hands of the house of Austria, the French dominions were surrounded on all sides by the possessions of that ambitious family and might be invaded by superior forces from every quarter. It concerned the king of France, therefore, to prevent the peaceable establishment of the emperor in his new conquests; and by both the location and the greater power of his state, he was much better enabled than James to give succor to the distressed palatine. But though these views escaped neither Louis nor Cardinal Richelieu, who now began to acquire an ascendance in the French court, that minister was determined to pave the way for his enterprises by first subduing the Protestant Huguenots, and from there to proceed by mature counsels to humble the house of Austria. The prospect, however, of a conjunction with England was presently embraced, and all imaginable encouragement was given to every proposal for conciliating a marriage between Charles and the princess Henrietta.

Notwithstanding the useful experience which James might have acquired of the insurmountable antipathy entertained by his subjects against an alliance with Catholics, he still persevered in the opinion that his son would be degraded by receiving into his bed a princess of less than royal extraction. After the rupture with Spain, therefore, nothing remained but an alliance with France; and to that court he immediately applied himself. The same allurements which had so long entangled him in the Spanish negotiation had no place here; the portion promised was much inferior, and the peaceable restoration of the palatine could not be expected from that quarter. But James was afraid lest his son be altogether disappointed of a bride; and therefore, as soon as the French king demanded, for the honor of his Crown, the same terms which had been granted to the Spanish, he was prevailed with to comply. And as the prince, during his abode in Spain, had given a verbal promise to allow the infanta the education of her children till the age of thirteen, this article was here inserted in the treaty; and to that imprudence is generally imputed the present distressed condition of his posterity. The court of England, however, it must be confessed, always claimed, even in their memorials to the French court, that all the favorable conditions granted to the Catholics were inserted in the marriage treaty merely to please the pope, and that their strict execution was, by an agreement with France, secretly dispensed with.

As much as the conclusion of the marriage treaty was acceptable to the king, all the military enterprises were to the same degree disagreeable, both from the extreme difficulty of the undertaking in which he was engaged and from his own incapacity for such a scene of action.

During the Spanish negotiation, Heidelberg and Mannheim had been taken by the imperial forces, and Frankenthal, though the garrison was entirely English, was closely besieged by them. After reiterated remonstrances from James, Spain interposed and procured a suspension of arms for eighteen months. But as Frankenthal was the only place of Frederick's ancient dominions which was still in his hands, Ferdinand, desirous of withdrawing his forces from the Palatinate and of leaving that state in security, was unwilling that so important a fortress would remain in the possession of the enemy. To compromise all differences, it was agreed to sequestrate it into the hands of the infanta as a neutral person, upon the condition that after the expiration of the truce, it would be delivered to Frederick even if peace were not at that time concluded between him and Ferdinand. After the unexpected rupture with Spain, the infanta, when James demanded the execution of the treaty, offered him peaceable possession of Frankenthal and even promised a safe conduct for the garrison through the Spanish Netherlands. But there was some territory of the empire interposed between her state and the Palatinate, and no terms were stipulated for passage over that territory. By this chicanery, which certainly would not have been employed if amity with Spain had been preserved, the palatine was totally dispossessed of his patrimonial dominions.

Mansfeld's expedition

Neither the English nation nor James's warlike Council, however, were discouraged. They were still determined to reconquer the Palatinate, a state lying in the midst of Germany, possessed entirely by the emperor and the Duke of Bavaria, surrounded by potent enemies, and cut off from all communication with England. The Count of Mansfeld was taken into pay, and an English army of twelve thousand infantry and two hundred cavalry was levied by a general press throughout the kingdom. During the negotiation with France, vast promises had been made, though in general terms, by the French ministry: not only that a free passage would be granted to the English troops but also that powerful succors would join them in their march towards the Palatinate. In England, all these professions were hastily interpreted to be positive engagements. The troops under Mansfeld's command were embarked at Dover in December; but upon sailing over to Calais, they found no orders yet arrived for their admission. After waiting in vain for some time, they were obliged to sail towards Zeeland, where it had also been neglected to concert proper measures for their disembarkation; and some hesitations arose among the States on account of the scarcity of provisions. Meanwhile, a pestilential distemper crept in among the English forces, so long cooped up in narrow vessels. Half the army died while on board; the other half, weakened by sickness, appeared too small a body to march into the Palatinate. And thus ended this ill-concerted and fruitless expedition, the only disaster which happened to England during the prosperous and pacific reign of James.

1625

Death of the king

That reign was now drawing towards a conclusion. With peace, so successfully cultivated and so passionately loved by this monarch, his life also terminated. This spring, he was seized with tertian ague [intermittent fever due to malaria]. When encouraged by his courtiers with the common proverb that such a distemper during that season was health for a king, he replied that the proverb was meant of a young king. After some fits, he found himself extremely weakened and sent for the prince, whom he exhorted to bear a tender affection for his wife but to preserve a constancy in religion, to protect the Church of England, and to extend his care towards the unhappy family of the palatine. With decency and courage, he prepared himself for his end; and he expired on March 27, after a reign over England of twenty-two years and some days, and in the fifty-ninth year of his age. His reign over Scotland was almost of equal duration with his life. In all history, it would be difficult to find a reign less illustrious yet more unspotted and unblemished than that of James in both kingdoms.

His character

No prince so little enterprising and so inoffensive was ever so much exposed to the opposite extremes of calumny and flattery, of satire and panegyric. And the factions which began in his time, being still continued, have made his character be as much disputed to this day as is commonly that of princes who are our contemporaries. It must be admitted that he was possessed of many virtues, but scarcely any of them pure or free from the contagion of the neighboring vices. His generosity bordered on extravagance, his learning on pedantry, his pacific disposition on pusillanimity, his wisdom on cunning, his friendship on light fancy and boyish fondness. While he imagined that he was only maintaining his own authority, he may perhaps be suspected—in a few of his actions, and still more of his pretensions—to have somewhat encroached on the liberties of his people. While he endeavored by an exact neutrality to acquire the good will of all his neighbors, he was able to preserve fully the esteem and regard of none.

His capacity was considerable, but fitter to discourse on general maxims than to conduct any intricate business. His intentions were just, but more adapted to the conduct of private life than to the government of kingdoms. Awkward in his person and ungainly in his manners, he was ill qualified to command respect; partial and undiscerning in his affections, he was little fitted to acquire general love. He displayed more of a feeble temper than of a frail judgment; he lies exposed to our ridicule from his vanity but exempt from our hatred by his freedom from pride and arrogance. And upon the whole, it may be pronounced of his character that all his qualities were sullied with weakness and embellished by humanity. Of political courage he certainly was destitute, and from that chiefly is derived the strong prejudice which prevails against his personal bravery; such an inference, however, must be acknowledged from general experience to be extremely fallacious.

He was only once married, to Anne of Denmark, a woman eminent neither for her vices nor her virtues, who died on March 3, 1619, in the forty-fifth year of her age. She loved shows and expensive amusements but possessed little taste in her pleasures. A great comet appeared about the time of her death, and the vulgar viewed it as an omen of that event. So considerable in their eyes are even the most insignificant royal persons.

He left only one son, Charles, then in the twenty-fifth year of his age, and one daughter, Elizabeth, married to the elector palatine. She was aged twenty-nine years. Those alone remained of six legitimate children born to him. He never had any illegitimate; and he never showed any tendency, even the smallest, towards a passion for any mistress.

CHAPTER 50
1625 – 1627

*A Parliament at Westminster – A Parliament at Oxford –
Naval expedition against Spain – Second Parliament –
Impeachment of Buckingham – Violent measures of the
court – War with France – Expedition to the Isle of Rhé*

A Parliament at Westminster

NO sooner had Charles taken into his hands the reins of government than he showed an impatience to assemble the great council of the nation; and he would gladly, for the sake of dispatch, have
called together the same Parliament which had sat under his father
and which lay at that time under prorogation. But being told that this
measure would appear unusual, he issued writs for summoning a new
Parliament on May 7. It was not without regret that the arrival of the
princess Henrietta, whom he had espoused by proxy, obliged him to
delay by repeated prorogations their meeting till June 18, when they
assembled at Westminster for the dispatch of business. The young
prince, inexperienced and impolitic, regarded as sincere all the praises
and caresses with which he had been loaded while active in procuring
the rupture with the house of Austria. Although he labored under
great necessities, he hastened with alacrity to a period when he might
receive the most undoubted testimony of the dutiful attachment of his
subjects. His discourse to the Parliament was full of simplicity and
cordiality. He lightly mentioned the occasion which he had for supply.
He employed no intrigue to influence the suffrages of the members.
He would not even allow the officers of the Crown who had seats in
the house to mention any particular sum which might be expected by
him. Sure of the affections of the Commons, he was resolved that

their bounty should be entirely their own deed, unasked, unsolicited, the genuine fruit of sincere confidence and regard.

The House of Commons, accordingly, took into consideration the business of supply. They knew that all the money granted by the last Parliament had been expended on naval and military armaments, and that great anticipations were likewise made on the revenues of the Crown. They were not ignorant that Charles was loaded with a large debt contracted by his father, who had borrowed money both from his own subjects and from foreign princes. They had learned by experience that the public revenue could only with difficulty maintain the dignity of the Crown even under the ordinary charges of government. They were aware that the present war was the result of their own very recent and importunate applications and entreaties, and that they had solemnly engaged to support their sovereign in the management of it. They were acquainted with the difficulty of military enterprises directed against the whole house of Austria; against the king of Spain, possessed of the greatest riches and most extensive dominions of any prince in Europe; against the emperor Ferdinand, up to this time the most fortunate monarch of his age, who had subdued and astonished Germany by the rapidity of his victories. They saw that deep impressions must be made by the English sword and a vigorous offensive war be waged against these mighty potentates before they would resign a principality which they had now fully subdued and which they held in secure possession, surrounded as it was with all their other territories.

To answer, therefore, all these great and important ends, to satisfy their young king in the first request which he made them, to prove their recognition of the many royal virtues, particularly economy, with which Charles was endowed, the House of Commons, conducted by the wisest and ablest statesmen that had ever flourished in England, thought proper to confer on the king a supply of two subsidies, amounting to £112,000.

This measure, which reveals a cruel mockery of Charles rather than any serious design of supporting him, appears so extraordinary when considered in all its circumstances that it naturally summons up our attention and raises an inquiry concerning the causes of a conduct unprecedented in an English Parliament. So numerous an assembly, composed of persons of various dispositions, was not, it is probable, wholly influenced by the same motives; and few declared openly their true reason. We shall, therefore, approach nearer to the truth if we mention all the views which the present conjuncture could suggest to them.

It is not to be doubted that spleen and ill will against the Duke of Buckingham had an influence with many. So vast a fortune, so rapidly gained and so little merited, could not fail to excite public envy; and however men's hatred might have been suspended for a moment while the duke's conduct seemed to gratify their passions and their prejudices, it was impossible for him long to preserve the affections of the people. His influence over the modesty of Charles exceeded even that which he had acquired over the weakness of James; no public measure was conducted but by his counsel and direction. His vehement temper prompted him to raise suddenly to the highest elevation his flatterers and dependants; and upon the least occasion of displeasure, he threw them down with equal impetuosity and violence. Implacable in his hatred, fickle in his friendships, all men either were regarded as his enemies or dreaded soon to become such. The whole power of the kingdom was grasped by his insatiable hand as long as he both possessed the entire confidence of his master and held invested in his single person the most considerable offices of the Crown.

However the ill humor of the Commons might have been increased by these considerations, we are not to suppose them the sole motives. The last Parliament of James, amidst all their joy and festivity, had given him a supply very inadequate to his demand and to the occasion. And as every House of Commons which was elected during forty years succeeded to all the passions and principles of their predecessors, we ought to account for this obstinacy from the general situation of the kingdom during that whole period rather than from any circumstances which attended this particular conjuncture.

The nation was very little accustomed at that time to the burden of taxes and had never opened their purses in any degree for supporting their sovereign. Even Elizabeth, notwithstanding her vigor and frugality and the necessary wars in which she was engaged, had reason to complain of the Commons in this particular; nor could the authority of that princess, which was otherwise almost absolute, ever extort from them the requisite supplies. Habits more than reason we find in everything to be the governing principle of mankind. Accordingly, the diminishing over time of the value of subsidies must be considered as a loss to the king; the Parliament, swayed by custom, would not augment their number in the same proportion.

The Puritanical party, though disguised, had a great authority over the kingdom, and many of the leaders among the Commons had covertly embraced the rigid tenets of that sect. All these were disgusted with the court, both by the prevalence of the principles of civil liberty essential to their party and on account of the restraint under which they were held by the established hierarchy. To fortify himself against the resentment of James, Buckingham had made insincere efforts to gain the favor of the people and had entered into the cabals of the Puritans. But being secure of the confidence of Charles, he had since abandoned this party; and on that account, he was the more exposed to their hatred and resentment. Though the religious tenets of many of the Puritans, when expounded, appear pretty frivolous, we are not from that to imagine that they were pursued only by persons of weak understandings. Some men of the greatest abilities and most extensive knowledge that the nation at this time produced could not enjoy any peace of mind because they were obliged to hear prayers offered up to the Divinity by a priest covered with a white linen vestment.

The match with France and the articles in favor of Catholics which were suspected to be in the treaty were likewise causes of disgust to this whole party; though it must be observed that the connections with that Crown were much less obnoxious to the Protestants, and less agreeable to the Catholics, than the alliance formerly projected with Spain, and were therefore received rather with pleasure than dissatisfaction.

To all these causes we must yet add another, of considerable moment. The House of Commons, we may observe, was almost entirely governed by a set of men of the most uncommon capacity and the largest views, men who were now formed into a regular party and united by fixed aims and projects as well as by the hardships which some of them had undergone in prosecution of them. Among these we may mention the names of Sir Edward Coke, Sir Edwin Sandys, Sir Robert Phelips, Sir Francis Seymour, Sir Dudley Digges, Sir John Eliot, Sir Thomas Wentworth, Mr. Selden, and Mr. Pym. Animated with a warm regard to liberty, these generous patriots saw with regret an unbounded power exercised by the Crown and were resolved to seize the opportunity which the king's necessities offered them of reducing the prerogative within more reasonable compass. Though their ancestors had blindly given way to practices and precedents favorable to kingly power and had been able, notwithstanding, to preserve some small remains of liberty, it would be impossible, they thought, to maintain any shadow of popular government in opposition to such unlimited authority in the sovereign when all these pretensions were methodized and prosecuted by the increasing knowledge of the age. It was necessary to fix a choice: either to abandon entirely the privileges of the people or to secure them by firmer and more precise barriers than the constitution had up to this time provided for them. In this dilemma, men of such aspiring geniuses and such independent fortunes could not long deliberate; they boldly embraced the side of freedom and resolved to grant no supplies to their necessitous prince without extorting concessions in favor of civil liberty. The end they deemed beneficent and noble; the means, regular and constitutional. To grant or refuse supplies was the undoubted privilege of the Commons. And as all human governments, particularly those of a mixed frame, are in continual fluctuation, it was, in their opinion, as natural and allowable for popular assemblies to take advantage of favorable incidents in order to secure the subject as it was for monarchs to do so in order to extend their own authority. They beheld with pleasure the king involved in a foreign war which rendered him every day more dependent on the Parliament; while at the same time, the location of the kingdom, even without any military preparations, gave it sufficient security against all invasion from foreigners. Perhaps too, it was partly from expectations of this nature that the popular leaders had been so urgent for a rupture with Spain; nor is it credible that religious zeal could so much have blinded all of them as to make them perceive in such a measure any appearance of necessity or any hopes of success.

But however natural all these sentiments might appear to the country party, it is not to be imagined that Charles would entertain the same ideas. Strongly prejudiced in favor of Buckingham, whom he had heard so highly extolled in Parliament, he could not conjecture the cause of so sudden an alteration in their opinions. And when the war which they themselves had so earnestly solicited was at last commenced, the immediate desertion of their sovereign could not seem other than very unaccountable. Even if no further motive had been suspected, the refusal of supply in such circumstances would naturally appear to him cruel and deceitful; but when he perceived that this measure proceeded from an intention of encroaching on his authority, he could not fail to regard these aims as highly criminal and traitorous. Those lofty ideas of monarchical power which were very commonly adopted during that age, and to which the ambiguous nature of the English constitution gave so plausible an appearance, were firmly fixed in Charles; and however moderate his temper, the natural and unavoidable prepossessions of self-love joined to the late uniform precedents in favor of prerogative had made him regard his political tenets as certain and uncontroverted. Taught to consider even the ancient laws and constitution more as lines to direct his conduct than as barriers to withstand his power, a conspiracy to erect new ramparts in order to straiten his authority appeared but one degree removed from open sedition and rebellion. So atrocious in his eyes was such a design that he was even unwilling, it seems, to impute it to the Commons; and though he was constrained to adjourn the Parliament on July 11 by reason of the plague which at that time raged in London, he immediately reassembled them at Oxford on August 1 and made a new attempt to gain from them some supplies in such an urgent necessity.

A Parliament at Oxford

Charles now found himself obliged to depart from that delicacy which he had formerly maintained. By himself or his ministers, he set forth particular details regarding both the alliances which he had formed and the military operations which he had projected. He told the Parliament that by a promise of subsidies, he had engaged the king of Denmark to take part in the war. That this monarch intended to enter Germany by the north and to rouse to arms those princes who impatiently longed for an opportunity of asserting the liberty of the empire. That Mansfeld had undertaken to penetrate into the Palatinate with an English army, and by that quarter to excite the members of the Evangelical Union. That the Dutch States had to be supported in the unequal warfare which they maintained with Spain. That no less a sum than £700,000 a year had been computed to be requisite for all these purposes. That the maintenance of the fleet and the defense of Ireland demanded an annual expense of £400,000. That he himself had already exhausted and anticipated his whole revenue in the public service and had scarcely left an amount sufficient for the daily subsistence of himself and his family. That on his accession to the Crown, he found a debt of more than £300,000 contracted by his father in support of the palatine. And that while Prince of Wales, he had himself contracted debts, notwithstanding his great frugality, to the amount of £70,000, which he had expended entirely on naval and military armaments. After mentioning all these facts, the king even stooped to use entreaties. He said that this request was the first that he had ever made them, that he was young and in the commencement of his reign, and that if he now met with kind and dutiful usage, it would endear to him the use of Parliaments and would forever preserve an entire harmony between him and his people.

To these reasons the Commons remained inexorable. Notwithstanding that the king's measures, on the supposition of a foreign war which they had constantly demanded, were altogether unexceptionable, they obstinately refused any further aid. Some members favorable to the court insisted on an addition of two fifteenths to the former supply; but even this pittance was refused, though it was known that a fleet and army were lying at Portsmouth in great want of pay and provisions, and that the treasurer of the navy and Buckingham, the admiral, had advanced on their own credit nearly £100,000 for the sea service. Besides all their other motives, the House of Commons had made a discovery which, as they lacked but a pretense for their refusal, inflamed them against the court and against the Duke of Buckingham.

When James deserted the Spanish alliance and courted that of France, he had promised to furnish Louis, who was entirely destitute of naval force, with one ship of war together with seven armed vessels hired from the merchants. These the French court had claimed they would employ against the Genoese, who, being firm and useful allies to the Spanish monarchy, were naturally regarded with an evil eye both by the king of France and of England. When these vessels, by Charles's orders, arrived at Dieppe, there arose a strong suspicion that they were to serve against the Huguenot city of La Rochelle. The sailors were inflamed. That race of men, who are at present both careless and ignorant in all matters of religion, were at that time only ignorant. They drew up a remonstrance to Pennington, their commander; and signing all their names in a circle so he could not discover the ringleaders, they laid it under his prayer book. Pennington declared that he would rather be hanged in England for disobedience than fight against his brother Protestants in France. The whole squadron sailed immediately to the Downs. There they received new orders from Buckingham, lord admiral, to return to Dieppe. As the duke knew that authority alone would not suffice, he employed much art and many subtleties to engage them to obedience; and a rumor which was spread that peace had been concluded between the French king and the Huguenots assisted him in his purpose. When they arrived at Dieppe, they found that they had been deceived. Sir Ferdinando Gorges, who commanded one of the vessels, broke through and returned to England. All the officers and sailors of all the other ships, notwithstanding great offers made them by the French, immediately deserted.

One gunner alone preferred duty towards his king to the cause of religion; and he was afterwards killed in charging a cannon before La Rochelle. The care which historians have taken to record this frivolous event proves with what pleasure the news was received by the nation.

The House of Commons, when informed of these transactions, showed the same attachment to the Protestant religion as had the sailors; nor was their zeal much better guided by reason and sound policy. It was not considered that it was highly probable that the king and the duke themselves had here been deceived by the artifices of France and had no hostile intention against the Huguenots. That if it were otherwise, their measures might yet be justified by the most obvious and most received maxims of civil policy. That if the force of Spain were really so exorbitant as the Commons imagined, the French monarch was the only prince that could oppose its progress and preserve the balance of Europe. That his power was at present fettered by the Huguenots, who, being possessed of many privileges and even of fortified towns, formed an empire within his empire and kept him in perpetual jealousy [apprehension] and uneasiness. That an insurrection had been at that time wantonly and voluntarily formed by their leaders, who, being disgusted in some court intrigue, took advantage of the never-failing pretense of religion in order to cover their rebellion. That the Dutch, influenced by these designs, had ordered a squadron of twenty ships to join the French fleet employed against the inhabitants of La Rochelle. That the Spanish monarch, aware of the same consequences, secretly supported the Protestants in France. And that all princes had always sacrificed to reasons of state the interests of their religion in foreign countries. All these obvious considerations had no influence. Great murmurs and discontents still prevailed in Parliament. The Huguenots, though they had no ground of complaint against the French court, were thought to be as much entitled to assistance from England as if they had taken arms in defense of their liberties and religion against the persecuting rage of the Catholics. And it plainly appears from this incident, as well as from many others, that of all European nations, the British were at that time, and till long after, the most under the influence of that religious spirit which tends to inflame bigotry rather than increase peace and mutual charity.

On this occasion, the Commons renewed their eternal complaints against the growth of popery, which was always the chief of their grievances and now their only one. They demanded a strict execution of the penal laws against the Catholics and remonstrated against some late pardons granted to priests. They attacked Richard Montague, one of the king's chaplains, on account of a moderate book which he had lately published; to their great disgust, it saved virtuous Catholics as well as other Christians from eternal torments. Charles gave them a gracious and a compliant answer to all their remonstrances. He was, however, in his heart extremely averse to these furious measures. Though a determined Protestant by principle as well as inclination, he entertained no violent horror against popery; and a little humanity, he thought, was due by the nation to the religion of their ancestors. It suited neither with Charles's sentiments nor the humor of the age to allow Catholics that degree of liberty which is now indulged to them (though a party much more obnoxious than during the reign of the Stuarts). An abatement of the more rigorous laws was all he intended; and his engagements with France, notwithstanding that their regular execution had never been promised or expected, required of him some indulgence. But so unfortunate was this prince that no measure embraced during his whole reign was ever attended with more unhappy and more fatal consequences.

The extreme rage against popery was a sure characteristic of Puritanism. The House of Commons revealed other infallible symptoms of the prevalence of that party. They petitioned the king for reinstating such able clergy as had been silenced for lack of conformity to the ceremonies. They also enacted laws for the strict observance of Sunday, which the Puritans affected to call the Sabbath and which they sanctified by the most melancholy indolence. It is to be observed that the different appellations of this festival were at that time known symbols of the different parties.

The king, finding that the Parliament was resolved to grant him no supply and would furnish him with nothing but empty protestations of duty or disagreeable complaints of grievances, took advantage of the plague which began to appear at Oxford and immediately dissolved them on that pretense on August 12. By finishing the session with a dissolution instead of a prorogation, he sufficiently expressed his displeasure at their conduct.

Naval expedition against Spain

To supply the lack of parliamentary aids, Charles issued privy seals for borrowing money from his subjects. The advantage reaped by this expedient was a small compensation for the disgust which it occasioned. By means of that supply, however, and by other expedients, he was, though with difficulty, enabled to equip his fleet. It consisted of eighty vessels, great and small, and carried on board an army of ten thousand men. Sir Edward Cecil, lately created Viscount Wimbledon, was entrusted with the command. Immediately, on October 1, he sailed for Cadiz; on arrival, he found the bay full of Spanish ships of great value. He either neglected to attack these ships or attempted it preposterously. The army was landed and a fort taken; but the undisciplined soldiers, finding a store of wine, could not be restrained from the utmost excesses. Further stay appearing fruitless, they were reembarked; and the fleet put to sea with an intention of intercepting the Spanish galleons. But the plague having seized the seamen and soldiers, they were obliged to abandon all hopes of this prize and return to England in November. Loud complaints were made against the court for entrusting so important a command to a man like Cecil, whom the people, judging by the event, deemed of slender capacity, though he possessed great experience.

Second Parliament

Charles, having failed of so rich a prize, was obliged again to have recourse to a Parliament. Though the ill success of

1626

his enterprises diminished his authority and showed every day more plainly the imprudence of the Spanish war, though the increase of his necessities rendered him more dependent and more exposed to the encroachments of the Commons, he was resolved to try once more that regular and constitutional expedient for supply. Perhaps too, a little political art which he practiced at that time was much trusted to. He had named four popular leaders of the Commons—Sir Edward Coke, Sir Robert Phelips, Sir Thomas Wentworth, and Sir Francis Seymour—sheriffs of counties; and though the question had been formerly much contested, he thought that he had by that means incapacitated them from being elected members of the Commons. But his intention being so evident, the Commons rather were put more upon their guard. Enough patriots still remained to keep up the ill humor of the house, and other men needed but little instruction or rhetoric to recommend to them practices which increased their own importance and consideration. The weakness of the court also could not more clearly appear than by its being reduced to use so ineffectual an expedient in order to obtain an influence over the Commons.

This Parliament, assembled on February 6, therefore immediately adopted the views of the last one as if the same men had been everywhere elected and no time had intervened since their meeting. When the king laid before the house his necessities and asked for supply, they immediately voted him three subsidies and three fifteenths. Though they afterwards added one subsidy more, the sum was little proportioned to the greatness of the occasion and ill fitted to promote those prospects of success and glory for which the young prince in his first enterprise so ardently longed. But this circumstance was not the most disagreeable one. The supply was only voted by the Commons; the passing of that vote into a law was reserved till the end of the session. A condition was thereby made, in a very undisguised manner, with their sovereign. Under color of redressing grievances, which during this short reign could not have been very numerous, they were to proceed in regulating and controlling every part of government which displeased them. And if the king either cut them short in this undertaking or refused compliance with their demands, he could not expect any supply from the Commons. Great dissatisfaction was expressed by Charles at a treatment which he deemed so harsh and undutiful. But his urgent necessities obliged him to submit; and he waited with patience, observing to what side they would turn themselves.

Impeachment of Buckingham

The Duke of Buckingham, formerly obnoxious to the public, became every day more unpopular due to the signs which appeared both of his lack of temper and prudence and of the uncontrolled ascendance which he had acquired over his master. He was obliged this session to sustain two violent attacks, one from the Earl of Bristol, another from the House of Commons.

As long as James lived, Bristol, secure of the concealed favor of that monarch, had expressed all duty and obedience in expectation that an opportunity would offer of reinstating himself in his former credit and authority. Even after Charles's accession, he did not despair. He submitted to the king's commands of remaining at his country seat and of absenting himself from Parliament. He made many attempts to regain the good opinion of his master; but finding them all fruitless and observing Charles to be entirely governed by Buckingham, his implacable enemy, he resolved no longer to abide by any limits on his conduct with respect to the court. He saw a new spirit and a new power arising in the nation, and to these he was determined to trust for his security and protection in the future.

When the Parliament was summoned, Charles, by a stretch of prerogative, had given orders that the customary writ not be sent to Bristol. That nobleman applied to the House of Lords by petition and craved that body's good offices with the king for obtaining what was his due as a peer of the realm. His writ was sent to him, but accompanied with a letter from the lord keeper, Coventry, commanding him in the king's name to absent himself from Parliament. Bristol conveyed this letter to the Lords and asked for advice on how to proceed in so delicate a situation. The king's prohibition was withdrawn, and Bristol took his seat. Provoked at these repeated instances of rigor, which the court denominated contumacy, Charles ordered his attorney general to enter an accusation of high treason against Bristol. By way of recrimination, Bristol accused Buckingham of high treason. Both the earl's defense of himself and accusation of the duke remain; together with some original letters still extant, these contain the fullest and most authentic account of all the negotiations with the house of Austria. From the whole, the great imprudence of the duke manifestly appears, and the sway of his ungovernable passions; but it would be difficult to see in them any action which could be deemed a crime in the eye of the law, much less could subject him to the penalty of treason.

The impeachment of the Commons was still less dangerous to the duke, were it estimated by the standard of law and equity. The house, after having voted, upon some queries of Dr. Turner's, "that common fame was a sufficient ground of accusation by the Commons," proceeded to frame regular articles against Buckingham. They accused him of having united many offices in his person; of having bought two of them; of neglecting to guard the seas, with the result that many merchant ships had fallen into the hands of the enemy; of delivering ships to the French king in order to serve against the Huguenots; of being employed in the sale of honors and offices; of accepting extensive grants from the Crown; of procuring many titles of honor for his kindred; and of administering medicine to the late king without telling his physicians. All these articles appear, from comparing the accusation and reply, to be either frivolous or false, or both. The only charges which could be regarded as important were that he had extorted a sum of £10,000 from the East India company and that he had confiscated some goods belonging to French merchants on pretense of their being the property of Spanish ones. The impeachment never came to a full determination, so it is difficult for us to give a decisive opinion with regard to these articles. But it must be confessed that the duke's answer in these particulars, as in all the rest, is so clear and satisfactory that it is impossible to refuse our assent to it. His faults and blemishes were in many respects very great, but rapacity and avarice were vices with which he was entirely unacquainted.

It is remarkable that the Commons, though so much at a loss to find articles of charge against Buckingham, never adopted Bristol's accusation or impeached the duke for his conduct in the Spanish treaty, the most blamable circumstance in his whole life. He had reason to believe the Spaniards sincere in their professions; yet in order to gratify his private passions, he had hurried his master and his country into a war pernicious to the interests of both. But so firmly fixed throughout the nation were the prejudices with regard to Spanish deceit and falsehood that very few of the Commons seem as yet to have been convinced that they had been seduced by Buckingham's narrative, a certain proof that a discovery of this nature was not, as is imagined by several historians, the cause of so sudden and surprising a variation in the measures of the Parliament.

While the Commons were thus warmly engaged against Buckingham, the king seemed desirous of embracing every opportunity by which he could express a contempt and disregard for them. No one was at that time sufficiently aware of the great weight which the Commons bore in the balance of the constitution. The history of England had never before afforded one instance where any great movement or revolution had proceeded from the lower house. And as their rank, considered both as a body and as individuals, was but the second in the kingdom, nothing less than fatal experience could engage the English princes to pay a due regard to the inclinations of that formidable assembly.

The Earl of Suffolk, chancellor of the University of Cambridge, died about this time; Buckingham, though lying under impeachment, was yet chosen in his place by means of court influence. The Commons resented and loudly complained of this affront; and the more to enrage them, the king himself wrote a letter to the university extolling the duke and giving them thanks for his election.

The lord keeper, in the king's name, expressly commanded the house not to meddle with his minister and servant Buckingham, and he ordered them to finish in a few days the bill which they had begun for the subsidies and to make some addition to them; otherwise they must not expect to sit any longer. And though these harsh commands were endeavored to be explained and mollified a few days later by a speech of Buckingham's, they failed not to leave a disagreeable impression behind them.

Besides a stately style, which Charles in general affected more to this Parliament than to the last, he went so far in a message as to threaten the Commons that if they did not furnish him with supplies, he would be obliged to try "new counsels." This language was sufficiently clear; yet lest any ambiguity might remain, Sir Dudley Carleton, vice-chamberlain, took care to explain it. "I pray you, consider," said he, "what these new counsels are, or may be. I fear to declare those that I conceive. In all Christian kingdoms, you know that parliaments were in use anciently, by which those kingdoms were governed in a most flourishing manner; until the monarchs began to know their own strength, and seeing the turbulent spirit of their parliaments, at length they, by little and little, began to stand on their prerogatives, and at last overthrew the parliaments throughout Christendom, except here only with us. Let us be careful then to preserve the king's good opinion of parliaments, which bringeth such happiness to this nation and makes us envied of all others, while there is this sweetness between his majesty and the Commons; lest we lose the repute of a free people by our turbulency in Parliament." These imprudent suggestions gave warning rather than struck terror. A precarious liberty, the Commons thought, which was to be preserved by unlimited complaisance, was no liberty at all. And it was necessary, while yet in their power, to secure the constitution by such invincible barriers that no king or minister would ever in the future dare to speak such a language to any Parliament, or even entertain such a project against them.

Two members of the house, Sir Dudley Digges and Sir John Eliot, who had been employed as managers of the impeachment against Buckingham, were thrown into prison. The Commons immediately declared that they would proceed no further upon business till they had satisfaction in their privileges. Charles alleged, as the reason of this measure, certain seditious expressions which had, he said, dropped from these members in their accusation of the duke. Upon inquiry, it appeared that no such expressions had been used. The members were released, and the king reaped no other benefit from this attempt than to exasperate the house still further and to show some degree of precipitancy and indiscretion.

Moved by this example, the House of Peers were roused from their inactivity and claimed liberty for the Earl of Arundel, who had been lately confined in the Tower. After many fruitless evasions, the king, though somewhat ungracefully, was at last obliged to comply. And in this incident it sufficiently appeared that the Lords, however little they were inclined to popular courses, were not lacking in a just sense of their own dignity.

The ill humor of the Commons, thus wantonly irritated by the court and finding no gratification in the legal impeachment of Buckingham, sought other objects on which it might exert itself. The never-failing cry of popery here served them instead. They again claimed the execution of the penal laws against Catholics, and they presented to the king a list of persons entrusted with offices, most of them insignificant, who were either convicted or suspected recusants. In this particular, they had perhaps some reason to blame the king's conduct. He had promised to the last House of Commons a redress of this religious grievance; but he was apt, in imitation of his father, to imagine that when the Parliament failed of supplying his necessities, they had freed him from his obligation of a strict performance. The Commons also attempted by these representations to throw a new odium upon Buckingham. His mother, who had great influence over him, was a professed Catholic, his wife was not free from suspicion, and the indulgence given to Catholics was of course supposed to proceed entirely from his credit and authority. So violent was the bigotry of the times that it was thought a sufficient reason for disqualifying one from holding an office if his wife, relations, or companions were papists, though he himself was a conformist.

It is remarkable that persecution was here chiefly pushed on by laymen, and that the church was willing to have granted more liberty than would be allowed by the Commons. The reconciling doctrines of Montague likewise met anew with severe censures from that zealous assembly.

The next attack made by the Commons, had it prevailed, would have proved decisive. They were preparing a remonstrance against the levying of tonnage and poundage without consent of Parliament. This article, together with the new impositions laid on merchandise by James, constituted nearly half of the Crown revenues; if they could deprive the king of these resources, they would reduce him to total subjection and dependence. As long as they held such a security, together with the supply already promised, they were sure that nothing could be refused them. Though they found themselves, after canvassing the matter nearly three months, utterly incapable of fixing any legal crime upon the duke, they regarded him as an unable and perhaps a dangerous minister; and they intended to present a petition, which would then have been equivalent to a command, for removing him from his majesty's person and councils.

The king was alarmed at the yoke which he saw prepared for him. Buckingham's sole guilt, he thought, was being his friend and favorite. All the other complaints against him were mere pretenses. A little before, he was the idol of the people. No new crime had since been discovered. After the most diligent inquiry, prompted by the greatest malice, the smallest appearance of guilt could not be fixed upon him. What idea, he asked, must all mankind entertain of his honor if he sacrificed his innocent friend to pecuniary considerations? What further authority would he retain in the nation were he capable, in the beginning of his reign and in so signal an instance, to give such cause of triumph to his enemies and discouragement to his adherents? To-day the Commons attempt to wrest his minister from him; tomorrow they will attack some branch of his prerogative. By their remonstrances and promises and protestations, they had engaged the Crown in a war. As soon as they saw a retreat impossible, without waiting for new incidents, without covering themselves with new pretenses, they immediately deserted him and refused him all reasonable supply. It was evident that they desired nothing so much as to see him plunged in inextricable difficulties, of which they intended to take advantage. To such deep perfidy, to such unbounded usurpations, it was necessary to oppose a proper firmness and resolution. All encroachments on supreme power could only be resisted successfully on the first attempt. The sovereign authority was with some difficulty reduced from its ancient and legal height; but when once pushed downwards, it soon became contemptible and would easily be carried to the lowest extremity by the continuance of the same effort, now encouraged by success.

Prompted by these plausible motives, Charles was determined to dissolve the Parliament immediately. When this resolution was known, the House of Peers, whose compliant behavior entitled them to some authority with him, endeavored to interpose, and they petitioned him to allow the Parliament to sit some time longer. "Not a moment longer," cried the king hastily; and he soon after, on June 15, ended the session by a dissolution.

As this measure was foreseen, the Commons took care to finish and disperse their remonstrance, which they intended as a justification of their conduct to the people. The king likewise published a declaration, in which he gave the reasons of his disagreement with the Parliament and of their sudden dissolution before they had time to conclude any one act. These papers furnished the partisans on both sides with ample matter of defense or of recrimination. But all impartial men judged, "That the Commons, though they had not as yet violated any law, yet, by their unpliableness and independence, were insensibly [imperceptibly; gradually] changing, perhaps improving, the spirit and genius, while they preserved the form, of the constitution. And that the king was acting altogether without any plan, running on in a road surrounded on all sides with the most dangerous precipices, and concerting no proper measures, either for submitting to the obstinacy of the Commons or for subduing it."

After a breach with the Parliament which seemed so difficult to repair, the only rational counsel which Charles could pursue was immediately to conclude a peace with Spain and to render himself as far as possible independent of his people, who revealed so little inclination to support him, or rather who seemed to have formed a determined resolution to abridge his authority. Nothing could be easier in the execution than this measure, nor more agreeable to his own and to national interest. But besides the treaties and engagements which he had entered into with Holland and Denmark, the king's thoughts were at this time averse to pacific counsels. There were two circumstances in Charles's character, seemingly incompatible, which attended him during the whole course of his reign and were in part the cause of his misfortunes: he was very steady, and even obstinate, in his purpose; and he was easily governed, by reason of his pliancy and of his deference to men much inferior to himself both in morals and understanding. His great ends he inflexibly maintained, but the means of attaining them he readily received from his ministers and favorites, though not always fortunate in his choice. The violent, impetuous Buckingham—inflamed with a desire of revenge for injuries which he himself had committed, animated with a love of glory which he had not talents to merit—had at this time, notwithstanding his profuse, licentious life, acquired an invincible ascendance over the virtuous and gentle temper of the king.

Violent measures of the court

The "new counsels" which Charles had mentioned to the Parliament were now to be tried in order to supply his necessities. Had he possessed any military force on which he could rely, it is not improbable that he would at once have taken off the mask and governed without any regard to parliamentary privileges, so high an idea had he received of kingly prerogative and so contemptible a notion of the rights of those popular assemblies from which, he very naturally thought, he had met with such ill usage. But his army was newly levied, ill paid, worse disciplined, and in no way superior to the militia, who were much more numerous and who were in a great measure under the influence of the country gentlemen. It behooved him, therefore, to proceed cautiously and to cover his enterprises under the pretense of ancient precedents, which, considering the great authority commonly enjoyed by his predecessors, could not be lacking to him.

A commission was openly granted to compound with the Catholics and agree for dispensing with the penal laws enacted against them. By this expedient, the king both filled his coffers and gratified his inclination of giving indulgence to these religionists. But he could not have employed any branch of prerogative which would have been more disagreeable, or would have appeared more exceptionable, to his Protestant subjects.

From the nobility, he desired assistance; from the city, he required a loan of £100,000. The former contributed slowly; but the latter, after covering themselves under many pretenses and excuses, gave him at last a flat refusal.

In order to equip a fleet, a distribution, by order of Council, was made to all the maritime towns; and each of them was required, with the assistance of the adjacent counties, to arm as many vessels as were appointed to them. The city of London was rated at twenty ships. This is the first appearance in Charles's reign of ship money, a taxation which had once been imposed by Elizabeth but which afterwards, when carried some steps further by Charles, created such violent discontents.

Of some, loans were required; to others, the way of benevolence was proposed: methods supported by precedent but always odious, even in times more submissive and compliant. In the most absolute governments, such expedients would be regarded as irregular and unequal.

These counsels for supply were conducted with some moderation till news arrived that a great battle had been fought on August 25 between the king of Denmark and the Count of Tilly, the imperial general, in which the former was totally defeated. Money now more than ever became necessary in order to repair so great a breach in the alliance and to support a prince who was so nearly allied to Charles and who had been engaged in the war chiefly by the intrigues, solicitations, and promises of the English monarch. After some deliberation, an act of Council was passed, stating that as the urgency of affairs did not admit the way of Parliament, the most speedy, equal, and convenient method of supply was by a general loan from the subject, in proportion as every man was assessed in the rolls of the last subsidy. That precise sum was required which each would have paid had the vote of four subsidies passed into a law; but care was taken to inform the people that the sums exacted were to be called not subsidies but loans. Had any doubt remained whether forced loans, however authorized by precedent and even by statute, were a violation of liberty and must by necessary consequence render all Parliaments superfluous, this was the proper expedient for opening the eyes of the whole nation. The example of Henry VIII, who had once in his arbitrary reign practiced a like method of levying a regular supply, was generally deemed a very insufficient authority.

The commissioners appointed to levy these loans were enjoined, among other articles of secret instruction, "If any shall refuse to lend, and shall make delays or excuses and persist in his obstinacy, that they examine him upon oath, whether he has been dealt with to deny or refuse to lend, or make an excuse for not lending? Who has dealt with him, and what speeches or persuasions were used to that purpose? And that they also shall charge every such person, in his majesty's name, upon his allegiance, not to disclose to any one what his answer was." So violent an inquisitorial power, so impracticable an attempt at secrecy, were the objects of indignation and even, in some degree, of ridicule.

That religious prejudices might support civil authority, sermons were preached by Robert Sibthorpe and Roger Maynwaring in favor of the general loan; and the court industriously spread them over the kingdom. Passive obedience was there recommended in its full extent, the whole authority of the state was represented as belonging to the king alone, and all limitations of law and a constitution were rejected as seditious and impious. So openly was this doctrine espoused by the court that Archbishop Abbot, a popular and virtuous prelate, was, because he refused to license Sibthorpe's sermon, suspended from the exercise of his office, banished from London, and confined to one of his country seats. Abbot's principles of liberty and his opposition to Buckingham had always rendered him very unwelcome at court and had acquired him the reputation of being a Puritan. For it is remarkable that the Puritanical party made the privileges of the nation as much a part of their religion as the church party did the prerogatives of the Crown; and nothing tended further to recommend among the people, who always take opinions in the lump, the whole system and all the principles of the former sect. The king soon found by fatal experience that this engine of religion, which with so little necessity was introduced into politics, was played with the most terrible success against him once it fell under more auspicious management.

While the king, instigated by anger and necessity, thus employed the whole extent of his prerogative, the spirit of the people was far from being subdued. Throughout England, many refused these loans; some were even active in encouraging their neighbors to insist upon their common rights and privileges. By warrant of the Council, these were thrown into prison. Most of them with patience submitted to confinement or applied by petition to the king, who commonly released them. Five gentlemen only—Sir Thomas Darnell, Sir John Corbet, Sir Walter Earl, Sir John Heveningham, and Sir Edmund Hampden—had spirit enough, at their own hazard and expense, to defend the public liberties and to demand release not as a favor from the court but as their due by the laws of their country. No particular cause was assigned for their imprisonment. The special command alone of the king and Council was pleaded. And it was asserted that by law, this was not sufficient reason for refusing bail or release to the prisoners.

This question was brought to a solemn trial before the King's Bench, and the whole kingdom was attentive to the adjudication of a cause which was of much greater consequence than the result of many battles.

By the debates on this subject, it appeared beyond controversy to the nation that their ancestors had been so jealous of personal liberty as to secure it against arbitrary power in the Crown by six separate statutes and by an article of the Great Charter itself, the most sacred foundation of the laws and constitution. But the kings of England, who had not been able to prevent the enacting of these laws, had sufficient authority to obstruct their regular execution when the tide of liberty was spent, and they deemed it superfluous to attempt the formal repeal of statutes which they found so many expedients and pretenses to elude. Turbulent and seditious times frequently occurred when the safety of the people absolutely required the confinement of factious leaders; and by the spirit of the old constitution, the prince of his own accord was accustomed to assume every branch of prerogative which was found necessary for the preservation of public peace and of his own authority. At other times, expediency would cover itself under the appearance of necessity; and in proportion as precedents multiplied, the will alone of the sovereign was sufficient to supply the place of expediency, of which he constituted himself the sole judge. In an age and nation where the power of a turbulent nobility prevailed and where the king had no settled military force, the only means that could maintain public peace was the exertion of such prompt and discretionary powers in the Crown; and the public itself had become so aware of the necessity that those ancient laws in favor of personal liberty, while often violated, had never been claimed as due or revived during the course of nearly three centuries. Though rebellious subjects had frequently resisted the king's authority in the open field, no person had been found so bold as to set himself in opposition to regal power and to claim the protection of the constitution against the will of the sovereign while confined and at mercy. It was not till this age—when the spirit of liberty was universally diffused, when the principles of government were nearly reduced to a system, when the tempers of men, more civilized, seemed less to require those violent exertions of prerogative—that these above-mentioned five gentlemen ventured, by a noble effort in this national cause, to bring the question to a final determination. And the king was astonished to observe that a power exercised by his predecessors almost without interruption was found upon trial to be directly opposite to the clearest laws and supported by few undoubted precedents in courts of judicature. These had scarcely in any instance refused bail upon commitments by special command of the king because the persons committed had seldom or never dared to demand it, or at least to insist on their demand.

Sir Randolph Crewe, chief justice, was viewed by the court as unfit for its purposes and had been displaced. Sir Nicholas Hyde, deemed more obsequious, had obtained that high office. Yet the judges, by his direction, went no further than to remand the gentlemen to prison and refuse the bail which was offered. Sir Robert Heath, the attorney general, insisted that the court, in imitation of the judges in the thirty-fourth year of Elizabeth, should enter a general judgment that no bail could be granted upon a commitment by the king or Council. But the judges wisely declined complying. The nation, they saw, was already to the last degree exasperated. In the pre-

1627

sent disposition of men's minds, universal complaints prevailed likening the kingdom to one reduced to slavery. And the most odious prerogative of the Crown, it was said—that of imprisoning the subject—was here openly, solemnly, and in numerous instances exercised for the most odious purpose: to extort loans, or rather subsidies, without consent of Parliament.

But this was not the only hardship of which the nation thought they had reason to complain. The army which had made the fruitless expedition to Cadiz was dispersed throughout the kingdom, and money was levied upon the counties for the payment of their quarters.

The soldiers were billeted in private houses, contrary to custom, which required that in all ordinary cases they should be quartered in inns and public houses. Those who had refused or delayed the loan were sure to be loaded with a great number of these dangerous and disorderly guests.

Many of those too of low condition who had shown a refractory disposition regarding the loan were pressed into the service and enlisted in the fleet or army. Sir Peter Heyman was dispatched on an errand to the Palatinate for the same reason. John Glanville, an eminent lawyer, had been obliged during the former interval of Parliament to accept an office in the navy.

The soldiers, ill paid and undisciplined, committed many crimes and outrages and much increased the public discontents. To prevent these disorders, martial law, so requisite to the support of discipline, was exercised upon the soldiers. Although the outrages of the army were complained of, this remedy was thought, by a contradiction which is natural when the people are exasperated, still more intolerable. Though the expediency, if we are not rather to say the necessity, of martial law had formerly been deemed by itself a sufficient ground for establishing it, men, now become more jealous of liberty and more refined reasoners in questions of government, regarded as illegal and arbitrary every exercise of authority which was not supported by express statute or uninterrupted precedent.

It may safely be affirmed that all men, except a few courtiers or ecclesiastics, were displeased with this high exertion of prerogative and this new spirit of administration. Though ancient precedents were pleaded in favor of the king's measures, a considerable difference, upon comparison, was observed between the cases. Acts of power, however irregular, might casually and at intervals be exercised by a prince for the sake of dispatch or expediency, and yet liberty still continue in some tolerable degree under his administration. But where all these were reduced into a system, were exerted without interruption, were studiously sought for in order to supply the place of laws and subdue the refractory spirit of the nation, it was necessary to find some speedy remedy or finally to abandon all hopes of preserving the freedom of the constitution. Nor did moderate men deem the provocation which the king had received, though great, sufficient to warrant all these violent measures. The Commons as yet had in no way invaded his authority; they had only exercised, as best pleased them, their own privileges. Was he justified, because he had met with harsh and unkind treatment from one house of Parliament, to make in revenge an invasion on the rights and liberties of the whole nation?

War with France

But great was the surprise of all men at this time when Charles—baffled in every attempt against the Austrian dominions, embroiled with his own subjects, unsupplied with any treasure but what he extorted by the most odious and most dangerous measures—as if the half of Europe now his enemy were not sufficient for the exercise of military prowess, wantonly attacked France, the other great kingdom in his neighborhood, and engaged at the same time in war against these two powers, Spain and France, whose interests were up to this time deemed so incompatible that they could never, it was thought, agree either in the same friendships or enmities. All authentic memoirs, both foreign and domestic, ascribe to Buckingham's counsels this war with France and represent him as actuated by motives which would appear incredible were we not acquainted with the violence and temerity of his character.

The three great monarchies of Europe were at this time ruled by young princes—Philip, Louis, and Charles—who were nearly of the same age and who had resigned the government of themselves and of their kingdoms to their creatures and ministers—Olivares, Richelieu, and Buckingham. The people, whom the moderate temper or narrow genius of their princes would have allowed to remain forever in tranquility, were strongly agitated by the rivalry and jealousy of the ministers. Above all, the towering spirit of Richelieu, incapable of rest, promised an active age and gave indications of great revolutions throughout all Europe.

This man had no sooner gotten possession of the reins of government by suppleness and intrigue than he formed at once three mighty

projects: to subdue the turbulent spirits of the French nobility, to reduce the rebellious Huguenots, and to curb the encroaching power of
the house of Austria. Undaunted and implacable, prudent and active,
he braved all the opposition of the French princes and nobles in the
prosecution of his vengeance; he discovered and dissipated all their
secret cabals and conspiracies. His sovereign himself he held in subjection while he exalted the throne. By means of his administration, the
people, while they lost their liberties, acquired learning, order, discipline, and renown. He changed that confused and inaccurate kind of
government of which France partook in common with other European kingdoms into a simple monarchy, at the very time when the incapacity of Buckingham encouraged the free spirit of the Commons to
establish in England a regular system of liberty.

However unequal the comparison between these ministers, Buckingham had entertained a mighty jealousy against Richelieu, a jealousy
founded on rivalry not of power and politics but of love and gallantry,
where the duke was as much superior to the cardinal as he was inferi-
or in every other particular.

At the time when Charles married by proxy the princess Henrietta,
the Duke of Buckingham had been sent to France in order to grace
the nuptials and conduct the new queen into England. The eyes of the
French court were directed by curiosity towards that man who had enjoyed the unlimited favor of two successive monarchs and who, from a
private station and in the earliest youth, had mounted to the absolute
government of three kingdoms. The beauty of his person, the grace-
fulness of his air, the splendor of his equipage, his fine taste in dress,
festivals, and carousals corresponded to the prepossessions entertained
in his favor; the affability of his behavior, the gaiety of his manners,
the magnificence of his expense increased still further the general admiration which was paid him. All business being already concerted,
the time was entirely spent in mirth and entertainments; and during
those splendid scenes among that gay people, the duke found himself
in a situation where he was perfectly qualified to excel. But his great
success at Paris proved as fatal as his former failure at Madrid. Encouraged by the smiles of the court, he dared to carry his ambitious
addresses to the queen herself; and he failed not to make an impression on a heart disposed to the tender passions. That attachment—at
least of the mind, which appears so delicious and is so dangerous—
seems to have been encouraged by the princess. The duke presumed
so far on her good graces that after his departure, he secretly returned

upon some pretense, and paying a visit to the queen, was dismissed with a reproof which savored more of kindness than of anger.

Information of this correspondence was soon carried to Richelieu. The vigilance of that minister was here further roused by jealousy. He too, either from vanity or politics, had ventured to pay his addresses to the queen. But a priest past middle age, of a severe character and occupied in the most extensive plans of ambition or vengeance, was in that contest but an unequal match for a young courtier entirely disposed to gaiety and gallantry. The cardinal's disappointment strongly inclined him to work against the amorous projects of his rival. When the duke was making preparations for a new embassy to Paris, a message was sent to him from Louis that he must not think of such a journey. In a romantic passion, he swore, "That he would see the queen, in spite of all the power of France," and from that moment he determined to engage England in a war with that kingdom.

He first took advantage of some quarrels excited by the queen of England's attendants; and he persuaded Charles to dismiss at once all her French servants, contrary to the articles of the marriage treaty. He encouraged the English ships of war and privateers to seize vessels belonging to French merchants; and these he forthwith condemned as prizes by a sentence of the Court of Admiralty. But finding that all these injuries produced only remonstrances and embassies, or at most reprisals, on the part of France, he resolved to second the intrigues of the Duke of Soubise and to undertake at once a military expedition against that kingdom.

Soubise, who, with his brother, the Duke of Rohan, was the leader of the Huguenot faction, was at that time in London and strongly solicited Charles to embrace the protection of these distressed religionists. He represented that after the inhabitants of La Rochelle had been repressed by the combined squadrons of England and Holland, after peace was concluded with the French king under Charles's mediation, the ambitious cardinal was still meditating the destruction of the Huguenots. That preparations were silently being made in every province of France for the suppression of their religion. That forts were erected in order to bridle La Rochelle, the most considerable bulwark of the Protestants. That the reformed in France cast their eyes on Charles as the head of their faith and considered him as a prince engaged by interest as well as inclination to support them. And that so long as their party continued, Charles might rely on their attachment as much as on that of his own subjects; but if their liberties were once ravished from them, the power of France, freed from this impediment, would soon become formidable to England and to all the neighboring nations.

Expedition to the Isle of Rhé

Though Charles probably bore but small favor to the Huguenots, who so much resembled the Puritans in discipline and worship, in religion and politics, he yet allowed himself to be gained by these arguments, reinforced by the solicitations of Buckingham. A fleet of a hundred sail and an army of seven thousand men were fitted out for the invasion of France, and both of them entrusted to the command of the duke, who was altogether unacquainted both with land and sea service. The fleet appeared before La Rochelle on July 9; but so ill concerted were Buckingham's measures that the inhabitants of that city shut their gates and refused to admit allies of whose coming they were not previously informed. All his military operations showed equal incapacity and inexperience. Instead of attacking Oleron, a fertile and defenseless island, he bent his course to the Isle of Rhé, which was well garrisoned and fortified. Having landed his men, though with some loss, he failed to follow the blow but allowed Toiras, the French governor, five days' respite, during which St. Martin was provisioned for a siege. He left behind him the small fort of La Prée, which could at first have made no manner of resistance. Though resolved to starve St. Martin, he guarded the sea negligently and allowed provisions and ammunition to be thrown into it. Despairing to reduce it by famine, he attacked it without having made any breach and rashly threw away the lives of the soldiers. Having found that a French army had stolen over in small divisions and had landed at La Prée, the fort which he had at first overlooked, he began to think of a retreat, but made it so unskillfully that it was equivalent to a total rout. He was the last of the army that embarked on October 28, and he returned to England having lost two-thirds of his land forces, totally discredited both as an admiral and a general, and bringing no praise with him but the vulgar one of courage and personal bravery.

The Duke of Rohan, who had taken arms as soon as Buckingham appeared upon the coast, revealed the dangerous spirit of the Huguenots without being able to do any mischief; the inhabitants of La Rochelle, who had at last been induced to join the English, hastened the vengeance of Richelieu, exhausted their provisions in supplying their allies, and were threatened with an immediate siege. Such were the fruits of Buckingham's expedition against France.

CHAPTER 51
1628 – 1629

*Third Parliament – Petition of Right – Prorogation – Death
of Buckingham – New session of Parliament – Tonnage and
poundage – Arminianism – Dissolution of the Parliament*

THERE was reason to fear some disorder or insurrection from the discontents which prevailed among the
people in England. Their liberties, they believed, were ravished from
them; illegal taxes were extorted; their commerce, which had met with
a severe check from the Spanish war, was totally annihilated by the
French one; those military honors transmitted to them from their ancestors had received a grievous stain by two unsuccessful and ill-
conducted expeditions; rare was the illustrious family that did not
mourn the loss of a son or brother from the last of them; greater calamities were dreaded from the war with these powerful monarchies,
concurring with the internal disorders under which the nation labored. And these ills were ascribed not to the refractory disposition of
the two former Parliaments, to which they were partly owing, but solely to Charles's obstinacy in adhering to the counsels of Buckingham, a
man in no way entitled by his birth, age, services, or merit to that unlimited confidence reposed in him. To be sacrificed to the interest,
policy, and ambition of the great is so much the common lot of the
people that those who would attempt to complain of it may appear
unreasonable. But to be the victim of the frivolous gallantry and boyish caprices of a favorite seemed the object of particular indignation.

1628

Third Parliament
In this situation, it may be imagined, the king and the duke dreaded

above all things the assembling of a Parliament. But so little foresight had they possessed in their enterprising schemes that they found themselves under an absolute necessity of embracing that expedient. The money levied, or rather extorted, under color of prerogative had come in very slowly and had left such ill humor in the nation that it appeared dangerous to renew the experiment. The absolute necessity of supply, it was hoped, would engage the Commons to forget all past injuries; it was thought probable that having experienced the ill effects of former obstinacy, they would assemble with a resolution of making some reasonable compliances. The more to soften them, it was agreed on Sir Robert Cotton's advice that Buckingham would be the first person to propose in Council the calling of a new Parliament. Having laid in this stock of merit, he expected that all his former misdemeanors would be overlooked and forgiven, and that he would be regarded not as a tyrant and oppressor but as the first patriot in the nation.

The views of the popular leaders were much more judicious and profound. When the Commons assembled on March 17, they appeared to be men of the same independent spirit as their predecessors, and possessed of such riches that their property was computed to surpass three times that of the House of Peers. They were deputized by boroughs and counties all inflamed by the late violations of liberty. Many of the members themselves had been cast into prison and had suffered by the measures of the court. Yet notwithstanding these circumstances, which might have prompted them to embrace violent resolutions, they entered upon business with perfect temper and decorum. They considered that the king, disgusted at these popular assemblies and little prepossessed in favor of their privileges, lacked but a fair pretense for breaking with them and would seize the first opportunity offered by any incident or any undutiful behavior of the members. He fairly told them in his first speech that, "If they should not do their duties in contributing to the necessities of the state, he must, in discharge of his conscience, use those other means which God had put into his hands in order to save that which the follies of some particular men may otherwise put in danger. Take not this for a threatening," added the king, "for I scorn to threaten any but my equals; but as an admonition from him who, by nature and duty, has most care of your preservation and prosperity." The lord keeper, by the king's direction, appended, "This way of parliamentary supplies, as his majesty told you, he hath chosen, not as the only way, but as the fittest; not because he is destitute of others, but because it is most agreeable to the goodness of his own most gracious disposition, and to the desire and weal of his people. If this be deferred, necessity and the sword of the enemy make way for the others. Remember his majesty's admonition; I say, remember it." From these avowed maxims, the Commons foresaw that if the least handle were afforded, the king would immediately dissolve them and would from then on deem himself justified in violating all the ancient forms of the constitution in a manner still more open. No remedy could then be looked for but from insurrections and civil war, of which the result would be extremely uncertain and which must, in all events, prove calamitous to the nation. To correct the late disorders in the administration required some new laws which would no doubt appear harsh to a prince so enamored of his prerogative; and it was requisite to temper, by the decency and moderation of their debates, the rigor which must necessarily attend their determinations. Nothing can give us a higher idea of the capacity of those men who now guided the Commons and of the great authority which they had acquired than the forming and executing of so judicious and so difficult a plan of operations.

The decency, however, which the popular leaders had prescribed to themselves and recommended to others did not hinder them from making the loudest and most vigorous complaints against the grievances under which the nation had lately labored. Sir Francis Seymour said, "This is the great council of the kingdom; and here with certainty, if not here only, his majesty may see, as in a true glass, the state of the kingdom. We are called hither by his writs, in order to give him faithful counsel, such as may stand with his honor; and this we must do without flattery. We are also sent hither by the people, in order to deliver their just grievances; and this we must do without fear. Let us not act like Cambyses's judges, who, when their approbation was demanded by the prince to some illegal measure, said that, 'Though there was a written law, the Persian kings might follow their own will and pleasure.' This was base flattery, fitter for our reproof than our imitation; and as fear, so flattery taketh away the judgment. For my part, I shall shun both, and speak my mind with as much duty as any man to his majesty, without neglecting the public.

"But how can we express our affections while we retain our fears, or speak of giving till we know whether we have anything to give? For if his majesty may be persuaded to take what he will, what need we give?

"That this hath been done appeareth by the billeting of soldiers, a thing nowise [in no way] advantageous to the king's service and a burthen [burden] to the commonwealth; by the imprisonment of gentlemen for refusing the loan, who, if they had done the contrary for fear, had been as blamable as the projector [one who plans a project; promoter] of that oppressive measure. To countenance these proceedings, hath it not been preached in the pulpit, or rather prated, that, 'All we have is the king's by divine right'? But when preachers forsake their own calling and turn ignorant statesmen, we see how willing they are to exchange a good conscience for a bishopric.

"He, I must confess, is no good subject who would not willingly and cheerfully lay down his life when that sacrifice may promote the interests of his sovereign and the good of the commonwealth. But he is not a good subject, he is a slave who will allow his goods to be taken from him against his will, and his liberty against the laws of the kingdom. By opposing these practices, we shall but tread in the steps of our forefathers, who still preferred the public before their private interest; nay, before their very lives. It will in us be a wrong done to ourselves, to our posterities, to our consciences, if we forgo this claim and pretension."

"I read of a custom," said Sir Robert Phelips, "among the old Romans that, once every year, they held a solemn festival in which their slaves had liberty, without exception, to speak what they pleased, in order to ease their afflicted minds; and on the conclusion of the festival, the slaves severally returned to their former servitudes.

"This institution may, with some distinction, well set forth our present state and condition. After the revolution of some time, and the grievous sufferance of many violent oppressions, we have now at last, as those slaves obtained for a day, some liberty of speech; but shall not, I trust, be hereafter slaves; for we are born free. Yet what new illegal burthens our estates and persons have groaned under, my heart yearns to think of, my tongue falters to utter.

"The grievances by which we are oppressed, I draw under two heads: acts of power against law, and the judgments of lawyers against our liberty."

Having mentioned three illegal judgments passed within his memory—that by which the Scots born after James's accession were admitted to all the privileges of English subjects, that by which the new impositions had been warranted, and the late one, by which arbitrary imprisonments were authorized—he thus proceeded.

"I can live, though another who has no right be put to live along with me; nay, I can live, though burthened with impositions beyond what at present I labor under. But to have my liberty, which is the soul of my life, ravished from me, to have my person pent up in a jail, without relief by law, and to be so adjudged—O improvident ancestors! O unwise forefathers! To be so curious in providing for the quiet possession of our lands and the liberties of Parliament, and at the same time to neglect our personal liberty, and let us lie in prison, and that during pleasure, without redress or remedy! If this be law, why do we talk of liberties? Why trouble ourselves with disputes about a constitution, franchises, property of goods, and the like? What may any man call his own, if not the liberty of his person?

"I am weary of treading these ways, and therefore conclude to have a select committee in order to frame a petition to his majesty for redress of these grievances. And this petition, being read, examined, and approved, may be delivered to the king; of whose gracious answer we have no cause to doubt, our desires being so reasonable, our intentions so loyal, and the manner so dutiful. Neither need we fear that this is the critical Parliament, as has been insinuated, or that this is the way to distraction, but assure ourselves of a happy issue [result]. Then shall the king, as he calls us his great council, find us his true council, and own us his good council."

The same topics were reinforced by Sir Thomas Wentworth. After mentioning projectors and ill [evil] ministers of state, "These," said he, "have introduced a Privy Council, ravishing at once the spheres of all ancient government, destroying all liberty, imprisoning us without bail or bond. They have taken from us—What shall I say? Indeed, what have they left us? By tearing up the roots of all property, they have taken from us every means of supplying the king, and of ingratiating ourselves by voluntary proofs of our duty and attachment towards him.

"To the making whole all these breaches, I shall apply myself; and to all these diseases shall propound a remedy. By one and the same thing have the king and the people been hurt, and by the same must they be cured. We must vindicate—what? New things? No: our ancient, legal, and vital liberties, by reinforcing the laws enacted by our ancestors, by setting such a stamp upon them that no licentious spirit shall dare henceforth to invade them. And shall we think this a way to break a Parliament? No: our desires are modest and just. I speak both for the interest of king and people. If we enjoy not these rights, it will be impossible for us to relieve him. Let us never, therefore, doubt of a favorable reception from his goodness."

These sentiments were unanimously embraced by the whole house. Even the court party did not attempt to plead, in defense of the late measures, anything but the necessity to which the king had been reduced by the obstinacy of the two former Parliaments. A vote against arbitrary imprisonments and forced loans was passed, therefore, without opposition. And the spirit of liberty having obtained some contentment by this exertion, the reiterated messages of the king, who pressed for supply, were attended to with more temper. Five subsidies were voted him; though they were much inferior to his wants, he declared himself well satisfied with them, and tears of affection even started in his eye when he was informed of this concession. Buckingham's approbation too was mentioned by Secretary Coke, but the conjunction of a subject with the sovereign was ill received by the house. Though disgusted with the king, the jealousy which they felt for his honor was more strongly felt than that which his unbounded confidence in the duke would allow even himself to entertain.

Petition of Right

The supply, though voted, was not as yet passed into a law; and the Commons resolved to employ the interval in providing some barriers to their rights and liberties so lately violated. They knew that their own vote declaring the illegality of the former measures did not have sufficient authority by itself to secure the constitution against future invasion. Some act to that purpose needed to receive the sanction of the whole legislature, and they appointed a committee to prepare the model of so important a law. By collecting into one effort all the dangerous and oppressive claims of his prerogative, Charles had exposed them to the hazard of one assault; further, by presenting a nearer view of the consequences attending them, he had roused the independent spirit of the Commons. Forced loans, benevolences, taxes without consent of Parliament, arbitrary imprisonments, the billeting of soldiers, martial law: these were the grievances complained of, and against these an eternal remedy was to be provided. The Commons affirmed that they laid no claim to any unusual powers or privileges; they aimed only at securing those which had been transmitted to them from their ancestors. And their law they resolved to call a "Petition of Right," as implying that it contained a corroboration or explanation of the ancient constitution, not any infringement of royal prerogative or acquisition of new liberties.

While the committee was employed in framing the Petition of

Right, the favorers of each party, both in Parliament and throughout the nation, were engaged in disputes about this bill, which in all likelihood was to form a memorable era in the English government.

The partisans of the Commons argued in this manner that the statutes which secured English liberty had not now become obsolete: The English have always been free and have always been governed by law and a limited constitution. In particular, privileges which are founded on the Great Charter must always remain in force because they are derived from a source of never-failing authority, regarded in all ages as the most sacred contract between king and people. Such attention was paid to this charter by our generous ancestors that they got the confirmation of it reiterated thirty separate times, and even secured it by a rule which, though popular, seems in the execution impracticable. They have established it as a maxim, "That even a statute which should be enacted in contradiction to any article of that charter cannot have force or validity." But with regard to that important article which secures personal liberty, they were always so far from attempting any legal infringement of it that they have corroborated it by six statutes and put it out of all doubt and controversy. If in practice it has often been violated, abuses can never come in the place of rules, nor can any rights or legal powers be derived from injury and injustice. But the title of the subject to personal liberty not only is founded on ancient—and, therefore, the more sacred—laws; it is confirmed by the whole analogy of the government and constitution. A free monarchy in which every individual is a slave is a glaring contradiction; and it is requisite, where the laws assign privileges to the different orders of the state, that it likewise secure the independence of the members. If any difference could be made in this particular, it would be better to abandon even life or property to the arbitrary will of the prince, for no greater danger to the laws and to the privileges of the people would ensue from that concession. To take the life of a man not condemned by any legal trial is so egregious an exercise of tyranny that it must both shock the natural humanity of princes and convey an alarm throughout the whole commonwealth. To confiscate a man's fortune, besides being a most atrocious act of violence, exposes the monarch so much to the imputation of avarice and rapacity that it will seldom be attempted in any civilized government. But confinement, though a less striking, is no less severe a punishment; nor is there any spirit so erect and independent as not to be broken by the long continuance of the silent and inglorious sufferings of a jail. The power of imprison-

143

ment, therefore, being the most natural and potent engine of arbitrary government, it is absolutely necessary to remove it from a government which is free and legal.

The partisans of the court reasoned after a different manner. The true rule of government, they said, during any period is that to which the people from time immemorial have been accustomed and to which they naturally pay a prompt obedience. A practice which has always struck their senses, and of which they have seen and heard innumerable precedents, has an authority with them much superior to that which attends maxims derived from antiquated statutes and moldy records. In vain do the lawyers establish it as a principle that a statute can never be abrogated by opposite custom but must be expressly repealed by a contrary statute. While they claim to inculcate an axiom belonging to English jurisprudence, they violate the most established principles of human nature; and by necessary consequence, they even reason in contradiction to law itself, which they would represent as so sacred and inviolable. A law, to have any authority, must be derived from a legislature which has right. And from where do all legislatures derive their right but from long custom and established practice? If a statute contrary to public good has at any time been rashly voted and assented to, either from the violence of faction or the inexperience of senates and princes, it cannot be more effectually abrogated than by a train of contrary precedents, which prove that it has been tacitly set aside by common consent as inconvenient and impracticable. Such has been the case with all those statutes enacted during turbulent times in order to limit royal prerogative and cramp the sovereign in his protection of the public and his execution of the laws. But above all branches of prerogative, that which is most necessary to be preserved is the power of imprisonment. Faction and discontent, like diseases, frequently arise in every political body; and during these disorders, it is only by the salutary exercise of this discretionary power that rebellions and civil wars can be prevented. To circumscribe this power is to destroy its nature; entirely to abrogate it is impracticable; and the attempt itself must prove dangerous, if not pernicious, to the public. In critical and turbulent times, the supreme magistrate, either from prudence or duty, will never allow the state to perish while there remains a remedy which, however irregular, it is still in his power to apply. And if, moved by a regard to public good, he employs any exercise of power condemned by recent and express statute, how greedily, in such dangerous times, will factious leaders seize this pretense of throwing on his government the imputation of tyranny and despotism? Were the alternative quite necessary, it would surely be much better for human society to be deprived of liberty than to be destitute of government.

Impartial reasoners will confess that this subject is not without its difficulties on both sides. Where a general and rigid law is enacted against arbitrary imprisonment, it would appear that government cannot, in times of sedition and faction, be conducted but by temporary suspensions of the law; and such an expedient was never thought of during the age of Charles. The meetings of Parliament were too precarious, and their determinations might be too dilatory, to serve in cases of urgent necessity. Nor was it then conceived that the king did not possess of his own accord sufficient power for the security and protection of his people, or that the authority of these popular assemblies was ever to become so absolute that the prince must always conform himself to them and could never have any occasion to guard against their practices as much as against those of his other subjects.

Though the House of Lords was alert to the reasons urged in favor of the pretensions of the Commons, they deemed the arguments pleaded in favor of the Crown still more cogent and convincing. That assembly seems to have acted, in the main, a reasonable and a moderate part during this whole period; and if their bias inclined a little too much, as is natural, to the side of monarchy, they were far from entertaining any design of sacrificing to arbitrary will the liberties and privileges of the nation. When Ashley, the king's serjeant [barrister], asserted in pleading before the Peers that the king must sometimes govern by acts of state as well as by law, this position gave such offense that he was immediately committed to prison and was not released but upon his recantation and submission. Being, however, afraid lest the Commons would go too far in their projected petition, the Peers proposed a plan of one more moderate, which they recommended to the consideration of the other house. It consisted merely in a general declaration that the Great Charter and the six statutes conceived to be explanations of it still stood in force to all intents and purposes; that in consequence of the charter and the statutes, and by the tenor of the ancient customs and laws of the realm, every subject had a fundamental property in his goods and a fundamental liberty of his person; that this property and liberty were as entire at present as during any former period of the English government; that in all common cases, the common law ought to be the standard of proceedings; "And in case

145

that, for the security of his majesty's person, the general safety of his people, or the peaceable government of the kingdom, the king shall find just cause, for reasons of state, to imprison or restrain any man's person, he was petitioned graciously to declare that, within a convenient time, he shall and will express the cause of the commitment or restraint, either general or special, and upon a cause so expressed, will leave the prisoner immediately to be tried according to the common law of the land."

Archbishop Abbot was employed by the Lords to recommend, in a conference, this plan of a petition to the House of Commons. The prelate, as was no doubt foreseen from his known principles, was not extremely urgent in his applications; and the lower house was fully convinced that the general declarations signified nothing, and that the latter clause left their liberties rather in a worse condition than before. They proceeded, therefore, with great zeal in framing the model of a petition which would contain expressions more precise and more favorable to public freedom.

The king could easily see the consequence of these proceedings. Though he had offered at the beginning of the session to give his consent to any law for the security of the rights and liberties of the people, he had not expected that such inroads would be made on his prerogative. In order, therefore, to divert the Commons from their intention, he sent a message in which he acknowledged past errors and promised that hereafter there would be no just cause of complaint. And he added, "That the affairs of the kingdom press him so, that he could not continue the session above a week or two longer. And if the house be not ready by that time to do what is fit for themselves, it shall be their own fault." On a subsequent occasion, he asked them, "Why demand explanations, if you doubt not the performance of the statutes according to their true meaning? Explanations will hazard an encroachment upon the prerogative, and it may well be said, 'What need a new law to confirm an old, if you repose confidence in the declarations which his majesty made to both houses?'" The truth is, the Great Charter and the old statutes were sufficiently clear in favor of personal liberty. But as all kings of England had always, in cases of necessity or expediency, been accustomed at intervals to elude them, and as Charles had lately violated them in a number of instances, the Commons judged it requisite to enact a new law which might not be eluded or violated by any interpretation, construction, or contrary precedent. Nor was it sufficient, they thought, that the king promised to return into the way of his predecessors. His predecessors in all times had enjoyed too much discretionary power; and by his recent abuse of it, the whole world had reason to see the necessity of entirely retrenching it.

The king still persevered in his endeavors to elude the petition. He sent a letter to the House of Lords in which he went so far as to make a particular declaration, "That neither he nor his Privy Council shall or will, at any time hereafter, commit or command to prison, or otherwise restrain, any man for not lending money, or for any other cause which, in his conscience, he thought not to concern the public good, and the safety of king and people." And he further declared, "That he never would be guilty of so base an action as to pretend [claim] any cause of whose truth he was not fully satisfied." But this promise, though reinforced by the recommendation of the upper house to the Commons, made no more impression than all the former messages.

We may reckon among the other evasions of the king the proposal of the House of Peers to append to the intended Petition of Right the following clause: "We humbly present this petition to your majesty, not only with a care of preserving our own liberties, but with due regard to leave entire that sovereign power with which your majesty is entrusted for the protection, safety, and happiness of your people." Less penetration than was possessed by the leaders of the House of Commons could easily discover the trap that this clause was, and how much it was calculated to elude the whole force of the petition.

These obstacles, therefore, being surmounted, the Petition of Right passed the Commons and was sent to the upper house. The Peers, who were probably well pleased in secret that all their solicitations had been eluded by the Commons, quickly passed the petition without any material alteration; and nothing but the royal assent was lacking to give it the force of a law. The king, accordingly, came to the House of Peers and sent for the Commons; being seated in his chair of state, the petition was read to him. Great was now the astonishment of all men when, instead of the usual concise and clear form by which a bill is either confirmed or rejected, Charles said, in answer to the petition, "The king willeth that right be done according to the laws and customs of the realm, and that the statutes be put into execution, that his subjects may have no cause to complain of any wrong or oppression contrary to their just rights and liberties, to the preservation whereof he holds himself in conscience as much obliged as of his own prerogative."

It is surprising that Charles, who had seen so many instances of the jealousy [suspicious dread] of the Commons, who had himself so much roused that jealousy by his frequent evasive messages during this session, could imagine that they would rest satisfied with an answer so vague and indeterminate. It was evident that the unusual form alone of the answer must arouse their attention, that the disappointment must inflame their anger, and that therefore it was necessary, as the petition seemed to bear hard on royal prerogative, to come early to some fixed resolution either gracefully to comply with it or courageously to reject it.

It happened as might have been foreseen. The Commons returned in very ill humor. When in that disposition, their zeal for religion and their enmity against the unfortunate Catholics usually ran extremely high. But they had already, in the beginning of the session, presented their petition of religion and had received a satisfactory answer, though they expected that the execution of the laws against papists would in the future be no more exact and rigid than they had previously found it. To give vent to their present indignation, they fell with their utmost force on Dr. Maynwaring.

There is nothing which tends more to excuse, if not to justify, the extreme rigor of the Commons towards Charles than his open encouragement and avowal of such general principles as were altogether incompatible with a limited government. Maynwaring had preached a sermon which the Commons found, upon inquiry, to be printed by special command of the king; and when this sermon was looked into, it contained doctrines subversive of all civil liberty. It taught that though property was commonly lodged in the subject, yet whenever any exigency required supply, all property was transferred to the sovereign; that the consent of Parliament was not necessary for the imposition of taxes; and that the divine laws required compliance with every demand, however irregular, which the prince might make upon his subjects. For these doctrines the Commons impeached Maynwaring. The sentence pronounced upon him by the Peers was that he would be imprisoned during the pleasure of the house, be fined £1,000 to the king, make submission and acknowledgment of his offense, be suspended for three years, be incapable of holding any ecclesiastical dignity or secular office, and that his book be called in and burned.

It may be worthy of notice that no sooner was the session ended than this man, so justly obnoxious to both houses, received a pardon and was promoted to a living of considerable value. Some years later, he was raised to the see of St. Asaph. If the republican spirit of the

Commons increased the monarchical spirit of the court beyond all reasonable bounds, this latter, carried to so high a pitch, tended still further to augment the former. And thus extremes were everywhere affected, and the just medium was gradually deserted by all men.

From Maynwaring, the House of Commons proceeded to censure the conduct of Buckingham, whose name they had cautiously forborne to mention before then. In vain did the king send them a message in which he told them that the session was drawing near to a conclusion and desired that they not enter upon new business nor cast any aspersions on his government and ministry. Though the court endeavored to explain and soften this message by a subsequent message—as Charles was apt hastily to correct any hasty step which he had taken—it served rather to inflame than appease the Commons, as if the method of their proceedings had here been prescribed to them. It was foreseen that a great tempest was ready to burst on the duke; and in order to divert it, the king thought proper, upon a joint application of the Lords and Commons, to endeavor giving them satisfaction with regard to the Petition of Right. Therefore, he came to the House of Peers, and pronouncing the usual form of words, "Let it be law, as is desired," gave full sanction and authority to the petition. The acclamations with which the house resounded and the universal joy diffused over the nation showed how much this petition had been the object of all men's vows and expectations.

It may be affirmed without any exaggeration that the king's assent to the Petition of Right produced such a change in the government as was almost equivalent to a revolution, and by circumscribing the royal prerogative in so many articles, gave additional security to the liberties of the subject. Yet the Commons were far from being satisfied with this important concession. Their ill humor had been so much irritated by the king's frequent evasions and delays that it could not be presently appeased by an assent which he allowed to be so reluctantly extorted from him. Perhaps too, the popular leaders, implacable and artful, saw the opportunity favorable, and turning against the king those very weapons with which he had furnished them, resolved to pursue the victory. The bill for the five subsidies which had been formerly voted, however, immediately passed the house, because the granting of that supply was, in a manner, tacitly contracted for upon the royal assent to the petition. Had faith been here violated, no further confidence could have existed between king and Parliament. Having made this concession, the Commons continued to carry their scrutiny into every part of government. In some particulars, their industry was laudable; in some, it may be liable to censure.

A little after writs were issued for summoning this Parliament, a commission had been granted to Sir Thomas Coventry, lord keeper, the Earl of Marlborough, treasurer, the Earl of Manchester, president of the Council, the Earl of Worcester, privy seal, the Duke of Buckingham, high admiral, and all the considerable officers of the Crown, in the whole thirty-three. By this commission, which from the number of persons named in it could be no secret, the commissioners were empowered to meet and to concert among themselves the methods of levying money by impositions or otherwise "where form and circumstance must be dispensed with, rather than the substance be lost or hazarded," as expressed in the commission. In other words, this was a scheme for finding expedients which might raise the prerogative to the greatest height and render Parliaments entirely useless. The Commons applied for canceling the commission, and were no doubt desirous that all the world would conclude the king's principles to be extremely arbitrary and would observe what little regard he was disposed to pay to the liberties and privileges of his people.

A commission had likewise been granted and some money remitted in order to raise a thousand German cavalrymen and transport them into England. These were supposed to be levied in order to support the projected impositions or excises, though the number seems insufficient for such a purpose. The Commons took notice of this design in severe terms; and no measure, surely, could be projected more generally odious to the whole nation. It must, however, be confessed that the king was right to the extent that he had now at last fallen on the only effectual method for supporting his prerogative. But at the same time, he should have perceived that till provided with a sufficient military force, all his attempts in opposition to the rising spirit of the nation must in the end prove wholly fruitless, and that the higher he screwed up the springs of government while he had so little real power to retain them in that forced situation, with more fatal violence must they fly out when any accident occurred to restore them to their natural action.

The Commons next resumed their censure of the conduct and behavior of Buckingham, against whom they were implacable. They agreed to present a remonstrance to the king in which they recapitulated all national grievances and misfortunes and omitted no circumstance which could render the whole administration despicable and odious. The compositions with Catholics, they said, amounted to no less than a toleration, hateful to God, full of dishonor and disprofit to his majesty, and of extreme scandal and grief to his good people. They took notice of the violations of liberty above mentioned, against which the Petition of Right seemed to have provided a sufficient remedy. They mentioned the decay of trade, the unsuccessful expeditions to Cadiz and the Isle of Rhé, the encouragement given to Arminians, the commission for transporting German cavalrymen, that for levying illegal impositions; and all these grievances they ascribed solely to the ill conduct of the Duke of Buckingham. This remonstrance was perhaps not the less provoking to Charles because, joined to the extreme acrimony of the subject, there were preserved in it, as in most of the remonstrances of that age, an affected civility and submission in the language. And as it was the first return which he met with for his late beneficial concessions and for his sacrifices of prerogative—the greatest by far ever made by an English sovereign—nothing could be more the object of just and natural indignation.

Prorogation

It was not without good grounds that the Commons were so fierce and assuming. Though they had already granted the king the supply of five subsidies, they still retained a security in their hands which they thought assured them success in all their applications. Tonnage and poundage had not yet been granted by Parliament, and the Commons had artfully this session concealed their intention of invading that branch of revenue till the royal assent had been obtained to the Petition of Right, which they justly deemed of such importance. They then openly asserted that the levying of tonnage and poundage without consent of Parliament was a palpable violation of the ancient liberties of the people and an open infringement of the Petition of Right, so lately granted. The king, in order to prevent the finishing and presenting of this remonstrance, came suddenly to the Parliament on June 26 and ended this session by a prorogation.

Being freed for some time from the embarrassment of this assembly, Charles began to look towards foreign wars, where all his efforts were equally unsuccessful as in his domestic government. The Earl of Denbigh, brother-in-law to Buckingham, was dispatched to the relief of La Rochelle, now closely besieged by land and threatened with a blockade by sea. But he returned without effecting anything; and having declined to attack the enemy's fleet, he brought on the English arms the imputation either of cowardice or ill conduct. In order to repair this dishonor, Buckingham went to Portsmouth, where he had prepared a considerable fleet and army on which all the subsidies given by Parliament had been expended. This supply had very much disappointed the king's expectations. The same mutinous spirit which prevailed in the House of Commons had diffused itself over the nation, and the commissioners appointed for making the assessments had connived at all frauds which might diminish the supply and reduce the Crown to still greater necessities. This national discontent, communicated to a desperate enthusiast, soon broke out in an event which may be considered as remarkable.

Death of Buckingham

There was one Felton, of a good family but of an ardent, melancholic temper, who had served under Buckingham in the station of lieutenant. His captain being killed in the retreat at the Isle of Rhé, Felton had applied for that rank in the company; when disappointed, he threw up his commission and retired in discontent from the army. While private resentment was boiling in his sullen, unsociable mind, he heard the nation resound with complaints against the duke and became acquainted with the remonstrance of the Commons, in which his enemy was represented as the cause of every national grievance and as the great enemy of the public. Religious fanaticism further inflamed these vindictive reflections, and he fancied that he would do heaven acceptable service if at one blow he dispatched this dangerous foe to religion and to his country. Full of these dark views, he secretly arrived at Portsmouth at the same time as the duke and watched for an opportunity of effecting his bloody purpose.

Buckingham had been engaged in conversation with Soubise and other French gentlemen; and a difference of sentiment having arisen, the dispute, though conducted with temper and decency, had produced some of those vehement gesticulations and lively exertions of voice in which that nation, more than the English, are apt to indulge themselves. The conversation being finished, Buckingham drew towards the door; and in that passage, turning to speak to Sir Thomas Fryer, a colonel in the army, he was suddenly, over Sir Thomas's shoulder, struck upon the breast with a knife. Without uttering other words than, "The villain has killed me," in the same moment pulling out the knife, he breathed his last.

No man had seen the blow nor the person who gave it; but in the confusion, everyone made his own conjecture, and all agreed that the murder had been committed by the French gentlemen whose angry tone of voice had been heard, while their words had not been understood, by the bystanders. In the hurry of revenge, they would have instantly been put to death had they not been saved by some of more temper and judgment, who, though they had the same opinion of their guilt, thought proper to reserve them for a judicial trial and examination.

Near the door there was found a hat, inside of which was sewed a paper containing four or five lines of that remonstrance of the Commons which declared Buckingham an enemy to the kingdom; and under these lines was a short ejaculation, or attempt towards a prayer. It was easily concluded that this hat belonged to the assassin, but the question of who that person was still remained, for the writing did not reveal the name; whoever he was, it was natural to believe that he had already fled far enough not to be found without a hat.

In this hurry, a man without a hat was seen walking very composedly before the door. One crying out, "Here is the fellow who killed the duke," everybody ran to ask, "Which is he?" The man very sedately answered, "I am he." The more furious immediately rushed upon him with drawn swords. Others, more deliberate, defended and protected him. He himself, with open arms, calmly and cheerfully exposed his breast to the swords of the most enraged, being willing to fall a sudden sacrifice to their anger rather than be reserved for that public justice which he knew must be executed upon him.

He was now known to be that Felton who had served in the army. After he was carried into a private room, it was thought proper to dissemble so far as to tell him that Buckingham was only grievously wounded but not without hopes of recovery. Felton smiled and told them that the duke, he knew full well, had received a blow which had terminated all their hopes. When asked at whose instigation he had performed the horrid deed, he replied that they needed not to trouble themselves in that inquiry; that no man living had credit enough with him to have disposed him to such an action; that he had not even told of his purpose to anyone; that the resolution proceeded only from himself and the impulse of his own conscience; and that his motives would appear if his hat were found, for believing he would perish in the attempt, he had there taken care to explain them.

When the king was informed of this assassination, he received the news in public with an unmoved and undisturbed countenance, and the courtiers who studied his looks concluded that secretly he was not displeased to be rid of a minister so generally odious to the nation. But Charles's command of himself proceeded entirely from the gravity and composure of his temper. He was still as much as ever attached to his favorite; during his whole life, he retained an affection for Buckingham's friends and a prejudice against his enemies. He urged too that Felton should be put to the question in order to extort from him a discovery of his accomplices. But the judges declared that though that practice had formerly been very usual, it was altogether illegal; so much more exact reasoners with regard to law had they become from the jealous scruples of the House of Commons.

Meanwhile, the distress of La Rochelle had risen to the utmost extremity. That vast genius of Richelieu which made him form the greatest enterprises led him to attempt their execution by means equally great and extraordinary. In order to deprive La Rochelle of all succor, he had dared to project the throwing across the harbor a breakwater of a mile's extent in that boisterous ocean; and having executed his project, he now held the town closely blockaded on all sides. The inhabitants, though pressed with the greatest rigors of famine, still refused to submit, being supported partly by the lectures of their zealous preachers, partly by the daily hopes of relief from England. After Buckingham's death, the command of the fleet and army was conferred on the Earl of Lindsey, who, arriving before La Rochelle, made some attempts to break through the breakwater and force his way into the harbor. But by the delays of the English, that work was now fully finished and fortified; and the Rochellers, finding their last hopes failing them, were reduced to surrender at discretion [unconditionally] on October 18, even in sight of the English admiral. Of fifteen thousand persons shut up in the city, only four thousand survived the fatigues and famine which they had undergone.

This was the first necessary step towards the prosperity of France. Foreign enemies as well as domestic factions being deprived of this resource, that kingdom began now to shine forth in its full splendor. By a steady prosecution of wise plans both of war and policy, it gradually gained an ascendance over the rival power of Spain, and every order of the state and every sect were reduced to pay submission to the lawful authority of the sovereign. The victory, however, over the Huguenots was at first pushed by the French king with great moderation. A toleration was still continued to them, the only avowed and open toleration which at that time was granted in any European kingdom.

New session of Parliament

The failure of an enterprise in which the English nation so much interested themselves from religious sympathy could not but diminish the king's authority in the Parliament during

the approaching session. But the Commons, when assembled on January 20, found many other causes of complaint. Buckingham's conduct and character with some had afforded a reason, with others a pretense, for discontent against public measures. But after his death, new reasons and new pretenses for general dissatisfaction were not lacking. Maynwaring's pardon and promotion were taken notice of. Sibthorpe and Cosin, two clergymen who for like reasons were no less obnoxious to the Commons, had met with like favor from the king. Montague, who had been censured for moderation towards the Catholics—the greatest of crimes—had been created bishop of Chichester. They also found, upon inquiry, that by the king's orders, all the copies of the Petition of Right which were dispersed had annexed to them the first answer which had given so little satisfaction to the Commons, an expedient by which Charles endeavored to persuade the people that he had in no way receded from his former claims and pretensions, particularly with regard to the levying of tonnage and poundage. Selden also complained in the house that one Savage had been punished, contrary to the Petition of Right, with the loss of his ears by a discretionary or arbitrary sentence of the Star Chamber. So apt were they on their part to stretch the petition into such consequences as might deprive the Crown of powers which from immemorial custom were supposed inherent in it.

Tonnage and poundage

But the great article on which the House of Commons broke with the king, and which finally created in Charles a disgust to all Parliaments, was their claim with regard to tonnage and poundage. On this occasion, therefore, it is necessary to give an account of the controversy.

The duty of tonnage and poundage in more ancient times had been commonly a temporary grant of Parliament, but it had been conferred on Henry V and all the succeeding princes for life in order to enable them to maintain a naval force for the defense of the kingdom. The necessity of levying this duty had been so apparent that each king had always claimed it from the moment of his accession, and the first Parliament of each reign had usually by vote conferred on the prince what they found him already in possession of. Agreeably to the inaccurate nature of the old constitution, this abuse, however considerable, had never been perceived nor remedied, though nothing could have been easier than for the Parliament to have prevented it. If this duty had been granted to each prince during his own life and for a year after his demise to the successor, all inconveniences would have been obviated, and yet the duty never for a moment levied without proper authority. But contrivances of that nature were not thought of during those rude ages. And as so complicated and jealous a government as the English cannot persist without many such refinements, it is easy to see how favorable every inaccuracy must formerly have proved to royal authority, which on all emergencies was obliged to supply by discretionary power the great deficiency of the laws.

The Parliament did not grant the duty of tonnage and poundage to Henry VIII till the sixth year of his reign. Yet this prince, who had not then raised his power to its greatest height, continued to levy the imposition during that whole time. In their very grant, the Parliament blamed the merchants who had neglected to make payment to the Crown; and though one expression of that bill may seem ambiguous, they employed the plainest terms in calling tonnage and poundage the king's due, even before that duty was conferred on him by parliamentary authority. Four reigns and more than a century had since elapsed, and this revenue had continued to be levied before it was voted by Parliament. So long had the inaccuracy continued without being noticed or corrected!

During that short interval which passed between Charles's accession and his first Parliament, he had followed the example of his predecessors; and no fault was found with his conduct in this particular. But what was most remarkable in the proceedings of that House of Commons, and what proved beyond controversy that they had seriously formed a plan for reducing their prince to subjection, was that instead of granting this supply during the king's lifetime, as it had been enjoyed by all his immediate predecessors, they voted it only for a year and reserved to themselves the power of renewing or refusing the same concession after that period elapsed. But the House of Peers, who saw that this duty had now become more necessary than ever to supply the growing necessities of the Crown and who did not approve of this encroaching spirit in the Commons, rejected the bill; and the dissolution of that Parliament followed so soon that no attempt seems to have been made for obtaining tonnage and poundage in any other form.

Charles, meanwhile, continued still to levy this duty by his own authority; and the nation was so accustomed to that exertion of royal power that no scruple was at first entertained of submitting to it. But the succeeding Parliament excited doubts in everyone. The Commons there took some steps towards declaring it illegal to levy tonnage and poundage without consent of Parliament, and they openly showed their intention of employing this engine in order to extort from the Crown concessions of the most important nature. But Charles was not yet sufficiently tamed to compliance, and the abrupt dissolution of that Parliament, as above related, put an end to their further pretensions for the time.

The following interval between the second and third Parliament was distinguished by so many exertions of prerogative that men had little leisure to attend to the affair of tonnage and poundage, where the abuse of power in the Crown might seem to be of a more disputable nature. But during the above-mentioned session, after the Commons had remedied all these grievances by means of their Petition of Right, which they deemed so necessary, they afterwards proceeded to take the matter into consideration, and they showed the same intention as formerly: of exacting very large compliances on the part of the Crown in return for the grant of this revenue. Their sudden prorogation prevented them from bringing their pretensions to a full conclusion.

When Charles opened this session, he had foreseen that the same controversy would arise; and therefore, he took care very early, among many mild and reconciling expressions, to inform the Commons, "That he had not taken these duties as appertaining to his hereditary prerogative, but that it ever was, and still is, his meaning to enjoy them as a gift of his people. And that, if he had hitherto levied tonnage and poundage, he pretended [claimed] to justify himself only by the necessity of so doing, not by any right which he assumed." This concession, which probably arose from the king's moderate temper, now freed from the impulse of Buckingham's violent counsels, might have satisfied the Commons had they entertained no other purpose than that of ascertaining their own powers and privileges. But they carried their pretensions much higher. They insisted as a necessary preliminary that the king first entirely desist from levying these duties, after which they were to take it under consideration how far they would restore him to the possession of a revenue of which he had clearly divested himself. But besides that this extreme rigor had never been exercised towards any of his predecessors and that many obvious inconveniences must follow from the intermission of the customs, there were other reasons which deterred Charles from complying with so hard a condition. It was probable that the Commons might renew their former project of making this revenue only temporary and thereby reduce their prince to perpetual dependence. They certainly would cut off the new impositions, which Mary and Elizabeth, but especially James, had levied and which formed no despicable part of the public revenue. And they openly declared that they had at present many important pretensions, chiefly with regard to religion, and that if compliance with these were refused, no supply must be expected from the Commons.

It is easy to see in what an inextricable labyrinth Charles was now involved. By his own concessions, by the general principles of the English government, and by the form of every bill which had granted this duty, tonnage and poundage was derived entirely from the free gift of the people, and consequently might be withdrawn at their pleasure. If unreasonable in their refusal, they still refused nothing but what was their own. If public necessity required this supply, it might be thought also to require the king's compliance with those conditions which were the price of obtaining it. Though the motive for granting it had been the enabling of the king to guard the seas, it did not follow that because he guarded the seas, he was therefore entitled to this revenue without further formality, since the people had still reserved to themselves the right of judging how far that service merited such a supply. But Charles, notwithstanding his public declaration, was far from assenting to this conclusion in its full extent. The plain consequence, he saw, of all these rigors, refinements, and inferences was that he, without any public necessity and without any fault of his own, must suddenly, even from his accession, become a magistrate of a very different nature from any of his predecessors; he must fall into a total dependence on subjects over whom former kings, especially those immediately preceding, had exercised an authority almost unlimited. Entangled in a chain of consequences which he could not easily break, he was inclined to go higher and deny the first principle rather than admit of conclusions which to him appeared so absurd and unreasonable. Agreeably to the ideas entertained till then both by natives and foreigners, he considered the monarch to be the essence and soul of the English government; whatever other power aspired to annihilate or even abridge the royal authority must necessarily, he thought, either in its nature or exercise, be deemed no better than a usurpation. Willing to preserve the ancient harmony of the constitution, he had always intended to comply, as far as he *easily* could, with the ancient forms of administration. But when these forms appeared to him to have no other tendency, by the inveterate obstinacy of the Commons, than to disturb that harmony and to introduce a new constitution, he concluded that in this violent situation, what was subordinate must necessarily yield to what was principal, and the privileges of the people, for a time, give place to royal prerogative. To be degraded from the rank of a monarch into a slave of his insolent, ungrateful subjects seemed of all indignities the greatest; and nothing, in his judgment, could exceed the humiliation attending such a state but the meanness of tamely submitting to it without making some efforts to preserve the authority transmitted to him by his predecessors.

Though these were the king's reflections and resolutions before the Parliament assembled, he did not immediately disclose them upon their delay in voting him this supply. He thought that he could better justify any strong measure which he might afterwards be obliged to take if he allowed them to carry to the utmost extremities their attacks upon his government and prerogative. He contented himself for the present with soliciting the house by messages and speeches. But the Commons, instead of hearkening to his solicitations, proceeded to carry their scrutiny into his management of religion, which was the only grievance to which, in their opinion, they had not as yet applied a sufficient remedy by their Petition of Right.

Arminianism

It was not possible that this century, so fertile in religious sects and disputes, could escape the controversy concerning fatalism and free will, which had in all ages, being strongly interwoven both with philosophy and theology, thrown every school and every church into such inextricable doubt and perplexity. The first reformers in England, as in other European countries, had embraced the most rigid tenets of predestination and absolute decrees, and they had composed upon that system all the articles of their religious creed. But these principles having met with opposition from Arminius and his sectaries on the Continent, the controversy was soon brought into England and began there to diffuse itself. The Arminians, finding more encouragement from the superstitious spirit of the Church of England than from the fanaticism of the Puritans, gradually incorporated themselves with the

159

former; and some of that sect, by the indulgence of James and Charles, had attained the highest preferments in the hierarchy. But their success with the public had not been equal to that which they met with in the church and the court. Throughout the nation, they still lay under the reproach of innovation and heresy. The Commons now leveled against them their formidable censures and made them the objects of daily invective and declamation. Their protectors were stigmatized, their tenets canvassed, their views represented as dangerous and pernicious. To impartial spectators, surely, if any such had been at that time in England, it must have given great entertainment to see a popular assembly inflamed with faction and enthusiasm attempt to discuss questions to which the greatest philosophers in the tranquility of retreat had never before been able to find any satisfactory solution.

Amidst that complication of disputes in which men were then involved, we may observe that the appellation "Puritan" stood for three parties which, though commonly united, were yet actuated by very different views and motives. There were the political Puritans, who maintained the highest principles of civil liberty; the Puritans in discipline, who were averse to the ceremonies and episcopal government of the church; and the doctrinal Puritans, who rigidly defended the speculative system of the first reformers. In opposition to all these stood the court party, the church hierarchy, and the Arminians, only with the distinction that the latter sect, being introduced a few years before, did not as yet include all those who were favorable to the church and to monarchy. But as the controversies on every subject grew daily warmer, men united themselves more intimately with their friends and separated themselves wider from their antagonists, and the distinction gradually became quite uniform and regular.

This House of Commons, which, like all the ones preceding during the reigns of James and Charles, and even of Elizabeth, was much governed by the Puritanical party, thought that they could not better serve their cause than by branding and punishing the Arminian sect, which, introducing an innovation in the church, were the least favored and least powerful of all their antagonists. From this measure, it was easily foreseen that besides gratifying the animosity of the doctrinal Puritans, both the Puritans in discipline and those in politics would reap considerable advantages. Laud, Neile, Montague, and other bishops, who were the chief supporters of episcopal government and the most zealous partisans of the discipline and ceremonies of the church, were all supposed to be tainted with Arminianism. The same men and their disciples were the strenuous preachers of passive obedience and of entire submission to princes. And if these could once be censured and be expelled from the church and court, it was concluded that the hierarchy would receive a mortal blow, the ceremonies be less rigidly insisted on, and the king, deprived of his most faithful friends, be obliged to abate those high claims of prerogative on which at present he insisted.

But Charles was strongly determined to oppose such pretensions, not only from considerations of the political consequences which must result from a compliance with them but also from principles of piety and conscience. Neither the dissipation incident to youth nor the pleasures attending a high fortune had been able to prevent this virtuous prince from embracing the most sincere sentiments of religion; and that quality, which in that religious age should have been of infinite advantage to him, proved in the end the chief cause of his ruin, merely because the religion adopted by him was not of that precise mode and sect which began to prevail among his subjects. His piety, though remote from popery, had a tincture of superstition in it, and being averse to the gloomy spirit of the Puritans, was represented by them as tending towards the abominations of antichrist. Laud also had unfortunately acquired a great ascendance over him. And as all those prelates obnoxious to the Commons were regarded as his chief friends and most favored courtiers, he was resolved not to disarm and dishonor himself by abandoning them to the resentment of his enemies. Being totally unprovided with military force and finding a refractory, independent spirit to prevail among the people, he thought that the most solid basis of his authority consisted in the support which he received from the hierarchy.

In the debates of the Commons which are transmitted to us, it is easy to discern so early some sparks of that enthusiastic fire which later set the whole nation in combustion. One Rouse made use of an allusion which, though familiar, seems to have been borrowed from the writings of Lord Bacon. "If a man meet a dog alone," he said, "the dog is fearful, though ever so fierce by nature. But if the dog have his master with him, he will set upon that man from whom he fled before. This shows that lower natures, being backed by higher, increase in courage and strength; and certainly man, being backed with Omnipotency, is a kind of omnipotent creature. All things are possible to him that believes; and where all things are possible, there is a kind of omnipotency. Wherefore, let it be the unanimous consent and resolution of us all to make a vow and covenant henceforth to hold fast our God and our religion, and then shall we henceforth expect with certainty happiness in this world."

Oliver Cromwell, at that time a young man of no account in the nation, is mentioned in these debates as complaining of one who, he was told, preached flat popery. It is amusing to observe the first words of this fanatical hypocrite correspond so exactly to his character.

The inquiries and debates concerning tonnage and poundage went hand in hand with these theological or metaphysical controversies. The officers of the Custom House were summoned before the Commons to tell by what authority they had seized the goods of merchants who had refused to pay these duties. The barons of the Exchequer were questioned concerning their decrees on that head. One of the sheriffs of London was committed to the Tower for his activity in supporting the officers of the Custom House. The goods of John Rolle, a merchant and member of the House of Commons, were seized for his refusal to pay the duties; and complaints were made of this violence as if it were a breach of parliamentary privilege. Charles supported his officers in all these measures, and the quarrel grew every day higher between him and the Commons. Mention was made in the house of impeaching Sir Richard Weston, the treasurer; and the king began to entertain thoughts of finishing the session by a dissolution.

Dissolution of the Parliament

Sir John Eliot framed a remonstrance against levying tonnage and poundage without consent of Parliament and offered it to the clerk to read. It was refused. He read it himself. The question being then called for, the speaker, Sir John Finch, said, "That he had a command from the king to adjourn, and to put no question." Upon which he rose and left the chair. The whole house was in an uproar. The speaker was pushed back into the chair and forcibly held in it by Denzil Holles and Benjamin Valentine till a short remonstrance was framed and was passed by acclamation rather than by vote. Papists and Arminians were there declared capital enemies to the commonwealth. Those who levied tonnage and poundage were branded with the same epithet. And even the merchants who voluntarily paid these duties were denominated betrayers of English liberty and public enemies. The doors being locked, the gentleman usher of the House of Lords, who was sent by the king, could not get admittance till this remonstrance was finished. By the king's order, he took the mace from the table, which ended their proceedings. And a few days later, on March 10, the Parliament was dissolved.

The discontents of the nation ran high on account of this violent rupture between the king and Parliament. These discontents Charles inflamed by his affectation of a severity which he had not power, nor probably inclination, to carry to extremities. Sir Miles Hobart, Sir Peter Heyman, Selden, Coryton, Long, and Strode were committed to prison on account of the last tumult in the house, which was called sedition. They were released with great difficulty and after several delays, and the law was generally supposed to have been twisted in order to prolong their imprisonment. Sir John Eliot, Holles, and Valentine were summoned to their trial in the King's Bench for seditious speeches and behavior in Parliament, but they refused to answer before an inferior court for their conduct as members of a superior one; they were condemned to be imprisoned during the king's pleasure, to find sureties for their good behavior, and to be fined, the two former £1,000 apiece, the latter £500. This sentence, procured by the influence of the Crown, served only to show the king's disregard to the privileges of Parliament and to acquire an immense stock of popularity to the sufferers, who had so bravely, in opposition to arbitrary power, defended the liberties of their native country. The Commons of England, though an immense body and possessed of the greater part of national property, were naturally somewhat defenseless because of their personal equality and their lack of leaders. But the king's severity, if these prosecutions deserve the name, here pointed out leaders to them whose resentment was inflamed and whose courage was in no way daunted by the hardships which they had undergone in so honorable a cause.

So much did these prisoners glory in their sufferings that though they were promised liberty if they would present a petition to the king expressing their sorrow for having offended him, they would not agree even to that condition. They unanimously refused to find sureties for their good behavior and disdained to accept deliverance on such easy terms. Indeed, Holles was so industrious to continue his meritorious distress that when one offered to bail him, he would not yield to the rule of court and be himself bound with his friend. Even Long, who had actually found sureties in the chief justice's chamber, declared in court that his sureties would no longer continue. Yet because Sir John Eliot happened to die while in custody, a great clamor was raised against the administration, and he was universally regarded as a martyr to the liberties of England.

CHAPTER 52
1629 – 1637

Peace with France and Spain – State of the court and ministry – Character of the queen – Strafford – Laud – Innovations in the church – Irregular levies of money – Severities in the Star Chamber and High Commission – Ship money – Trial of Hampden

THERE now opens to us a new scene. Charles, naturally disgusted with Parliaments—who, he found, were determined to proceed against him with unmitigated rigor, both in invading his prerogative and refusing him all supply—resolved not to call any more till he could see greater indications of a compliant disposition in the nation. Having lost his great favorite, Buckingham, he became his own minister, and never afterwards reposed in anyone such unlimited confidence. As he chiefly follows his own genius and disposition, his measures are from now on less rash and hasty, though the general tenor of his administration still lacks somewhat of being entirely legal, and perhaps more of being entirely prudent.

We shall endeavor to exhibit a just idea of the events which followed for some years so far as they regard foreign affairs, the state of the court, and the government of the nation. The incidents are neither numerous nor illustrious, but the knowledge of them is necessary for understanding the subsequent transactions which are so memorable.

Peace with France and Spain
Charles, destitute of all supply, was necessarily reduced to embrace a measure which ought to have been the result of reason and sound pol-

icy: he made peace with the two Crowns against which he had till then waged a war entered into without necessity and conducted without glory. Notwithstanding the distracted and helpless condition of England, no attempt was made either by France or Spain to invade their enemy, nor did they entertain any further project than to defend themselves against the feeble and ill-concerted expeditions of that kingdom. Pleased that the jealousies and quarrels between king and Parliament had disarmed so formidable a power, they carefully avoided any enterprise which might rouse either the terror or anger of the English and dispose them to domestic union and submission. The endeavors to regain the good will of the nation were carried so far by the king of Spain that he generously released and sent home all the English prisoners taken in the expedition against Cadiz. The example was imitated by France after the retreat of the English from the Isle of Rhé. When princes were in such dispositions and had so few pretensions on each other, it could not be difficult to conclude a peace. The treaty was first signed with France, on April 14. The situation of the king's affairs did not entitle him to demand any conditions for the Huguenots, and they were abandoned to the will of their sovereign. Peace was afterwards concluded with Spain on November 5, 1630, where no conditions were made in favor of the

1630

palatine except that Spain promised in general to use their good offices for his restoration. The influence of these two wars on domestic affairs and on the dispositions of king and people was of the utmost consequence, but no alteration was made by them on the foreign interests of the kingdom.

Nothing more happy can be imagined than the situation in which England then stood with regard to foreign affairs. Europe was divided between the rival families of Bourbon and Austria, whose opposite interests, and still more their mutual jealousies, secured England's tranquility. Their forces were so nearly counterpoised that no apprehensions were entertained of any event which could suddenly disturb the balance of power between them. The Spanish monarch, deemed the most powerful, lay at greatest distance; and by that means, the English possessed the advantage of being drawn by political motives into a more intimate union and confederacy with the neighboring potentate. The dispersed locations of the Spanish dominions rendered the naval power of England formidable to them and kept that empire in continual dependence. France, more vigorous and more compact, was every day rising in policy and discipline, and reached at last an equality of power with the house of Austria. But as its progress was slow and gradual, England still retained the power to check its superiority by a timely interposition. And thus Charles, could he have avoided all dissensions with his own subjects, was in a situation to make himself be courted and respected by every power in Europe; and what has scarcely ever since been attained by the princes of England, he could either be active with dignity or neutral with security.

A neutrality was embraced by the king, and he seems to have paid little attention to foreign affairs during the rest of his reign, except so far as he was engaged by honor and by friendship for his sister and the palatine to endeavor the procuring of some relief for that unhappy family. He joined his good offices to those of France and mediated a peace between the kings of Sweden and Poland in hopes of engaging the former to embrace the protection of the oppressed Protestants in the empire. This was the famed Gustavus Adolphus, whose heroic genius, seconded by the wisest policy, made him in a little time the most distinguished monarch of the age and rendered his country, formerly unknown and neglected, of great weight in the balance of Europe. To encourage and assist him in his projected invasion of Germany, Charles agreed to furnish him with six thousand men; but that he might preserve the appearance of neutrality, he made use of the Marquess of Hamilton's name. That nobleman entered into an engagement with Gustavus; and enlisting these troops in England and Scotland at Charles's expense, he landed them in the Elbe. The decisive Battle of Leipzig was fought soon after, where the conduct of Tilly and the valor of the imperialists were overcome by the superior conduct of Gustavus and the superior valor of the Swedes. What remained of this hero's life was one continued series of victories, for which he was less beholden to fortune than to those personal endowments which he derived from nature and from industry. That rapid progress of conquest which we so much admire in ancient history was here renewed in modern annals, and without that cause to which in former ages it had always been owing. Military nations were not now engaged against an undisciplined and unwarlike people, nor heroes set in opposition to cowards. The veteran troops of Ferdinand, conducted by the most celebrated generals of the age, were foiled in every encounter, and all Germany was overrun in an instant by the victorious Swede. But by this extraordinary and unexpected success of his ally, Charles failed of the purpose for which he framed the alliance. Gustavus, elated by prosperity, began to form more extensive plans of ambition; in freeing Germany from the yoke of Ferdinand, he intended to reduce it to subjection under his own. He refused to restore the palatine to his principality except on conditions which would have kept him in total dependence. And thus the negotiation was protracted till the Battle of Lutzen, where the Swedish monarch perished in the midst of a complete victory over his enemies.

We have carried on these transactions a few years beyond the present period so that we might not be obliged to return to them, nor be from here on interrupted in our account of Charles's court and kingdoms.

State of the court and ministry

When we consider Charles as presiding in his court, as associating with his family, it is difficult to imagine a character at once more respectable and more amiable. A kind husband, an indulgent father, a gentle master, a steadfast friend: to all these eulogies his conduct in private life fully entitled him. As a monarch too, in the exterior qualities, he excelled; in the essential ones, he was not defective. His address and manner, though perhaps inclining a little towards stateliness and formality, in the main corresponded to his high rank and gave grace to that reserve and gravity which were natural to him. The moderation and equity which shone forth in his temper seemed to secure him against rash and dangerous enterprises. The good sense which he displayed in his discourse and conversation seemed to warrant his success in every reasonable undertaking. Other endowments likewise he had attained which in a private gentleman would have been highly ornamental and which in a great monarch might have proved extremely useful to his people. He was possessed of an excellent taste in all the fine arts, and the love of painting was in some degree his favorite passion. Learned beyond what is common in princes, he was a good judge of writing in others and enjoyed no mean talent in composition himself. In any other age or nation, this monarch would have been secure of a prosperous and a happy reign. But the high idea of his own authority which he had imbibed made him incapable of giving way to the spirit of liberty which began to prevail among his subjects. His politics were not supported by such vigor and foresight as might have enabled him to subdue their pretensions and maintain his prerogative at the high pitch to which it had been raised by his predecessors. And above all, the spirit of enthusiasm, being universally diffused, defeated all the hopes of human prudence and disturbed the operation of every motive which usually influences society.

But the misfortunes arising from these causes were yet remote. Charles now enjoyed himself in the full exercise of his authority, in a social intercourse with his friends and courtiers, and in a moderate use of those pleasures of which he was most fond.

Character of the queen

After the death of Buckingham, who had somewhat alienated Charles from the queen, she is to be considered as his chief friend and favorite. That rustic contempt of the fair sex which James affected, and which, banishing them from his court, made it resemble more a fair or an exchange than the seat of a great prince, was very wide of the disposition of this monarch. But though full of complaisance to the whole sex, Charles reserved all his passion for his consort, to whom he attached himself with unshaken fidelity and confidence. By her sense and spirit as well as by her beauty, she justified the fondness of her husband; though it is allowed that, being somewhat of a passionate temper, she precipitated him into hasty and imprudent measures. Her religion likewise, to which she was much addicted, must be regarded as a great misfortune, since it augmented the jealousy which prevailed against the court and engaged her to procure for the Catholics some indulgences which were generally distasteful to the nation.

Strafford

In the former situation of the English government, when the sovereign was in a great measure independent of his subjects, the king chose his ministers either from personal favor or from an opinion of their abilities without any regard to their parliamentary interest or talents. It has since been the maxim of princes, wherever popular leaders encroach too much on royal authority, to confer offices on them in expectation that they will afterwards become more careful not to diminish that power which has become their own. These politics were now embraced by Charles, a sure proof that a covert revolution had happened in the constitution and had necessitated the prince to adopt new maxims of government. But the views of the king were at this time so repugnant to those of the Puritans that the leaders whom he favored lost from that moment all credit with their party and were even pursued with implacable hatred and resentment as traitors. This was the case with Sir Thomas Wentworth, whom the king created first a baron, then a viscount, and afterwards Earl of Strafford; made him president of the Council of York and deputy of Ireland; and regarded him as'his chief minister and counselor. By his eminent talents and abilities, Strafford merited all the confidence which his master reposed in him. His character was stately and austere, more fitted to procure esteem than love. His fidelity to the king was unshaken. But as he now employed all his counsels to support the prerogative, which he had formerly bent all his endeavors to diminish, his virtue seems not to have been entirely pure but to have been susceptible of strong impressions from private interest and ambition. Sir Dudley Digges was about the same time created master of the rolls; Noy, attorney general; Littleton, solicitor general. All these had likewise been parliamentary leaders and were men eminent in their profession.

Laud

In all ecclesiastical affairs, and even in many civil ones, William Laud, bishop of London, had great influence over the king. This man was virtuous, if severity of manners alone and abstinence from pleasure could deserve that name. He was learned, if polemical knowledge could entitle him to that praise. He was disinterested, but with unceasing industry he endeavored to exalt the priestly and prelatical rank, which was his own. His zeal was unrelenting in the cause of religion—that is, in imposing by rigorous measures his own tenets and pious ceremonies on the obstinate Puritans, who had profanely dared to oppose him. In prosecution of his holy purposes, he overlooked every human consideration—or in other words, the heat and indiscretion of his temper made him neglect the considerations of prudence and rules of good manners. He was in this respect happy: all his enemies were also imagined by him the declared enemies to loyalty and true piety, so every exercise of his anger became in his eyes a merit and a virtue. This was the man who acquired so great an ascendance over Charles and who led him by the pliancy of his temper into conduct which proved so fatal to himself and to his kingdoms.

Innovations in the church

The humor of the nation ran at that time to the extreme opposite of superstition; and it was with difficulty that the ancient ceremonies, to which men had been accustomed and which had been sanctified by the practice of the first reformers, could be retained in divine service. Yet this was the time which Laud chose for the introduction of new ceremonies and observances. These were sure to displease as innovations; but besides that, there lay in the opinion of the public another very forcible objection against them. Laud and the other prelates who embraced his measures were generally well instructed in sacred antiquity and had adopted many of those religious sentiments which prevailed during the fourth and fifth centuries, when the Christian church, as is well known, was already sunk into those superstitions which were afterwards continued and augmented by the policy of Rome. The revival, therefore, of the ideas and practices of that age could not fail to give the English faith and liturgy some resemblance to the Catholic superstition, which the kingdom in general and the Puritans in particular held in the greatest horror and detestation. Men also were apt to think that such insignificant observances would not be imposed with such unrelenting zeal on the refractory nation without some secret purpose, and that Laud's scheme was to lead back the English by gradual steps to the religion of their ancestors. They failed to consider that the very insignificance of these ceremonies recommended them to the superstitious prelate and made them appear the more particularly sacred and religious, as they could serve to no other purpose. Nor was the resemblance to the Romish ritual any objection with Laud and his brethren; it was rather a merit. They bore a much greater kindness to the "Mother Church," as they called it, than to the sectaries and Presbyterians; and they frequently recommended it as a "true Christian church," an appellation which they refused, or at least scrupled, to give to the others. So openly were these tenets espoused that not only the discontented Puritans believed the Church of England to be relapsing fast into Romish superstition. The court of Rome itself entertained hopes of regaining its authority in England; and in order to forward Laud's supposed good intentions, an offer was twice made to him in private of a cardinal's hat, which he declined. His answer was, as he said himself, "That something dwelt within him which would not suffer his compliance till Rome were other than it is."

A court lady, daughter of the Earl of Devonshire, having turned Catholic, was asked by Laud the reason for her conversion. "'Tis chiefly," she said, "because I hate to travel in a crowd." The meaning of this expression being demanded, she replied, "I perceive your grace and many others are making haste to Rome; and therefore, in order to prevent my being crowded, I have gone before you." Though Laud did not deserve the appellation of papist, it must be confessed that the spirit of his religion was the same as that of the Romish, though in a lesser degree. The same profound respect was exacted to the priestly rank, the same submission required to the creeds and decrees of synods and councils, the same pomp and ceremony was affected in worship, and the same superstitious regard to days, postures, meats, and vestments was enforced. It is no wonder, therefore, that this prelate was everywhere among the Puritans regarded with horror as the forerunner of antichrist.

As a specimen of the new ceremonies to which Laud sacrificed his own quiet and that of the nation, it may not be amiss to relate those which he was accused of employing in the consecration of St. Catharine's Church and which were the object of such general scandal and offense.

On the bishop's approach to the west door of the church, a loud voice cried, "Open, open, ye everlasting doors, that the king of glory may enter in!" Immediately the doors of the church flew open and the bishop entered. Falling upon his knees, with eyes elevated and arms expanded, he uttered these words: "This place is holy; the ground is holy. In the name of the Father, Son, and Holy Ghost, I pronounce it holy."

Going towards the chancel, he several times took up from the floor some of the dust and threw it in the air. When he approached with his attendants near to the communion table, he bowed frequently towards it. And on their return, they went round the church, repeating as they marched along some of the psalms, and then said a form of prayer which concluded with these words: "We consecrate this church, and separate it unto thee as holy ground, not to be profaned any more to common uses."

After this, the bishop, standing near the communion table, solemnly pronounced many imprecations upon any who might afterwards pollute that holy place by musters of soldiers, or keeping in it profane law courts, or carrying burdens through it. On the conclusion of every curse, he bowed towards the east and cried, "Let all the people say, Amen."

The imprecations being all so piously finished, there were poured out a number of blessings upon those who had any hand in framing and building that sacred and beautiful edifice, and upon those who had given to it, or would hereafter give, any chalices, plate, ornaments, or utensils. At every benediction, he in like manner bowed towards the east and cried, "Let all the people say, Amen."

The sermon followed, after which the bishop consecrated and administered the sacrament in the following manner: As he approached the communion table, he made many lowly reverences; and coming up to that part of the table where the bread and wine lay, he bowed seven times. After the reading of many prayers, he approached the sacramental elements and gently lifted up the corner of the napkin in which the bread was placed. When he beheld the bread, he suddenly let fall the napkin, flew back a step or two, bowed three separate times towards the bread, then drew nigh again, opened the napkin, and bowed as before. Next he laid his hand on the cup, which had a cover upon it and was filled with wine. He let go of the cup, fell back, and bowed thrice towards it. He approached again, and lifting up the cover, peeped into the cup. Seeing the wine, he let fall the cover, started back, and bowed as before. Then he received the sacrament and gave it to others. And many prayers being said, the solemnity of the consecration ended. The walls, and floor, and roof of the fabric were then supposed to be sufficiently holy.

Orders were given and rigorously insisted on that the communion table be removed from the middle of the area, where it previously had stood in all churches except in cathedrals. It was placed at the east end, railed in, and denominated an "altar"; the clergyman who officiated received commonly the appellation of "priest." It is easy to imagine the discontents excited by this innovation and the suspicions which it gave rise to.

The kneeling at the altar and the using of copes (a species of embroidered vestment) in administering the sacrament were also known to be great objects of scandal, as being popish practices. But the opposition increased rather than abated the zeal of the prelate for the introduction of these garments and ceremonies.

All kinds of ornament, especially pictures, were necessary for supporting that mechanical devotion which was intended to be raised in this model of religion. But as these had been so much employed by the church of Rome and had given rise to so much superstition, or what the Puritans called idolatry, it was impossible to introduce them into English churches without exciting general murmurs and complaints. But Laud, possessed of present authority, persisted in his purpose and made several attempts towards acquiring these ornaments. Some of the pictures introduced by him were also found, upon inquiry, to be the very same that might be met with in the Roman Missal. The crucifix too, that eternal consolation of all pious Catholics and terror to all sound Protestants, was not forgotten on this occasion.

It was much noticed that Sheffield, the recorder of Salisbury, was tried in the Star Chamber for having broken, contrary to the bishop of Salisbury's express injunctions, a painted window of St. Edmund's Church in that city. He boasted that he had destroyed these monuments of idolatry. But for this effort of his zeal, he was fined £500, removed from his office, condemned to make a public acknowledgment, and bound to his good behavior.

Not only were those of the clergy who neglected to observe every ceremony suspended and deprived by the High Commission Court; oaths were imposed by many of the bishops on the churchwardens, and the latter were sworn to inform against anyone who acted contrary to the ecclesiastical canons. Such a measure, though practiced during the reign of Elizabeth, gave much offense, as resembling too nearly the practice of the Romish Inquisition.

To show the greater alienation from the churches reformed after the presbyterian model, Laud advised that the discipline and worship of the Church of England should be imposed on the English regiments and trading companies abroad. All foreigners of the Dutch and Walloon congregations were commanded to attend the established church, and indulgence was granted to none after the children of the first denizens. Viscount Scudamore too, the king's ambassador at Paris, had orders to withdraw himself from the communion of the Huguenots. Even men of sense were apt to blame this conduct, not only because it gave offense in England, but because it lost the Crown the advantage of being considered in foreign countries as the head and support of the Reformation.

On pretense of pacifying disputes, orders were issued from the Privy Council forbidding on both sides all preaching and printing with regard to the disputed points of predestination and free will. But it was complained of, and probably with reason, that the impartiality was altogether confined to the orders, and that the execution of them was only meant against the Calvinists.

In return for Charles's indulgence towards the Church of England, Laud and his followers took care to magnify on every occasion the regal authority and to treat with the utmost disdain or detestation all Puritanical pretensions to a free and independent constitution. But while these prelates were so liberal in raising the Crown at the expense of public liberty, they did not scruple to encroach on the most incontestable royal rights in order to exalt the hierarchy and procure to their own order dominion and independence. All the doctrines which the Romish church had borrowed from some of the fathers and which freed the spiritual from subordination to the civil power were now adopted by the Church of England and interwoven with its political and religious tenets. A divine and apostolic charter was insisted on in preference to a legal and parliamentary one. The priestly rank was magnified as sacred and indefeasible. All right to spiritual authority, or even to private judgment in spiritual subjects, was refused to profane laymen. Ecclesiastical courts were held by the bishops in their own name, without any notice taken of the king's authority. And Charles, though extremely jealous of every claim in popular assemblies, seemed rather to encourage than repress those encroachments of his clergy. Having felt many perceptible inconveniences from the independent spirit of Parliaments, he attached himself entirely to those who professed a devoted obedience to his crown and person. Nor did he foresee that the ecclesiastical power which he exalted, not admitting of any precise boundary, might in time become more dangerous to public peace, and no less fatal to royal prerogative, than the other.

As early as the coronation, Laud was the person, according to general opinion, who introduced a novelty which, though overlooked by Charles, made a deep impression on many of the bystanders. After the usual ceremonies, these words were recited to the king: "Stand and hold fast from henceforth the place to which you have been heir by the succession of your forefathers, being now delivered to you by the authority of Almighty God, and by the hands of us and all the bishops and servants of God. And as you see the clergy to come nearer the altar than others, so remember that, in all places convenient, you give them greater honor; that the Mediator of God and man may establish you on the kingly throne, to be a mediator betwixt the clergy and the laity; and that you may reign forever with Jesus Christ, the King of kings and Lord of lords."

The principles which exalted prerogative were not entertained by the king merely as soft and agreeable to his royal ears; they were also put in practice during the time that he ruled without Parliaments. Though frugal and regular in his expense, he lacked money for the support of government; and he levied it either by the revival of obsolete laws or by violations—some more open, some more disguised—of the privileges of the nation. Though humane and gentle in his temper, he gave way to a few severities in the Star Chamber and High Commission which seemed necessary to support the present mode of administration and repress the rising spirit of liberty throughout the kingdom. Under these two heads may be reduced all the remarkable transactions of this reign for some years. For in peaceable and prosperous times, where a neutrality in foreign affairs is observed, almost everything that is remarkable is in some degree blamed or blamable. And lest the hope of relief or protection from Parliament might encourage opposition, Charles issued a proclamation in which he declared, "That, whereas, for several ill ends, the calling again of a parliament is divulged [proclaimed]; though his majesty has shown, by frequent meetings with his people, his love to the use of parliaments: yet the late abuse having, for the present, driven him unwillingly out of that course, he will account it presumption for anyone to prescribe to him any time for the calling of that assembly." This was generally construed as a declaration that during this reign, no more Parliaments were intended to be summoned. And every measure of the king's confirmed a suspicion so disagreeable to the greatest part of the people.

Irregular levies of money

Tonnage and poundage continued to be levied by the royal authority alone. The former additional impositions were still exacted. Even new impositions were laid on several kinds of merchandise.

The Custom House officers received orders from the Council to enter into any house, warehouse, or cellar, to search any trunk or chest, and to break open any bulk whatever in default of the payment of customs.

In order to exercise the militia and to keep them in good order, each county was assessed a certain sum by an edict of the Council for maintaining a muster-master appointed for that service.

Compositions were openly made with recusants, and the popish religion became a regular part of the revenue. This was all the persecution which it underwent during the reign of Charles.

A commission was granted for compounding with those possessed of Crown lands upon defective titles, and some money was exacted from the people on this pretense.

There was a law of Edward II that whoever was possessed of £20 a year in land would be obliged, when summoned, to appear and to receive the order of knighthood. Twenty pounds at that time was equivalent to two hundred in the seventeenth century—partly by the change of denomination, partly by that in the value of money—and it seemed just that the king should not strictly insist on the letter of the law and oblige people of so small revenue to accept that expensive honor. Edward VI and Queen Elizabeth, who had both of them made use of this expedient for raising money, had summoned only those who were possessed of £40 a year and upwards to receive knighthood or to compound for their neglect, and Charles imitated their example in granting the same indulgence. Commissioners were appointed for fixing the rates of composition, and instructions were given to these commissioners not to accept a smaller sum than would have been due by the party upon a tax of three subsidies and a half. Nothing proves more plainly how ill disposed the people were to the measures of the Crown than to observe that they loudly complained of an expedient founded on positive statute and warranted by such recent precedents. The law was claimed to be obsolete, though only one reign had intervened since the last execution of it.

Severities in the Star Chamber and High Commission

Barnard, lecturer of St. Sepulchre's, London, used this expression in his prayer before sermon: "Lord, open the eyes of the queen's majesty, that she may see Jesus Christ, whom she has pierced with her infidelity, superstition, and idolatry." He was questioned in the High Commission Court for this insult on the queen but was dismissed upon his submission. Leighton, who had written libels against the king, the queen, the bishops, and the whole administration, was condemned by a very severe, if not a cruel, sentence; but the execution of it was suspended for some time in expectation of his submission. All the severities, indeed, of this reign were exercised against those who triumphed in their sufferings, who courted persecution and braved authority. And on that account, their punishment may be deemed the more just but the less prudent. To have neglected them entirely, had it been consistent with order and public safety, would have been the wisest measure that could have been embraced, and would perhaps have been the most severe punishment that could have been inflicted on these zealots.

In order to gratify the clergy with a magnificent structure, subscriptions were put in motion for repairing and | *1631* | rebuilding St. Paul's Cathedral, and the king encouraged this laudable undertaking by his favor and example. By order of the Privy Council, St. Gregory's Church was removed as an impediment to the project of extending and beautifying the cathedral. Some houses and shops likewise were pulled down, and compensation was made to the owners. As there was no immediate prospect of assembling a Parliament, such acts of power in the king became necessary, and in no former age would the people have entertained any scruple with regard to them. It must be remarked that the Puritans were extremely averse to the raising of this ornament to the capital; it savored, as they claimed, of popish superstition.

A new tax, a stamp duty on cards, was imposed; although liable to no objection by itself, it appeared of dangerous consequence when considered as arbitrary and illegal.

Monopolies were revived: an oppressive method of levying money, being unlimited as well as destructive of industry. The last Parliament of James, which abolished monopolies, had left an equitable exception in favor of new inventions; and on pretense of these and of erecting new companies and corporations, this grievance was now renewed. The manufacture of soap was given to a company who paid a sum for their patent. Leather, salt, and many other commodities, even down to linen rags, were likewise put under restrictions.

It is affirmed by Clarendon that so little benefit was reaped from these projects that of £200,000 thereby levied on the people, scarcely £1,500 came into the king's coffers. Though we ought not to suspect the noble historian of exaggerations to the disadvantage of Charles's measures, this fact, it must be admitted, appears somewhat incredible. The same author adds that the king's intention was to teach his subjects how unthrifty a thing it was to refuse reasonable supplies to the Crown. To offend a whole nation in order to punish it, and to hope by acts of violence to break their refractory spirits without being possessed of any force to prevent resistance: an imprudent project!

The Council of York had first been erected after a rebellion by a patent from Henry VIII without any authority of Parliament; and this exercise of power, like many others, was indulged to that arbitrary monarch. This council had long acted chiefly as a criminal court. But in addition to some innovations introduced by James, Charles thought proper, some time after Wentworth was made president, to extend its powers and to give it a large civil jurisdiction, and that discretionary in some respects. It is not improbable that the king's intention was only to prevent inconveniences which arose from the bringing of every cause from the most distant parts of the kingdom into Westminster Hall. But the consequence of this measure was the putting of all the northern counties out of the protection of ordinary law and subjecting them to an authority somewhat

1632

arbitrary. Some irregular acts of that council were this year complained of.

The Court of Star Chamber extended its authority; and it was cause of complaint that it encroached upon the jurisdiction of the other courts, imposing heavy fines and inflicting severe punishment beyond the usual course of justice. Sir David Foulis was fined £5,000 chiefly because he had dissuaded a friend from compounding with the commissioners of knighthood.

William Prynne, a barrister of Lincoln's Inn, had written an enormous quarto of a thousand pages which he called *Histriomastix*. Its professed purpose was to decry stage plays, comedies, interludes, music, and dancing, but the author likewise took occasion to declaim against hunting, public festivals, Christmas-keeping, bonfires, and maypoles. His zeal against all these levities, he wrote, was first moved by observing that plays sold better than the choicest sermons, and that they were frequently printed on finer paper than the Bible itself. Besides that, the players were often papists and desperately wicked; the playhouses, he affirmed, were Satan's chapels, and the playgoers little better than incarnate devils; and so many steps in a dance, so many paces to hell. The chief crime of Nero he represented to have been his frequenting and acting of plays, and those who nobly conspired his death were principally moved to it, as he affirmed, by their indignation at that enormity. The rest of his thousand pages were of a like strain. He had obtained a license from Archbishop Abbot's chaplain, yet he was indicted in the Star Chamber as a libeler. It was thought somewhat hard that general invectives against plays would be interpreted into satires against the king and queen merely because they frequented these amusements and because the queen sometimes acted a part in pastorals and interludes which were represented at court. The author, it must be granted, had in plainer terms blamed the hierarchy, the ceremonies, the innovations in religious worship, and the new superstitions introduced by Laud; and this, together with the obstinacy and petulance of his behavior before the Star Chamber, probably was the reason why his sentence was so severe. He was condemned to be expelled from the bar; to stand on the pillory in two places, Westminster and Cheapside; to lose both his ears, one in each place; to pay £5,000 fine to the king; and to be imprisoned for life.

This same Prynne was a great hero among the Puritans; and it was chiefly with an intention of mortifying that sect that he was condemned by the Star Chamber to so ignominious a punishment, though he was of an honorable profession. The thoroughgoing Puritans were distinguishable by the sourness and austerity of their manners and by their aversion to all pleasure and society. To inspire them with better humor, both for their own sake and that of the public, was certainly a laudable intention in the court; but whether pillories, fines, and prisons were proper expedients for that purpose may admit of some question.

Another expedient which the king tried in order to infuse cheerfulness into the national devotion was not much more successful. He renewed his father's edict for allowing sports and recreations on Sunday to those who attended public worship, and he ordered his proclamation for that purpose to be publicly read by the clergy after divine service. Those who were puritanically affected refused obedience and were punished by suspension or deprivation [removal from their positions]. The differences between the sects were sufficiently great before; it was unnecessary to widen them further by these inventions.

Some encouragement and protection which the king and the bishops gave to wakes, church-ales, bride-ales, and other cheerful festivals of the common people were the objects of like scandal to the Puritans.

This year Charles made a journey to Scotland, attended by the court, in order to hold a Parliament there and to pass through the ceremony of his coronation, on June 12. The nobility and gentry of both kingdoms rivaled each other in expressing all duty and respect to the king and in showing mutual friendship and regard to each other. No one could have suspected from exterior appearances that such dreadful scenes were approaching.

Besides obtaining some supply, one chief article of business (for it deserves the name) which the king transacted in this Parliament was to procure authority for ordering the garments of clergymen. The act did not pass without opposition and difficulty. The dreadful surplice was before men's eyes; and they feared, with some reason, that under sanction of this law it would soon be introduced among them. Though the king believed that his prerogative entitled him to a power, in general, of directing whatever belonged to the exterior government of the church, this was deemed a matter of too great importance to be ordered without the sanction of a particular statute.

Immediately after the king's return to England, he heard of the death of Abbot, the archbishop of Canterbury. Without delay, he conferred that dignity on his favorite, Laud, who by this accession of authority was now enabled to maintain ecclesiastical discipline with greater rigor and to aggravate the general discontent of the nation.

Laud obtained the bishopric of London for his friend William Juxon; and about a year after the death of Sir Richard Weston, who had been created Earl of Portland, he had interest enough to engage the king to make that prelate high treasurer. Juxon was a person of great integrity, mildness, and humanity, and endowed with a good understanding. Yet this last promotion gave general offense. His birth and rank were deemed too obscure for a man raised to one of the highest offices of the Crown. And the clergy, it was thought, were already too much elevated by former instances of the king's attachment to them and had no need of this further encouragement to assume dominion over the laity. The Puritans likewise were much dissatisfied with Juxon, notwithstanding his eminent virtues, because he was a lover of profane field sports and hunting.

Ship money

Ship money was now introduced. The first writs of this kind had been directed to seaport towns only. But ship money was at this time levied on the whole kingdom, and each county was rated at a particular sum, which was afterwards assessed upon individuals. The amount of the whole tax was very moderate, little exceeding £200,000. It was levied upon the people with equality. The money was entirely expended on the navy, to the great honor and advantage of the kingdom. As England had no standing army, while all the other powers of Europe were strongly armed, a fleet seemed absolutely necessary for its security. And it was obvious that a navy must be built and equipped at leisure, during peace; it could not possibly be fitted out on a sudden emergency. Yet all these considerations could not reconcile the people to the imposition. It was entirely arbitrary; by the same right, any other tax might be imposed. And men thought that a powerful fleet, though very desirable both for the credit and safety of the kingdom, was an unequal recompense for their liberties, which they feared were thus sacrificed to the obtaining of it.

England, it must be granted, was in this respect unhappy in its present situation: the king entertained a very different idea of the constitution from that which began, in general, to prevail among his subjects. He did not regard national privileges as so sacred and inviolable that nothing but the most extreme necessity could justify an infringement of them. He considered himself as the supreme magistrate, to

1634

whose care heaven, by his birthright, had committed his people, whose duty it was to provide for their security and happiness, and who was vested with ample discretionary powers for that salutary purpose. If the observance of ancient laws and customs was consistent with the present convenience of government, he thought himself obliged to comply with that rule as the easiest and the safest course, procuring the most prompt and willing obedience. But when a change of circumstances—especially if derived from the obstinacy of the people—required a new plan of administration, he thought that national privileges must yield to supreme power; nor could any order of the state oppose any right to the will of the sovereign directed to the good of the public. It would be rash to affirm that these principles of government were derived from the uniform tenor of the English laws. The fluctuating nature of the constitution, the impatient humor of the people, and the variety of events had doubtless produced exceptions and contradictions in different ages. These observations alone may be established on both sides: that the appearances were sufficiently strong in favor of the king to provide a defense of his following such maxims, and that public liberty must be so precarious under this exorbitant prerogative as to render the people's opposition to it not only excusable but laudable.

Some laws had been enacted during the reign of Henry VII against depopulation, or the converting of arable lands into pasture. By a decree of the Star Chamber, Sir Anthony Roper was fined £4,000 for an offense of that nature. This severe sentence was intended to terrify others into composition, and more than £30,000 was levied by that expedient. Like compositions—or in default of them, heavy fines—were required for encroachments on the king's forests, whose bounds, by decrees deemed arbitrary, were extended much beyond what was usual. The bounds of one forest, that of Rockingham, were increased from six miles to sixty. The same refractory humor which made the people refuse voluntary supplies to the king disposed them, with better reason, to murmur against these irregular methods of taxation.

Morley was fined £10,000 for reviling, challenging, and striking, in the court of Whitehall, Sir George Theobald, one of the king's servants. This fine was thought exorbitant; but whether it was compounded, as was usual in fines imposed by the Star Chamber, we are not informed.

Allison had reported that the archbishop of York had incurred the king's displeasure by asking for a limited toleration for the Catholics and an allowance to build some churches for the exercise of their religion. For this slander against the archbishop, he was condemned in the Star Chamber to be fined £1,000, to be committed to prison, to be bound to his good behavior during life, to be whipped, and to be set on the pillory at Westminster and in three other towns in England. Robins, who had been an accomplice in the guilt, was condemned by a sentence equally severe. Such events are rather to be considered as rare and detached incidents, collected by the severe scrutiny of historians, than as proofs of the prevailing spirit of the king's administration, which seems to have been more gentle and equitable than that of most of his predecessors. There were on the whole only five or six such instances of rigor during the course of the fifteen years which elapsed before the meeting of the Long Parliament. And it is also certain that scandal against the great, though seldom prosecuted at present, is, however, in the eye of the law a great crime and subjects the offender to very heavy penalties.

There are other instances of the high respect paid to the nobility and to the great in that age, when the powers of monarchy, though disputed, still maintained themselves in their pristine vigor. Clarendon tells us a pleasant incident to this purpose: A boatman in service to a man of quality squabbled with a citizen about his fare, showed his badge—the crest of his master, which happened to be a swan—and from that insisted on better treatment from the citizen. But the other replied carelessly that he did not trouble his head about that goose. For this offense he was summoned before the Marshal's Court, was fined as having contemptuously defamed the nobleman's crest by calling the swan a goose, and was, in effect, reduced to beggary.

Sir Richard Grenville had thought himself ill used by the Earl of Suffolk in a lawsuit, and he was accused before the Star Chamber of having said of that nobleman that he was a base lord. The evidence against him was somewhat lame; yet for this slight offense, insufficiently proved, he was condemned to pay a fine of £8,000, one half to the earl, the other to the king.

Sir George Markham, following a chase where Lord Darcy's huntsman was exercising his hounds, kept closer to the dogs than was thought proper by the huntsman, who, besides other rudeness, gave him foul language, which Sir George returned with a stroke of his whip. The fellow threatened to complain to his master. The knight replied that if his master would justify such insolence, he would serve him in the same manner, or words to that effect. Sir George was summoned before the Star Chamber and fined £10,000. "So fine a thing was it in those days to be a lord!" was Lord Lansdowne's natural reflection in relating this incident. The people, in vindicating their liberties from the authority of the Crown, also threw off the yoke of the nobility. It is proper to note that this last incident happened early in the reign of James. The present practice of the Star Chamber was far from being an innovation, though the present dispositions of the people made them complain more at this servitude.

Charles had imitated the example of Elizabeth and James and had issued proclamations forbidding the land- | 1635 | ed gentlemen and the nobility to live idly in London and ordering them to retire to their country seats. For disobedience to this edict, many were indicted by the attorney general and were fined in the Star Chamber. This occasioned discontents, and the sentences were complained of as illegal. But if proclamations had authority, of which nobody claimed to doubt, must they not be put in execution? In no instance, I must confess, does it more manifestly appear what confused and uncertain ideas were entertained concerning the English constitution during that age.

Ray, having exported fuller's earth contrary to the king's proclamation, was condemned in the Star Chamber to the pillory and a fine of £2,000. Like fines were levied on Terry, Eman, and others for disobeying a proclamation which forbade the exportation of gold. In order to account for the subsequent convulsions, even these incidents are not to be overlooked as frivolous or contemptible. Such severities were later magnified into the greatest enormities.

There remains a proclamation of this year prohibiting hackney coaches from standing in the street. We are told that there were not more than twenty coaches of that kind in London. There are at present nearly eight hundred.

The effects of ship money now began to appear. A formidable fleet of sixty sail, the greatest that England had | 1636 | ever known, was equipped under the Earl of Northumberland, who had orders to attack the herring busses of the Dutch, which fished in what were called the British seas. The Dutch were content to pay £30,000 for a license during this year. They openly denied, however, the claim of dominion in the seas beyond the firths, bays, and shores, and it may be questioned whether the laws of nations warrant any further pretensions.

This year the king, with the assistance of the emperor of Morocco, sent a squadron against Salé and destroyed that den of pirates, by whom the English commerce and even the English coasts had long been infested.

Burton, a divine, and Bastwick, a physician, were tried in the Star Chamber for seditious and schismatic libels $\boxed{1637}$ and were condemned to the same punishment that had been inflicted on Prynne. Prynne himself was tried for a new offense, and together with another fine of £5,000, was condemned to lose what remained of his ears. Not only had these writers attacked the ceremonies, rites, and government of the church with great severity, and even an intemperate zeal; the very answers which they gave to the court were so full of contumacy and of invectives against the prelates that no lawyer could be prevailed on to take their cases. The rigors which they underwent, however, being so unworthy to men of their professions, gave general offense; and the patience, or rather alacrity, with which they suffered increased still further the indignation of the public. The severity of the Star Chamber, which was generally ascribed to Laud's passionate disposition, was perhaps in itself somewhat blamable; but it will naturally appear enormous to us, who enjoy in the utmost latitude that liberty of the press which is deemed so necessary in every monarchy confined by strict legal limitations. But as these limitations were not regularly fixed during the age of Charles nor at any time before, so was this liberty totally unknown; and it was generally deemed, as was religious toleration, incompatible with all good government. No age or nation among the moderns had ever set an example of such an indulgence, and it seems unreasonable to judge of the measures embraced during one period by the maxims which prevail in another.

Burton, in his book in which he complained of innovations, mentioned among others that a certain Wednesday had been appointed for a fast, and that the fast was ordered to be celebrated without any sermons. He claimed that the intention of that novelty was, by the example of a fast without sermons, to suppress all the Wednesday lectures in London. It is observable that the church of Rome and that of England, being both of them lovers of form, ceremony, and order, are more friends to prayer than preaching; while the Puritanical sectaries find that the latter method of address, being directed to a numerous audience present and visible, is more inflaming and animating, and so they have always regarded it as the chief part of divine service. Such circumstances, though minute, it may not be improper to transmit to posterity, so that those who are curious of tracing the history of the human mind may observe how far its several singularities coincide in different ages.

Certain zealots had erected themselves into a society for buying in of impropriations [property interests in streams of tithe income, owned by laymen] and transferring them to the church, and great sums of money had been bequeathed to the society for these purposes. But it was soon observed that the only use which they made of their funds was to establish, in all the considerable churches, lecturers—men who, without being subjected to episcopal authority, employed themselves entirely in preaching and spreading the fire of Puritanism. Laud took care, by a decree which was passed in the Court of Exchequer and which was much complained of, to abolish this society and to stop their progress. It was, however, still observed that throughout England the lecturers were, all of them, puritanically affected, and from them the clergymen, who contented themselves with reading prayers and homilies to the people, commonly received the reproachful appellation of "dumb dogs."

The Puritans, restrained in England, shipped themselves off for America and laid there the foundations of a government which possessed all the liberty, both civil and religious, of which they found themselves bereaved in their native country. But their enemies, unwilling that they might anywhere enjoy ease and contentment, and perhaps dreading the dangerous consequences of so disaffected a colony, prevailed on the king to issue a proclamation barring these devotees access even into those inhospitable deserts. Eight ships lying in the Thames and ready to sail were detained by order of the Council; and in these were embarked Sir Arthur Haselrig, John Hampden, John Pym, and Oliver Cromwell, who had resolved to abandon their native country forever and fly to the other extremity of the globe, where they might enjoy lectures and discourses of any length or form which pleased them. The king later had full leisure to repent this exercise of his authority.

The bishop of Norwich, by rigorously insisting on uniformity, had banished many industrious tradesmen from that city and chased them into Holland. The Dutch began to be more intent on commerce than on orthodoxy and thought that the knowledge of useful arts and obedience to the laws formed a good citizen, though attended with errors in subjects where it is not allowable for human nature to expect any positive truth or certainty.

Complaints about this time were made that the Petition of Right was in some instances violated, and that bail or release had been refused to Jennings, Pargiter, and Danvers upon their commitment by the king and Council.

John Williams, bishop of Lincoln, a man of spirit and learning, a popular prelate who had been lord keeper, was fined £10,000 by the Star Chamber, committed to the Tower during the king's pleasure, and suspended from his office. This severe sentence was founded on frivolous pretenses and was more ascribed to Laud's vengeance than to any guilt of the bishop. Laud had owed his first promotion to the good offices of Williams with King James. But so implacable was the haughty Laud that he raised up a new prosecution against Williams on the strangest pretense imaginable. In order to levy the fine above mentioned, some officers had been sent to seize all the furniture and books of his episcopal palace of Lincoln; and in rummaging through the house, they found in a corner some neglected letters which had been thrown aside as useless. These letters were written by one Osbaldeston, a schoolmaster, and were addressed to Williams. Mention was there made of "a little great man"; and in another passage, the same person was denominated "a little urchin." By inferences and constructions, these epithets were applied to Laud; and on no better foundation, Williams was tried anew for having received scandalous letters and not revealing that private correspondence. Another fine of £8,000 was levied on him for this offense. Osbaldeston was likewise brought to trial and condemned to pay a fine of £5,000 and to have his ears nailed to the pillory before his own school. He saved himself by flight and left a note in his study in which he said, "that he was gone beyond Canterbury."

These prosecutions of Williams seem to have been the most iniquitous measure pursued by the court during the time that the use of Parliaments was suspended. Williams had been indebted for all his fortune to the favor of James; but having quarreled first with Buckingham, then with Laud, he threw himself into the country party and with great firmness and vigor opposed all the measures of the king. For a creature of the court to become its obstinate enemy, a bishop to favor Puritans: these circumstances excited indignation and engaged the ministers into those severe measures. Not to mention what some writers relate: that before the sentence was pronounced against him, Williams was offered a pardon upon his submission, which he refused to make. The court was apt to think that so refractory a spirit must by any expedient be broken and subdued.

In a former trial which Williams underwent (for these were not the first), there was mentioned in court a story which, as it reveals the nature of the parties, may be worth relating. Sir John Lambe was urging Williams to prosecute the Puritans, and the prelate asked what sort of people these same Puritans were. Sir John replied, "That to the world they seemed to be such as would not swear, whore, or be drunk; but they would lie, cozen [cheat], and deceive. That they would frequently hear two sermons a day, and repeat them too, and that sometimes they would fast all day long." This portrait must be conceived to be satirical, yet it may be allowed that that sect was more averse to such irregularities as proceed from the excess of gaiety and pleasure than to those enormities which are the most destructive of society. The former were opposite to the very genius and spirit of their religion, the latter were only a transgression of its precepts. And it was not difficult for a gloomy enthusiast to convince himself that a strict observance of the one would atone for any violation of the other.

In 1632, the treasurer, the Earl of Portland, had insisted to the vintners that they should submit to a tax of a penny a quart upon all the wine which they retailed. But they rejected the demand. In order to punish them, a decree suddenly passed in the Star Chamber, without much inquiry or examination, prohibiting them to sell or dress food products in their houses. Two years later, they were questioned for the breach of this decree; and in order to avoid punishment, they agreed to lend the king £6,000. Being threatened during the subsequent years with fines and prosecutions, they at last compounded the matter and submitted to pay half of that duty which was at first demanded of them. It required little foresight to perceive that the king's right of issuing proclamations must, if prosecuted, result in a power of taxation.

John Lilburne was accused before the Star Chamber of publishing and dispersing seditious pamphlets. He was ordered to be examined; but he refused to take the oath, usual in that court, that he would answer interrogatories even though they might lead him to accuse himself. For this contempt, as it was interpreted, he was condemned to be whipped, pilloried, and imprisoned. While he was whipped at the cart and stood on the pillory, he harangued the populace and declaimed violently against the tyranny of bishops. From his pockets also he scattered pamphlets, said to be seditious because they attacked the hierarchy. The Star Chamber, which was sitting at that very time, ordered him immediately to be gagged. He ceased not, however, though both gagged and pilloried, to stamp with his foot and gesticulate, in order to show the people that if he had it in his power he would still harangue them. This behavior gave fresh provocation to the Star Chamber; and they condemned him to be imprisoned in a dungeon and to be loaded with irons. It was found difficult to break the spirits of men who placed both their honor and their conscience in suffering.

The indignation of the church appeared in another instance less tragic. Archy, the king's fool, who by his office had the privilege of jesting on his master and the whole court, happened unluckily to try his wit upon Laud, who was too sacred a person to be played with. News having arrived from Scotland of the first commotions excited by the liturgy, Archy, seeing the primate pass by, called to him, "Who's fool now, my lord?" For this offense Archy was ordered by sentence of the Council to have his coat pulled over his head and to be dismissed from the king's service.

Here is another instance of that rigorous subjection in which all men were held by Laud. Some young gentlemen of Lincoln's Inn, heated by their cups, having drunk confusion [ruin] to the archbishop, were at his instigation cited before the Star Chamber. They applied to the Earl of Dorset for protection. "Who bears witness against you?" asked Dorset. "One of the drawers," they said. "Where did he stand when you were supposed to drink this health?" added the earl. "He was at the door," they replied, "going out of the room." "Tush!" cried he, "the drawer was mistaken: you drank confusion to the archbishop of Canterbury's enemies, and the fellow was gone before you pronounced the last word." This hint supplied the young gentlemen with a new method of defense; and the modesty of their carriage—Dorset having advised them to behave with great humility and great submission to the primate—the ingenuity of their apology [excuse], and the patronage of that noble lord saved them from any severer punishment than a reproof and admonition, with which they were dismissed.

Trial of Hampden

This year John Hampden, by his spirit and courage, acquired universal popularity throughout the nation and has merited great renown with posterity for the bold stand which he made in defense of the laws and liberties of his country. After the imposing of ship money, Charles, in order to discourage all opposition, had proposed this question to the judges: "Whether, in a case of necessity, for the defense of the kingdom, he might not impose this taxation; and whether he were not sole judge of the necessity." These guardians of law and liberty replied with great complaisance, "That in a case of necessity he might impose that taxation, and that he was sole judge of the necessity." Hampden had been rated at twenty shillings for an estate which he possessed in the county of Buckingham. Yet notwithstanding this declared opinion of the judges, notwithstanding the great power and sometimes rigorous maxims of the Crown, notwithstanding the small prospect of relief from Parliament, he resolved to stand a legal prosecution and expose himself to all the indignation of the court rather than tamely submit to so illegal an imposition. The case was argued for twelve days in the Exchequer chamber before all the judges of England, and the nation regarded with the utmost anxiety every circumstance of this celebrated trial. The outcome was easily foreseen. But the principles and reasonings and behavior of the parties engaged in the trial were much canvassed and inquired into, and nothing could equal the favor paid to the one side except the hatred which attended the other.

It was urged by Hampden's counsel and by his partisans in the nation that the plea of necessity was in vain introduced into a trial of law, since it was the nature of necessity to abolish all law and by irresistible violence to dissolve all the weaker and more artificial ties of human society. Not only the prince is exempted from the ordinary rules of administration in cases of extreme distress; all orders of men are then leveled, and any individual may consult the public safety by any expedient which his situation enables him to employ. But an ordinary danger or difficulty, much less a necessity which is merely fictitious and pretended, is not sufficient to produce an effect so violent and so hazardous to every community. Where the peril is urgent and extreme, it will be palpable to every member of the society; and though all ancient rules of government are in that case abrogated, men will readily of their own accord submit to that irregular authority which is exerted for their preservation. But what is there in common between such suppositions and the present condition of the nation? England enjoys a profound peace with all its neighbors. And what is more, all its neighbors are engaged in furious and bloody wars among themselves; they further assure its tranquility by their mutual enmities. The very writs themselves which are issued for the levying of ship money contradict the supposition of necessity and pretend [claim] only that the seas are infested with pirates, a slight and temporary inconvenience which may well await a legal supply from Parliament. The writs likewise allow several months for equipping the ships, which proves a very calm and deliberate species of necessity, and one that admits of delay much beyond the forty days requisite for summoning that assembly. It is strange too that an extreme necessity, which is always apparent and usually comes to a sudden crisis, would now have continued without interruption for nearly four years and would have remained invisible to the whole kingdom during so long a time. And as to the pretension that the king is sole judge of the necessity, what is this but to subject all the privileges of the nation to his arbitrary will and pleasure? To expect that the public will be convinced by such reasoning must aggravate the general indignation by adding to violence against men's persons and their property so cruel a mockery of their understanding.

In vain are precedents of ancient writs produced. These writs, when examined, are only found to require the seaports—sometimes at their own charge, sometimes at the charge of the counties—to send their ships for the defense of the nation. Even the prerogative which empowered the Crown to issue such writs is abolished, and its exercise almost entirely discontinued from the time of Edward III; and all the authority which remained or was afterwards exercised was to press ships into the public service, to be paid for by the public. How wide are these precedents from a power of obliging the people at their own charge to build new ships, to provision and pay them, for the public— nay, to furnish money to the Crown for that purpose? What security exists either against the further extension of this claim or against diverting to other purposes the public money so levied? The plea of necessity would warrant any other taxation as much as that of ship money; wherever any difficulty shall occur, the administration, instead of endeavoring to elude or overcome it by gentle and prudent measures, will instantly represent it as a reason for infringing all ancient laws and institutions. And if such maxims and such practices prevail, what has become of national liberty? What authority is left to the Great Charter, to the statutes, and to the very Petition of Right, which in the present reign had been so solemnly enacted by the concurrence of the whole legislature?

The defenseless condition of the kingdom while unprovided with a navy; the inability of the king to equip and maintain one from his established revenues, employed with the utmost care and frugality; the impossibility of obtaining on reasonable terms any voluntary supply from Parliament: all these are reasons of state, not topics of law. If these reasons appear to the king so urgent as to dispense with the legal rules of government, let him enforce his edicts by his Court of Star Chamber, the proper instrument of irregular and absolute power, not prostitute the character of his judges by a decree which is not, and cannot possibly be, legal. By this means, the boundaries between ordinary law and extraordinary exertions of prerogative will at least be kept more distinct, and men will know that the national constitution is only suspended during a present and difficult emergency but has not undergone a total and fundamental alteration.

Notwithstanding these reasons, the prejudiced judges, four excepted, gave sentence in favor of the Crown. By the trial, however, Hampden obtained the end for which he had so generously sacrificed his safety and his quiet: the people were roused from their lethargy and became aware of the danger to which their liberties were exposed. These national questions were canvassed in every company; and the more they were examined, the more manifestly did it appear to many that liberty was totally subverted and an unusual and arbitrary authority exercised over the kingdom. Slavish principles, they said, concur with illegal practices; ecclesiastical tyranny gives aid to civil usurpation; iniquitous taxes are supported by arbitrary punishments; and all the privileges of the nation, transmitted through so many ages, secured by so many laws, and purchased by the blood of so many heroes and patriots, now lie prostrate at the feet of the monarch. What though public peace and national industry increased the commerce and opulence of the kingdom? This advantage was temporary and was due not to any encouragement given by the Crown but only to the spirit of the English, the remains of their ancient freedom. What though the personal character of the king, amidst all his misguided counsels, might merit indulgence or even praise? He was but one man; and the privileges of the people, the inheritance of millions, were too valuable to be sacrificed to his prejudices and mistakes. Such, or more severe, were the sentiments promoted by a great party in the nation. No excuse on the king's part, no alleviation, however reasonable, could be hearkened to or admitted. And to redress these grievances, a Parliament was impatiently longed for; or some other incident, however calamitous, that might secure the people against those oppressions which they felt—or the greater ills which they feared—from the combined encroachments of church and state.

CHAPTER 53
1637 – 1640

*Discontents in Scotland – Introduction of the canons and
liturgy – A tumult at Edinburgh – The Covenant –
A General Assembly – Episcopacy abolished – War –
A pacification – Renewal of the war – Fourth English
Parliament – Dissolution – Discontents in England – Rout
at Newburn – Treaty at Ripon – Great Council of the Peers*

THE grievances under which the English labored, when considered
in themselves and without regard to the constitution, scarcely deserve the name. They were neither burdensome on the people's prop-
erties nor in any way shocking to the natural humanity of mankind.
Even the imposition of ship money, independent of the consequences, was a great and evident advantage to the public by the judicious use
which the king made of the money levied by that expedient. And
though it was justly feared that such precedents, if patiently submitted
to, would end in a total disuse of Parliaments and in the establishment of arbitrary authority, Charles dreaded no opposition from the
people, who are not commonly much affected by future consequences
and require some striking motive to engage them in a resistance of established government. All ecclesiastical affairs were settled by law and
uninterrupted precedent, and the church had become a considerable
barrier to the power, both legal and illegal, of the Crown. Peace too,
industry, commerce, opulence; indeed, even justice and lenity of administration, notwithstanding some very few exceptions: all these were
enjoyed by the people, and every other blessing of government except
liberty, or rather the present exercise of liberty and its proper security.
It seemed probable, therefore, that affairs might long have continued

on the same footing in England, had it not been for the proximity of Scotland, a country more turbulent and less disposed to submission and obedience. It was there that the commotions first arose, and it is therefore time for us to return there and to give an account of the state of affairs in that kingdom.

Discontents in Scotland

Though the pacific and not unskillful government of James and the great authority which he had acquired had much allayed the feuds among the great families of Scotland and had established law and order throughout the kingdom, the Scottish nobility were still possessed of the chief power and influence over the people. Their property was extensive, their hereditary jurisdictions and the feudal tenures increased their authority, and the attachment of the gentry to the heads of families established a kind of voluntary servitude under the chieftains. Besides that long absence had much loosened the king's connections with the nobility, who resided chiefly at their country seats, they were in general at this time much disgusted with the court, though from slight causes. Charles, from the natural piety or superstition of his temper, was extremely attached to the ecclesiastics. And as it is natural for men to persuade themselves that their interest coincides with their inclination, he had established it as a fixed maxim of policy to increase the power and authority of that order. The prelates, he thought, established regularity and discipline among the clergy; the clergy inculcated obedience and loyalty among the people. And as that rank of men had no separate authority and no dependence but on the Crown, the royal power, it would seem, might with the greater safety be entrusted in their hands. Many of the prelates, therefore, were raised to the chief dignities of the state. John Spottiswoode, archbishop of St. Andrews, was created chancellor of Scotland, nine of the bishops were privy councilors, the bishop of Ross rose to the office of treasurer, some of the prelates possessed places in the Exchequer, and it was even endeavored to revive the first institution of the College of Justice and to share equally between the clergy and laity the whole judicial authority. These advantages possessed by the church, and which the bishops did not always enjoy with suitable modesty, disgusted the haughty nobility, who, deeming themselves much superior in rank and quality to this new order of men, were displeased to find themselves inferior in power and influence. Interest joined itself to ambition and begat a jealousy [suspicion] that the episcopal sees, which at

the Reformation had been pillaged by the nobles, would again be enriched at the expense of that order. By a most useful and beneficial
law, the impropriations had already been ravished from the great men,
competent salaries had been assigned to the impoverished clergy from
the tithes of each parish, and the proprietor of the land was empowered to purchase what remained at a low valuation. The king likewise,
warranted by ancient law and practice, had declared for a general resumption of all Crown lands alienated by his predecessors; and
though he took no step towards the execution of this project, the very
pretension to such power had excited jealousy and discontent.

Notwithstanding the tender regard which Charles bore to the
whole church, he had been able in Scotland to acquire only the affection of the superior rank among the clergy. The ministers in general
equaled, if not exceeded, the nobility in their prejudices against the
court, against the prelates, and against episcopal authority. Though
the establishment of the hierarchy might seem advantageous to the inferior clergy, both as it erected dignities to which all of them might aspire and as it bestowed a luster on the whole body and allured men of
family into it, these views had no influence on the Scottish ecclesiastics. In the present disposition of men's minds, there was another circumstance which drew consideration and counterbalanced power and
riches, the usual foundations of distinction among men: the fervor of
piety and the rhetoric, however barbarous, of religious lectures and
discourses. Checked by the prelates in the license of preaching, the
clergy regarded episcopal jurisdiction both as a tyranny and a usurpation, and they maintained that a parity among ecclesiastics was a divine privilege which no human law could alter or infringe. While such
ideas prevailed, the most moderate exercise of authority would have
given disgust; much more so did that extensive power which the king's
indulgence encouraged the prelates to assume. The jurisdiction of
presbyteries, synods, and other democratic courts was, in effect, abolished by the bishops, and the General Assembly itself had not been
summoned for several years. A new oath was arbitrarily imposed on
new clergy, by which they swore to observe the Articles of Perth and
submit to the liturgy and canons. And in a word, the whole system of
church government had been changed by means of the innovations
introduced by James and Charles during a course of thirty years.

The people, under the influence of the nobility and clergy, could
not fail to partake of the discontents which prevailed among these two
orders; and where real grounds of complaint were lacking, they greedi-

ly laid hold of imaginary ones. The same horror against popery with which the English Puritans were possessed was observable among the populace in Scotland; and among these, being more uncultivated and uncivilized, it seemed rather to be inflamed into a higher degree of ferocity. The spirit of religion which prevailed in the court and among the prelates was of an opposite nature, and having some affinity to the Romish worship, led them to mollify as much as possible these severe prejudices and to speak of the Catholics in more charitable language and with more reconciling expressions. A panic fear of popery was easily raised from this foundation; and every new ceremony or ornament introduced into divine service was part of that great mystery of iniquity which was to overspread the nation from the encouragement of the king and the bishops. The few innovations which James had made were considered as preparations for this grand design; and the further alterations attempted by Charles were represented as a plain declaration of his intentions. Through the whole course of this reign, nothing had more fatal influence in both kingdoms than this groundless apprehension, which with so much industry was propagated and with so much credulity was embraced by all ranks of men.

Amidst these dangerous complaints and terrors of religious innovation, the civil and ecclesiastical liberties of the nation were imagined, and with some reason, not to be altogether free from invasion.

The establishment of the High Commission by James without any authority of law seemed a considerable encroachment of the Crown; it erected the most dangerous and arbitrary of all courts by a method equally dangerous and arbitrary. All the steps towards the settlement of episcopacy had indeed been taken with consent of Parliament: the Articles of Perth were confirmed in 1621, and the king had obtained a general ratification of every ecclesiastical establishment in 1633. But these laws had less authority with the nation as they were known to have passed contrary to the sentiments even of those who voted for them and were in reality extorted by the authority and importunity of the sovereign. The means, however, which both James and Charles had employed in order to influence the Parliament were entirely regular, and no reasonable pretense had been afforded for representing these laws as null or invalid.

But there prevailed among the greater part of the nation another principle of the most important and most dangerous nature, and one which, if admitted, destroyed entirely the validity of all such statutes. The ecclesiastical authority was supposed totally independent of the civil; and no act of Parliament, nothing but the consent of the church itself, was represented as sufficient ground for the introduction of any change in religious worship or discipline. And though James had obtained the vote of assemblies for receiving episcopacy and his new rites, it must be confessed that such irregularities had prevailed in constituting these ecclesiastical courts, and such violence in conducting them, that there were some grounds for denying the authority of all their acts. Charles, aware that an extorted consent attended with such odious circumstances would be prejudicial to his measures, instead had wholly laid aside the use of assemblies; he was resolved to govern the church, in conjunction with the bishops, by an authority to which he thought himself fully entitled and which he believed inherent in the Crown.

The king's great aim was to complete the work so happily begun by his father: to establish discipline upon a regular system of canons, to introduce a liturgy into public worship, and to render the ecclesiastical government of all his kingdoms regular and uniform. Some views of policy might move him to this undertaking, but his chief motives were derived from principles of zeal and conscience.

Introduction of the canons and liturgy

The canons for establishing ecclesiastical jurisdiction were promulgated in 1635 and were received by the nation without much apparent opposition, yet with great inward apprehension and discontent. Men felt displeasure at seeing the canons highly exalt the royal authority and represent it as absolute and uncontrollable. They saw these speculative principles reduced to practice and a whole body of ecclesiastical laws established without any previous consent either of church or state. They dreaded lest, by a parity of reason, like arbitrary authority from like pretenses and principles would be assumed in civil matters. They noticed that the delicate boundaries which separate church and state were already passed, and many civil ordinances established by the canons under color of ecclesiastical institutions. And they were apt to deride the negligence with which these important edicts had been compiled when they found that the new liturgy, or service book, was everywhere required, under severe penalties, to be used by them though it had not yet been composed or published. It was, however, soon expected; and in the reception of it—as the people are always most affected by what is external and exposed to the senses—it was thought that the chief difficulty would consist.

The liturgy which the king, from his own authority, imposed on Scotland was copied from that of England. But lest a servile imitation might shock the pride of his ancient kingdom, a few alterations, in order to save appearances, were made in it; and in that shape it was transmitted to the bishops at Edinburgh. But the Scots had universally entertained a notion that though riches and worldly glory had been shared out to them with a sparing hand, they could boast of spiritual treasures more abundant and more genuine than were enjoyed by any nation under heaven. Even their southern neighbors, they thought, though separated from Rome, still retained a great tincture of the primitive pollution; and their liturgy was represented as a species of mass, though with some less show and embroidery. Great prejudices, therefore, were entertained against it, even considered in itself; much more so when it was regarded as a preparation to introduce soon into Scotland all the abominations of popery. And as the very few alterations which distinguished the new liturgy from the English seemed to approach nearer to the Catholic doctrine of the real presence, this circumstance was deemed an undoubted confirmation of every suspicion with which the people were possessed.

A tumult at Edinburgh

Easter Day was by proclamation appointed for the first reading of the new service in Edinburgh. But in order to judge more surely of men's dispositions, the Council delayed the matter till July 23; and they even gave notice the Sunday before of their intention to commence the use of the new liturgy. As no considerable symptoms of discontent appeared, they thought that they might safely proceed in their purpose; and accordingly, in the Cathedral Church of St. Giles, the dean of Edinburgh, arrayed in his surplice, began the service, the bishop himself and many of the Privy Council being present. But no sooner had the dean opened the book than a multitude of the meanest sort, most of them women, clapping their hands, cursing, and crying out, "A pope, a pope! Antichrist! Stone him!" raised such a tumult that it was impossible to proceed with the service. The bishop, mounting the pulpit in order to appease the populace, had a stool thrown at him; the Council was insulted; and it was with difficulty that the magistrates were able—partly by authority, partly by force—to expel the rabble and to shut the doors against them. The tumult, however, still continued without; stones were thrown at the doors and windows; and when the service was ended, the bishop, going home, was attacked and narrowly escaped from the hands of the enraged multitude. In the afternoon the privy seal, because he carried the bishop in his coach, was so pelted with stones, hooted at with execrations, and pressed upon by the eager populace that if his servants with drawn swords had not kept them off, the bishop's life would have been exposed to the utmost danger.

Though it was violently suspected that the low populace, who alone appeared, had been instigated by some of higher condition, yet no proof of it could be produced; and everyone spoke with disapprobation of the licentiousness of the giddy multitude. It was not thought safe, however, to hazard a new insult by any new attempt to read the liturgy; and the people seemed for the time to be appeased and satisfied. But as it was known that the king still persevered in his intentions of imposing that mode of worship, men fortified themselves still further in their prejudices against it; and great multitudes traveled to Edinburgh in order to oppose the introduction of so hated a novelty. It was not long before they broke out in the most violent disorder. The bishop of Galloway was attacked in the streets and chased into the chamber where the Privy Council was sitting. The Council itself was besieged and violently attacked; the Town Council met with the same fate; and nothing could have saved the lives of all of them but their application to some popular lords, who protected them and dispersed the multitude. In this sedition the actors were of some better condition than in the former, though nobody of rank seemed as yet to favor them.

All men, however, began to unite and to encourage each other in opposition to the religious innovations introduced into the kingdom. Petitions to the Council were signed and presented by persons of the highest quality; the women took part, and as was usual, with violence; the clergy everywhere loudly declaimed against popery and the liturgy, which they represented as the same; the pulpits resounded with vehement invectives against antichrist; and the populace who first opposed the service was often compared to Balaam's ass, an animal in itself stupid and senseless but whose mouth had been opened by the Lord to the admiration of the whole world. In short, fanaticism mingled with faction, private interest with the spirit of liberty, and symptoms appeared on all hands of the most dangerous insurrection and disorder.

Archbishop Spottiswoode, the primate of Scotland, a man of wisdom and prudence who was all along averse to the introduction of the liturgy, represented to the king the state of the nation. The Earl of Traquair, the treasurer, set out for London in order to lay the matter more fully before him. Every circumstance, whether the condition of England or of Scotland were considered, should have engaged him to desist from so hazardous an attempt. Yet Charles was inflexible. In his whole conduct of this affair, there appear no marks of the good sense with which he was endowed; a lively instance of that species of character, so frequently to be met with, where there are sound faculties and judgment in every discourse and opinion but indiscretion and imprudence in many actions. Men's views of things are the result of their understanding alone; their conduct is regulated by their understanding, their temper, and their passions.

The Covenant

To so violent a combination of a whole kingdom, Charles had nothing to oppose but a proclamation, issued on

1638

February 19, in which he pardoned all past offenses and exhorted the people to be more obedient for the future and to submit peaceably to the use of the liturgy. This proclamation was instantly countered with a public protestation, presented by the Earl of Home and Lord Lindsay; and this was the first time that men of quality had appeared in any violent act of opposition. But this proved a crisis. The insurrection, which had been advancing by a gradual and slow progress, now blazed up at once. No disorder, however, attended it. On the contrary, a new order immediately took place. Four "Tables," as they were called, were formed in Edinburgh. One consisted of nobility, another of gentry, a third of ministers, a fourth of burgesses. The Table of gentry was divided into many subordinate Tables, according to their different counties. The whole authority of the kingdom was placed in the hands of the four Tables. Orders were issued by them and everywhere obeyed with the utmost regularity. And among the first acts of their government was the production of the Covenant.

This famous Covenant consisted first of a renunciation of popery, formerly signed by James in his youth, and composed of many invectives fitted to inflame the minds of men against their fellow creatures, whom heaven has enjoined them to cherish and to love. There followed a bond of union, by which the subscribers obliged themselves to resist religious innovations and to defend each other against all opposition whatsoever. And all this was purposed for the greater glory of God and the greater honor and advantage of their king and country.

The people, without distinction of rank or condition, of age or sex, flocked to the subscription of this Covenant. Few in their judgment disapproved of it, and still fewer dared openly condemn it. Most of the king's ministers and counselors themselves were seized by the general contagion. And none but rebels to God and traitors to their country, it was thought, would withdraw themselves from so salutary and so pious a combination.

The treacherous, the cruel, the unrelenting Philip, accompanied with all the terrors of a Spanish Inquisition, was scarcely opposed with more determined fury in the Low Countries during the preceding century than the mild, the humane Charles, attended with his inoffensive liturgy, was now opposed by the Scots.

The king began to fear the consequences. In June, he sent the Marquess of Hamilton as commissioner with authority to treat with the Covenanters. He required the Covenant to be renounced and recalled. And he thought that on his part he had made very satisfactory concessions when he offered to suspend the canons and the liturgy till they could be received in a fair and legal way and to reform the High Commission so that it would no longer give offense to his subjects. Such general declarations could not give full satisfaction to any, much less to those who carried their pretensions so much higher. The Covenanters found themselves seconded by the zeal of the whole Scottish nation. More than sixty thousand people were assembled in a tumultuous manner in Edinburgh and the neighborhood. Charles possessed no regular forces in either of his kingdoms. And the discontents in England, though not overt, were believed so violent that the king, it was thought, would find it very difficult to employ in such a cause the power of that kingdom. The more, therefore, the popular leaders in Scotland considered their situation, the less apprehension did they entertain of royal power, and the more rigorously did they insist on entire satisfaction. In answer to Hamilton's demand of renouncing the Covenant, they plainly told him that they would sooner renounce their baptism. And the clergy invited the commissioner himself to subscribe it by informing him, "With what peace and comfort it had filled the hearts of all God's people; what resolutions and beginnings of reformation of manners were sensibly [appreciably] perceived in all parts of the nation, above any measure they had ever before found or could have expected; how great glory the Lord had received thereby; and what confidence they had that God would make Scotland a blessed kingdom."

Hamilton returned to London; made another fruitless journey with new concessions to Edinburgh; returned again to London; and was immediately sent back, on September 17, with still more substantial concessions. The king was now willing to abolish entirely the canons, the liturgy, and the High Commission Court. He was even resolved to limit greatly the power of the bishops and was content if he could retain that order in the Church of Scotland on any terms. And to guarantee all these gracious offers, he gave Hamilton authority to summon first an Assembly, then a Parliament, where every national grievance might be redressed and remedied. These successive concessions of the king, which yet came still short of the rising demands of the malcontents, revealed his own weakness, encouraged their insolence, and gave no satisfaction. The offer, however, of an Assembly and a Parliament, in which they expected to be entirely masters, was willingly embraced by the Covenanters.

Charles, perceiving what advantage his enemies had reaped from their Covenant, resolved to have a covenant on his side; and he ordered one to be drawn up for that purpose. It consisted of the same violent renunciation of popery above mentioned; though the king did not approve of this, he thought it safest to adopt in order to remove all the suspicions entertained against him. As the Covenanters had been careful not to except the king in their bond of mutual defense against all opposition, Charles formed a bond which was annexed to this renunciation and which expressed the duty and loyalty of the subscribers to his majesty. But the Covenanters, perceiving that this new covenant was only meant to weaken and divide them, received it with the utmost scorn and detestation. And they proceeded without delay to model the future Assembly, from which such great achievements were expected.

A General Assembly

The genius of that religion which prevailed in Scotland, and which every day was covertly gaining ground in England, was far from inculcating deference and submission to the ecclesiastics, merely as such. Or rather, by nourishing in every individual the highest raptures and ecstasies of devotion, it consecrated every individual, in a sense, and in his own eyes bestowed a rank on him much superior to what forms and ceremonious institutions alone could confer. Though so much tumult was excited about religious worship and discipline, the clergy of Scotland were both poor and few in number; nor are they in general to be considered, at least in the beginning, as the ringleaders of the sedition which was raised on their account. On the contrary, several incidents caused the laity to fear a spirit of moderation in the clergy; and the former resolved to domineer entirely in the Assembly which was summoned and to hurry on the ecclesiastics by the same furious zeal with which they were themselves transported.

Before the establishment of prelacy, it had been usual for each presbytery to send to the Assembly, besides two or three ministers, one lay commissioner; and as all the boroughs and universities likewise sent commissioners, the lay members in that ecclesiastical court nearly equaled the ecclesiastics. James, apprehensive of zeal in the laity, had abolished the Assembly. Not only was this institution now revived by the Covenanters, they also introduced an innovation which served still further to reduce the clergy to subjection. By an edict of the Tables, whose authority was supreme, an elder from each parish was ordered to attend the presbytery and to give his vote in the choice both of the commissioners and ministers who would be deputized to the Assembly. As it was not usual for the ministers on the list of candidates to claim a vote, all the elections by that means fell into the hands of the laity. The most furious of all ranks were chosen. And the more to overawe the clergy, a new device was fallen upon: choosing for every commissioner four or five lay assessors, who, though they could have no vote, might yet interpose with their advice and authority in the Assembly.

Episcopacy abolished
The Assembly met at Glasgow. Besides a great concourse of the people, all the nobility and gentry of any family or interest were present, either as members, assessors, or spectators; and it was apparent that the resolutions taken by the Covenanters could here meet with no manner of opposition. A firm determination had been entered into of utterly abolishing episcopacy; as a preparation for it, there was laid before the presbytery of Edinburgh and solemnly read in all the churches of the kingdom an accusation against the bishops as guilty, all of them, of heresy, simony, bribery, perjury, cheating, incest, adultery, fornication, common swearing, drunkenness, gaming, breach of the Sabbath, and every other crime that had occurred to the accusers. The bishops sent a protest declining the authority of the Assembly; the commissioner too protested against the court as illegally constituted and elected, and in his majesty's name dissolved it. This measure was

foreseen and little regarded. The court still continued to sit and to finish their business. All the acts of Assembly since the accession of James to the Crown of England were, upon pretty reasonable grounds, declared null and invalid. The acts of Parliament which affected ecclesiastical affairs were supposed on that very account to have no manner of authority. And thus, episcopacy, the High Commission, the Articles of Perth, the canons, and the liturgy were abolished and declared unlawful, and the whole structure which James and Charles had long been rearing with so much care and policy fell at once to the ground. The Covenant likewise was ordered to be signed by everyone, under pain of excommunication.

The independence of the ecclesiastical from the civil power was the old presbyterian principle, which had been *1639* zealously adopted at the Reformation and which, though James and Charles had obliged the church publicly to disclaim it, had covertly been adhered to by all ranks of people. It was commonly asked whether Christ or the king were superior. And as the answer seemed obvious, it was inferred that the Assembly, being Christ's council, was superior in all spiritual matters to the Parliament, which was only the king's. But as the Covenanters were aware that this consequence, though it seemed to them irrefutable, would not be assented to by the king, it became necessary to maintain their religious tenets by military force and not to trust entirely to supernatural assistance, of which, however, they held themselves well assured. They cast their eyes on all sides, abroad and at home, to wherever they could expect any aid or support.

After France and Holland had entered into a league against Spain and framed a treaty of partition by which they were to conquer and to divide between them the Low Country provinces, England was invited to preserve a neutrality between the contending parties while the French and Dutch would attack the maritime towns of Flanders. But the king replied to d'Estrées, the French ambassador who opened the proposal, that he had a squadron ready and would cross the seas if necessary with an army of fifteen thousand men in order to prevent these projected conquests. This answer—which proves that Charles, though he expressed his mind with an imprudent candor, had at last acquired a just idea of national interest—irritated Cardinal Richelieu; and in revenge, that politic and enterprising minister carefully fomented the first commotions in Scotland and secretly supplied the

Covenanters with money and arms in order to encourage them in their opposition against their sovereign.

War

But the chief resource of the Scottish malcontents was in themselves and in their own vigor and abilities. No regular established commonwealth could take measures more just or execute them with greater promptness than did this tumultuous combination, inflamed with bigotry for religious trifles and faction without a reasonable object. Nearly the whole kingdom was engaged; and the men of greatest abilities soon acquired the ascendant, which their family influence enabled them to maintain. The Earl of Argyll, though he long seemed to temporize, had at last embraced the Covenant; and he became the chief leader of that party: a man equally supple and inflexible, cautious and determined, and entirely qualified to make a figure during a factious and turbulent period. The Earls of Rothes, Cassilis, Montrose, and Lothian, the Lords Lindsay, Loudoun, Yester, and Balmerino distinguished themselves in that party. Many Scottish officers had acquired reputation in the German wars, particularly under Gustavus Adolphus, and these were invited over to assist their country in its present necessity. The command was entrusted to Alexander Leslie, a soldier of experience and abilities. Forces were regularly enlisted and disciplined. Arms were commissioned and imported from foreign countries. A few castles which belonged to the king, being unprovided with victuals, ammunition, and garrisons, were soon seized. And the whole country being in the hands of the Covenanters, except a small part where the Marquess of Huntly still adhered to the king, it was in a very little time put in a tolerable posture of defense.

The fortifications of Leith were begun and carried on with great rapidity. Besides the inferior sort and those who labored for pay, incredible numbers of volunteers, even noblemen and gentlemen, put their hand to the work and deemed the most abject employment to be dignified by the sanctity of the cause. Women too of rank and condition, forgetting the delicacy of their sex and the decorum of their rank, were intermingled with the lowest rabble and carried on their shoulders the rubbish requisite for completing the fortifications.

We must not omit another auxiliary of the Covenanters, and no inconsiderable one: a prophetess, who was much followed and admired by all ranks of people. Her name was Michelson, a woman full of whimsies—partly hysterical, partly religious—and inflamed with a zealous concern for the ecclesiastical discipline of the Presbyterians. She spoke at certain times only, and often had interruptions of days and weeks. But when she began to renew her ecstasies, warning of the happy event was conveyed over the whole country, thousands crowded about her house, and every word which she uttered was received with veneration as the most sacred oracles. The Covenant was her perpetual theme. The true, genuine Covenant, she said, was ratified in heaven; the king's covenant was an invention of Satan; when she spoke of Christ, she usually gave him the name of the Covenanting Jesus. Rollo, a popular preacher and zealous Covenanter, was her great favorite, and he paid her no less veneration. Being desired by the spectators to pray with her and speak to her, he answered, "That he durst [dared] not, and that it would be ill manners in him to speak while his master, Christ, was speaking in her."

Charles had agreed to reduce episcopal authority so much that it would no longer have been of any service to support the Crown, and this sacrifice of his own interests he was willing to make in order to attain public peace and tranquility. But he could not consent to abolish entirely an order which he thought as essential to the being of a Christian church as his Scottish subjects deemed it incompatible with that sacred institution. If we would be impartial, we must either blame or excuse this narrowness of mind equally on both sides, and thereby anticipate by a little reflection that judgment which time, by introducing new subjects of controversy, will undoubtedly render quite familiar to posterity.

So great was Charles's aversion to violent and sanguinary measures and so strong his affection to his native kingdom that it is probable that the contest in his breast was nearly equal between these laudable passions and his attachment to the hierarchy. The latter affection, however, prevailed for the time and made him hasten those military preparations which he had projected for subduing the refractory spirit of the Scottish nation. By regular economy, he had not only paid all the debts contracted during the Spanish and French wars but had amassed a sum of £200,000, which he reserved for any sudden exigency. The queen had great influence with the Catholics, both from the sympathy of religion and from the favors and indulgences which she had been able to procure to them. She now employed her credit and persuaded them that it was reasonable to give large contributions as a mark of their duty to the king during this urgent necessity. A considerable supply was obtained by this means, to the great scandal of the

Puritans, who were offended at seeing the king on such good terms with the papists and complained that others would give what they themselves were disposed to refuse him.

Charles's fleet was formidable and well supplied. Having put five thousand land forces on board, he entrusted it to the Marquess of Hamilton, who had orders to sail to the Firth of Forth and to cause a diversion in the forces of the malcontents. An army was levied of nearly twenty thousand foot and more than three thousand horse and was put under the command of the Earl of Arundel, a nobleman of great family but celebrated neither for military nor political abilities. The Earl of Essex, a man of strict honor and extremely popular among the soldiery especially, was appointed lieutenant general. The Earl of Holland was general of the horse. The king himself joined the army on May 29, and he summoned all the peers of England to attend him. The whole had the appearance of a splendid court rather than of a military armament; and in this situation, carrying more show than real force with it, the camp arrived at Berwick.

The Scottish army was as numerous as that of the king but inferior in cavalry. The officers had more reputation and experience; and the soldiers, though undisciplined and ill armed, were animated as much by the national aversion to England and the dread of becoming a province to their old enemy as by an insurmountable fervor of religion. The pulpits had greatly assisted the officers in levying recruits and had thundered out anathemas against all those "who went not out to assist the Lord against the mighty." Yet so prudent were the leaders of the malcontents that they immediately sent submissive messages to the king and craved to be admitted to a treaty [conference].

Charles knew that the force of the Covenanters was considerable, their spirits high, their zeal furious, and that as they were not yet daunted by any ill success, no reasonable terms could be expected from them. With regard to a treaty, therefore, great difficulties occurred on both sides. If he submitted to the pretensions of the malcontents, not only would the prelacy be sacrificed to their religious prejudices, but royal authority too, which had only very lately and with much difficulty been thoroughly established in Scotland, would suffer such a check that he must expect ever after to retain in that kingdom no more than the appearance of majesty. The great men, having proved by so conspicuous a trial the impotence of law and prerogative, would return to their former licentiousness; the preachers would retain their innate arrogance; and the people, unprotected by justice, would recognize no other authority than that which they found to domineer over them. England also, it was much to be feared, would imitate so bad an example, and having already a strong propensity towards republican and puritanical factions, would expect by the same seditious practices to attain the same indulgence. To advance so far without bringing the rebels to a total submission, or at least to reasonable concessions, was to promise them in all future time an impunity for rebellion.

On the other hand, Charles considered that Scotland had never before, under any of his ancestors, been so united and so animated in its own defense; yet it had often been able to foil or elude the force of England when the latter had been combined heartily in one cause and inured by long practice to the use of arms. How much greater difficulty would he find at present to subdue by violence a people inflamed with religious prejudices, while he could only oppose to them a nation enervated by long peace and lukewarm in his service—or what was more to be dreaded, many of them engaged in the same party with the rebels. If the war were protracted beyond a single campaign (and who could expect to finish it in that period?), his treasures would fail him; and for supply, he would need recourse to an English Parliament, which by fatal experience he had always found more ready to encroach on the prerogatives than to supply the necessities of the Crown. And what if he received a defeat from the rebel army? This misfortune was far from being impossible. They were engaged in a national cause and strongly actuated by mistaken principles. His army was retained entirely by pay and looked on the quarrel with the same indifference which naturally belongs to mercenary troops without possessing the discipline by which such troops are commonly distinguished. And the consequences of a defeat, while Scotland was enraged and England discontented, were so dreadful that no motive could persuade him to hazard it.

A pacification

It is evident that Charles had fallen into such a situation that whichever side he embraced, his errors necessarily would be dangerous. It is no wonder, therefore, that he was in great perplexity. But he did worse than embrace the worst side; for properly speaking, he embraced no side at all. He decided suddenly to issue a peace agreement in which it was stipulated that he would withdraw his fleet and army, that within forty-eight hours the Scots would dismiss their forces, and that the king's forts would be restored to him, his authority would be acknowledged, and a General Assembly and a Parliament would be immediately summoned in order to resolve all differences. What the *reasons* were which engaged the king to admit such strange articles of peace it is in vain to inquire, for there scarcely could be any. The *causes* of that event may admit of a more easy explication.

The malcontents had been very industrious in representing to the English the grievances under which Scotland labored and the ill counsels which had been suggested to their sovereign. Their liberties, they said, were invaded; the prerogatives of the Crown extended beyond all former precedent; illegal courts erected; the hierarchy exalted at the expense of national privileges; and so many new superstitions introduced by the haughty, tyrannical prelates as begat a just suspicion that a project was seriously formed for the restoration of popery. The king's conduct in Scotland had been in everything except in establishing the ecclesiastical canons surely more legal than in England; yet there was such a general resemblance in the complaints of both kingdoms that the English readily assented to all the representations of the Scottish malcontents and believed that nation to have been driven by oppression into the violent counsels which they had embraced. Far from being willing, therefore, to second the king in subduing the free spirit of the Scots, they rather pitied that unhappy people, who had been pushed to those extremities. And they thought that the example of such neighbors as well as their assistance might sometime be advantageous to England and encourage it to recover by a vigorous effort its violated laws and liberties. The gentry and nobility—who attended in great numbers the English camp while being without attachment to the court or command in the army—greedily seized, propagated, and gave authority to these sentiments. A retreat, very little honorable, which the Earl of Holland, with a considerable detachment of the English forces, had made before a detachment of the Scottish caused all these humors to blaze up at once. And the king, whose character was not sufficiently vigorous or decisive and who was apt to take the easy course of embracing hasty counsels, suddenly assented to a measure which was recommended by all about him and which favored his natural propensity towards the misguided subjects of his native kingdom.

Renewal of the war

Charles, having so far advanced in pacific measures, ought to have prosecuted them with a steady resolution and to have submitted to every tolerable condition demanded by the Assembly and Parliament; nor should he have recommenced hostilities but on account of such enormous and unexpected pretensions as would have justified his cause, if possible, to the whole English nation. He adopted this plan to the extent, indeed, that he agreed not only to confirm his former concessions of abrogating the canons, the liturgy, the High Commission, and the Articles of Perth, but also to abolish the order of bishops itself, for which he had so zealously contended. But this concession was gained by the utmost constraint which he could impose on his disposition and prejudices; he even secretly retained an intention of seizing favorable opportunities to recover the ground which he had lost. And one step further he could not prevail with himself to advance. The Assembly, when it met on August 17, paid no deference to the king's prepossessions but gave full indulgence to their own. They voted episcopacy to be unlawful in the Church of Scotland; he was willing to allow it contrary to the constitutions of that church. They stigmatized the liturgy and canons as popish; he agreed simply to abolish them. They denominated the High Commission as tyranny; he was content to set it aside. The Parliament which sat after the Assembly advanced pretensions which tended to diminish the civil power of the monarch; and what probably affected Charles still more, they were proceeding to ratify the acts of the Assembly. Traquair, the commissioner, then prorogued them by the king's instructions. And on account of these claims, which might have been foreseen, the war was renewed, with great advantages on the side of the Covenanters and disadvantages on that of the king.

No sooner had Charles concluded the pacification without conditions than the necessity of his affairs and his lack of money obliged him to disband his army; and as the soldiers had been held together solely by mercenary interests, it was not possible without great trouble, expense, and loss of time to assemble them again. The more prudent Covenanters had concluded that as their pretensions were so contrary to the interests, and still more to the inclinations, of the king, it was likely that they would again be obliged to support their cause by arms; they were therefore careful, in dismissing their troops, to preserve nothing but the appearance of a pacific disposition. The officers had orders to be ready on the first summons, the soldiers were warned not to think the nation secure from an English invasion, and the religious zeal which animated all ranks of men made them immediately fly to their standards as soon as the trumpet was sounded by their spiritual and temporal leaders. The credit which they had acquired in their last expedition by obliging their sovereign to depart from all his pretensions gave courage to everyone in undertaking this new enterprise.

Fourth English Parliament

The king with great difficulty found means to draw together an army; but he soon discovered that, all savings | *1640* | being gone and great debts contracted, his revenue would be insufficient to support them. An English Parliament, therefore, formerly so unkind and intractable, must now—after more than eleven years' intermission, after the king had tried many irregular methods of taxation, after multiplied disgusts given to the Puritanical party—be summoned to assemble amidst the most pressing necessities of the Crown.

As the king resolved to try whether this House of Commons would be more compliant than its predecessors and grant him supply on any reasonable terms, the time appointed for the meeting of Parliament, April 13, was late, and very near the time allotted for opening the campaign against the Scots. After the past experience of their ill humor and of their encroaching disposition, he thought that he could not in prudence trust them with a long session till he had seen some better proofs of their good intentions. The urgency of the occasion and the little time allowed for debate were reasons which he reserved against the malcontents in the house. And an incident had happened which he believed had now furnished him with still more cogent arguments.

The Earl of Traquair had intercepted a letter written to the king of France by the Scottish malcontents and had conveyed this letter to the king. Charles, partly repenting of the large concessions made to the Scots, partly disgusted at their fresh insolence and pretensions, seized this opportunity of breaking with them. He ordered Lord Loudoun, commissioner from the Covenanters and one of the persons who had signed the treasonable letter, thrown into the Tower. And he now laid the matter before the Parliament, whom he hoped to inflame by the resentment, and alarm by the danger, of this application to a foreign power. By the mouth of the lord keeper, Finch, he revealed his wants and informed them that he had been able to assemble his army and to maintain them not by any revenue which he possessed but by means of a large debt of more than £300,000, which he had contracted and for which he had given security upon the Crown lands. He represented that it was necessary to grant supplies for the immediate and urgent demands of his military armaments. That the season was far advanced, the time precious, and none of it must be lost in deliberation. That though his coffers were empty, they had not been exhausted by unnecessary pomp or sumptuous buildings or any other kind of magnificence. That whatever supplies had been levied on his subjects had been employed for their advantage and preservation, and like vapors rising out of the earth and gathered into a cloud, had fallen in sweet and refreshing showers on the same fields from which they had at first been exhaled. That though he desired such immediate assistance as might prevent for the time a total disorder in the government, he was far from any intention of precluding them from their right to inquire into the state of the kingdom and to offer him petitions for the redress of their grievances. That as much as was possible of this season would afterwards be allowed them for that purpose. That as he expected only such supply at present as the current service necessarily required, it would be requisite to assemble them again next winter, when they would have full leisure to conclude whatever business had this session been left imperfect and unfinished. That the Parliament of Ireland had twice put such trust in his good intentions as to grant him in the beginning of the session a large supply and had always experienced good effects from the confidence reposed in him. And that in every circumstance, his people would find his conduct suitable to a just, pious, and gracious king, and such as was fitted to promote an entire harmony between prince and Parliament.

However plausible these topics, they made small impression on the House of Commons. By some illegal, and several suspicious, measures of the Crown, and by the courageous opposition which particular persons amidst dangers and hardships had made to them, the minds of men throughout the nation had taken such a turn as to ascribe every honor to the refractory opposers of the king and the ministers. These were the only patriots, the only lovers of their country, the only heroes, and perhaps too the only true Christians. A reasonable compliance with the court was slavish dependence; a regard to the king, servile flattery; a confidence in his promises, shameful prostitution. This general cast of thought, which has more or less prevailed in England during nearly a century and a half and which has been the cause of much good and much ill in public affairs, never predominated more than during the reign of Charles. The present House of Commons, being entirely composed of country gentlemen who came into Parliament with all their native prejudices about them and whom the Crown had no means of influencing, could not fail to contain a majority of these stubborn patriots.

Affairs likewise were drawing so near to a crisis by means of the Scottish insurrection and the general discontents in England that the leaders of the house, sagacious and penetrating, began to foresee the consequences and to hope that the time so long wished for, when royal authority must fall into a total subordination under popular assemblies and when public liberty must acquire a full ascendant, was now come. By reducing the Crown to necessities, they had previously found that the king had been pushed into violent counsels which had greatly served the purposes of his adversaries. And by multiplying these necessities, it was foreseen that his prerogative, undermined on all sides, must at last be overthrown and be no longer dangerous to the privileges of the people. Whatever, therefore, tended to resolve the differences between king and Parliament and to preserve the government uniformly in its present channel was zealously opposed by these popular leaders, and their past conduct and sufferings gave them credit sufficient to effect all their purposes.

The House of Commons, moved by these and many other obvious reasons, instead of taking notice of the king's complaints against his Scottish subjects or his applications for supply, entered immediately upon grievances; and a speech by Pym on that subject was much more hearkened to than that which the lord keeper had delivered to them in the name of their sovereign. The subject of Pym's harangue has been sufficiently explained above where we gave an account of all the grievances—imaginary in the church, more real in the state—of which the nation at that time so loudly complained. The house began with examining the behavior of the speaker on the last day of the former Parliament, when he refused on account of the king's command to put the question, and they declared it a breach of privilege. They proceeded next to inquire into the imprisonment and prosecution of Sir John Eliot, Holles, and Valentine; the affair of ship money was canvassed; and plentiful subject of inquiry was suggested on all hands. Grievances were regularly classed under three heads: those with regard to privileges of Parliament, to the property of the subject, and to religion. The king, seeing a large and inexhaustible field opened, pressed them again for supply. Finding his message ineffectual, he came to the House of Peers and desired their good offices with the Commons. The Peers appreciated the king's urgent necessities and thought that supply on this occasion ought, both in reason and in decency, to go before grievances. They ventured to represent their sense of the matter to the Commons, but their intercession did harm. The Commons had always claimed as their particular province the granting of supplies; and though the Peers had here gone no further than offering advice, the lower house immediately thought proper to vote so unprecedented an interposition to be a breach of privilege. Charles, in order to bring the matter of supply to some conclusion, solicited the house by new messages. Finding that ship money gave great alarm and disgust, he not only informed them that he never intended to make a constant revenue of it and that all the money levied had been regularly, with other great sums, expended on equipping the navy, he now went so far as to offer them a total abolition of that obnoxious claim by any law which the Commons would think proper to present to him. In return he only asked for his necessities, a supply of twelve subsidies (about £600,000), and that payable in three years; but at the same time, he let them know that, considering the situation of his affairs, a delay would be equivalent to a denial. The king, though the majority was against him, never had more friends in any House of Commons, and the debate was carried on for two days with great zeal and warmth on both sides.

It was urged by the partisans of the court that the happiest occasion which the fondest wishes could suggest was now presented for removing all disgusts and jealousies between king and people and for reconciling their sovereign forever to the use of Parliaments. That if they on their part laid aside all enormous claims and pretensions and provided in a reasonable manner for the public necessities, they needed entertain no suspicion of any insatiable ambition or illegal usurpation in the Crown. That though due regard had not always been paid to the rights of the people during this reign, yet no invasion of those rights had been altogether deliberate and voluntary, much less the result of wanton tyranny and injustice, and still less of a formal design to subvert the constitution. That to repose a reasonable confidence in the king and generously to supply his present wants, which proceeded neither from prodigality nor misconduct, would be the true means of gaining on his generous nature and extorting by a gentle force such concessions as were requisite for the establishment of public liberty. That he had promised—not only on the word of a prince but also on that of a gentleman (the expression which he had been pleased to use)—that after the supply was granted, the Parliament would still have liberty to continue their deliberations; could it be suspected that any man, any prince, much less this one, whose word was as yet sacred and inviolate, would for so small a motive forfeit his honor and with it all future trust and confidence by breaking a promise so public and so solemn? That even if the Parliament were deceived in reposing this confidence in him, they neither lost anything nor incurred any danger, since it was manifestly necessary for the security of public peace to supply him with money in order to suppress the Scottish rebellion. That he had suited his first demands to their prejudices so much that he only asked a supply for a few months and was willing after so short a trust from them to fall again into dependence and to trust them for his further support and subsistence. That if he now seemed to desire something further, he also made them in return a considerable offer and was willing for the future to depend on them for a revenue which was quite necessary for public honor and security. And that the nature of the English constitution supposed a mutual confidence between king and Parliament; if they would refuse it on their part, especially with circumstances of such outrage and indignity, what could be expected but a total dissolution of government and violent factions, followed by the most dangerous convulsions and internal disorders?

In opposition to these arguments, it was urged by the malcontent party that the court had revealed on their part but few symptoms of that mutual confidence to which they now so kindly invited the Commons. That eleven years' intermission of Parliaments—the longest that was to be found in the English annals—was a sufficient indication of the jealousy entertained against the people, or rather of designs formed for the suppression of all their liberties and privileges. That the ministers might well plead necessity, for nothing indeed could be a stronger proof of some invincible necessity than their embracing a measure for which they had conceived so violent an aversion as the assembling of an English Parliament. That this necessity, however, was purely ministerial, not national; and if the same grievances, ecclesiastical and civil, under which this nation itself labored had pushed the Scots to extremities, was it requisite that the English forge their own chains by imposing chains on their unhappy neighbors? That the ancient practice of Parliament was to give grievances precedence over supply; and this order, so carefully observed by their ancestors, was founded on a jealousy inherent in the constitution and never indicated any unusual distrust of the present sovereign. That a practice which had been upheld during the most favorable times to liberty could not in common prudence be departed from where such undeniable reasons for suspicion had been afforded. That it was ridiculous to plead the advanced season and the urgent occasion for supply when it plainly appeared that in order to afford a pretense for this topic and to seduce the Commons, great political contrivance had been employed. That the writs for elections were issued early in the winter; and if the meeting of Parliament had not purposely been delayed till so near the commencement of military operations, there would have been leisure sufficient to have redressed all national grievances and to have proceeded afterwards to an examination of the king's occasion for supply. That the intention of so gross an artifice was to engage the Commons to violate the regular order of Parliament under pretense of necessity; and once a precedent of that kind was established, no inquiry into public measures would afterwards be permitted. That scarcely any argument more unfavorable could be pleaded for supply than an offer to abolish ship money, a taxation the most illegal and the most dangerous that had ever in any reign been imposed upon the nation. And that by bargaining for the remission of that duty, the Commons would, in a manner, ratify the authority by which it had been levied, or at least give encouragement for advancing new pretensions of a like nature in hopes of resigning them on like advantageous conditions.

These reasons, joined to so many occasions of ill humor, seemed to influence the greater number. But to make the matter worse, Sir Harry Vane, the secretary, told the Commons, without any authority from the king, that nothing less than twelve subsidies would be accepted as a compensation for the abolition of ship money. This assertion, proceeding from the indiscretion—if we are not rather to call it the treachery—of Vane, displeased the house by showing a stiffness and rigidity in the king which was deemed inexcusable in a claim so ill grounded. We are informed likewise that some men who were thought to understand the state of the nation affirmed in the house that the amount of twelve subsidies was a greater sum than could be found in all England. Such were the happy ignorance and inexperience of those times with regard to taxes!

Dissolution

The king was in great doubt and perplexity. He saw that his friends in the house were outnumbered by his enemies and that the same counsels which had always bred such opposition and disturbance were still predominant. Instead of hoping that any supply would be granted him to carry on war against the Scots, whom the majority of the house regarded as their best friends and firmest allies, he expected every day that they would present him a petition for making peace with those rebels. And he was informed that if the house met again, a vote to blast his revenue of ship money would certainly pass and thereby renew all the opposition which he had surmounted with so much difficulty in levying that taxation. Where great evils lie on all sides, it is difficult to follow the best counsel; it is no wonder that the king, whose capacity was not equal to situations of such extreme delicacy, hastily formed and executed the resolution of dissolving this Parliament. This was a measure, however, of which he soon after repented, and which the subsequent events, more than any convincing reason, inclined everyone to condemn. The last Parliament, which ended with such rigor and violence, had yet at first covered its intentions with greater appearance of moderation than this Parliament had assumed.

An abrupt and violent dissolution naturally excites discontents among the people, who usually put entire confidence in their representatives and expect from them the redress of all grievances. As if there were not already sufficient grounds of complaint, the king persevered still in those counsels which from experience he might have been aware were so dangerous and unpopular. Belasyse and Sir John Hotham were summoned before the Privy Council, and refusing to give any account of their conduct in Parliament, were committed to prison. All the petitions and complaints which had been sent to the Commons committee of religion were demanded from John Crew, chairman of that committee; and on his refusal to deliver them, he was sent to the Tower. The studies, and even the pockets, of the Earl of Warwick and Lord Brooke were searched before the expiration of privilege in expectation of finding treasonable papers. These acts of authority were interpreted, with some appearance of reason, to be invasions on the right of national assemblies. But the king, after the first provocation which he met with, never sufficiently respected the privileges of Parliament, and by his example he further confirmed their resolution to pay like disregard to the prerogatives of the Crown should they acquire power.

Though the Parliament was dissolved, the Convocation was still allowed to sit, a practice of which there were but few instances since the Reformation and which was for that reason supposed by many to be irregular. Besides granting to the king a supply from the spirituality and framing many canons, the Convocation, jealous of innovations like those which had taken place in Scotland, imposed an oath on the clergy and the graduates in the universities by which each one swore to "maintain the established government of the church by archbishops, bishops, deans, chapters, etc." These steps, in the present discontented humor of the nation, were commonly deemed illegal because they were not ratified by consent of Parliament, in whom all authority was now supposed to be centered. In addition, nothing could afford more subject of ridicule than an oath which contained an "et cetera" in the midst of it.

Discontents in England

The people, who generally abhorred the Convocation as much as they revered the Parliament, could scarcely be restrained from insulting and abusing this assembly, and the king was obliged to give them guards in order to protect them. An attack too was made during the night upon Laud in his palace of Lambeth by more than five hundred persons, and he found it necessary to fortify himself for his defense. A multitude consisting of two thousand sectaries entered St. Paul's, where the High Commission then sat, tore down the benches, and cried out, "No bishop, no High Commission." All these instances of discontent were presages of some great revolution, had the court possessed sufficient skill to discern the danger or sufficient power to provide against it.

In this disposition of men's minds, it was in vain that the king issued a declaration in order to convince his people of the necessity which he lay under of dissolving the last Parliament. The chief topic on which he insisted was that the Commons imitated the bad example of all their predecessors of late years in making continual encroachments on his authority, in censuring his whole administration and conduct, in discussing every circumstance of public government, and in their indirect bargaining and contracting with their king for supply, as if nothing ought to be given him but what he might purchase either by abandoning some of his royal prerogative or by diminishing and lessening his standing revenue. These practices, he said, were contrary to the maxims of their ancestors and were totally incompatible with monarchy.

The king, disappointed of parliamentary subsidies, was obliged to have recourse to other expedients in order to supply his urgent necessities. The ecclesiastical subsidies served him in some stead, and it seemed but just that the clergy should contribute to a war which was in a great measure of their own raising. He borrowed money from his ministers and courtiers; he was so much beloved among them that more than £300,000 was subscribed in a few days—though nothing surely could be more disagreeable to a prince full of dignity than to be a burden on his friends instead of being a support to them. Some attempts were made towards forcing a loan from the citizens; but such were repelled by the spirit of liberty, which had now become unconquerable. A loan of £40,000 was extorted from the Spanish merchants, who had bullion in the Tower exposed to the attempts of the king. Coat and conduct money for the soldiery was levied on the counties; an ancient practice, but one supposed to be abolished by the Petition of Right. All the pepper was bought from the East India Company upon trust and sold at a great discount for ready money. A scheme was proposed for coining two or three hundred thousand pounds of base money. Such were the extremities to which Charles was reduced. Amidst the present distresses, the fresh difficulties which were every day raised with regard to the payment of ship money obliged him to exert continual acts of authority, augmented the discontents of the people, and increased his indigence and necessities.

These expedients, however, enabled the king, though with great difficulty, to march his army, consisting of nineteen thousand foot and two thousand horse. The Earl of Northumberland was appointed general; the Earl of Strafford, who was called over from Ireland, lieutenant general; Lord Conway, general of the horse. A small fleet was thought sufficient to serve the purposes of this expedition.

Rout at Newburn

So great are the effects of zeal and unanimity that the Scottish army, though more numerous, were sooner ready than the king's; and they marched to the borders of England. They were engaged to proceed not only by their general knowledge of the covert discontents of the English but also by a letter—purportedly in the name of six of the most considerable noblemen of England, actually forged by Lord Savile—which invited the Scots to assist their neighbors in procuring a redress of grievances. Notwithstanding these warlike preparations and hostile attempts, the Covenanters still preserved the most pathetic and most submissive language; they entered England, they said, with no other view than to obtain access to the king's presence and lay their humble petition at his royal feet. At Newburn upon Tyne, on August 28, they were opposed by a detachment of four thousand five hundred men under Conway, who seemed resolute to dispute with them the passage of the river. The Scots first entreated them with great civility not to stop them in their march to their gracious sovereign, then attacked them with great bravery, killed several, and chased the rest from their ground. Such a panic seized the whole English army that the forces at Newcastle upon Tyne fled immediately to Durham; and not yet thinking themselves safe, they deserted that town and retreated into Yorkshire.

The Scots took possession of Newcastle upon Tyne; though sufficiently elated with their victory, they preserved exact discipline and persevered in their resolution of paying for everything, in order still to maintain the appearance of an amicable correspondence with England. They also dispatched messengers to the king, who had arrived at York; they took care, after the advantage which they had obtained, to redouble their expressions of loyalty, duty, and submission to his person, and they even made apologies, full of sorrow and contrition, for their late victory.

Charles was in a very distressed condition. The nation was universally and highly discontented. The army was discouraged and began likewise to be discontented, both from the contagion of general disgust and as an excuse for their misbehavior, which they were desirous of representing rather as lack of will than of courage to fight. The Treasury too was quite exhausted, and every expedient for supply had been tried to the uttermost. No event had happened but what might have been foreseen as necessary, or at least as very probable; yet such was the king's situation that no provision could be made, nor was even any resolution taken, against such an exigency.

Treaty at Ripon

In order to prevent the advance of the Scots upon him, the king agreed to frame a treaty and named sixteen English noblemen to meet with eleven Scottish commissioners at Ripon. The Earls of Hertford, Bedford, Salisbury, Warwick, Essex, Holland, Bristol, and Berkshire, the Lords Kimbolton, Wharton, Dunsmore, Paget, Brooke, Savile, Paulet, and Howard of Escrick were chosen by the king; all of them popular men and consequently supposed in no way averse to the Scottish invasion or unacceptable to that nation.

An address arrived from the city of London petitioning for a Parliament, the great point to which all men's projects at this time tended. Twelve noblemen presented a petition to the same purpose. But the king contented himself with summoning a Great Council of the Peers at York, a measure which had formerly been taken in cases of sudden emergency but which at present could serve to little purpose. Perhaps the king, who dreaded above all things the House of Commons and who expected no supply from them on any reasonable terms, thought that in his present distresses he might be enabled to levy supplies by the authority of the Peers alone. But employing for so long the plea of a necessity which appeared distant and doubtful rendered it impossible for him to avail himself of a necessity which now at last had become real, urgent, and inevitable.

By Northumberland's sickness, the command of the army had devolved on Strafford. This nobleman possessed more vigor of mind than the king or any of the Council. He advised Charles to put all to hazard rather than submit to such unworthy terms as were likely to be imposed upon him. The loss sustained at Newburn, he said, was inconsiderable; and though a panic had for the time seized the army, that event was nothing strange among newly levied troops. The Scots, being in the same condition, would no doubt be liable in their turn to a like accident. His opinion, therefore, was that the king should push forward and attack the Scots and bring the affair to a quick decision. Even if he were ever so unsuccessful, nothing worse could befall him than what from his inactivity he would certainly be exposed to. To show how easy it would be to execute this project, he ordered an assault to be made on some quarters of the Scots, and he gained an advantage over them. No cessation of arms had as yet been agreed to during the treaty [negotiations] at Ripon, yet great clamor prevailed on account of this act of hostility. And when it was known that the officer who conducted the attack was a papist, a violent outcry was raised against the king for employing that hated sect in the murder of his Protestant subjects.

It may be worthy of notice that several mutinies had arisen among the English troops when marching to join the army, and some officers had been murdered merely on suspicion of their being papists. The Petition of Right had abolished all martial law; and by an inconvenience which naturally attended the still new and unformed plan of regular and rigid liberty, it was found absolutely impossible for the generals to govern the army by all the authority which the king could legally confer upon them. The lawyers had declared that martial law could not be exercised except in the very presence of an enemy; and because it had been found necessary to execute a mutineer, the generals thought it advisable for their own safety to apply for a pardon from the Crown. This weakness, however, was carefully concealed from the army; and Lord Conway said that if any lawyer were so imprudent as to reveal the secret to the soldiers, it would be necessary instantly to refute it and to hang the lawyer himself by sentence of a court martial.

Great Council of the Peers

An army newly levied, undisciplined, frightened, seditious, ill paid, and governed by no proper authority was very unfit for withstanding a victorious and high-spirited enemy and retaining in subjection a discontented and zealous nation. Charles, in despair of being able to stem the torrent, at last determined to yield to it; and as he foresaw that the Great Council of the Peers would advise him to call a Parliament, he told them in his first speech, on September 24, that he had already taken this resolution. He informed them likewise that the queen, in a letter which she had written to him, had very earnestly recommended that measure. This good prince, who was extremely attached to his consort and who passionately wished to render her popular in the nation, did not forget the interests of his domestic tenderness amidst all his distress.

To maintain both armies (for the king was obliged to pay his enemies in order to save the northern counties), Charles wrote to the city desiring a loan of £200,000. And the Peers at York, whose authority was now much greater than that of their sovereign, joined in the same request. So low had this prince already fallen in the eyes of his own subjects!

As many difficulties occurred in the negotiations with the Scots, it was proposed to transfer the conference from Ripon to London. This proposal was willingly embraced by the Scots, who were now sure of treating with advantage in a place where the king, they foresaw, would be, in a manner, a prisoner, in the midst of his implacable enemies and their determined friends.

CHAPTER 54
1640 – 1641

*Meeting of the Long Parliament – Strafford impeached –
Laud impeached – Lord Keeper Finch flies – Secretary
Windebank flies – Great authority of the Commons – The
bishops attacked – Tonnage and poundage – Triennial Bill –
Strafford's trial – Bill of attainder – Execution of Strafford –
High Commission and Star Chamber abolished –
King's journey to Scotland*

T HE causes of disgust which for more than thirty years had daily
been multiplying in England were now come to full maturity and
threatened the kingdom with some great revolution or convulsion.
The uncertain and undefined limits of prerogative and privilege had
been eagerly disputed during that whole period; and in every controversy between prince and people, the question, however doubtful, had
always been decided by each party in favor of its own pretensions.
Moved perhaps too easily by the appearance of necessity, the king had
even assumed powers incompatible with the principles of limited government and had rendered it impossible for his most zealous partisans
entirely to justify his conduct except by topics so unpopular that they
were, in the present disposition of men's minds, more fitted to inflame than appease the general discontent. Law and religion, those
great supports of public authority, had likewise lost much of their influence over the people by the unbounded compliance of judges and
prelates; or rather, they had in a great measure gone over to the side of
faction and authorized the spirit of opposition and rebellion. The nobility also, whom the king had no means of retaining by offices and
preferments suitable to their rank, had been seized with the general

discontent and unwarily threw themselves into the scale, which already began to swing much to one side. Aware of some encroachments which had been made by royal authority, men entertained no jealousy [suspicious fear] of the Commons, whose enterprises for the acquisition of power had always been covered with the appearance of public good and had till now gone no further than some disappointed efforts and endeavors. The progress of the Scottish malcontents reduced the Crown to an entire dependence for supply. Their union with the popular party in England brought great accession of authority to the latter. The near prospect of success roused all latent murmurs and pretensions which had previously been held in such rigorous constraint. And the torrent of general inclination and opinion ran so strongly against the court that the king was in no situation to refuse any reasonable demands of the popular leaders either for defining or limiting the powers of his prerogative. In his present situation, even many exorbitant claims would probably be made and must necessarily be complied with.

The triumph of the malcontents over the Church of England was not yet so immediate or certain. Though the political and religious Puritans mutually lent assistance to each other, there were many who joined the former yet declined all connection with the latter. The hierarchy had been established in England ever since the Reformation; the Romish church in all ages had carefully maintained that form of ecclesiastical government; the ancient fathers too bore testimony to episcopal jurisdiction; and though parity may seem at first to have had place among Christian pastors, the period during which it prevailed was so short that few undisputed traces of it remained in history. The bishops and their more zealous partisans inferred from this the divine indefeasible right of prelacy. Others regarded that institution as venerable and useful. And if the love of novelty led some to adopt the new rites and discipline of the Puritans, the reverence to antiquity retained many in their attachment to the liturgy and government of the church. It behooved, therefore, the zealous innovators in Parliament to proceed with some caution and reserve. They justly regarded the king to be, from principle, inclination, and policy, the determined patron of the hierarchy. By promoting all measures which reduced the powers of the Crown, they hoped to disarm the king's defense of the prelacy. By declaiming against the supposed encroachments and tyranny of the prelates, they endeavored to carry the nation from a hatred of their persons to an opposition against their office and rank.

And when men once were enlisted in party, it would not be difficult, they thought, to lead them by degrees into many measures for which they formerly entertained the greatest aversion. Though the new sectaries did not at first compose the majority of the nation, they were inflamed, as is usual among innovators, with extreme zeal for their opinions. Their insurmountable passion, disguised to themselves as well as to others under the appearance of holy fervors, was well qualified to make proselytes and to seize the minds of the ignorant multitude. And one furious enthusiast was able by his active industry to surmount the indolent efforts of many sober and reasonable antagonists.

With the nation so generally discontented and so little suspicious of any design to subvert the church and monarchy, it is no wonder that almost all elections ran in favor of those who had encouraged the national prejudices by their high pretensions to piety and patriotism. It is a usual compliment to respect the king's inclination in the choice of a speaker, and Charles had intended to advance Thomas Gardiner, recorder of London, to that important trust. But so little credit did the Crown at that time possess in the nation that Gardiner's election to Parliament was defeated, not only in London but in every other place where it was attempted. The king was obliged to make the choice of speaker fall on William Lenthall, a lawyer of some character but not sufficiently qualified for so high and difficult an office.

Meeting of the Long Parliament

The eager expectations of men with regard to a Parliament summoned at so critical a juncture and during such general discontents, a Parliament which, from the situation of public affairs, could not be abruptly dissolved and which was to execute everything left unfinished by former Parliaments: these motives, so important and interesting, engaged the attendance of all the members; and the House of Commons was never observed to be, from the beginning, so full and numerous. Without any interval, therefore, they entered upon business on November 3; and by unanimous consent, they immediately struck a blow which may almost be regarded as decisive.

The Earl of Strafford was considered the king's chief minister, both on account of the credit which he possessed with his master and of his own great and uncommon vigor and capacity. By a concurrence of accidents, this man labored under the severe hatred of all three nations which composed the British monarchy. The Scots, whose authority now ran extremely high, looked on him as the capital enemy of their country and one whose counsels and influence they had most reason to fear. He had engaged the Parliament of Ireland to advance large subsidies in order to support a war against them; he had levied an army of nine thousand men with which he had menaced all their western coast; he had obliged the Scots who lived under his government to renounce the Covenant, their national idol; he had in Ireland proclaimed the Scottish Covenanters rebels and traitors even before the king had issued any such declaration against them in England; and he had always dissuaded his master against the late treaty and suspension of arms, which he regarded as dangerous and dishonorable. So avowed and violent were the Scots in their resentment of all these measures that they had refused to send commissioners to treat at York, as was at first proposed, because, they said, the lieutenant of Ireland, their capital enemy, had there the chief command and authority as general of the king's forces.

Strafford, first as deputy, then as lord lieutenant, had governed Ireland for eight years with great vigilance, energy, and prudence but with very little popularity. In a nation so averse to the English government and religion, these very virtues were sufficient to draw on him the public hatred. The manners too and character of this great man, though to all full of courtesy and to his friends full of affection, were at bottom haughty, rigid, and severe. His authority and influence during the time of his government had been unlimited; but no sooner did adversity seize him than the concealed aversion of the nation blazed up at once, and the Irish Parliament used every expedient to aggravate the charge against him.

The universal discontent which prevailed in England against the court was all pointed towards the Earl of Strafford, without any particular reason but because he was the minister of state whom the king most favored and most trusted. His extraction was honorable, his paternal fortune considerable, yet envy attended his sudden and great elevation. And his former associates in popular counsels, finding that he owed his advancement to the desertion of their cause, represented him as the great apostate of the commonwealth, whom it behooved them to sacrifice as a victim to public justice.

Strafford, aware of the load of popular prejudices under which he labored, would gladly have declined attendance in Parliament. He begged the king's permission to withdraw himself to his government of Ireland, or at least to remain at the head of the army in Yorkshire, where he hoped many opportunities would offer, by reason of his distance, to elude the attacks of his enemies. But Charles, who had entire confidence in the earl's capacity, thought that his counsels would be extremely useful during the critical session which approached. And when Strafford still insisted on the danger of his appearing amidst so many enraged enemies, the king, little apprehensive that his own authority was so suddenly to expire, promised him protection and assured him that not a hair of his head would be touched by the Parliament.

Strafford impeached

No sooner was Strafford's arrival known than a concerted attack was made upon him in the House of Commons. On November 11, Pym, in a long, studied discourse divided into many heads, as was his manner, enumerated all the grievances under which the nation labored; and by connecting and interweaving such oppressions, he inferred that a deliberate plan had been formed of changing entirely the frame of government and subverting the ancient laws and liberties of the kingdom. If anything, he said, could increase our indignation against so enormous and criminal a project, it would be to find, during the reign of the best of princes, that the constitution had been endangered by the worst of ministers and that the virtues of the king had been seduced by wicked and pernicious counsel. We must inquire, he added, from what fountain these waters of bitterness flow; and though doubtless many evil counselors will be found to have contributed their endeavors, yet there is one who challenges [claims; demands] the infamous preeminence, and who, by his courage, enterprise, and capacity, is entitled to the first place among these betrayers of their country. He is the Earl of Strafford, lieutenant of Ireland and president of the Council of York, who in both places and in all other provinces where he has been entrusted with authority has raised ample monuments of tyranny and will appear from a survey of his actions to be the chief promoter of every arbitrary counsel. Some instances both of imperious expressions and actions were given by Pym, who afterwards entered into a more personal attack on that minister and endeavored to expose his whole character and manners. The austere genius of Strafford, occupied in the pursuits of ambition, had not rendered his breast altogether inaccessible to the tender passions or secured him from the dominion of the fair; and in that sullen age, when the irregularities of pleasure were more reproachful than the most odious crimes, these weaknesses were thought worthy of being mentioned together with his treasons before so great an assembly. And upon the whole, the orator concluded that it belonged to the house to provide a remedy proportionate to the disease and to prevent the further mischiefs justly to be feared from the influence which this man had acquired over the measures and counsels of their sovereign.

Sir John Clotworthy, an Irish gentleman, Sir John Hotham of Yorkshire, and many others entered into the same topics; after several hours spent in bitter invective, during which the doors were locked in order to prevent all discovery of their purpose, it was moved, in consequence of the resolution secretly taken, that Strafford should immediately be impeached of high treason. This motion was received with universal approbation; there was not one person in all the debate who offered to stop the torrent by any testimony in favor of the earl's conduct. Lord Falkland alone, though known to be his enemy, modestly desired the house to consider whether it would not better suit the gravity of their proceedings first to digest by a committee many of those particulars which had been mentioned before they sent up an accusation against him. It was ingeniously answered by Pym that such a delay might probably blast all their hopes and put it out of their power to proceed any further in the prosecution; that when Strafford learned that so many of his enormities were discovered, his conscience would dictate his condemnation, and so great was his power and credit that he would immediately procure the dissolution of the Parliament or attempt some other desperate measure for his own preservation; that the Commons were only accusers, not judges, and it was the province of the Peers to determine whether such an admixture of enormous crimes in one person did not amount to the highest crime known by the law. Without further debate, the impeachment was voted. Pym was chosen to carry it up to the Lords; most of the house accompanied him on so agreeable an errand. And Strafford, who had just entered the House of Peers and who little expected so speedy a prosecution, was immediately upon this general charge ordered into custody, with several symptoms of violent prejudice in his judges as well as in his prosecutors.

Laud impeached

In the inquiry concerning grievances and in the censure of past measures, Laud could not long escape the severe scrutiny of the Commons, who were led, in their accusation of that prelate, as much by their prejudices against his whole order as by the extreme antipathy which his intemperate zeal had drawn upon him. After a deliberation which scarcely lasted half an hour, an impeachment of high treason was voted against this subject, the first both in rank and in favor throughout the kingdom. Though this incident, considering the example of Strafford's impeachment and the present disposition of the nation and Parliament, must have been no surprise to him, yet he was betrayed into some passion when the accusation was presented. The Commons themselves, he said, though his accusers, did not believe him guilty of the crimes with which they charged him. The next day, upon more mature deliberation, he desired leave to retract this indiscretion; but so little favorable were the Peers that they refused him this advantage or indulgence. Laud also was immediately sequestered from Parliament and committed to custody upon this general charge.

Lord Keeper Finch flies

The principal charge insisted on against these two great men was the design which the Commons supposed to have been formed of subverting the laws and constitution of England and introducing arbitrary and unlimited authority into the kingdom. Of all the king's ministers, no one was so obnoxious in this respect as the lord keeper, Finch. He had been speaker in the king's third Parliament, and it was he who had left the chair and refused to put the question when ordered by the house. The extrajudicial opinion of the judges in the case of ship money had been procured by his intrigues, persuasions, and even menaces. In all unpopular and illegal measures, he was always most active; and he was even believed to have declared publicly that while he was keeper, an order of Council would always with him be equivalent to a law. To appease the rising displeasure of the Commons, he desired to be heard at their bar. He prostrated himself with all humility before them, but this submission availed him nothing. An impeachment was resolved on, and he thought it proper to withdraw secretly and retire into Holland in order to escape their fury. As he was not deemed equal to Strafford, or even to Laud, either in capacity or in fidelity to his master, it was generally believed that his escape had been connived at by the popular leaders. His impeachment, however, was carried up to the House of Peers in his absence.

Secretary Windebank flies

Sir Francis Windebank, the secretary, was a creature of Laud's, a sufficient reason for his being extremely obnoxious to the Commons. He was suspected too of the crime of secret popery, and it was known that—from complaisance to the queen, and indeed, in compliance with the king's maxims of government—he had granted many indulgences to Catholics and had signed warrants for the pardon of priests and their delivery from confinement. Grimston, a popular member, called him, in the house, the very pander and broker to the whore of Babylon. Finding that the scrutiny of the Commons was pointing towards him, and being aware that England was no longer a place of safety for men of his kind, he suddenly made his escape into France.

Thus, in a few weeks, this House of Commons, not opposed but rather seconded by the Peers, had produced such a revolution in the government that the two most powerful and most favored ministers of the king were thrown into the Tower and daily expected to be tried for their life. Two other ministers had by flight alone saved themselves from a like fate. All the king's servants saw that no protection could be given them by their master. A new jurisdiction was erected in the nation; and before that tribunal, all those trembled who had before exulted most in their credit and authority.

Great authority of the Commons

What rendered the power of the Commons more formidable was the extreme shrewdness with which it was conducted. Not content with the authority which they had acquired by attacking these great ministers, they were resolved to render the most considerable bodies of the nation vulnerable to them. Though the idol of the people, they determined to fortify themselves likewise with terrors and to overawe those who might still be inclined to support the falling ruins of monarchy.

During the late military operations, several powers had been exercised by the lieutenants and deputy lieutenants of counties. These powers, though necessary for the defense of the nation and even warranted by all former precedent, had not been authorized by statute; they were now voted to be illegal, and the persons who had assumed them were declared "delinquents." This term was newly come into vogue and expressed a degree and species of guilt not exactly known or ascertained. In consequence of that determination, many of the nobility and prime gentry of the nation unexpectedly found themselves involved in the crime of delinquency while only exerting, as they justly thought, the legal powers of magistracy. And the Commons reaped multiple advantages by this vote: they disarmed the Crown, they established the maxims of rigid law and liberty, and they spread the terror of their own authority.

The writs for ship money had been directed to the sheriffs, who were obliged under severe penalties to assess the sums upon individuals and to levy them by their authority. Yet all the sheriffs and all those who had been employed in that illegal service were voted by a very rigorous sentence to be delinquents. By the maxims of law, the king could do no wrong; in case of any violation of the constitution, only his ministers and servants, of whatever degree, were culpable.

All the tax farmers and officers of the customs who had been employed during so many years in levying tonnage and poundage and the new impositions were likewise declared criminals; they were afterwards glad to compound for a pardon by paying a fine of £150,000.

Every discretionary or arbitrary sentence of the Star Chamber and High Commission—courts which from their very constitution were arbitrary—underwent a severe scrutiny, and all those who had concurred in such sentences were voted to be liable to the penalties of law. Every minister of the king, every member of the Council, found himself exposed by this decision.

The judges who had given their vote against Hampden in the trial of ship money were accused before the Peers and obliged to find surety for their appearance. Berkeley, a judge of the King's Bench, was seized by order of the Commons even when sitting in his tribunal; and all men saw with astonishment the irresistible authority of their jurisdiction.

The sanction of the Lords and Commons as well as that of the king was declared necessary for the confirmation of ecclesiastical canons. It must be confessed that this judgment—however reasonable, or at least useful—would have been difficult to justify by any precedent. But the present was no time for question or dispute. Abolishing all legislative power except that of Parliament was requisite for completing the new plan of liberty and rendering it quite uniform and systematic. Almost all the bench of bishops and the most considerable of the inferior clergy who had voted in the late Convocation found themselves exposed by these new principles to the imputation of delinquency.

The most unpopular and the least justifiable of all Charles's measures was the revival of monopolies, so solemnly abolished after reiterated endeavors by a recent act of Parliament. Aware of the unhappiness this measure had created, the king had of his own accord recalled many of these oppressive patents during the time of his first expedition against Scotland. The rest were now annulled by authority of Parliament, and everyone who was concerned in them declared delinquents. The Commons carried their detestation of this odious measure so far that they assumed a power which had formerly been seldom practiced and expelled all their members who were monopolists or projectors [promoters], an artifice by which they both increased their own privileges and weakened still further the very small party which the king secretly retained in the house. Sir Henry Mildmay, a notorious monopolist who recently had associated himself with the ruling party, was allowed to keep his seat. In all questions of elections, indeed, no steady rule of decision was observed, and nothing further was regarded than the affections and attachments of the parties. Men's passions were too much heated to be shocked with any instance of injustice which served ends so popular as those which were pursued by this House of Commons.

The whole sovereign power being thus in effect transferred to the Commons, and the government being changed in a moment, without any seeming violence or disorder, from a monarchy almost absolute to a pure democracy, the popular leaders seemed willing for some time to suspend their active vigor and to consolidate their authority before they proceeded to any violent exercise of it. Every day produced some new harangue on past grievances. The detestation of former usurpations was further enlivened, the jealousy of liberty roused, and agreeably to the spirit of free government, no less indignation was excited by the sight of a violated constitution than by the ravages of the most enormous tyranny.

This was the time when genius and capacity of all kinds, freed from the restraint of authority and nourished by unbounded hopes and projects, began to exert themselves and be distinguished by the public. Then was celebrated the sagacity of Pym, more fitted for use than ornament; matured, not chilled, by his advanced age and long experience. Then was displayed the mighty ambition of Hampden, taught disguise, not moderation, from former constraint; supported by courage, conducted by prudence, embellished by modesty; but whether founded in a love of power or zeal for liberty is still, from his untimely end, left doubtful and uncertain. Then too were known the dark, ardent, and dangerous character of St. John; the impetuous spirit of Holles, violent and sincere, open and entire in his enmities and in his friendships; the enthusiastic genius of young Vane, extravagant in the ends which he pursued, sagacious and profound in the means which he employed; incited by the appearances of religion, negligent of the duties of morality.

So little apology would be received for past measures, so contagious the general spirit of discontent, that even men of the most moderate tempers and the most attached to the church and monarchy exerted themselves with the utmost vigor in the redress of grievances and in prosecuting the authors of them. The lively and animated Digby displayed his eloquence on this occasion, as did the firm and undaunted Capell and the modest and candid Palmer. In this list too of patriot royalists are found the virtuous names of Hyde and Falkland. Though in their ultimate views and intentions these men differed widely from the former, in their present actions and discourses an entire concurrence and unanimity was observed.

By the daily harangues and invectives against illegal usurpations, not only the House of Commons inflamed themselves with the highest animosity against the court: the nation caught new fire from the popular leaders and seemed now to have made the first discovery of the many supposed disorders in the government. Previously, when the law in several instances seemed to be violated, they went no further than some private and calm murmurs; but now that the constitution was thought to be restored to its former integrity and vigor, they mounted up into rage and fury. The capital especially, being the seat of Parliament, was highly animated with the spirit of mutiny and disaffection. Tumults were daily raised, seditious assemblies encouraged, and every man, neglecting his own business, was wholly intent on the defense of liberty and religion. By stronger contagion, the popular affections were communicated from breast to breast in this place of general rendezvous and society.

The harangues of members, now first published and dispersed, kept alive the discontents against the king's administration. The pulpits, delivered over to Puritanical preachers and lecturers whom the Commons arbitrarily settled in all the considerable churches, resounded with faction and fanaticism. Vengeance was fully taken for the long silence and constraint in which, by the authority of Laud and the High Commission, these preachers had been retained. The press, freed from all fear or reserve, swarmed with productions made dangerous by their seditious zeal and calumny more than by any art or eloquence of composition. Noise and fury, cant and hypocrisy, formed the sole rhetoric which could be heard or attended to during this tumult of various prejudices and passions.

The sentences which had been executed against Prynne, Bastwick, and Burton were now revised by Parliament. These libelers, far from being tamed by the rigorous punishments which they had undergone, still showed a disposition of repeating their offense; and the ministers were afraid lest new satires would issue from their prisons and still further inflame the prevailing discontents. By an order, therefore, of Council, they had been carried to remote prisons: Bastwick to Scilly, Prynne to Jersey, Burton to Guernsey. All access to them was denied, and the use of books, and of pen, ink, and paper, was refused them. The sentence for these additional punishments was immediately reversed in an arbitrary manner by the Commons. Even the first sentence, upon examination, was declared illegal, and the judges who passed it were ordered to make reparation to the sufferers. When the prisoners landed in England, they were received and entertained with the highest demonstrations of affection and were attended by a mighty confluence of company. They were borne with great magnificence, and liberal presents were bestowed on them. On their approach to any town, all the inhabitants crowded to receive them and welcomed their reception with shouts and acclamations. Their train still increased as they drew nigh to London. Some miles from the city, the zealots of their party met them in great multitudes and attended their triumphant entrance: boughs were carried in this tumultuous procession, the roads were strewed with flowers, and the highest exultations of joy were intermingled with loud and virulent invectives against the prelates who had so cruelly persecuted such godly personages. The more ignoble these men were, the more perceptible was the insult upon royal authority and the more dangerous was the spirit of disaffection and mutiny which it revealed among the people.

Lilburne, Leighton, and everyone who had been punished for seditious libels during the preceding administration now recovered their liberty and were decreed damages from the judges and ministers of justice.

Not only the present disposition of the nation assured impunity to all libelers: a new method of framing and dispersing libels was invented by the leaders of popular discontent. Petitions to Parliament craving redress against particular grievances were drawn; when a sufficient number of subscriptions were procured, the petitions were presented to the Commons and immediately published. These petitions became distinct bonds of association among the subscribers and seemed to give undoubted sanction and authority to the complaints which they contained.

It is claimed by historians favorable to the royal cause, and was even asserted by the king himself in a declaration, that a most disingenuous, or rather criminal, practice prevailed in conducting many of these addresses. A petition was first framed: moderate, reasonable, such as men of rank willingly subscribed. The names were afterwards torn off and affixed to another petition which served better the purposes of the popular faction. We may judge the wild fury which prevailed throughout the nation when so scandalous an imposture, affecting such numbers of people, could be openly practiced without drawing infamy and ruin upon the managers.

So many grievances were offered, both by the members and by outsiders' petitions, that the house was divided into more than forty committees, each of them charged with the examination of some particular violation of law and liberty which had been complained of. Besides the general committees of religion, trade, privileges, and laws, many subdivisions of these were framed, and a strict scrutiny was everywhere carried on. It is to be noticed that before the beginning of the seventeenth century, when the Commons assumed less influence and authority, complaints of grievances were usually presented to the house by any members who had had particular opportunity of observing them. These general committees, each of which was a kind of inquisitorial court, had not then been established; and we find that the king in a former declaration complained loudly of this innovation, so little favorable to royal authority. But the use of these committees was never so much multiplied as at present; and the Commons, though themselves the greatest innovators, employed the usual artifice of complaining against innovations and claiming to recover the ancient and established government.

From the reports of the committees, the house daily passed votes which mortified and astonished the court and inflamed and animated the nation. Ship money was declared illegal and arbitrary, the sentence against Hampden cancelled, the Court of York abolished, compositions for knighthood stigmatized, the enlargement of the forests condemned, patents for monopolies annulled, and every late measure of administration treated with reproach and obloquy. Today a sentence of the Star Chamber was exclaimed against, tomorrow a decree of the High Commission. Every discretionary act of Council was represented as arbitrary and tyrannical; and the general inference was still inculcated that a formed design had been laid to subvert the laws and constitution of the kingdom.

From necessity, the king remained entirely passive during all these violent operations. The few servants who continued faithful to him were seized with astonishment at the rapid progress made by the Commons in power and popularity; they were glad to avoid punishment by their inactive and inoffensive behavior. The torrent rising to so dreadful and unexpected a height, despair seized all those who, from interest or habit, were most attached to monarchy. And as for those who maintained their duty to the king merely from their regard to the constitution, they seemed by their concurrence to swell that inundation which began already to deluge everything. "You have taken the whole machine of government in pieces," said Charles in a discourse to the Parliament, "a practice frequent with skillful artists when they desire to clear the wheels from any rust which may have grown upon them. The engine," he continued, "may again be restored to its former use and motions provided it be put up entire, so as not a pin of it be wanting." But this was far from the intention of the Commons. The machine, they thought with some reason, was encumbered with many wheels and springs which retarded and crossed its operations and destroyed its utility. Happy would it have been had they proceeded with moderation and been contented, in their present plenitude of power, to remove such parts only as might justly be deemed superfluous and incongruous.

In order to maintain that high authority which they had acquired, the Commons, besides confounding and overawing their opponents, judged it requisite to inspire courage into their friends and adherents—particularly into the Scots and the religious Puritans, to whose assistance and good offices they were already so much beholden.

No sooner were the Scots masters of the northern counties than they laid aside their first professions—which they had not, indeed, means to support—of paying for everything; and in order to prevent the destructive expedient of plunder and free quarters, the country consented to give them a regular contribution of £850 a day, full payment for their subsistence. The Parliament, to relieve the northern counties from so grievous a burden, agreed to remit pay to the Scottish as well as to the English army; because subsidies would be levied too slowly for so urgent an occasion, money was borrowed from the citizens upon the security of particular members. Two subsidies, a very small sum, were at first voted; and as the intention of this supply was to indemnify the members who by their private credit had supported public credit, this pretense was immediately laid hold of, and the money was ordered to be paid not into the Treasury but to commissioners appointed by Parliament. This practice, as it diminished the authority of the Crown, was willingly embraced; and it was afterwards continued by the Commons with regard to every branch of revenue which they granted to the king. It was evident that the invasion of the Scots had been the cause of assembling the Parliament. The presence of their army reduced the king to that total subjection in which he was now held. For this reason, the Commons openly professed their intention of retaining these invaders till all their own enemies could be suppressed and all their purposes effected. "We cannot yet spare the Scots," said Strode plainly in the house, "the sons of Zeruiah are still too strong for us": an allusion to a passage of Scripture, in accord with the mode of that age. Eighty thousand pounds a month were requisite for the maintenance of the two armies, a sum much greater than the subject had ever been accustomed in any former period to pay to the public. And though several subsidies, together with a poll tax, were from time to time voted to answer the charge, the Commons still took care to be in debt, in order to render the continuance of the session the more necessary.

The Scots being such useful allies to the malcontent party in England, it is no wonder that they were courted with the most unlimited complaisance and the most important services. The king, having in his first speech called them "rebels," observed that he had given great offense to the Parliament, and he was immediately obliged to soften and even retract the expression. The Scottish commissioners, of whom the most considerable were the Earl of Rothes and Lord Loudoun, found every advantage in conducting their treaty [negotiations], yet made no haste in bringing it to a conclusion. They were lodged in the city and kept an intimate correspondence both with those magistrates who were extremely disaffected and with the popular leaders in both houses. St. Antholin Church was assigned them for their devotions, and their chaplains here began openly to practice the Presbyterian form of worship, which, except in foreign languages, had never before been allowed any indulgence or toleration. So violent was the general propensity towards this new religion that multitudes of all ranks crowded to the church. Those who were so happy as to find access early in the morning kept their places the whole day; those who were excluded clung to the doors or windows in hopes of catching at least some distant murmur or broken phrases of the holy rhetoric. All the eloquence of Parliament, now well refined from pedantry, animated with the spirit of liberty, and employed in the most important interests, was not attended to with such insatiable avidity as were these lectures, delivered with ridiculous cant and a provincial accent, full of barbarism and of ignorance.

The most effectual expedient for paying court to the zealous Scots was to promote the Presbyterian discipline and worship throughout England, and to this innovation the popular leaders among the Commons and their more devoted partisans were sufficiently inclined of their own accord. Taking advantage of the present disorders, the Puritanical party, whose progress, though covert, had till now been gradual in the kingdom, began openly to profess their tenets and to make furious attacks on the established religion. The prevalence of that sect in the Parliament revealed itself from the beginning by barely noticed but decisive symptoms. Marshall and Burgess, two Puritanical clergymen, were chosen to preach before them; and they entertained the members with discourses seven hours in length. It being the custom of the house always to take the sacrament before they enter upon business, they ordered as a necessary preliminary that the communion table be moved from the east end of St. Margaret's [the parish church of the House of Commons] into the middle of the area. The name of the "spiritual lords" was commonly left out in acts of Parliament; and the laws ran in the name of king, Lords, and Commons. The clerk of the upper house, in reading bills, turned his back on the bench of bishops; nor was his insolence ever taken notice of. On a day appointed for a solemn fast and humiliation, all the orders of temporal peers, contrary to former practice, took the place of the spiritual ones in going to church; Lord Spencer remarked that the humiliation that day seemed confined to the prelates alone.

The bishops attacked

Every meeting of the Commons produced some vehement harangue against the usurpations of the bishops, against the High Commission, against the late Convocation, against the new canons. So disgusted were all lovers of civil liberty at the doctrines promoted by the clergy that these invectives were received without restraint; and no distinction at first appeared between those who desired only to repress the exorbitances of the hierarchy and those who aspired totally to annihilate episcopal jurisdiction. Encouraged by these favorable appearances, petitions against the church were framed in different parts of the kingdom. The epithet of "the ignorant and vicious priesthood" was commonly applied to all churchmen addicted to the established discipline and worship—though the episcopal clergy in England during that age seem to have been, as they are at present, sufficiently learned and exemplary. An address against episcopacy was presented by twelve clergymen to the committee of religion and was claimed to be signed by many hundreds of the Puritanical persuasion. But what made most noise was the city petition for a total alteration of church government, a petition to which fifteen thousand subscriptions were annexed and which was presented by Alderman Pennington, the city member. It is remarkable that among the many ecclesiastical abuses there complained of, an allowance given by the licensers of books to publish a translation of Ovid's *Art of Love* was not forgotten by those rustic censors.

Notwithstanding the favorable disposition of the people, the leaders in the house resolved to proceed with caution. They introduced a bill for prohibiting all clergymen the exercise of any civil office. As a consequence, the bishops were to be deprived of their seats in the House of Peers. This was a measure not unacceptable to the zealous friends of liberty, who observed with regret the devoted attachment of that order to the will of the monarch. But when this bill was presented to the Peers, it was rejected by a great majority: the first check which the Commons had received in their popular career, and a sign of what they might afterwards expect from the upper house, whose inclinations and interests could never be totally separated from the throne. But to show how little they were discouraged, the Puritans immediately brought in another bill for the total abolition of episcopacy; though they thought proper to let that bill sleep at present, in expectation of a more favorable opportunity of reviving it.

Among other acts of regal executive power which the Commons were every day assuming, they issued orders for demolishing all images, altars, and crucifixes. The zealous Sir Robert Harley, to whom the execution of these orders was committed, removed all crosses even out of streets and markets; and from his abhorrence of that superstitious figure, he would not anywhere allow one piece of wood or stone to lie over another at right angles.

The bishop of Ely and other clergymen were attacked on account of innovations. Cosin, who had long been vulnerable, was exposed to new censures. This clergyman, who was dean of Peterborough, was extremely zealous for ecclesiastical ceremonies. Far from permitting the communicants to break the sacramental bread with their fingers—a privilege on which the Puritans strenuously insisted—he would not so much as allow it to be cut with an ordinary household instrument: a consecrated knife alone could perform that sacred office, and such could never afterwards be profaned by any vulgar service.

Cosin likewise was accused of having said, "The king has no more authority in ecclesiastical matters than the boy who rubs my horse's heels." The expression was intemperate, but it is certain that all those high churchmen who were so industrious in reducing the laity to submission were extremely fond of their own privileges and independence and were desirous of exempting the mitre from all subjection to the Crown.

A committee was elected by the lower house as a court of inquisition upon the clergy; it was commonly denominated the committee of "scandalous ministers." The politicians among the Commons were apprised of the great importance of the pulpit for guiding the people, the bigots were enraged against the prelatical clergy, and both of them knew that no established government could be overthrown by strictly observing the principles of justice, equity, or clemency. The proceedings, therefore, of this famous committee, which continued for several years, were cruel, arbitrary, and made great havoc both on the church and the universities. They began with harassing, imprisoning, and molesting the clergy and ended with sequestrating and ejecting them. In order to join contumely to cruelty, they gave the sufferers the epithet of "scandalous" and endeavored to render them as odious as they were miserable. The greatest vices, however, which they could reproach a great part of them for were bowing at the name of Jesus, placing the communion table in the east, reading the king's orders for sports on Sunday, and other practices which the established government, both in church and state, had strictly required of them.

It may be worth observing that all historians who lived near that age—and, what perhaps is more decisive, all authors who have casually made mention of those public transactions—still represent the civil disorders and convulsions as proceeding from religious controversy and consider the political disputes about power and liberty as entirely subordinate to the other. It is true that had the king been able to support government and at the same time to abstain from all invasion of national privileges, it seems not probable that the Puritans ever could have acquired such authority as to overturn the whole constitution. Yet so entire was the subjection into which Charles was now fallen that had not the wound been poisoned by the infusion of theological hatred, it must have admitted of an easy remedy. Disuse of Parliaments, imprisonments and prosecution of members, ship money, an arbitrary administration: these were loudly complained of. But the grievances which tended chiefly to inflame the Parliament and nation, especially the latter, were the surplice, the rails placed about the altar, the bows exacted on approaching it, the liturgy, the breach of the Sabbath, embroidered copes, lawn sleeves, the use of the ring in marriage and of the cross in baptism. On account of these were the popular leaders content to throw the government into such violent convulsions; and to the disgrace of that age and of Britain, it must be acknowledged that the disorders in Scotland entirely, and those in England mostly, proceeded from so mean and contemptible an origin.

Some persons, partial to the patriots of this age, have ventured to put them in a balance with the most illustrious characters of antiquity and mentioned the names of Pym, Hampden, and Vane as a just parallel to those of Cato, Brutus, and Cassius. Profound capacity, indeed, undaunted courage, extensive enterprise: in these particulars, perhaps the Roman do not much surpass the English worthies. But what a difference when the discourse, conduct, conversation, and private as well as public behavior of both are inspected! Compare only one circumstance and consider its consequences. The leisure of those noble ancients was totally employed in the study of Grecian eloquence and philosophy, in the cultivation of polite letters and civilized society. The whole discourse and language of the moderns were polluted with mysterious jargon and full of the lowest and most vulgar hypocrisy.

The laws as they stood at present protected the Church of England, but they exposed the Catholics to the utmost rage of the Puritans; and these unhappy religionists, so obnoxious to the prevailing sect, could not hope to remain long unmolested. The voluntary contribution which they had made in order to assist the king in his war against the Scottish Covenanters was inquired into and represented as the greatest enormity. By an address from the Commons, all Catholic officers were removed from the army; and application was made to the king for seizing two-thirds of the lands of recusants, a proportion to which by law he was entitled but which he had always allowed them to possess upon easy compositions. The execution of the severe and bloody laws against priests was insisted on; and one Goodman, a Jesuit who was found in prison, was condemned to a capital punishment. Charles, however, agreeably to his usual principles, scrupled to sign the warrant for his execution; and the Commons expressed great resentment on the occasion. In a singular petition, Goodman begged to be hanged rather than prove a source of contention between the king and his people. He escaped with his life; but it seems more probable that he was overlooked amidst affairs of greater consequence than that such unrelenting hatred would be softened by any consideration of his courage and generosity.

An ambassador from the pope—first Con, a Scotsman; afterwards Rossetti, an Italian—had for some years openly resided at London and frequented the court. The queen's zeal and her authority with her husband had been the cause of this imprudence, so offensive to the nation. But the spirit of bigotry now rose too high to permit any longer such indulgences.

Hayward, a justice of peace, was wounded when employed in the exercise of his office by one James, a Catholic madman; this enormity was ascribed to the popery, not to the frenzy, of the assassin, and great alarms seized the nation and Parliament. A universal conspiracy of the papists was supposed to have taken place, and every man for some days imagined that he had a sword at his throat. Though some persons of family and distinction were still attached to the Catholic superstition, it is certain that the numbers of that sect did not amount to the fortieth part of the nation. The frequent panics to which men during this period were so subject on account of the Catholics were less the effects of fear than of extreme rage and aversion entertained against them.

The queen mother of France, having been forced into banishment by some court intrigues, had retired into England and expected shelter amidst her present distresses in the dominions of her daughter and son-in-law. But though she behaved in the most inoffensive manner, she was insulted by the populace on account of her religion and was even threatened with worse treatment. The Earl of Holland, lieutenant of Middlesex, had ordered a hundred musketeers to guard her; but finding that they had imbibed the same prejudices with the rest of their countrymen and were unwillingly employed in such a service, he laid the case before the House of Peers; for the king's authority was now entirely annihilated. He spoke of the indignity of so great a princess, mother to the king of France and to the queens of Spain and England, being affronted by the multitude. He observed the indelible reproach which would fall upon the nation if that unfortunate queen suffered any violence from the misguided zeal of the people. He urged the sacred rights of hospitality due to everyone, and much more to a person in distress, of so high a rank, and so nearly connected with the nation. The Peers thought proper to communicate the matter to the Commons, whose authority over the people was absolute. The Commons agreed to the necessity of protecting the queen mother but at the same time prayed that she might be desired to depart the kingdom, "For the quieting those jealousies in the hearts of his majesty's well-affected subjects, occasioned by some ill instruments [evil agents] about that queen's person, by the flowing of priests and papists to her house, and by the use and practice of the idolatry of the mass, and exercise of other superstitious services of the Romish church, to the great scandal of true religion."

Charles, in the former part of his reign, had endeavored to overcome the intractable and encroaching spirit of the Commons by a perseverance in his own measures, by a stately dignity of behavior, and by maintaining at their utmost height, and even perhaps stretching beyond former precedent, the rights of his prerogative. Finding by experience how unsuccessful those measures had proved and observing the low condition to which he was now reduced, he resolved to alter his whole conduct and to regain the confidence of his people by pliableness, by concessions, and by a total conformity to their inclinations and prejudices. It may safely be averred that this new extreme into which the king had fallen from lack of proper counsel or support became no less dangerous to the constitution and pernicious to public peace than the other in which he had so long and so unfortunately persevered.

Tonnage and poundage

The pretensions with regard to tonnage and poundage were revived, and with certain assurance of success, by the Commons. The levying of these duties as formerly—without consent of Parliament, and even increasing them at pleasure—was too great an incongruity in a free constitution, where the people by their fundamental privileges cannot be taxed but by their own consent, to be endured any longer by these jealous patrons of liberty. In the preamble, therefore, to the bill by which the Commons granted these duties to the king, they took care, in the strongest and most positive terms, to assert their own right of bestowing this gift and to divest the Crown of all independent title of assuming it. And that they might increase, or rather finally fix, the entire dependence and subjection of the king, they voted these duties only for two months, and afterwards renewed their grant from time to time for very short periods. Charles, in order to show that he entertained no intention ever again to separate himself from his Parliament, passed this important bill without any scruple or hesitation.

Triennial Bill

With regard to the bill for triennial Parliaments, the king made a little difficulty. By an old statute passed during the reign of Edward III, it had been enacted that Parliaments should be held once every year, or more frequently if necessary. But as no provision had been made in case of failure and no precise method pointed out for execution, this statute had been considered merely as a general declaration and was dispensed with at pleasure. These defects were rectified by those vigilant patriots who now assumed the reins of government. It was enacted that if the chancellor, who was first bound under severe penalties, failed to issue writs by September 3 in every third year, any twelve or more of the Peers would be empowered to exert this authority. In default of the Peers, that the sheriffs, mayors, bailiffs, etc. would summon the voters. And in their default, that the voters themselves would meet and proceed to the election of members in the same manner as if writs had been regularly issued from the Crown. Nor could the Parliament, after it was assembled, be adjourned, prorogued, or dissolved without their own consent during the space of fifty days. By this bill, some of the noblest and most valuable prerogatives of the Crown were retrenched; but at the same time, nothing could be more necessary than such a statute for completing a regular plan of law and liberty. A great reluctance to assemble Parliaments must be expected in the king where these assemblies, as of late, establish it as a maxim to carry their scrutiny into every part of government. During long intermissions of Parliament, grievances and abuses would naturally creep in, as was found by recent experience; and it would even become necessary for the king and Council to exert a great discretionary authority and in every urgency to supply by acts of state the legislative power whose meeting was so uncertain and precarious. Charles, finding that nothing less would satisfy his Parliament and people, at last gave his assent to this bill, which produced so great an innovation in the constitution. Solemn thanks were presented to him by both houses. Great rejoicings were expressed both in the city and throughout the nation.

And mighty professions were everywhere made of gratitude and mutual returns of supply and confidence. This concession of the king, it must be granted, was not entirely voluntary; it was of a nature too important to be voluntary. The sole inference which his partisans were entitled to draw from the submissions so frankly made to present necessity was that he had certainly adopted a new plan of government and was resolved to acquire the confidence and affections of his people by every indulgence in the future.

Charles thought that what concessions were made to the public were of little consequence if no gratifications were bestowed on individuals who had acquired the direction of public counsels and determinations. A change of ministers as well as of measures was therefore resolved on. In one day, several new privy counselors were sworn: the Earls of Hertford, Bedford, Essex, Bristol; the Lords Say, Savile, Kimbolton. A few days later, the Earl of Warwick was admitted. All these noblemen were of the popular party; and some of them later, when matters were pushed to extremities by the Commons, proved the greatest support of monarchy.

Juxon, bishop of London, who had never desired the treasurer's staff, now earnestly solicited for leave to resign it and retire to the care of that turbulent diocese committed to him. The king gave his consent; and it is remarkable that during all the severe inquiries later carried on against the conduct of ministers and prelates, the mild and prudent virtues of this man, who bore both these hated ranks, remained unmolested. It was intended that Bedford, a popular man of great authority as well as wisdom and moderation, would succeed Juxon. But that nobleman, unfortunately both for king and people, died about this very time. By some promotions, place was made for St. John, who was created solicitor general. Holles was to be made secretary of state in the place of Windebank, who had fled; Pym, chancellor of the Exchequer in the place of Lord Cottington, who had resigned; Lord Say, master of the wards, in the place of the same nobleman; the Earl of Essex, governor; and Hampden, tutor to the prince.

What retarded the execution of these projected changes was the difficulty of satisfying all those who, from their activity and authority in Parliament, had pretensions for offices and who still had it in their power to embarrass and distress the public measures. Those whom the king intended to distinguish by his favor were unwilling to undergo the reproach of having driven a separate bargain and of sacrificing the cause of the nation to their own ambitious purposes. And as they were aware that they must owe their preferment entirely to their weight and consideration in Parliament, most of them were resolved still to adhere to that assembly and both to promote its authority and to preserve their own credit in it. On all occasions, they had no other advice to give the king than to allow himself to be directed by his great council, or in other words, to resign himself passively to their guidance and government. And Charles found that instead of acquiring friends by bestowing honors and offices, he would only arm his enemies with more power to hurt him.

The end on which the king was most intent in changing ministers was to save the life of the Earl of Strafford by mollifying with these indulgences the rage of his most furious prosecutors. But so high was that nobleman's reputation for experience and capacity that all the new counselors and intended ministers plainly saw that if he escaped their vengeance, he must return into favor and authority. They regarded his death as the only security which they could have, both for the establishment of their present power and for success in their future enterprises. His impeachment, therefore, was pushed on with the utmost vigor, and after long and solemn preparations, was brought to a final conclusion.

Strafford's trial

Immediately after Strafford was sequestered from Parliament and confined in the Tower, a committee of thirteen was chosen by the lower house and entrusted with the office of preparing a charge against him. These, joined to a small committee of the Lords, were vested with authority to examine all witnesses, to call for every paper, and to use any means of scrutiny with regard to any part of the earl's behavior and conduct. After so general and unbounded an inquisition, exercised by such powerful and implacable enemies, a man must have been very cautious or very innocent during the whole course of his life not to afford some cause of accusation against him.

This committee, by direction from both houses, took an oath of secrecy: a practice which was very unusual and which gave them the appearance of conspirators more than ministers of justice. But the intention of this strictness was to render it more difficult for the earl to elude their search or prepare for his justification.

Application was made to the king that he allow this committee to examine privy counselors with regard to opinions delivered at the board. Charles unwarily made this concession, which from then on banished all mutual confidence from the deliberations of Council, where every man is supposed to have entire freedom, without fear of future punishment or inquiry, of proposing any expedient, questioning any opinion, or supporting any argument.

Sir George Radcliffe, the earl's intimate friend and confidant, was accused of high treason, sent for from Ireland, and committed to close custody. As no charge ever appeared or was prosecuted against him, it is impossible to give a more charitable interpretation to this measure than that the Commons thereby intended to deprive Strafford, in his present distress, of the assistance of his best friend, who was most enabled by his testimony to justify the innocence of his patron's conduct and behavior.

When intelligence arrived in Ireland of the plans laid for Strafford's ruin, the Irish House of Commons, though they had very lately bestowed ample praises on his administration, entered into all the violent counsels against him and prepared a representation of the miserable state into which they supposed the kingdom to be fallen by his misconduct. They sent over a committee to London to assist in the prosecution of their unfortunate governor; and every measure of the Irish Parliament was governed and directed by intimations from this committee, who entered into close confederacy with the popular leaders in England. Impeachments—which were never prosecuted—were carried up against Sir Richard Bolton, the chancellor; Sir Gerard Lowther, chief justice; and John Bramhall, bishop of Derry. This step, which was an exact counterpart to the proceedings in England, served also the same purposes: it deprived the king of the ministers whom he most trusted, it discouraged and terrified all the other ministers, and it prevented those persons who were best acquainted with Strafford's counsels from giving evidence in his favor before the English Parliament.

The bishops, being forbidden by the ancient canons to assist in trials for life and being unwilling by any opposition to irritate the Commons, who were already much prejudiced against them, thought it proper to withdraw. The Commons also voted that the newly created peers ought to have no voice in this trial, on the grounds that because the accusation was agreed to while they were commoners, their consent to it was implied with that of all the Commons of England. Notwithstanding this decision, which was meant only to deprive Strafford of so many friends, Lord Seymour and some

1641

others still continued to keep their seats, and their right to them was not questioned any further.

To bestow greater solemnity on this important trial, which began on March 22, temporary galleries were erected in Westminster Hall; there both houses sat, the one as accusers, the other as judges. Besides the chair of state, a close gallery was prepared for the king and queen, who attended during the whole trial.

An accusation carried on by the united effort of three kingdoms against one man—unprotected by power, unassisted by counsel, disfavored by authority—was likely to prove a very unequal contest. Yet such were the capacity, genius, and presence of mind displayed by this magnanimous statesman that while argument, reason, and law had any place, he obtained an undisputed victory. And he perished at last, overwhelmed and still unsubdued, only by the open violence of his fierce and unrelenting antagonists.

The articles of impeachment against Strafford were twenty-eight in number and regarded his conduct as president of the Council of York, as deputy or lieutenant of Ireland, and as counselor or commander in England. But though four months were employed by the managers in framing the accusation and all Strafford's answers were extemporary, it appears from comparison that not only was he free from the crime of treason—of which there is not the least appearance—but that his conduct, making allowance for human infirmities exposed to such severe scrutiny, was innocent, and even laudable.

The powers of the northern council while he was president had been extended by the king's instructions beyond what formerly had been practiced. But as that court was at first instituted by a stretch of royal prerogative, it had been usual for the prince to vary his instructions, and the largest authority committed to it was altogether as legal as the most moderate and most limited. Nor was it reasonable to conclude that Strafford had used any art to procure those extensive powers, since he never once sat as president or exercised one act of jurisdiction after he was invested with the authority so much complained of.

In the government of Ireland, his administration had promoted equally his master's interest and that of the subjects committed to his care. He had paid off a large debt; he had left a considerable sum in the Exchequer; the revenue, which never before answered the charges of government, was now raised to be equal to them. A small standing army, formerly kept in no order, was augmented and governed by exact discipline; and a great force was raised and paid there for the support of the king's authority against the Scottish Covenanters.

Industry and all the arts of peace were introduced among that rude people. The shipping of the kingdom augmented a hundredfold; the customs tripled upon the same rates; the exports doubled in value to the imports; manufactures, particularly that of linen, were introduced and promoted. Agriculture, by means of the English and Scottish plantations, was gradually advancing; the Protestant religion was encouraged without the persecution or discontent of the Catholics.

The springs of authority he had enforced without overstraining them. Discretionary acts of jurisdiction, indeed, he had often exerted by holding courts martial, billeting soldiers, deciding causes upon paper petitions before the Council, issuing proclamations, and punishing their infraction. But discretionary authority during that age was usually exercised even in England. In Ireland, it was still more requisite among a rude people not yet thoroughly subdued, averse to the religion and manners of their conquerors, and ready on all occasions to relapse into rebellion and disorder. While the managers of the Commons demanded at every moment that the deputy's conduct should be examined by the line of rigid law and severe principles, he appealed still to the practice of all former deputies and to the uncontrollable necessity of his situation.

So great was his art of managing elections and balancing parties that he had engaged the Irish Parliament to vote whatever was necessary both for the payment of former debts and for support of the newly levied army; nor had he ever been reduced to the illegal expedients practiced in England for the supply of public necessities. No imputation of rapacity could justly lie against his administration. Some instances of imperious expressions and even actions may be met with. The case of Lord Mountnorris, of all those which were collected with so much industry, is the most flagrant and the least excusable.

It had been reported at the table of Lord Chancellor Loftus that Annesley, one of the deputy's attendants, had, while moving a stool, sorely hurt the foot of his master, who was at that time afflicted with the gout. "Perhaps," said Mountnorris, who was present at table, "it was done in revenge of that public affront which my lord deputy formerly put upon him. But he has a brother who would not have taken such a revenge." This casual and seemingly innocent, or at least ambiguous, expression was reported to Strafford, who, on pretense that such a suggestion might prompt Annesley to avenge himself in another manner, ordered Mountnorris, who was an officer, to be tried by a court martial for mutiny and sedition against his general. The court, which consisted of the chief officers of the army, found the crime to be capital and condemned that nobleman to lose his head.

In vain did Strafford plead in his own defense against this article of impeachment that the sentence of Mountnorris was the deed—and that too unanimous—of the court, not the act of the deputy; that he neither spoke to any member of the court nor voted in the cause, but sat openly as a party and then immediately withdrew to leave them to their freedom; that aware of the iniquity of the sentence, he procured his majesty's free pardon to Mountnorris; and that he did not even keep that nobleman a moment in suspense with regard to his fate, but instantly told him that he himself would sooner lose his right hand than execute such a sentence, nor was his lordship's life in any danger. In vain did Strafford's friends add as a further apology that Mount-norris was a man of an infamous character, who paid court by the lowest adulation to all deputies while present and blackened their character by the vilest calumnies when absent; and that Strafford, expecting like treatment, had used this expedient for no other purpose than to subdue the petulant spirit of the man. These excuses alleviate the guilt; but there still remains enough to prove that the mind of the deputy, though great and firm, had been not a little debauched by the riot of absolute power and uncontrolled authority.

When Strafford was called over to England, he found everything falling into such confusion by the open rebellion of the Scots and the covert discontents of the English that if he had counseled or executed any violent measure, he might perhaps have been able to defend his conduct from the great law of necessity, which admits not, while the necessity is extreme, of any scruple, ceremony, or delay. But in fact no illegal advice or action was proved against him; the whole amount of his guilt during this period was some peevish, or at most imperious, expressions which, amidst such desperate extremities and during a bad state of health, had unhappily fallen from him.

If Strafford's apology was, in the main, so satisfactory when he pleaded to each particular article of the charge, his victory was still more decisive when he brought the whole together and repelled the imputation of treason, the crime which the Commons would infer from the full view of his conduct and behavior. Of all species of guilt, Strafford argued, the law of England had with the most scrupulous exactness defined that of treason, because on that side it was found most necessary to protect the subject against the violence of the king and of his ministers. In the famous statute of Edward III, all the kinds of treason are enumerated, and every other crime besides those expressly mentioned is carefully excluded from that appellation. But with regard to the present charge—"An endeavor to subvert the fundamental laws"—the statute of treasons is totally silent. Arbitrarily to introduce it into the fatal catalogue is itself a subversion of all law, and under color of defending liberty, reverses a statute the best fitted for the security of liberty that had ever been enacted by an English Parliament.

As this species of treason discovered by the Commons is entirely new and unknown to the laws, he continued, so is the species of proof by which they pretend [attempt; claim] to fix that guilt upon the accused. They have invented a kind of "accumulative or constructive" evidence, by which many actions, either totally innocent in themselves or criminal in a much inferior degree, shall, when united, amount to treason and subject the person to the highest penalties inflicted by the law. A hasty and unguarded word, a rash and passionate action, assisted by the malevolent fancy of the accuser and tortured by doubtful constructions, is transmuted into the deepest guilt; and the lives and fortunes of the whole nation, no longer protected by justice, are subjected to arbitrary will and pleasure.

"Where has this species of guilt lain so long concealed?" said Strafford in conclusion. "Where has this fire been so long buried during so many centuries that no smoke should appear, till it burst out at once to consume me and my children? Better it were to live under no law at all, and by the maxims of cautious prudence to conform ourselves the best we can to the arbitrary will of a master, than fancy we have a law on which we can rely, and find at last that this law shall inflict a punishment precedent to the promulgation and try us by maxims unheard of till the very moment of the prosecution. If I sail on the Thames and split my vessel on an anchor, in case there be no buoy to give warning, the party shall pay me damages. But if the anchor be marked out, then is the striking on it at my own peril. Where is the mark set upon this crime? Where the token by which I should discover it? It has lain concealed, under water; and no human prudence, no human innocence, could save me from the destruction with which I am at present threatened.

"It is now full two hundred and forty years since treasons were defined; and so long has it been since any man was touched to this extent upon this crime before myself. We have lived, my lords, happily to ourselves at home. We have lived gloriously abroad to the world. Let us be content with what our fathers have left us. Let not our ambition carry us to be more learned than they were in these killing and destructive arts. Great wisdom it will be in your lordships, and just providence for yourselves, for your posterities, for the whole kingdom, to cast from you into the fire these bloody and mysterious volumes of arbitrary and constructive treasons, as the primitive Christians did their books of curious arts, and betake yourselves to the plain letter of the statute, which tells you where the crime is and points out to you the path by which you may avoid it.

"Let us not, to our own destruction, awake those sleeping lions by rattling up a company of old records which have lain for so many ages by the wall, forgotten and neglected. To all my afflictions, add not this, my lords, the most severe of any: that I, for my other sins, not for my treasons, be the means of introducing a precedent so pernicious to the laws and liberties of my native country.

"However, these gentlemen at the bar say they speak for the commonwealth, and they believe so. Yet, under favor, it is I who, in this particular, speak for the commonwealth. Precedents like those which are endeavored to be established against me must draw along [result in] such inconveniences and miseries that in a few years the kingdom will be in the condition expressed in a statute of Henry IV; and no man shall know by what rule to govern his words and actions.

"Impose not, my lords, difficulties insurmountable upon ministers of state, nor disable them from serving with cheerfulness their king and country. If you examine them, and under such severe penalties, by every grain, by every little weight, the scrutiny will be intolerable. The public affairs of the kingdom must be left waste, and no wise man who has any honor or fortune to lose will ever engage himself in such dreadful, such unknown perils.

"My lords, I have now troubled your lordships a great deal longer than I should have done. Were it not for the interest of these pledges, which a saint in heaven left me, I should be loath—"; here he pointed to his children, and his weeping stopped him. "What I forfeit for myself, it is nothing. But I confess, that my indiscretion should forfeit for them, it wounds me very deeply. You will be pleased to pardon my infirmity; something I should have said, but I see I shall not be able, and therefore I shall leave it.

"And now, my lords, I thank God I have been, by his blessing, sufficiently instructed in the extreme vanity of all temporary enjoyments compared to the importance of our eternal duration. And so, my lords, even so; with all humility and with all tranquility of mind, I submit, clearly and freely, to your judgments. And whether that righteous doom shall be to life or death, I shall repose myself, full of gratitude and confidence, in the arms of the great Author of my existence."

"Certainly," says Whitelocke with his usual candor, "never any man acted such a part, on such a theatre, with more wisdom, constancy, and eloquence, with greater reason, judgment, and temper, and with a better grace in all his words and actions, than did this great and excellent person; and he moved the hearts of all his auditors, some few excepted, to remorse and pity." It is remarkable that the historian who expresses himself in these terms was himself chairman of that committee which conducted the impeachment against this unfortunate statesman. The accusation and defense lasted eighteen days. The managers divided the several articles among them and attacked the prisoner with all the weight of authority, with all the vehemence of rhetoric, with all the accuracy of long preparation. Strafford was obliged to speak with deference and reserve towards his most inveterate enemies: the Commons, the Scottish nation, and the Irish Parliament. He took only a very short time on each article to recollect himself. Yet he alone, without assistance, mixing modesty and humility with firmness and vigor, made such a defense that the Commons saw it impossible ever to obtain a sentence against him by a legal prosecution.

Bill of attainder

But the death of Strafford was too important a stroke of party to be left unattempted by any expedient, however extraordinary. Besides the great genius and authority of that minister, he had threatened some of the popular leaders with an impeachment; and had he not himself been suddenly prevented by the impeachment of the Commons, he would have that very day, it was thought, charged Pym, Hampden, and others with treason for having invited the Scots to invade England. A bill of attainder was therefore brought into the lower house immediately after finishing these pleadings; and preparatory to it, a new proof of the earl's guilt was produced in order to remove such scruples as might be entertained with regard to a method of proceeding so unusual and irregular.

Sir Henry Vane, secretary, had taken some notes of a debate in Council after the dissolution of the last Parliament. Being at a distance, he had sent the keys of his cabinet, it was claimed, to his son, Sir Henry, in order to search for some papers which were necessary for completing a marriage settlement. Young Vane, falling upon his father's notes, deemed the matter of the utmost importance and immediately communicated it to Pym, who now produced the paper before the House of Commons. The question before the Council was: "Offensive or defensive war with the Scots." The king proposes this difficulty: "But how can I undertake offensive war if I have no more money?" The answer ascribed to Strafford was in these words: "Borrow of the city a hundred thousand pounds. Go on vigorously to levy ship money. Your majesty having tried the affections of your people, you are absolved and loose from all rules of government, and may do what power will admit. Your majesty, having tried all ways, shall be acquitted before God and man. And you have an army in Ireland, which you may employ to reduce this kingdom to obedience. For I am confident the Scots cannot hold out five months." There followed some counsels of Laud and Cottington equally violent with regard to the king's being absolved from all rules of government.

This paper, with all the circumstances of its discovery and communication, was claimed to be equivalent to two witnesses and to be an unanswerable proof of those pernicious counsels of Strafford which tended to the subversion of the laws and constitution. It was replied by Strafford and his friends that old Vane was his most inveterate and declared enemy; and if the secretary himself, as was by far most probable, had willingly delivered to his son this paper of notes to be communicated to Pym, this implied such a breach of oaths and of trust as rendered him totally unworthy of all credit. That the secretary's deposition was at first exceedingly dubious: upon two examinations he could not remember any such words; even the third time, his testimony was not positive, but imported only that Strafford had spoken such or suchlike words; and words may be very like in sound and differ much in sense; nor ought the lives of men to depend upon grammatical criticisms of any expressions, much less of those which had been delivered by the speaker without premeditation and committed by the hearer for any time, however short, to the uncertain record of memory. That in the present case, changing "this kingdom" into "that kingdom"—a very slight alteration!—the earl's discourse could regard nothing but Scotland, and implies no advice unworthy of an English counselor. That even retaining the expression "this kingdom," the words may fairly be understood to refer to Scotland, which alone was the kingdom that the debate regarded and which alone had thrown off allegiance and could be reduced to obedience. That it could be proved, by the evidence of all the king's ministers as well as by the known disposition of the forces, that the intention never was to land the Irish army in England, but in Scotland. That of six other counselors present, Laud and Windebank could give no evidence; Northumberland, Hamilton, Cottington, and Juxon could recollect no such expression; and the advice was too remarkable to be easily forgotten. That it was in no way probable such a desperate counsel would be openly delivered at the board and before Northumberland, a person of that high rank and whose attachments to the court were so much weaker than his connections with the country. That though Northumberland, and he alone, had recollected some such expression as that "of being absolved from rules of government," yet in such desperate extremities as those into which the king and kingdom were then fallen, a maxim of that nature, allowing it to be delivered by Strafford, may be defended upon principles the most favorable to law and liberty. And that nothing could be more iniquitous than to extract an accusation of treason from an opinion simply proposed at the council table, where all freedom of debate ought to be permitted and where it was not unusual for the members, in order to draw forth the sentiments of others, to propose counsels very remote from their own secret advice and judgment.

The evidence of Secretary Vane, though exposed to such insurmountable objections, was the real cause of Strafford's unhappy fate; it made the bill of attainder pass the Commons with no greater opposition than that of fifty-nine dissenting votes. But there remained two other branches of the legislature—the king and the Lords—whose assent was requisite; and these, it was easily foreseen, would reject the bill without scruple or deliberation if left to their free judgment. To overcome this difficulty, the popular leaders employed expedients for which they were beholden partly to their own industry, partly to the indiscretion of their adversaries.

Next Sunday, after the bill passed the Commons, the Puritanical pulpits resounded with declamations concerning the necessity of executing justice upon great delinquents. The populace took the alarm. About six thousand men armed with swords and cudgels flocked from the city and surrounded the Houses of Parliament. The names of the fifty-nine Commons members who had voted against the bill of attainder were posted up under the title of "Straffordians, and betrayers of their country." These were exposed to all the insults of the ungovernable multitude. When any of the lords passed, the cry for justice against Strafford resounded in their ears; and those suspected of friendship to that obnoxious minister were sure to meet with menaces, accompanied with symptoms of the most desperate resolutions in the furious populace.

Complaints in the House of Commons being made against these violences as the most flagrant breach of privilege, the ruling members showed plainly, by their affected coolness and indifference, that the popular tumults were not disagreeable to them. But a new discovery made about this time served to throw everything into still greater flame and combustion.

Some principal military officers—Percy, Jermyn, O'Neill, Goring, Wilmot, Pollard, Ashburnham—partly attached to the court, partly disgusted with the Parliament, had formed a plan of engaging the English army into the king's service, as they had observed displeasure in the army at some marks of preference given by the Commons to the Scots. For this purpose they entered into an association, took an oath of secrecy, and kept a close correspondence with some of the king's servants. The form of a petition to the king and Parliament was concerted; and it was intended to get this petition subscribed by the army. The petitioners there represented the great and unexampled concessions made by the king for the security of public peace and liberty; the endless demands of certain insatiable and turbulent spirits, whom nothing less than a total subversion of the ancient constitution would content; the frequent tumults which these factious malcontents had excited, and which endangered the liberty of Parliament. To prevent these mischiefs, the army offered to come up and guard that assembly. "So shall the nation," as they expressed themselves in the conclusion, "not only be vindicated from preceding innovations, but be secured from the future [innovations] which are threatened, and which are likely to produce more dangerous effects than the former." The draft of this petition being conveyed to the king, he was prevailed on, somewhat imprudently, to countersign it himself as a mark of his approbation. But as several difficulties occurred, the project was laid aside for two months before any public discovery was made of it.

It was Goring who betrayed the secret to the popular leaders. The alarm which this intelligence conveyed may easily be imagined. Petitions from the military to the civil power are always looked on as disguised, or rather undisguised, commands; they are of a nature widely different from petitions presented by any other rank of men. Pym opened the matter in the house. On the first intimation of a discovery, Percy concealed himself, and Jermyn withdrew overseas. This further confirmed the suspicion of a dangerous conspiracy. Goring delivered his evidence before the house; Percy wrote a letter to his brother, Northumberland, confessing most of the particulars. Both their testimonies agreed with regard to the oath of secrecy; and as this circumstance had been denied by Pollard, Ashburnham, and Wilmot in all their examinations, it was regarded as a new proof of some desperate resolutions which had been taken.

To convey more quickly the terror and indignation at this plot, the Commons voted that a protestation should be signed by all the members. It was sent up to the Lords and signed by all of them except Southampton and Robartes. Orders were given by the Commons alone, without other authority, that it should be subscribed by the whole nation. The protestation was in itself very inoffensive, even insignificant, and contained nothing but general declarations that the subscribers would defend their religion and liberties. But it tended to increase the popular panic, as it intimated, and declared more expressly in the preamble, that these blessings were now exposed to the utmost peril.

Alarms were every day given of new conspiracies. In Lancashire, great multitudes of papists were assembling. Secret meetings were held by them in caves and underground in Surrey. They had entered into a plot to blow up the Thames with gunpowder in order to drown London. Provisions of arms were being made overseas. Sometimes France, sometimes Denmark was forming designs against the kingdom. And the populace, who are always terrified by present dangers and enraged by distant ones, were still further animated in their demands of justice against the unfortunate Strafford.

The king came to the House of Lords; and though he expressed his resolution, for which he offered them any security, never again to employ Strafford in any branch of public business, he professed himself totally dissatisfied with regard to the circumstance of treason; and on that account, he declared his difficulty in giving his assent to the bill of attainder. The Commons took fire and voted it a breach of privilege for the king to take notice of any bill pending before the houses. Charles did not perceive that his attachment to Strafford was the chief motive for the bill, and that the greater proofs he gave of anxious concern for this minister, the more inevitable did he render his destruction.

About eighty peers had constantly attended Strafford's trial; but such apprehensions were entertained on account of the popular tumults that only forty-five were present when the bill of attainder was brought into the house. Yet of these, nineteen had the courage to vote against it; a certain proof that if entire freedom had been allowed, the bill would have been rejected by a great majority.

In carrying up the bill to the Lords, St. John, the solicitor general, advanced two topics well suited to the fury of the times: that if the testimony against Strafford were not clear, the use of a bill of attainder provided private satisfaction to each man's conscience even if no evidence at all be produced; and that the earl had no right to plead law, because he had broken the law. It is true, he added, we give law to hares and deer, for they are beasts of chase. But it was never accounted either cruel or unfair to destroy foxes or wolves wherever they can be found, for they are beasts of prey.

After popular violence had prevailed over the Lords, the same battery was next applied to force the king's assent. The populace flocked about Whitehall and accompanied their demand of justice with the loudest clamors and most open menaces. Rumors of conspiracies against the Parliament were anew spread abroad, invasions and insurrections were talked of, and the whole nation was raised into such a ferment as threatened some great and imminent convulsion. On whichever side the king cast his eyes, he saw no resource or security. All his servants, consulting their own safety rather than their master's honor, declined interposing with their advice between him and his Parliament. The queen, terrified with the appearance of so mighty a danger and bearing formerly no good will to Strafford, was in tears and pressed him to satisfy his people in this demand, which it was hoped would finally content them. Juxon alone, whose courage was not inferior to his other virtues, ventured to advise him that if in his conscience he did not approve of the bill, he should by no means assent to it.

Strafford, hearing of Charles's irresolution and anxiety, took a very extraordinary step: he wrote a letter in which he entreated the king, for the sake of public peace, to put an end to his unfortunate— however innocent—life and to quiet the tumultuous people by granting them the request for which they were so importunate. "In this," he added, "my consent will more acquit you to God than all the world can do besides. To a willing man there is no injury. And as, by God's grace, I forgive all the world with a calmness and meekness of infinite contentment to my dislodging soul; so, sir, to you, I can resign the life of this world with all imaginable cheerfulness, in the just acknowledgment of your exceeding favors." Perhaps Strafford hoped that this unusual instance of generosity would engage the king still more strenuously to protect him. Perhaps he gave his life for lost; and finding himself in the hands of his enemies and observing that Balfour, the lieutenant of the Tower, was devoted to the popular party, he absolutely despaired of ever escaping the multiplied dangers with which he was every way environed. We might ascribe this step to a noble effort of disinterestedness not unworthy of the great mind of Strafford if the measure which he advised had not been, in the event, as pernicious to his master as it was immediately fatal to himself.

After the most violent anxiety and doubt, Charles at last granted a commission to four noblemen to give the royal assent, in his name, to the bill of attainder. He probably flattered himself, in this extremity of distress, that as neither his will consented to the deed nor was his hand immediately engaged in it, he was the more free from all the guilt which attended it. These commissioners he empowered at the same time to give his assent to the bill which rendered the Parliament perpetual.

The Commons, from policy rather than necessity, had embraced the expedient of paying the two armies by borrowing money from the city; and these loans they had repaid afterwards by taxes levied upon the people. The citizens, either of their own accord or by suggestion, began to start difficulties with regard to a further loan which was demanded. We would make no scruple of trusting the Parliament, they said, were we certain that the Parliament were to continue till our repayment. But in the present precarious situation of affairs, what security can be given us for our money? In pretense of obviating this objection, a bill providing that the Parliament could not be dissolved, prorogued, or adjourned without their own consent was suddenly brought into the house and passed with great unanimity and rapidity. It was hurried in like manner through the House of Peers and was instantly carried to the king for his assent. Charles, in the agony of grief, shame, and remorse for Strafford's doom, failed to perceive that this other bill was of still more fatal consequence to his authority: the power of his enemies, already uncontrollable, was now rendered perpetual. In comparison with the bill of attainder, by which he deemed himself an accomplice in his friend's murder, this concession did not loom large in his eyes. If this circumstance lessens our idea of his resolution or penetration, it serves to prove the integrity of his heart and the goodness of his disposition. It is indeed certain that strong compunction for his consent to Strafford's execution attended this unfortunate prince during the remainder of his life; and even at his own fatal end, the memory of this guilt recurred upon him with great sorrow and remorse. All men were so aware of the extreme duress which was done to him that his reputation suffered little from this unhappy measure; and though he abandoned his best friend, yet he was still able to preserve in some degree the attachment of all his adherents.

Secretary Carleton was sent by the king to inform Strafford of the final resolution which necessity had extorted from him. The earl seemed surprised, and starting up, exclaimed in the words of Scripture, "Put not your trust in princes, nor in the sons of men; for in them there is no salvation." He was soon able, however, to collect his courage; and he prepared himself to suffer the fatal sentence. Only three days' interval was allowed him. The king made a new effort in his behalf and sent by the hands of the young prince a letter addressed to the Peers; in it, he entreated them to confer with the Commons about a mitigation of Strafford's sentence and begged at least for some delay. He was refused in both requests.

Execution of Strafford

Strafford, in passing from his prison cell to Tower Hill, where the scaffold was erected, stopped under Laud's windows and asked the archbishop, with whom he had long lived in intimate friendship, for the assistance of his prayers in those awful moments which were approaching. The aged primate dissolved in tears, and having pronounced with a broken voice a tender blessing on his departing friend, sank into the arms of his attendants. Strafford, still superior to his fate, moved on with an elevated countenance and with an air of even greater dignity than what usually attended him. He lacked that consolation which commonly supports those who perish by the stroke of injustice and oppression; he was not buoyed up by glory nor by the affectionate compassion of the spectators; yet his mind, erect and undaunted, found resources within itself and maintained its unbroken resolution amidst the terrors of death and the triumphant exultations of his misguided enemies. His discourse on the scaffold was full of decency and courage. He feared, he said, "that the omen was bad for the intended reformation of the state, that it commenced with the shedding of innocent blood." He bid a last adieu to his brother and friends who attended him and sent a blessing to his nearer relations who were absent. "And now," he said, "I have nigh done! One stroke will make my wife a widow, my dear children fatherless, deprive my poor servants of their indulgent master, and separate me from my affectionate brother and all my friends! But let God be to you and them all in all!" Going to disrobe and prepare himself for the block, "I thank God," he said, "that I am nowise afraid of death, nor am daunted with any terrors; but do as cheerfully lay down my head at this time as ever I did when going to repose!" An end was put to his life by one blow of the executioner.

Thus perished, in the forty-ninth year of his age, the Earl of Strafford, one of the most eminent personages that has appeared in England. Though his death was loudly demanded as a satisfaction to justice and an atonement for the many violations of the constitution, it may safely be affirmed that the sentence by which he fell was an enormity greater than the worst of those which his implacable enemies prosecuted with so much cruel industry. The people in their rage had totally mistaken the proper object of their resentment. All the necessities—or more properly speaking, the difficulties—by which the king had been induced to use violent expedients for raising supply were the result of measures previous to Strafford's favor; and if they arose from ill conduct, he, at least, was entirely innocent. Even those violent expedients themselves—all of them—which occasioned the complaint that the constitution was subverted had been conducted, so far as appeared, without his counsel or assistance. And whatever his private advice might have been, he often and publicly inculcated in the king's presence the salutary maxim that if any inevitable necessity ever obliged the sovereign to violate the laws, this license ought to be practiced with extreme reserve, and as soon as possible, a just atonement be made to the constitution for any injury which it might sustain from such dangerous precedents. The first Parliament after the Restoration reversed the bill of attainder; and even a few weeks after Strafford's execution, this very Parliament remitted to his children the more severe consequences of his sentence, as if conscious of the violence with which the prosecution had been conducted.

In vain did Charles expect, as a return for so many instances of unbounded compliance, that the Parliament would at last show him some indulgence and would cordially fall into that unanimity to which, at the expense of his own power and of his friend's life, he so earnestly courted them. All his concessions were poisoned by their suspicion of his lack of cordiality; and the supposed attempt to engage the army against them served with many as a confirmation of this jealousy. It was natural for the king to seek some resource while all the world seemed to desert him or combine against him; and this probably was the entire motive of that embryo scheme which was formed with regard to the army. But the popular leaders still insisted that a desperate plot was laid to bring up the forces immediately and offer violence to the Parliament. According to Percy, the project of bringing the army to London was proposed to the king; but he rejected it as foolish, because the Scots, who were in arms and lying near them, would be at London as soon as the English army. By means of these suspicions, however, the same implacable spirit was still kept alive; and the Commons, without giving the king any satisfaction in the settlement of his revenue, proceeded to carry their inroads with great vigor into his now defenseless prerogative.

High Commission and Star Chamber abolished

The two ruling passions of this Parliament were zeal for liberty and an aversion to the church; and nothing could appear more exceptionable to both of these than the Court of High Commission, whose institution rendered it entirely arbitrary and assigned to it the defense of the ecclesiastical establishment. The Star Chamber also was a court which exerted high discretionary powers and had no precise rule or limit, either with regard to the causes which came under its jurisdiction or the decisions which it formed. A bill unanimously passed the houses to abolish these two courts; and in them to annihilate the principal and most dangerous articles of the king's prerogative. By the same bill, the jurisdiction of the Privy Council was regulated and its authority abridged. Charles hesitated before he gave his assent. But finding that he had gone too far to retreat, and that he possessed no resource in case of a rupture, he at last affixed the royal sanction to this excellent bill. But to show the Parliament that he was sufficiently apprised of the importance of his grant, he observed to them that this statute altered in a great measure the fundamental laws, ecclesiastical and civil, which many of his predecessors had established.

By removing the Star Chamber, the king's power of binding the people by his proclamations was indirectly abolished. Removing at last that important branch of prerogative—the strong symbol of arbitrary power, and unintelligible in a limited constitution—left the system of government more consistent and uniform. The Star Chamber alone was accustomed to punish infractions of the king's edicts. But as no courts of judicature now remained except those in Westminster Hall, which take cognizance only of common and statute law, the king could from then on issue proclamations, but no man was bound to obey them. It must, however, be confessed that the experiment here made by the Parliament was not a little rash and adventurous. No government at that time appeared in the world, nor is perhaps to be found in the records of any history, which continued in existence without the mixture of some arbitrary authority committed to some magistrate. And beforehand, it might reasonably appear doubtful whether human society could ever reach that state of perfection as to support itself with no other control than the general and rigid maxims of law and equity. But the Parliament justly thought that the king was too eminent a magistrate to be trusted with discretionary power, which he might so easily turn to the destruction of liberty. And in the event, it has since been found that though some perceptible inconveniences arise from the maxim of adhering strictly to law, yet the advantages overbalance them; and those should render the English grateful to the memory of their ancestors, who after repeated contests at last established that noble, though dangerous, principle.

At the request of the Parliament, Charles gave all the judges patents during their good behavior instead of during pleasure, a circumstance of the greatest moment towards securing their independence and barring the entrance of arbitrary power into the ordinary courts of judicature.

The Marshal's Court, which took cognizance of offensive words and was not thought sufficiently limited by law, was also for that reason abolished. The Stannary Courts, which exercised jurisdiction over the miners, being liable to a like objection, underwent a like fate. The abolition of the Council of the North and the Council of Wales followed from the same principles. The authority of the clerk of the market, who had a general inspection over the weights and measures throughout the kingdom, was transferred to the mayors, sheriffs, and ordinary magistrates.

In short, if we take a survey of the transactions of this memorable Parliament during the first period of its operations, we shall find that, excepting Strafford's attainder, which was a tangle of cruel iniquity, their merits in other respects so much outweigh their mistakes as to entitle them to praise from all lovers of liberty. Not only were former abuses remedied and grievances redressed, but great provision for the future was made by law against the return of like complaints. And if the means by which they obtained such advantages savor often of artifice and sometimes of violence, it is to be considered that revolutions of government cannot be effected by the mere force of argument and reasoning; and that once factions are excited, men cannot regulate the tempers of others or themselves firmly enough to insure themselves against all exorbitances.

King's journey to Scotland

The Parliament now came to a pause. The king had promised his Scottish subjects that he would this summer pay them a visit in order to settle their government; and though the English Parliament was very importunate with him that he should lay aside that journey, they could not prevail with him so much as to delay it. As his journey, begun on August 8, would necessarily pass through the troops of both nations, the Commons seem to have entertained great jealousy on that account; as much as they formerly delayed the disbanding of the armies, so much they now hurried it on. The arrears, therefore, of the Scots were paid in full, and those of the English in part. The Scots returned home, and the English were separated into their several counties and dismissed.

After this, on September 9, the Parliament adjourned until October 20, and a committee of both houses—a thing unprecedented—was appointed to sit during the recess with very ample powers. Pym was elected chairman of the committee of the lower house. Further attempts were made by the Parliament while it sat, and even by the Commons alone, to assume sovereign executive powers and publish their "ordinances" (as they called them, instead of "laws"). The committee too was ready to imitate the example.

A small committee of both houses was appointed to attend the king into Scotland—in order, it was pretended, to see that the articles of pacification were executed, but really to be spies upon him, to extend still further the ideas of parliamentary authority, and to eclipse the majesty of the king. The Earl of Bedford, Lord Howard, Sir Philip Stapleton, Sir William Airmine, Fiennes, and Hampden were the persons chosen.

Endeavors were used before Charles's departure to have a protector of the kingdom appointed with a power to pass laws without having recourse to the king. So little regard was now paid to royal authority or to the established constitution of the kingdom.

Amidst the great variety of affairs which occurred during this busy period, we have almost overlooked the marriage of the princess Mary with William, prince of Orange. Before concluding this alliance, the king communicated his intentions to the Parliament, who received the proposal with satisfaction. This was the commencement of the connections with the family of Orange, connections which later were attended with the most important consequences, both to the kingdom and to the house of Stuart.

CHAPTER 55
1641 – 1642

*Settlement of Scotland – State of Ireland – Conspiracy
in Ireland – Insurrection and massacre – Meeting of the
English Parliament – The Remonstrance – Reasons on
both sides – Impeachment of the bishops – Accusation
of the five members – Tumults – King leaves London –
Arrives at York – Preparations for civil war*

T HE Scots, who began these fatal commotions, thought that they
had finished a very perilous undertaking much to their profit and
reputation. Besides the large pay voted them for lying in good quarters
for a year, the English Parliament had conferred on them a present of
£300,000 for their brotherly assistance. In the articles of pacification,
they were declared to have always been good subjects, and their military expeditions were approved of as enterprises calculated and intended for his majesty's honor and advantage. To carry further the
triumph over their sovereign, these terms, so ignominious to him,
were ordered by a vote of Parliament to be read in all churches upon a
day of thanksgiving appointed for the national pacification. All their
claims for the restriction of prerogative were agreed to be ratified. And
what they valued more than all these advantages, they had a near prospect of spreading the Presbyterian discipline in England and Ireland
from the seeds which they had scattered of their religious principles.
Never did refined Athens so exult in diffusing the sciences and liberal
arts over a savage world, never did generous Rome so please itself in
the view of law and order established by its victorious arms, as the
Scots now rejoiced in communicating their barbarous zeal and theological fervor to the neighboring nations.

266

Settlement of Scotland

Charles, despoiled in England of a considerable part of his authority and dreading still further encroachments upon him, arrived in Scotland on August 14 with an intention of abdicating almost entirely the small share of power which there remained to him and of giving full satisfaction, if possible, to his restless subjects in that kingdom.

The Lords of Articles was an ancient institution in the Scottish Parliament. They were constituted after this manner: all the temporal lords chose eight bishops; all the bishops elected eight temporal lords; these sixteen named eight commissioners of counties and eight burgesses; and without the previous consent of the thirty-two, who were denominated Lords of Articles, no motion could be made in Parliament. As the bishops were entirely devoted to the court, it is evident that all the Lords of Articles, by necessary consequence, depended on the king's nomination; and the prince, therefore, possessed an indirect veto on bills before their introduction and a direct one after bills had passed through Parliament, the former a prerogative of much greater consequence than the latter. The bench of bishops being now abolished, the Parliament laid hold of the opportunity and totally set aside the Lords of Articles. And till this important point was obtained, the nation, properly speaking, could not be said to enjoy any regular freedom.

It is remarkable that notwithstanding this institution, to which there was no parallel in England, the royal authority was always deemed much lower in Scotland than in the former kingdom. Bacon represented it as one advantage to be expected from the union that the too extensive prerogative of England would be abridged by the example of Scotland, and the too narrow prerogative of Scotland be enlarged from the imitation of England. The English were at that time a civilized people and obedient to the laws. But among the Scots, it was of little consequence how the laws were framed or by whom voted while the exorbitant aristocracy had it so much in their power to prevent their regular execution.

The Peers and Commons formed only one house in the Scottish Parliament; and as it had been the practice of James, continued by Charles, to grace English gentlemen with Scottish titles, all the determinations of Parliament, it was to be feared, would in time depend upon the prince by means of these votes of foreigners who had no interest or property in Scotland. It was a law deserving approbation, therefore, that no man would be created a Scottish peer who possessed less than 10,000 marks (£500) of annual rent in Scotland.

A law for triennial Parliaments was likewise passed; and it was ordained that the last act of every Parliament would be to appoint the time and place for holding the Parliament next ensuing.

The king was deprived of the power formerly exercised of issuing proclamations which enjoined obedience under the penalty of treason, a prerogative which invested him with the whole legislative authority, even in matters of the highest importance.

So far was laudable. But the most fatal blow given to royal authority—and what in effect dethroned the prince in his native country—was the article that no member of the Privy Council (in whose hands during the king's absence the whole administration lay), no officer of state, and none of the judges would be appointed but by advice and approbation of Parliament. Charles even agreed to deprive of their seats four judges who had adhered to his interests, and their places were filled by others more agreeable to the ruling party. Several of the Covenanters were also sworn into the Privy Council. And all the ministers of state, counselors, and judges were by law to hold their places during life or good behavior.

While in Scotland, the king conformed himself entirely to the established church and assisted with great gravity at the long prayers and longer sermons with which the Presbyterians endeavored to regale him. He bestowed pensions and preferments on Henderson, Gillespie, and other popular preachers; and he practiced every art to soften, if not to gain, his greatest enemies. The Earl of Argyll was created a marquess, Lord Loudoun an earl, Leslie was dignified with the title of Earl of Leven. His friends he was obliged for the present to neglect and overlook; some of them were disgusted. And his enemies were not reconciled, but ascribed all his caresses and favors to artifice and necessity.

Argyll and Hamilton, being seized with an apprehension—real or pretended—that the Earl of Crawford and others meant to assassinate them, left the Parliament suddenly and retired into the country; but upon invitation and assurances, they returned in a few days. This event, which had neither cause nor effect that was visible, nor purpose, nor consequence, was commonly denominated "the Incident." Though the Incident had no effect in Scotland, it was attended with unexpected consequences in England. The English Parliament, which assembled on October 20, being willing to awaken the people's tenderness by exciting their fears, immediately raised an alarm, as if the malignants—so they called the king's party—had laid a plot to murder them and all the godly in both kingdoms. They applied, therefore, to Essex, whom the king had left general in the south of England; and he ordered a guard to attend them.

But while the king was employed in pacifying the commotions in Scotland and was preparing to return to England in order to apply himself to the same salutary work in that kingdom, he received intelligence of a dangerous rebellion broken out in Ireland, with circumstances of the utmost horror, bloodshed, and devastation. On every side, this unfortunate prince was pursued with murmurs, discontent, faction, and civil wars; and the fire from all quarters, even by the most independent accidents, at once blazed up about him.

State of Ireland

The great plan of James in the administration of Ireland, continued by Charles, was by justice and peace to reconcile that turbulent people to the authority of laws, and by introducing art and industry among them to cure them of that sloth and barbarism to which they had always been subject. In order to serve both these purposes, and at the same time secure the dominion of Ireland to the English Crown, great colonies of British had been carried over, and being intermixed with the Irish, had everywhere introduced a new face of things into that country. During a peace of nearly forty years, the inveterate quarrels between the nations seemed in a great measure to be obliterated; and though much of the landed property forfeited by rebellion had been conferred on the new planters, a more than equal return had been made by their instructing the natives in tillage, building, manufactures, and all the civilized arts of life. This had been the course of things during the successive administrations of Chichester, Grandison, Falkland, and above all, of Strafford. Under the government of this latter nobleman, the pacific plans, now come to great maturity and forwarded by his vigor and industry, seemed to have operated with full success and to have bestowed at last on that savage country the face of a European settlement.

After Strafford fell a victim to popular rage, the humors excited in Ireland by that great event could not suddenly be composed; rather, they continued to produce the greatest innovations in the government.

The British Protestants transplanted into Ireland, having every moment before their eyes all the horrors of popery, had naturally been carried into the opposite extreme and had universally adopted the highest principles and practices of the Puritans. Monarchy as well as the hierarchy had become odious to them; and every method of limiting the authority of the Crown and detaching themselves from the king of England was greedily adopted and pursued. They failed to consider that as they scarcely formed the sixth part of the people and were secretly obnoxious to the ancient inhabitants, their only method of supporting themselves was by maintaining royal authority and preserving a great dependence on their mother country. The English Commons likewise, in their furious prosecution of Strafford, had overlooked the most obvious consequences; and when they imputed to him as a crime every discretionary act of authority, they despoiled all succeeding governors of that power by which alone the Irish could be retained in subjection. And so strong was the current for popular government in all the three kingdoms that the most established maxims of policy were everywhere abandoned in order to gratify this ruling passion.

Charles, unable to resist, had been obliged to yield to the Irish as to the Scottish and English Parliaments; and he found too that their encroachments still rose in proportion to his concessions. Those subsidies which they themselves had voted they reduced by a subsequent vote to a fourth part; the Court of High Commission was determined to be a grievance; martial law was abolished; the jurisdiction of the Council was annihilated; proclamations and acts of state were declared of no authority; every order or institution which depended on monarchy was invaded; and the prince was despoiled of all his prerogative without the least pretext of any violence or illegality in his administration.

The standing army of Ireland was usually about three thousand men; but in order to assist the king in suppressing the Scottish Covenanters, Strafford had raised eight thousand more and had incorporated with them a thousand men drawn from the old army, a necessary expedient for bestowing order and discipline on the newly levied soldiers. The private men in this army were all Catholics, but the officers, both commission and noncommission, were Protestants and could entirely be depended on by Charles. The English Commons entertained the greatest apprehensions on account of this army and never ceased soliciting the king till he agreed to disband it. Nor would it consent to any proposal for augmenting the standing army to five thousand men, a number which the king deemed necessary for retaining Ireland in obedience.

Charles, thinking it dangerous to disperse eight thousand men accustomed to idleness and trained to the use of arms among a nation so turbulent and unsettled, agreed with the Spanish ambassador to have them transported into Flanders and enlisted in his master's service. The English Commons, pretending apprehensions lest regular bodies of troops disciplined in the Low Countries would prove still more dangerous, showed some aversion to this expedient; and the king reduced his allowance to four thousand men. But when the Spaniards had hired ships for transporting these troops, and the men were ready to embark, the Commons, willing to show their power and not displeased with an opportunity of curbing and affronting the king, prohibited everyone from furnishing vessels for that service. And thus, the project formed by Charles of freeing the country from these men was unfortunately disappointed.

The old Irish noticed all these false steps of the English and resolved to take advantage of them. Though their animosity against England seemed to be extinguished for lack of an occasion to exert itself, it was only composed into a temporary and deceitful tranquility. Their interests, both with regard to property and religion, secretly stimulated them to a revolt. No individual of any sept, according to the ancient customs, had the property of any particular estate; but as the whole sept had a title to a whole territory, they ignorantly preferred this barbarous community before the more secure and narrower possessions assigned them by the English. An indulgence amounting almost to a toleration had been given to the Catholic religion. But so long as the churches and the ecclesiastical revenues were kept from the Catholic priests, and they were obliged to endure the proximity of profane heretics, they were discontented; and they continually endeavored to retard any cordial reconciliation between the English and the Irish nations.

Conspiracy in Ireland

There was a gentleman called Rory O'Moore, who, though of a narrow fortune, was descended from an ancient Irish family and was much celebrated among his countrymen for valor and capacity. This man first formed the project of expelling the English and asserting the independence of his native country. He secretly went from chieftain to chieftain and roused up every latent principle of discontent. He maintained a close correspondence with Lord Maguire and Sir Phelim O'Neill, the most powerful of the old Irish. By conversation, by letters, by his emissaries, he represented to his countrymen the motives of a revolt. He observed to them that by the rebellion of the Scots and factions of the English, the king's authority in Britain was reduced to so low a condition that he never could exert himself with any vigor in maintaining the English dominion over Ireland. That the Catholics in the Irish House of Commons, assisted by the Protestants, had so much diminished the royal prerogative and the power of the lieutenant as to facilitate the success of any conspiracy or combination which could be formed. That the Scots, having so successfully thrown off dependence on the Crown of England and assumed the government into their own hands, had set an example to the Irish, who had so much greater oppressions to complain of. That the English planters, who had expelled them from their possessions, suppressed their religion, and bereaved them of their liberties, were but a handful in comparison with the natives. That the English in Ireland lived in the most supine security, interspersed with their numerous enemies, trusting to the protection of a small army, which was itself scattered in inconsiderable divisions throughout the whole kingdom. That a great body of men disciplined by the government were now thrown loose and were ready for any daring or desperate enterprise. That though the Catholics had till now enjoyed, from the moderation of their indulgent prince, the exercise of their religion in some tolerable measure, they must from now on expect that the government would be conducted by other maxims and other principles. That the Puritanical Parliament, having at length subdued their sovereign, would no doubt, as soon as they had consolidated their authority, extend their ambitious enterprises to Ireland and make the Catholics in that kingdom feel the same furious persecution to which their brethren in England were at present exposed. And that a revolt of the Irish, tending only to vindicate their native liberty against the violence of foreign invaders, could never at any time be deemed rebellion, much less during the present confusions, when their prince was in effect a prisoner, and obedience must be paid not to him but to those who had traitorously usurped his lawful authority.

By these considerations, O'Moore engaged all the heads of the native Irish into the conspiracy. It was hoped that the English of the Pale, as the old English planters were called, being all Catholics, would afterwards join the party which restored their religion to its ancient splendor and authority. The intention was that Sir Phelim O'Neill and the other conspirators would begin an insurrection on one day throughout the provinces and would attack all the English settlements; and that on the same day, Lord Maguire and Rory O'Moore would surprise the Castle of Dublin. The commencement of the revolt was fixed on the approach of winter, so that there might be more difficulty in transporting forces from England. They expected succors to themselves and supplies of arms from France, in consequence of a promise made to them by Cardinal Richelieu. And many Irish officers who served in the Spanish troops had engaged to join them as soon as they saw an insurrection entered upon by their Catholic brethren. News which every day arrived from England of the fury expressed by the Commons against all papists struck fresh terror into the Irish nation, and both stimulated the conspirators to execute their fatal purpose and gave them assured hopes of the concurrence of all their countrymen.

Such propensity to a revolt was apparent in all the Irish that it was deemed as unnecessary as it was dangerous to entrust the secret to many hands. As the appointed day drew nigh, the plans had not yet been betrayed to the government. The king indeed had received information from his ambassadors that something was in agitation among the Irish in foreign parts; but though he gave warning to the administration in Ireland, the intelligence was entirely neglected. Secret rumors likewise were heard of some approaching conspiracy, but no attention was paid to them. The Earl of Leicester, whom the king had appointed lieutenant, remained in London. The two justices of Ireland, Sir William Parsons and Sir John Borlase, were men of small abilities; and by an inconvenience common to all factious times, they owed their advancement to nothing but their zeal for the party by whom everything was now governed. Tranquil from their ignorance and inexperience, these men indulged themselves in the most profound repose on the very brink of destruction.

But they were awakened from their security on the very day before that which was appointed for the commencement of hostilities. The Castle of Dublin, by which the capital was commanded, contained arms for ten thousand men, with thirty-five pieces of cannon and a proportionate quantity of ammunition. Yet this important place was guarded, and that too without any care, by no greater force than fifty men. Maguire and O'Moore were already in town with a numerous band of their partisans; others were expected that night; and next morning, they were to enter upon what they deemed the easiest of all enterprises, the surprising of the castle. O'Connolly, an Irishman but a Protestant, betrayed the conspiracy to Parsons. The justices and Council fled immediately for safety into the castle and reinforced the guards. The alarm was conveyed to the city, and all the Protestants prepared for defense. O'Moore escaped; Maguire was taken; and MacMahon, one of the conspirators, being likewise seized, first revealed to the justices the project of a general insurrection and thereby redoubled the apprehensions which already were universally diffused throughout Dublin.

Insurrection and massacre

But though O'Connolly's disclosure saved the castle from a surprise, the confession extorted from MacMahon came too late to prevent the intended insurrection. O'Neill and his confederates had already taken arms in Ulster. The Irish, everywhere intermingled with the English, needed but a hint from their leaders and priests to begin hostilities against a people whom they hated for their religion and envied for their riches and prosperity. The houses, cattle, and goods of the unwary English were first seized. Those who heard of the commotions in their neighborhood, instead of deserting their habitations and assembling for mutual protection, remained at home in hopes of defending their property and fell thus separately into the hands of their enemies. After rapacity had fully exerted itself, cruelty—and the most barbarous that ever in any nation was known or heard of—began its operations. A universal massacre commenced of the English, now defenseless and passively resigned to their inhuman foes. No age, no sex, no condition was spared. The wife weeping for her butchered husband and embracing her helpless children was pierced with them and perished by the same stroke. The old, the young, the vigorous, the infirm, underwent a like fate and were confounded in one common ruin. In vain did flight save from the first assault; destruction was everywhere let loose and met the hunted victims at every turn. In vain was recourse had to relations, to companions, to friends; all connections were dissolved, and death was dealt by that hand from which protection was implored and expected. Without provocation, without opposition, the astonished English, living in profound peace and full security, were massacred by their nearest neighbors, with whom they had long upheld a continued intercourse of kindness and good offices.

But death was the lightest punishment inflicted by those rebels. All the tortures which wanton cruelty could devise, all the lingering pains of body, the anguish of mind, the agonies of despair, could not satiate revenge excited without injury and cruelty derived from no cause. To enter into particulars would shock the least delicate humanity. Such enormities, though attested by undoubted evidence, appear almost incredible. Neither depraved nature nor perverted religion encouraged by the utmost license reach to such a pitch of ferocity unless the pity inherent in human breasts be destroyed by that contagion of example which transports men beyond all the usual motives of conduct and behavior.

The weaker sex themselves, naturally tender to their own sufferings and compassionate to those of others, here emulated their more robust companions in the practice of every cruelty. Even children, taught by the example and encouraged by the exhortation of their parents, essayed their feeble blows on the dead carcasses of defenseless children of the English. The very avarice of the Irish was not a sufficient restraint to their cruelty. Such was their frenzy that the cattle which they had seized and by rapine made their own were, because they bore the name of English, wantonly slaughtered, or when covered with wounds, turned loose into the woods or deserts.

The stately buildings or commodious habitations of the planters, as if upbraiding the sloth and ignorance of the natives, were consumed with fire or laid level with the ground. And where the miserable owners, shut up in their houses and preparing for defense, perished in the flames together with their wives and children, a double triumph was afforded to their insulting foes.

If anywhere a number assembled together and were resolved, assuming courage from despair, to sweeten death by revenge on their assassins, they were disarmed by capitulations and promises of safety, confirmed by the most solemn oaths. But no sooner had they surrendered than the rebels, with perfidy equal to their cruelty, made them share the fate of their unhappy countrymen.

Others, more ingenious still in their barbarity, tempted their prisoners by the fond love of life to stain their hands in the blood of friends, brothers, parents; and having thus rendered them accomplices in guilt, gave them that death which they sought to shun by deserving it.

Amidst all these enormities, the sacred name of Religion resounded on every side, not to stop the hands of these murderers but to strengthen their blows and to steel their hearts against every movement of human or social sympathy. The English, as heretics abhorred of God and detestable to all holy men, were marked out by the priests for slaughter; and of all actions, to rid the world of these declared enemies to Catholic faith and piety was represented as the most meritorious. Nature, which in that rude people was sufficiently inclined to atrocious deeds, was further stimulated by precept, and national prejudices empoisoned by those more deadly and incurable aversions which arose from an enraged superstition. While death finished the sufferings of each victim, the bigoted assassins still cried with joy and exultation into his expiring ears that these agonies were but the commencement of torments infinite and eternal.

Such were the barbarities by which Sir Phelim O'Neill and the Irish in Ulster signalized their rebellion, an event memorable in the annals of humankind and worthy to be held in perpetual detestation and abhorrence. The generous nature of O'Moore was shocked at the recital of such enormous cruelties. He flew to O'Neill's camp; but he found that his authority, which was sufficient to excite the Irish to an insurrection, was too feeble to restrain their inhumanity. Soon after, he abandoned a cause polluted by so many crimes; and he retired into Flanders. Sir Phelim, recommended by the greatness of his family— and perhaps too by the unrestrained brutality of his nature—though without any courage or capacity, acquired the entire ascendant over the northern rebels. The English colonies were totally annihilated in the open country of Ulster; the Scots at first met with more favorable treatment. In order to engage them to a passive neutrality, the Irish pretended to distinguish between the British nations, and claiming friendship and consanguinity with the Scots, did not extend to them the fury of their massacres. Many of them found an opportunity to fly from the country. Others retired into places of security and prepared themselves for defense. And by this means the Scottish planters—most of them, at least—escaped with their lives.

From Ulster, the flames of rebellion diffused themselves in an instant over the other three provinces of Ireland. In all places death and slaughter were not uncommon, though the Irish in these other provinces claimed to act with moderation and humanity. But cruel and barbarous was their humanity! Not content with expelling the English from their houses, with despoiling them of their goodly manors, with wasting their cultivated fields, they stripped them of their very clothes and turned them out, naked and defenseless, to all the severities of the season. The heavens themselves, as if conspiring against that unhappy people, were armed with cold and tempest unusual to the climate and executed what the merciless sword had left unfinished. The roads were covered with crowds of naked English hastening towards Dublin and the other cities which yet remained in the hands of their countrymen. The feeble age of children, the tender sex of women, soon sunk under the multiplied rigors of cold and hunger. Here the husband, bidding a final adieu to his expiring family, envied them for a fate which he himself expected so soon to share. There the son, having long supported his aged parent, with reluctance obeyed his last commands, and abandoning him in this uttermost distress, kept the hopes of avenging that death which all his efforts could not prevent nor delay. The astonishing greatness of the calamity deprived the sufferers of any relief from the view of companions in affliction. With silent tears or lamentable cries, they hurried on through the hostile territories and found every heart which was not steeled by native barbarity guarded by the more implacable furies of mistaken piety and religion.

The saving of Dublin preserved in Ireland the remains of the English name. The gates of that city, though timorously opened, received the wretched supplicants and presented to the view a scene of human misery beyond what any eye had ever before beheld. Compassion seized the amazed inhabitants, aggravated with the fear of like calamities, as they observed the numerous foes without and within which everywhere environed them and reflected on the weak resources by which they were themselves supported. The more vigorous of the unhappy fugitives, to the number of three thousand, were enlisted into three regiments. The rest were distributed into the houses; and all care was taken by diet and warmth to reinvigorate their feeble and torpid limbs. Diseases of unknown name and species, derived from these multiplied distresses, seized many of them and put a speedy end to their lives; others, having now leisure to reflect on their mighty loss of friends and fortune, cursed the existence which they had saved. Abandoning themselves to despair, refusing all succor, they expired; their only consolation was that of receiving among their countrymen the honors of a grave, which had been denied to their slaughtered companions by the inhuman barbarians.

By some computations, those who perished by all these cruelties are supposed to be one hundred fifty or two hundred thousand. By the most moderate—and probably the most reasonable—account, they are made to amount to forty thousand; if this estimation itself be not, as is usual in such cases, somewhat exaggerated.

The justices ordered to Dublin all the bodies of the army which were not surrounded by the rebels; and they assembled a force of one thousand five hundred veterans. They soon enlisted and armed from the magazines over four thousand men more. They dispatched a body of six hundred men to throw relief into Drogheda, besieged by the Irish. But these troops, attacked by the enemy, were seized with a panic and were, most of them, put to the sword. Their arms fell into the hands of the Irish, supplying the latter with what they most wanted. The justices, willing to foment the rebellion with a view of profiting by the multiplied forfeitures, from then on thought of nothing more than providing for their own present security and that of the capital. The Earl of Ormonde, their general, remonstrated against such timid—not to say base and interested—counsels but was obliged to submit to authority.

The English of the Pale, who probably were not at first privy to the secret, pretended to blame the insurrection and to detest the barbarity with which it was accompanied. By their protestations and declarations, they engaged the justices to supply them with arms, which they promised to employ in defense of the government. But soon the interests of religion were found more prevalent over them than regard and duty to their mother country. They chose Lord Gormanston their leader, and joining the old Irish, rivaled them in every act of violence towards the English Protestants. Besides many smaller bodies dispersed over the kingdom, the principal army of the rebels amounted to twenty thousand men and threatened Dublin with an immediate siege.

Both the English and Irish rebels conspired in an imposture with which they seduced many of their deluded countrymen: they pretended authority from the king and queen, but chiefly from the latter, for their insurrection; and they affirmed that the cause of their taking arms was to vindicate royal prerogative, now invaded by the Puritanical Parliament. Sir Phelim O'Neill, having found a royal patent in the house of Lord Caulfield, whom he had murdered, tore off the seal and affixed it to a commission which he had forged for himself.

The king received an account of this insurrection by a messenger dispatched from the north of Ireland. He immediately communicated his intelligence to the Scottish Parliament. He expected that the mighty zeal expressed by the Scots for the Protestant religion would immediately engage them to fly to its defense where it was so violently invaded. He hoped that their horror against popery, a religion which now appeared in its most horrible aspect, would second all his exhortations. He had observed with what alacrity they had twice run to arms and assembled troops in opposition to the rights of their sovereign. He saw with how much greater facility they could now collect forces which had been very lately disbanded and which had been so long inured to military discipline. The cries of their frightened and distressed brethren in Ireland, he promised himself, would powerfully incite them to send over succors which could arrive so quickly and aid them with such promptitude in this uttermost distress. But the zeal of the Scots, as is usual among religious sects, was very feeble when not stimulated either by faction or by interest. They now considered themselves entirely as a republic and cared nothing for their prince's authority, which they had utterly annihilated. Conceiving hopes from the present distresses of Ireland, they resolved to make an advantageous bargain for the succors with which they could supply their neighboring nation. And they cast their eye towards the English Parliament, with whom they were already so closely connected and who alone could fulfill any articles which might be agreed on. Therefore, except dispatching a small body to support the Scottish colonies in Ulster, they would go no further at present than sending commissioners to London in order to treat with that power to whom the sovereign authority was now in reality transferred.

The king too, aware of his utter inability to subdue the Irish rebels, found himself obliged in this exigency to have recourse to the English Parliament and depend on their assistance for supply. After communicating to them the intelligence which he had received, he informed them that the insurrection was not, in his opinion, the result of any rash enterprise but of a formed conspiracy against the Crown of England. To their care and wisdom, therefore, he said, he committed the conduct and prosecution of the war, which, in a cause so important to national and religious interests, must of necessity be immediately entered upon and vigorously pursued.

Meeting of the English Parliament

The English Parliament was now assembled; and they revealed in every vote the same dispositions in which they had separated. The exalting of their own authority and the diminishing of the king's were still the objects pursued by the majority. Every attempt which had been made to gain the popular leaders and to attach them to the Crown by offices had failed of success, either for lack of skill in conducting it or by reason of the slender preferments which it was then in the king's power to confer. The ambitious and enterprising patriots disdained to accept a mere part of a precarious power while they deemed it so easy, by one bold and vigorous assault, to possess themselves forever of the entire sovereignty. Aware that the measures which they had till then pursued rendered them extremely obnoxious to the king, that many of those measures were in themselves exceptionable, and that some of them were, strictly speaking, illegal, they resolved to seek their own security as well as greatness by enlarging popular authority in England. The great necessities to which the king was reduced; the violent prejudices which generally, throughout the nation, prevailed against him; his pliancy in making the most important concessions; the example of the Scots, whose encroachments had totally subverted monarchy: all these circumstances further instigated the Commons in their invasion of royal prerogative. And the danger to which the constitution seemed to have been so lately exposed persuaded many that it never could be sufficiently secured but by the entire abolition of that authority which had invaded it.

But this project would not have been in the power, scarcely in the intention, of the popular leaders to execute had it not been for the passion which seized the nation for Presbyterian discipline and for the wild enthusiasm which at that time accompanied it. The license which the Parliament had bestowed on this spirit by checking ecclesiastical authority; the favor and encouragement with which they had honored it: these had already diffused its influence to a wonderful degree; and all orders of men had drunk deep of the intoxicating poison. In every discourse or conversation, this mode of religion entered; in all business it had a share; every elegant pleasure or amusement it utterly annihilated; many vices or corruptions of mind it promoted; even diseases and bodily distempers were not totally exempted from it; and it became requisite, we are told, for all physicians to be expert in the spiritual profession and to allay by theological considerations those religious terrors with which their patients were so generally haunted. Learning itself, which tends so much to enlarge the mind and humanize the temper, rather served on this occasion to exalt that epidemic frenzy which prevailed. Rude and imperfect as yet, it supplied the dismal fanaticism with a variety of views, founded it on some coherency of system, and enriched it with different figures of elocution: advantages with which a totally ignorant and barbarous people had been happily unacquainted.

At first from policy and inclination, now from necessity, the king attached himself extremely to the hierarchy. For like reasons, his enemies were determined to overpower the church and monarchy by one and the same effort.

While the Commons were in this disposition, the Irish rebellion was the event which tended most to promote the designs in which all their measures terminated. A horror against the papists, however innocent, they had constantly encouraged; a terror from the conspiracies of that sect, however improbable, they had at all times endeavored to excite. Here was broken out a rebellion, dreadful and unexpected, accompanied with circumstances the most detestable of which there ever was any record. And whatever was the particular guilt of the Irish Catholics, it was no difficult matter in the present disposition of men's minds to attribute guilt to that whole sect, who were already so much the object of general abhorrence. Accustomed in all invectives to join the prelatical party with the papists, the people immediately supposed this insurrection to be the result of their united counsels. And when they heard that the Irish rebels pleaded the king's commission as vindication for all their acts of violence, bigotry—ever credulous and malignant—assented without scruple to that gross imposture and loaded the unhappy prince with the whole enormity of a contrivance so barbarous and inhuman.

By the difficulties and distresses of the Crown, the Commons, who alone possessed the power of supply, had aggrandized themselves; and it seemed a particular happiness that the Irish rebellion had followed at so critical a juncture the pacification of Scotland. That expression of the king's by which he committed to them the care of Ireland they immediately laid hold of and interpreted in the most unlimited sense. They had on other occasions been gradually encroaching on the executive power of the Crown, which forms its principal and most natural branch of authority; but with regard to Ireland, they at once assumed it fully and entirely, as if delivered over to them by a regular gift or assignment. And to this usurpation the king was obliged passively to submit, both because of his inability to resist and lest he expose himself still more to the reproach of favoring the progress of that odious rebellion.

The project of introducing further innovations in England being once formed by the leaders among the Commons, it became a necessary consequence that all of their operations with regard to Ireland would be considered as subordinate to the former, on whose success, when once undertaken, their own grandeur, security, and even being must entirely depend. While they pretended the utmost zeal against the Irish insurrection, they took no steps towards its suppression but those that likewise tended to give them the superiority in those commotions which they foresaw must so soon be excited in England. The extreme contempt entertained for the natives in Ireland made the popular leaders believe that it would be easy at any time to suppress their rebellion and recover that kingdom. Nor were they willing to lose by too hasty success the advantage which that rebellion would afford them in their projected encroachments on the prerogative. By assuming the total management of the war, they acquired the courtship and dependence of everyone who had any connection with Ireland or who was desirous of enlisting in these military enterprises. They levied money under pretense of the Irish expedition but reserved it for purposes which concerned them more nearly. They took arms from the king's magazines but still kept them with a secret intention of employing them against the king himself. Whatever law they deemed necessary for aggrandizing themselves was voted under color of enabling them to recover Ireland; and if Charles withheld the royal assent, his refusal was imputed to those pernicious counsels which had at first excited the popish rebellion and which still threatened total destruction to the Protestant interest throughout all his dominions. And though no forces were for a long time sent over to Ireland, and very little money remitted during the extreme distress of that kingdom, so strong was the people's attachment to the Commons that the fault was never imputed to those pious zealots, whose votes breathed nothing but death and destruction to the Irish rebels.

The Remonstrance

To make the attack on royal authority by regular approaches, it was thought proper to frame a general remonstrance of the state of the nation. Accordingly, the committee which at the first meeting of Parliament had been chosen for that purpose, and which had since then made no progress in their work, received fresh injunctions to finish that undertaking.

The committee brought into the house that Remonstrance which has become so memorable and which was soon afterwards attended with such important consequences. It was not addressed to the king but was openly declared to be an appeal to the people. The harshness of the substance was equaled by the severity of the language. It consisted of many gross falsehoods intermingled with some evident truths; malignant insinuations were joined to open invectives; loud complaints of the past accompanied with jealous [distrustful] prognostications of the future. Whatever unfortunate, whatever invidious, whatever suspicious measure had been embraced by the king from the commencement of his reign was insisted on and aggravated with merciless rhetoric: the unsuccessful expeditions to Cadiz and the Isle of Rhé were mentioned; the sending of ships to France for the suppression of the Huguenots; the forced loans; the illegal confinement of men for not obeying illegal commands; the violent dissolution of four Parliaments; the arbitrary government which always followed; the questioning, fining, and imprisoning of members for their conduct in the house; the levying of taxes without consent of the Commons; the introducing of superstitious innovations into the church without authority of law; in short, everything which, either with or without reason, had given offense during the course of fifteen years, from the accession of the king to the calling of the present Parliament. And though all these grievances had been already redressed, and even laws enacted for future security against their return, the praise of these advantages was ascribed not to the king but to the Parliament who had extorted his consent to such salutary statutes. Their own merits too towards the king, they asserted, were no less eminent than towards the people. Though they had seized his whole revenue, rendered it totally precarious, and made even their temporary supplies be paid to their own commissioners, who were independent of him, they pretended that they had liberally supported him in his necessities. By an insult still more egregious, the very giving of money to the Scots for levying war against their sovereign they represented as an instance of their duty towards him. And all their grievances, they said, which amounted to no less than a total subversion of the constitution, proceeded entirely from the formed combination of a popish faction, who had always swayed the king's counsels, who had endeavored by an uninterrupted effort to introduce their superstition into England and Scotland, and who had now at last excited an open and bloody rebellion in Ireland.

This Remonstrance, so full of acrimony and violence, was a plain signal for some further attacks intended on royal prerogative and a declaration that the concessions already made, however important, were not to be regarded as satisfactory. What pretensions would be advanced, how unprecedented, how unlimited, were easily imagined; and nothing less was foreseen, whatever ancient names might be preserved, than an abolition almost total of the monarchical government of England. The opposition, therefore, which the Remonstrance met with in the House of Commons was great. For more than fourteen hours, the debate was warmly conducted; and from the weariness of the king's party, which probably consisted chiefly of the elderly people and men of cool spirits, the vote was at last, on November 22, carried by a small majority of eleven. Some time later, the Remonstrance was ordered to be printed and published without being carried up to the House of Peers for their assent and concurrence.

Reasons on both sides

When this Remonstrance was dispersed, it excited everywhere the same violent controversy which attended it when introduced into the House of Commons. This Parliament, said the partisans of that assembly, have at length profited by the fatal example of their predecessors and are resolved that the fabric which they have generously undertaken to rear for the protection of liberty shall not be left to future ages insecure and imperfect. At the time when the Petition of Right, that requisite vindication of a violated constitution, was extorted from the unwilling prince, who did not imagine that liberty was at last secured and that the laws would from then on maintain themselves in opposition to arbitrary authority? But what was the result? A *right* was indeed acquired to the people, or rather their ancient right was more exactly defined; but as the *power* of invading it still remained in the prince, no sooner did an opportunity offer than he totally disregarded all laws and preceding engagements [pledges] and made his will and pleasure the sole rule of government. It is in vain to hope that in his more advanced age he will sincerely renounce, from any subsequent reflection or experience, those lofty ideas of monarchical authority which he has derived from his early education, which are united in his mind with the irresistible illusions of self-love, and which are corroborated by his mistaken principles of religion. Such conversions, if ever they happen, are extremely rare; but to expect that they will be derived from necessity, from the jealousy and resentment of antagonists, from blame, from reproach, from opposition, must be the result of the fondest and most blind credulity. These violences, however necessary, are sure to irritate a prince against limitations so cruelly imposed upon him; and each concession which he is constrained to make is regarded as a temporary tribute paid to faction and sedition and is secretly attended with a resolution of seizing every favorable opportunity to retract it. Nor should we imagine that opportunities of that kind will not offer in the course of human affairs. Governments, especially those of a mixed kind, are in continual fluctuation; the humors of the people change perpetually from one extreme to another; and no resolution can be more wise as well as more just than that of employing the present advantages against the king who had formerly pushed much less tempting ones to the utmost extremities against his people and his Parliament. It is to be feared that if the religious rage which has seized the multitude be allowed to evaporate, they will quickly return to the ancient ecclesiastical establishment, and with it embrace those principles of slavery which it inculcates with such zeal on its submissive proselytes. Those patriots who are now the public idols may then become the objects of general detestation, and shouts of joy attend their ignominious execution equal with those which now second their advantages and triumphs. Nor ought the apprehension of such an event to be regarded in them as a selfish consideration; in their safety is involved the security of the laws. The patrons of the constitution cannot suffer without a fatal blow to the constitution; and it is but justice in the public to protect at any hazard those who have so generously exposed themselves to the utmost hazard for the public interest. What though monarchy, the ancient government of England, be impaired in many of its former prerogatives during these contests? The laws will flourish the more by its decay; and it is happy, even if matters are carried beyond the bounds of moderation, that the current at least runs towards liberty and that the error is on that side which is safest for the general interests of mankind and society.

The best arguments of the royalists against a further attack on the prerogative were founded more on opposite ideas which they had formed of the past events of this reign than on opposite principles of government. Some invasions, they said, and those too of importance, had undoubtedly been made on national privileges. But were we to look for the cause of these violences, we would never find it to consist in the wanton tyranny and injustice of the prince, not even in his ambition or immoderate appetite for authority. The hostilities with Spain in which the king on his accession found himself engaged, however imprudent and unnecessary, had proceeded from the advice, and even importunity, of the Parliament, who deserted him immediately after they had embarked him in those warlike measures. A young prince, jealous of honor, was naturally afraid of being foiled in his first enterprise and had not as yet attained such maturity of counsel as to perceive that his greatest honor lay in preserving the laws inviolate and gaining the full confidence of his people. The rigor of the subsequent Parliaments had been extreme with regard to many articles, particularly tonnage and poundage, and had reduced the king to an absolute necessity, if he would preserve entire the royal prerogative, of levying those duties by his own authority and of breaking through the forms, in order to maintain the spirit, of the constitution. Having once made so perilous a step, he was naturally induced to continue and to consult the public interest by imposing ship money and other moderate, though irregular, burdens and taxations. A sure proof that he had formed no system for enslaving his people is that the chief object of his government has been to raise a naval force, not an army; a project useful, honorable—nay, indispensably requisite—and in spite of his great necessities, brought almost to a happy conclusion. It is now full time to free him from all these necessities and to apply cordials and analgesics after those severities which have already had their full course against him. Never was a sovereign blessed with more moderation of temper, with more justice, more humanity, more honor, or a more gentle disposition. What pity that such a prince would so long have been harassed with rigors, suspicions, calumnies, complaints, encroachments, and been forced from that path in which the rectitude of his principles would have inclined him to have constantly trod! If some few instances are found of violations made on the Petition of Right, which he himself had granted, there is an easier and more natural way for preventing the return of like inconveniences than by a total abolition of royal authority. Let the revenue be settled suitably to the ancient dignity and splendor of the Crown, let the public necessities be fully supplied, let the remaining articles of prerogative be left untouched, and the king, as he has already lost the power, will lay aside the will of invading the constitution. From what quarter can jealousies now arise? What further security can be desired or expected? The king's preceding concessions, so far from being insufficient for public security, have rather erred on the other extreme; and by depriving him of all power of self-defense, these are the real cause why the Commons are emboldened to raise pretensions previously unheard of in the kingdom and to subvert the whole system of the constitution. But if they would be content with moderate advantages, is it not evident that besides other important concessions, the present Parliament may be continued till the government be accustomed to the new track and every part be restored to full harmony and concord? By the Triennial Act, a perpetual succession of Parliaments is established as everlasting guardians to the laws, while the king possesses no independent power or military force by which he can be supported in his invasion of them. No danger remains but what is inseparable from all free constitutions and what forms the very essence of their freedom: the danger of a change in the people's disposition and of general disgust contracted against popular privileges. To prevent such an evil, no expedient is more proper than to contain ourselves within the bounds of moderation and to consider that all extremes naturally and infallibly beget each other. In the same manner as the past usurpations of the Crown—however excusable on account of the necessity or provocations from which they arose—have excited an immeasurable appetite for liberty, let us beware lest our encroachments, by introducing anarchy, make the people seek shelter under the peaceable and despotic rule of a monarch. Authority is requisite to government as much as is liberty; and authority is even requisite to the support of liberty itself, by maintaining the laws which alone can regulate and protect liberty. What madness, while everything is so happily settled under ancient forms and institutions, now more exactly poised and adjusted, to try the hazardous experiment of a new constitution and renounce the mature wisdom of our ancestors for the crude whimsies of turbulent innovators! Besides the certain and inconceivable mischiefs of civil war, are not the perils apparent which the delicate frame of liberty must inevitably sustain amidst the furious shock of arms? Whichever side prevails, *she* can scarcely hope to remain inviolate; and she may suffer injuries no less, or perhaps greater, from the boundless pretensions of forces engaged in her cause than from the invasion of enraged troops enlisted on the side of monarchy.

The king, upon his return from Scotland on November 25, was received in London with the shouts and acclamations of the people and with every demonstration of regard and affection. Sir Richard Gurney, lord mayor, a man of moderation and authority, had promoted these favorable dispositions and had engaged the populace—who so lately had insulted the king, and who so soon after made furious war upon him—to give him these marks of their dutiful attachment. But all the pleasure which Charles reaped from this joyous reception was soon damped by the Remonstrance of the Commons, which was presented to him together with a petition of a like strain. The bad counsels which he followed were there complained of, his concurrence in the Irish rebellion plainly insinuated, the scheme laid for the introduction of popery and superstition inveighed against; and as a remedy for all these evils, he was desired to entrust every office and command to "persons in whom his Parliament should have cause to confide." By this phrase, which was so often repeated in all the memorials and addresses of that time, the Commons meant themselves and their adherents.

As soon as the Remonstrance of the Commons was published, the king dispersed an answer to it. He lay under great disadvantages in this contest. Not only were the ears of the people extremely prejudiced against him, but the best topics upon which he could justify, or at least defend, his former conduct were such as it was not safe or prudent for him at this time to employ. So high was the national idolatry towards Parliaments that to blame the past conduct of these assemblies would have been very ill received by the greatest part of the people. So loud were the complaints against regal usurpations that had the king asserted the prerogative of supplying by his own authority the deficiencies in government arising from the obstinacy of the Commons, he would have increased the clamors with which the whole nation already resounded. Charles, therefore, contented himself with observing in general that even during that period so much complained of, the people enjoyed a great measure of happiness, not only compared to their neighbors but even compared to those times which were justly accounted the most fortunate. He made warm protestations of sincerity in the reformed religion; he promised indulgence to tender consciences with regard to the ceremonies of the church; he mentioned his great concessions to national liberty; he blamed the infamous libels everywhere dispersed against his person and the national religion; he complained of the general reproaches thrown out in the Remonstrance with regard to ill counsels, though he had protected no minister from parliamentary justice, retained no unpopular servant, and conferred offices on no one who failed to enjoy a high reputation and estimation in the public. "If, notwithstanding this," he added, "any malignant party shall take heart, and be willing to sacrifice the peace and happiness of their country to their own sinister ends and ambition, under whatever pretense of religion and conscience; if they shall endeavor to lessen my reputation and interest, and to weaken my lawful power and authority; if they shall attempt, by discountenancing the present laws, to loosen the bands of government, that all disorder and confusion [tumult; ruin] may break in upon us; I doubt not but God in his good time will discover [uncover; reveal] them to me, and that the wisdom and courage of my high court of Parliament will join with me in their suppression and punishment." Nothing shows more clearly the hard situation in which Charles was placed than to observe that he was obliged to confine himself within the limits of civility towards subjects who had transgressed all bounds of regard, and even of good manners, in the treatment of their sovereign.

The first instance of those parliamentary encroachments which Charles was now to look for was the bill for pressing soldiers to the service of Ireland. This bill quickly passed the lower house. In the preamble, the king's power of pressing, a power exercised during all former times, was declared illegal and contrary to the liberty of the subject. By a necessary consequence, the prerogative of obliging men to accept of any branch of public service, which the Crown had always assumed, was abolished and annihilated; a prerogative, it must be granted, not very compatible with a limited monarchy. In order to elude this law, the king offered to raise ten thousand volunteers for the Irish service; but the Commons were afraid lest such an army would be too much at his devotion. Charles, still unwilling to submit to so considerable a diminution of power, came to the House of Peers and offered to pass the law without the preamble; by which means, he said, that ill-timed question with regard to the prerogative would for the present be avoided and the pretensions of each party be left entire. Both houses took fire at this measure. Charles might have foreseen it would be received with resentment from a similar instance that occurred while the bill of attainder against Strafford was pending. The Lords as well as Commons passed a vote declaring it to be a high breach of privilege for the king to take notice of any bill which was in agitation in either of the houses or to express his sentiments with regard to it before it be presented to him for his assent in a parliamentary manner. The king was obliged to compose all matters by an apology.

The general question, we may observe, with regard to privileges of Parliament has always been, and still continues to be, one of the greatest mysteries in the English constitution; and in some respects, notwithstanding the accurate nature of that government, these privileges are at present as undetermined as were formerly the prerogatives of the Crown. Such privileges as are founded on long precedent cannot be controverted. But even if it were certain that former kings had not in any instance taken notice of bills lying before the houses (which yet appears to have been very common), it does not follow, merely from their never exerting such a power, that they had renounced it or never were possessed of it. Parliament may be allowed to assume such privileges also as are essential to all free assemblies which deliberate, whatever precedents may prevail. But though the king's interposition, by an offer or advice, does in some degree overawe or restrain liberty, it may be doubted whether it imposes such evident violence as to entitle the Parliament, without any other authority or concession, to claim the privilege of excluding it. But this was the favorable time for extending privileges, and if none more exorbitant or unreasonable than this had been dared, few bad consequences would have followed. It is certain that the establishment of this rule contributes to the order and regularity as well as the freedom of parliamentary proceedings.

The interposition of peers in the election of commoners was likewise about this time declared a breach of privilege; it continues ever since to be condemned by votes of the Commons and universally practiced throughout the nation.

Every measure pursued by the Commons—and still more, every attempt made by their partisans—were full of the most inveterate hatred against the hierarchy and showed a determined resolution of subverting the whole ecclesiastical establishment. The vexations and persecutions which the clergy underwent from the arbitrary power of the lower house were numberless. The Peers, while the king was in Scotland, had passed an order for the observance of the laws with regard to public worship; the Commons then assumed such authority that they suspended those laws by a vote of their house alone, though the laws had been enacted by the whole legislature. They particularly forbade bowing at the name of Jesus, a practice which gave them the highest scandal and which was one of their capital objections against the established religion. They complained of the king's filling five vacant sees and considered it as an insult upon them that he would complete and strengthen an order which they intended soon to abolish entirely. They had accused thirteen bishops of high treason for enacting canons without consent of Parliament, though from the foundation of the monarchy no other method had ever been practiced; and they now insisted that the Peers, upon this general accusation, sequester those bishops from their seats in Parliament and commit them to prison. Their bill for taking away the bishops' votes had last winter been rejected by the Peers; but they again introduced the same bill, though no prorogation had intervened, and they endeavored by some minute alterations to elude that rule of Parliament which opposed them. And when they sent up this bill to the Lords, they made a demand—the most absurd in the world—that the bishops, being all of them parties, be refused a vote with regard to that question. After the resolution was once formed by the Commons of invading the established government of church and state, it could not be expected from then on that their proceedings in such a violent attempt would be altogether regular and equitable. But it must be confessed that in their attack on the hierarchy, they still more openly passed all bounds of moderation; as they supposed, no doubt, that the sacredness of the cause would sufficiently atone for employing the most irregular and unprecedented means. This principle, which prevails so much among zealots, never displayed itself so openly as during the transactions of this whole period.

But notwithstanding these efforts of the Commons, they could not expect the concurrence of the upper house either to this law or to any other which they might introduce for the further limitation of royal authority. The majority of the Peers adhered to the king and plainly foresaw the depression of nobility as a necessary consequence of popular usurpations on the Crown. The insolence, indeed, of the Commons and their haughty treatment of the Lords had already risen to a great height and gave sufficient warning of their future attempts upon that order. They muttered somewhat of their regret that they alone would be obliged to save the kingdom and that the House of Peers would have no part in the honor. Indeed, they went so far as openly to tell the Lords, "That they themselves were the representative body of the whole kingdom, and that the peers were nothing but individuals who held their seats in a particular capacity. And therefore, if their lordships will not consent to the passing of acts necessary for the preservation of the people, the Commons, together with such of the lords as are more sensible [aware] of the danger, must join together and represent the matter to his majesty." So violent was the democratic, enthusiastic spirit diffused throughout the nation that a total overthrow of all rank and order was justly to be feared; and the wonder was not that the majority of the nobles would seek shelter under the throne but that any of them would venture to desert it. But the tide of popularity seized many and carried them wide of the most established maxims of civil policy. Among the opponents of the king were ranked the Earl of Northumberland, lord admiral, a man of the first family and fortune, and endowed with that dignified pride which so well became his rank and station; the Earl of Essex, who inherited all his father's popularity, and having from his early youth sought renown in arms, united to a middling capacity that rigid inflexibility of honor which forms the proper ornament of a nobleman and a soldier; and Lord Kimbolton, soon after Earl of Manchester, a person distinguished by humanity, generosity, affability, and every amiable virtue. These men, finding that their credit ran high with the nation, ventured to encourage those popular disorders which they vainly imagined they possessed authority sufficient to regulate and control.

In order to obtain a majority in the upper house, the Commons had recourse to the populace, who on other occasions had done them such important service. Amidst the greatest security, they affected continual fears of destruction to themselves and the nation, and they seemed to quake at every breath or rumor of danger. They again excited the people by never-ceasing inquiries after conspiracies, by reports of insurrections, by feigned intelligence of invasions from abroad, by discoveries of dangerous combinations at home among papists and their adherents. When Charles dismissed the guard which they had ordered during his absence, they complained; and upon his promising them a new guard under the command of the Earl of Lindsey, they absolutely refused the offer and were well pleased to insinuate by this instance of indignation that their danger chiefly arose from the king himself. They ordered halberts to be brought into the hall where they assembled and thus armed themselves against those conspiracies with which they pretended they were hourly threatened. All stories of plots, however ridiculous, were willingly attended to and were dispersed among the multitude, to whose capacity they were well adapted. Beale, a tailor, informed the Commons that while walking in the fields, he had hearkened to the discourse of certain persons unknown to him and had heard them talk of a most dangerous conspiracy. One hundred eight ruffians, as he learned, had been appointed to murder one hundred eight lords and commoners, and were promised rewards for these assassinations: ten pounds for each lord, forty shillings for each commoner. Upon this notable intelligence, orders were issued for seizing priests and Jesuits, a conference was desired with the Lords, and the deputy lieutenants of some suspected counties were ordered to put the people in a posture of defense.

The pulpits likewise were called in aid and resounded with the dangers which threatened religion from the desperate attempts of papists and malignants. Multitudes flocked towards Westminster and insulted the prelates and such of the lords as adhered to the Crown. The Peers voted a declaration against those tumults and sent it to the lower house, but these refused their concurrence. Some seditious apprentices, being seized and committed to prison, immediately received their liberty by an order of the Commons. The sheriffs and justices having appointed constables with strong watches to guard the Parliament, the Commons sent for the constables and required them to discharge the watches, convened the justices, voted their orders a breach of privilege, and sent one of them to the Tower. Encouraged by these intimations of their pleasure, the populace crowded about Whitehall and threw out insolent menaces against Charles himself. During this time of disorder and danger, several reduced officers and young gentlemen of the Inns of Court offered their service to the king. Between them and the populace there passed frequent skirmishes, which ended not without bloodshed. By way of reproach, these gentlemen gave the rabble the appellation of "Roundheads," on account of the short-cropped hair which they wore; these called the others "Cavaliers." And thus the nation, which was before sufficiently provided with religious as well as civil causes of quarrel, was also supplied with party names under which the factions might rendezvous and signalize their mutual hatred.

Impeachment of the bishops
Meanwhile, the tumults still continued, and even increased, about Westminster and Whitehall. The cry incessantly resounded against "bishops and rotten-hearted lords." The former especially, being distinguishable by their religious habit and being the object of violent hatred to all the sectaries, were exposed to the most dangerous insults. John Williams, now created archbishop of York, having been abused by the populace on December 27, hastily called a meeting of his brethren. By his advice, a protestation was drawn and addressed to the king and the House of Lords. The bishops there set forth that though they had an undoubted right to sit and vote in Parliament, yet in coming to there, they had been menaced, assaulted, and affronted by the unruly multitude, and they could no longer with safety attend their duty in the house. For this reason, they protested against all laws, votes, and resolutions which would pass during the time of their constrained absence as null and invalid. This protestation—which, though just and legal, was certainly ill timed—was signed by twelve bishops and com-

municated to the king, who hastily approved of it. As soon as it was presented to the Lords, that house desired a conference with the Commons, whom they informed of this unexpected protestation. The opportunity was seized with joy and triumph. An impeachment of high treason was immediately sent up against the bishops as endeavoring to subvert the fundamental laws and to invalidate the authority of the legislature. On the first demand, they were sequestered from Parliament and committed to custody. No man in either house ventured to speak a word in their vindication, so much displeased was everyone at the egregious imprudence of which they had been guilty. One person alone said that he did not believe them guilty of high treason; rather, they were stark mad, and therefore he desired that they might be sent to Bedlam.

Accusation of the five members

A few days later, the king was betrayed into another indiscretion, much more fatal: an indiscretion to which all
| 1642 |

the ensuing disorders and civil wars ought immediately and directly to be ascribed. This was the impeachment of Lord Kimbolton and the five members.

When the Commons employed language so severe and indecent in their Remonstrance, they were not actuated entirely by insolence and passion; their purposes were more solid and profound. They thought that in so violent an attempt as an invasion of the ancient constitution, the more leisure was afforded the people to reflect, the less would they be inclined to second that rash and dangerous enterprise. That the House of Lords would certainly refuse its concurrence, nor were there any hopes of prevailing on that house but by instigating the populace to tumult and disorder. That the employing of such odious means for so invidious an end would, in the long run, lose them all their popularity and turn the tide of favor to the contrary party. And that if the king only remained in tranquility and cautiously eluded the first violence of the tempest, he would certainly prevail in the end and be able at least to preserve the ancient laws and constitution. They were, therefore, resolved to excite him, if possible, to some violent passion, in hopes that he would commit indiscretions of which they might make advantage.

It was not long before they succeeded beyond their fondest wishes. Charles was enraged to find that all his concessions but increased their demands; that the people, who were returning to a sense of duty towards him, were again roused to sedition and tumults; that the blackest calumnies were propagated against him, and even the Irish massacre ascribed to his counsels and machinations; and that a method of address was adopted not only unsuitable towards so great a prince but which no private gentleman could bear without resentment. When he considered all these increasing acts of insolence in the Commons, he was apt to ascribe them in a great measure to his own indolence and pliancy. The queen and the ladies of the court further stimulated his passion and represented that if he exerted the vigor and displayed the majesty of a monarch, the daring usurpations of his subjects would shrink before him. Lord Digby, a man of fine abilities but full of levity and hurried on by precipitate passions, suggested like counsels. And Charles—who, though commonly moderate in his temper, was always disposed to hasty resolutions—gave way to the fatal importunity of his friends and servants.

Sir Edward Herbert, attorney general, appeared in the House of Peers and entered, in his majesty's name, an accusation of high treason against Lord Kimbolton and five commoners: Denzil Holles, Sir Arthur Haselrig, Hampden, Pym, and Strode. The articles were that they had traitorously endeavored to subvert the fundamental laws and government of the kingdom, to deprive the king of his regal power, and to impose on his subjects an arbitrary and tyrannical authority. That they had endeavored, by many foul aspersions on his majesty and his government, to alienate the affections of his people and make him odious to them. That they had attempted to draw his late army to disobedience of his royal commands and to side with them in their traitorous designs. That they had invited and encouraged a foreign power to invade the kingdom. That they had aimed at subverting the rights and very being of Parliament. That in order to complete their traitorous designs, they had endeavored, as far as in them lay, to compel the Parliament by force and terror to join with them, and to that end had actually raised and supported tumults against the king and Parliament. And that they had traitorously conspired to levy, and actually had levied, war against the king.

The whole world stood amazed at this important accusation, so suddenly entered upon without concert, deliberation, or reflection. Some of these articles of accusation, men said, to judge by appearance, seem to be common between the impeached members and the Parliament; nor did these persons appear any further active in the enterprises of which they were accused than so far as they concurred with the majority in their votes and speeches. Though proofs might perhaps be produced of their privately inviting the Scots to invade England, how could such an attempt be considered as treason after the Act of Oblivion which had passed, and after both houses, with the king's concurrence, had voted that nation £300,000 for their brotherly assistance? While the House of Peers is scarcely able to maintain its independence or to reject the bills sent it by the Commons, will it—supposing the Lords were so inclined—ever be permitted by the populace to pass a sentence which must totally subdue the lower house and put an end to its ambitious undertakings? These five members—at least Pym, Hampden and Holles—are the very heads of the popular party; and if these be taken off, what fate must be expected by their followers, who are many of them accomplices in the same treason? The punishment of leaders is always the last triumph over a broken and routed party; surely such was never before attempted in opposition to a faction during the full tide of its power and success.

But men had not leisure to wonder at the indiscretion of this measure; their astonishment was excited by new attempts still more precipitate and imprudent. A sergeant-at-arms, in the king's name, demanded of the house the five members; and he was sent back without any positive answer. Messengers were employed to search for them and arrest them. Their trunks, chambers, and studies were sealed and locked. The house voted all these acts of violence to be breaches of privilege and commanded everyone to defend the liberty of the members. The king, irritated by all this opposition, resolved next day to come in person to the house with an intention to demand—perhaps seize in their presence—the persons whom he had accused.

This resolution was revealed to the Countess of Carlisle, sister to Northumberland, a lady of spirit, wit, and intrigue. She privately sent intelligence to the five members, and they had time to withdraw a moment before the king entered. He was accompanied by his ordinary retinue of more than two hundred men, armed as usual: some with halberts, some with walking swords. The king left them at the door, and he himself advanced alone through the hall while all the members rose to receive him. The speaker, William Lenthall, withdrew from his chair, and the king took possession of it. The speech which he made was as follows: "Gentlemen, I am sorry for this occasion of coming to you. Yesterday I sent a serjeant-at-arms to demand some who, by my order, were accused of high treason. Instead of obedience, I received a message. I must here declare to you that though no king that ever was in England could be more careful of your privileges than I shall be, yet in cases of treason no person has privilege. Therefore am I come to tell you that I must have these men wheresoever I can find them. Well, since I see all the birds are flown, I do expect that you will send them to me as soon as they return. But I assure you, on the word of a king, I never did intend any force, but shall proceed against them in a fair and legal way, for I never meant any other. And now, since I see I cannot do what I came for, I think this is no unfit occasion to repeat what I have said formerly, that whatever I have done in favor and to the good of my subjects, I do intend to maintain it."

When the king was looking around for the accused members, he asked the speaker, who stood below, whether any of these persons were in the house. The speaker, falling on his knee, prudently replied, "I have, sir, neither eyes to see nor tongue to speak in this place, but as the house is pleased to direct me, whose servant I am. And I humbly ask pardon that I cannot give any other answer to what your majesty is pleased to demand of me."

The Commons were in the utmost disorder; and when the king was departing, some members cried aloud, so as he might hear them, "Privilege! Privilege!" And the house immediately adjourned till next day.

That evening, the accused members, to show the greater apprehension, removed into the city, which was their fortress. The citizens were the whole night in arms. Some people, who were appointed for that purpose or perhaps actuated by their own terrors, ran from gate to gate, crying out that the Cavaliers were coming to burn the city and that the king himself was at their head.

Next morning, Charles sent to the mayor and ordered him to call a Common Council immediately. About ten o'clock, he himself, attended only by three or four lords, went to Guildhall. He told the Common Council that he was sorry to hear of the apprehensions entertained of him; that he was come to them without any guard in order to show how much he relied on their affections; and that he had accused certain men of high treason, against whom he would proceed in a legal way, and therefore presumed that they would not meet with protection in the city. After many other gracious expressions, he told one of the sheriffs, who of the two was thought the least inclined to his service, that he would dine with him. He departed the hall without receiving the applause which he expected. In passing through the streets, he heard the cry, "Privilege of Parliament! Privilege of Parlia-

ment!" resounding from all quarters. One of the populace, more insolent than the rest, drew nigh to his coach and called out with a loud
voice, "To your tents, O Israel!"—the words employed by the mutinous
Israelites when they abandoned Rehoboam, their rash and ill-
counseled sovereign.

When the House of Commons met, they affected the greatest dismay; and adjourning themselves for some days, they ordered a committee to sit in Merchant Tailors Hall in the city. The committee
made an exact inquiry into all circumstances attending the king's entry into the house: every passionate speech, every menacing gesture of
any, even the meanest, of his attendants, was recorded and exaggerated. An intention of offering violence to the Parliament—of seizing the
accused members in the very house and of murdering all who would
make resistance—was inferred. And that "unparalleled breach of privilege," as it was called, was still ascribed to the counsel of papists and
their adherents. This expression, which then recurred every moment
in speeches and memorials, and which at present is so apt to excite
laughter in the reader, begat at that time the deepest and most real
consternation throughout the kingdom.

A letter was pretended to be intercepted and was communicated to
the committee, who pretended to lay great stress upon it. One Catholic there congratulated another on the accusation of the members and
represented that incident as a branch of the same pious contrivance
which had excited the Irish insurrection and by which the profane
heretics would soon be exterminated in England.

Tumults

The house again met; and after confirming the votes of the committee, they instantly adjourned, as if exposed to the most imminent perils from the violence of their enemies. This practice they continued for
some time. When the people were wrought up to a sufficient degree of
rage and terror by these affected panics, it was thought proper that the
accused members take their seats in the house with a triumphant and
military procession. The river was covered with boats and other vessels, laden with small pieces of ordnance and prepared for fight. Philip
Skippon, whom the Parliament had appointed by their own authority
major general of the city militia, conducted the members at the head
of this tumultuous army to Westminster Hall. And when the populace
passed Whitehall by land and by water, they still asked with insulting

shouts, "What has become of the king and his Cavaliers? And whither are they fled?"

King leaves London

The king, apprehensive of danger from the enraged multitude, had retired to Hampton Court, deserted by all the world and overwhelmed with grief, shame, and remorse for the fatal measures into which he had been hurried. His distressed situation he could no longer ascribe to the rigors of destiny or the malignity of enemies: his own precipitancy and indiscretion must bear the blame of whatever disasters would from now on befall him. The most faithful of his adherents, between sorrow and indignation, were confounded with reflections on what had happened and what was likely to follow. Seeing every prospect blasted, faction triumphant, and the discontented populace inflamed to a degree of fury, they utterly despaired of success in a cause to whose ruin friends and enemies seemed equally to conspire.

The prudence of the king in his conduct of this affair was justified by no one. The legality of his proceedings met with many and just defenses, though generally offered to unwilling ears. No maxim of law, it was said, is more established or more universally allowed than that privilege of Parliament does not extend to treason, felony, or breach of peace; nor has either house during former ages ever pretended to interpose on behalf of its members in any of those cases. Though some inconveniences might result from the observance of this maxim, that would not be sufficient, without other authority, to abolish a principle established by uninterrupted precedent and founded on the tacit consent of the whole legislature. But what are the inconveniences so much dreaded? The king may seize any members of the opposite faction on pretense of treason and for a time gain to his partisans the majority of voices. But if he seize only a few, will he not lose more friends by such a gross artifice than he confines enemies? If he seize a great number, is not this expedient force, open and barefaced? And what remedy at all times serves against such force but to oppose to it a force which is superior? Even allowing that the king intended to employ violence, not authority, for seizing the members—though at that time and ever afterwards, he positively asserted the contrary—yet his conduct will admit of excuse. That the hall where the Parliament assembles is an inviolable sanctuary was never yet pretended. And if the Commons complain of the affront offered them by an attempt to arrest their members in their very presence, the blame must lie entirely on themselves, who had formerly refused compliance with the king's message when he peaceably demanded these members. The sovereign is the great executor of the laws, and his presence was here legally employed both to prevent opposition and to protect the house against those insults which their disobedience had so well merited.

Charles knew to how little purpose he might urge these reasons against the present fury of the Commons. He proposed, therefore, by a message that they agree upon a legal method by which he might carry on his prosecution against the members lest further misunderstandings happen with regard to privilege. They desired him to lay the grounds of accusation before the house; and they pretended that they must first judge whether it were proper to give up their members to a legal trial. The king then informed them that he would waive, for the present, all prosecution. By successive messages, he afterwards offered a pardon to the members; offered to concur in any law that would acquit or secure them; and offered any reparation to the house for the beach of privilege, of which, he acknowledged, they had reason to complain. They were resolved to accept of no satisfaction unless he would reveal his advisers in that illegal measure, a condition to which they knew that he could not possibly submit without rendering himself forever vile and contemptible. Meanwhile, they continued to thunder against the violation of parliamentary privileges and to inflame the whole nation by their violent outcries. The secret reason of their displeasure, however obvious, they carefully concealed. In the king's accusation of the members, they plainly saw his judgment of late parliamentary proceedings; and every adherent of the ruling faction dreaded the same fate, should royal authority be reestablished in its ancient luster. By the most unhappy conduct, Charles had extremely augmented in his opponents the will to hurt him while he had also increased their ability to do so.

The more to excite the people, whose dispositions were already very seditious, the expedient of petitioning was renewed. A petition from the county of Buckingham was presented to the house by six thousand subscribers, who promised to live and die in defense of the privileges of Parliament. The city of London, the county of Essex, that of Hertford, Surrey, Berks, imitated the example. A petition from the apprentices was graciously received. Indeed, one was encouraged from the porters, whose numbers amounted, as they said, to fifteen thousand. The address of that great body contained the same articles as all the others: the privileges of Parliament, the danger of religion, the rebellion of Ireland, the decay of trade. The porters further desired that justice might be done upon offenders as the atrociousness of their crimes had deserved. And they added, "That if such remedies were any longer suspended, they should be forced to extremities not fit to be named, and make good the saying, 'That necessity has no law.'"

Another petition was presented by several poor people, or beggars, in the name of many thousands more, in which the petitioners proposed as a remedy for the public miseries, "That those noble worthies of the House of Peers, who concur with the happy votes of the Commons, may separate themselves from the rest, and sit and vote as one entire body." The Commons gave thanks for this petition.

The very women were seized with the same rage. A brewer's wife, followed by many thousands of her sex, brought a petition to the house in which the petitioners expressed their terror of the papists and prelates and their dread of like massacres, rapes, and outrages with those which had been committed upon their sex in Ireland. They had been necessitated, they said, to imitate the example of the woman of Tekoah. And they claimed equal right with the men of declaring by petition their sense of the public cause because Christ had purchased them at as dear a rate and the happiness of both sexes consists equally in the free enjoyment of Christ. Pym came to the door of the house; and having told the female zealots that their petition was thankfully accepted and was presented in a seasonable time, he begged that their prayers for the success of the Commons might follow their petition. Such low arts of popularity were affected! And by such illiberal cant were the unhappy people incited to civil discord and convulsions!

In the meantime, not only were all petitions which favored the church or monarchy discouraged from whatever hand they came, but the petitioners were sent for, imprisoned, and prosecuted as delinquents. And this unequal conduct was openly avowed and justified. Those who desire a change, it was said, must express their sentiments; for how otherwise shall they be known? But those who favor the established government in church or state should not petition, because they already enjoy what they wish for.

The king had possessed a great party in the lower house, as appeared in the vote for the Remonstrance; and this party, had every new cause of disgust been carefully avoided, would soon have become the majority from the odium attending the violent measures embraced by the popular leaders. A great majority he always possessed in the House of Peers even after the bishops were confined or chased away, and this majority could not have been overcome but by outrages which in the end would have drawn disgrace and ruin on those who incited them. By the present fury of the people, as by an inundation, all these obstacles were swept away, and every rampart of royal authority laid level with the ground. The victory was pursued with impetuosity by the sagacious Commons, who knew the importance of a favorable moment in all popular commotions. They extended the terror of their authority over the whole nation, and all opposition—even all blame vented in private conversation—was treated as the most atrocious crimes by these severe inquisitors. Scarcely was it permitted to find fault with the conduct of any particular member if he made a figure in the house; reflections thrown out on Pym were at this time treated as breaches of privilege. The populace outdoors were ready to execute the will of their leaders from the least hint; nor was it safe for any member who attempted to control or oppose the general torrent to approach either house. In so undisguised a manner was this violence conducted that Holles, in a speech to the Peers, desired to know the names of such members who would vote contrary to the sentiments of the Commons. And Pym said in the lower house that the people must not be restrained in the expressions of their just desires.

By the flight or terror or despondency of the king's party, an undisputed majority remained everywhere to their opponents; and the bills sent up by the Commons which had previously stopped with the Peers, and would certainly have been rejected, now passed and were presented for the royal assent. These were the pressing bill with its preamble and the bill against the votes of the bishops in Parliament. The king's authority was at that time reduced to the lowest ebb. The queen too, being secretly threatened with an impeachment and finding no resource in her husband's protection, was preparing to retire into Holland. The rage of the people, on account of her religion as well as her spirit and energy, was universally leveled against her. The most rudely contemptuous usage she had till then borne with silent indignation. The Commons, in their fury against priests, had seized her very confessor; nor would they release him upon her repeated applications. Even a visit of the prince to his mother had been openly complained of, and remonstrances against it had been presented to her. Apprehensive of attacks still more violent, she was desirous of facilitating her escape; and she prevailed with the king to pass these bills in hopes of appeasing for a time the rage of the multitude.

The king immediately found these new concessions, however important, to have no other effect than had all the preceding ones: they were made the foundation of demands still more exorbitant. From the pliancy of his disposition, from the weakness of his situation, the Commons believed that he could now refuse them nothing. And they regarded the least moment of relaxation in their invasion of royal authority as highly impolitic during the uninterrupted torrent of their successes. The very moment they were informed of these last acquisitions, they affronted the queen by opening some intercepted letters written to her by Lord Digby. They carried up an impeachment against Sir Edward Herbert, attorney general, for obeying his master's commands in accusing their members. And they prosecuted with fresh vigor their plan of the militia, on which they rested all future hopes of an uncontrolled authority.

The Commons perceived that monarchical government, which during so many ages had been established in England, would soon regain some degree of its former dignity after the present tempest had blown over; nor would all their newly invented limitations be able totally to suppress an authority to which the nation had always been accustomed. The sword alone, to which all human ordinances must submit, could guard their acquired power and fully ensure to them personal safety against the rising indignation of their sovereign. This point, therefore, became the chief object of their aims. A large magazine of arms being placed in the town of Hull, they dispatched to that place Sir John Hotham, a gentleman of considerable fortune in the neighborhood and of an ancient family; and they gave him the authority of governor. They sent orders to George Goring, governor of Portsmouth, to obey no commands but such as he would receive from the Parliament. Not content with having obliged the king to displace Thomas Lunsford, whom he had appointed governor of the Tower, they never ceased soliciting him till he had also displaced Sir John Byron, a man of unexceptionable character, and had bestowed that command on Sir John Conyers, in whom alone, they said, they could repose confidence. After making a fruitless attempt, in which the Peers refused their concurrence, to give public warning that the people should put themselves in a posture of defense against the enterprises of "papists and other ill-affected persons," they now resolved to seize at once the whole power of the sword by a bold and decisive stroke and to confer it entirely on their own creatures and adherents.

The severe votes passed in the beginning of this Parliament against lieutenants and their deputies for exercising powers assumed by all their predecessors had totally disarmed the Crown and had not left in any magistrate military authority sufficient for the defense and security of the nation. To remedy this inconvenience now appeared necessary. A bill was introduced and passed the two houses which restored to lieutenants and deputies the same powers of which the votes of the Commons had bereaved them; but at the same time, the names of all the lieutenants were inserted in the bill, and these consisted entirely of men in whom the Parliament could confide. And for their conduct they were accountable, by the express terms of the bill, not to the king but to the Parliament.

The policy pursued by the Commons, which had till then succeeded to admiration, was to astonish the king by the boldness of their enterprises, to intermingle no sweetness with their severity, to employ expressions no less violent than their pretensions, and to make him perceive in what little estimation they held both his person and his dignity. To a bill so destructive of royal authority, they prefixed, with an insolence seemingly wanton, a preamble equally dishonorable to the personal character of the king. These are the words: "Whereas there has been of late a most dangerous and desperate design upon the House of Commons, which we have just cause to believe [is] an effect of the bloody counsels of papists and other ill-affected persons, who have already raised a rebellion in the kingdom of Ireland. And whereas, by reason of many discoveries, we cannot but fear they will proceed, not only to stir up the like rebellions and insurrections in this kingdom of England; but also to back them with forces from abroad, etc."

Here Charles first ventured to put a stop to his concessions, and that not by a refusal but a delay. When this demand was made—a demand which, if granted, the Commons justly regarded as the last they would ever have occasion to make—he was at Dover, attending the queen and the princess of Orange in their embarkation. He replied that he had not now leisure to consider a matter of so great importance and must, therefore, respite his answer till his return. The Parliament instantly, on February 22, dispatched another message to him with solicitations still more importunate. They expressed their great grief on account of his majesty's answer to their just and necessary petition. They represented that any delay during dangers and distractions so great and pressing was not less unsatisfactory and destructive than an absolute denial. They insisted that it was their duty to see put in execution a measure so necessary for public safety. And they affirmed that the people in many counties had applied to them for that purpose; and in some places they were, of their own accord and by their own authority, providing against those urgent dangers with which they were threatened.

Even after this insolence, the king dared not, in his response on February 28, venture upon a flat denial. Besides excepting to the preamble, which threw such dishonor upon him, and protesting the innocence of his intentions when he entered the House of Commons, he only desired that the military authority, if it were defective, first be conferred upon the Crown; and he promised to bestow commissions, but such as would be revocable at pleasure, on the same persons whom the Parliament had named in the bill. By a former message, he had expressed his wishes that they would lay before him in one view all the concessions which they deemed requisite for the settlement of the nation. They pretended that they were exposed to perils so dreadful and imminent that they had not leisure for such a work. The expedient proposed by the king seemed a sufficient remedy during this state of affairs and yet maintained the prerogatives of the Crown entire and unbroken.

But the intentions of the Commons were wide of this purpose, and their panics could be cured by one remedy alone. They instantly, on March 1, replied that the dangers and distempers of the nation were such as could endure no longer delay; and unless the king speedily complied with their demands, they would be constrained, for the safety of prince and people, to dispose of the militia by the authority of both houses, and they were resolved to do it accordingly. They asserted that those parts of the kingdom which had, from their own authority, put themselves in a posture of defense during these prevailing fears and jealousies had acted suitably to the declarations and directions of both houses and conformably to the laws of the kingdom. And while they thus menaced the king with their power, they invited him to fix his residence at London, where, they knew, he would be entirely at mercy.

"I am so much amazed at this message," said the king in his prompt reply, "that I know not what to answer. You speak of jealousies and fears! Lay your hands on your hearts, and ask yourselves, whether I may not likewise be disturbed with fears and jealousies. And if so, I assure you that this message has nothing lessened them.

"As to the militia, I thought so much of it before I gave that answer, and am so much assured, that the answer is agreeable to what in justice or reason you can ask, or I in honor grant, that I shall not alter it in any point.

"For my residence near you, I wish it might be safe and honorable, and that I had no cause to absent myself from Whitehall. Ask yourselves whether I have not.

"What would you have? Have I violated your laws? Have I denied to pass any bill for the ease and security of my subjects? I do not ask what you have done for me.

"Have any of my people been transported with fears and apprehensions? I offer as free and general a pardon as yourselves can devise. All this considered, there is a judgment of heaven upon this nation if these distractions continue.

"God so deal with me and mine as all my thoughts and intentions are upright for the maintenance of the true Protestant profession, and for the observance and preservation of the laws; and I hope God will bless and assist those laws for my preservation."

No sooner did the Commons despair of obtaining the king's consent to their bill than they instantly voted that those who advised his majesty's answer were enemies to the state and mischievous projectors against the safety of the nation; that this denial was of such dangerous consequence that if his majesty persisted in it, it would hazard the peace and tranquility of all his kingdoms, unless some speedy remedy be applied by the wisdom and authority of both houses; and that such of the subjects as had put themselves in a posture of defense against the common danger had done nothing but what was justified and approved by the house.

Lest the people might be averse to the seconding of all these usurpations, they were plied anew with rumors of danger, with the terrors of invasion, with the dread of English and Irish papists; and the most unaccountable panics were spread throughout the nation. Lord Digby having entered Kingston in a coach and six attended by a few livery servants, the intelligence was conveyed to London; and it was immediately voted that he had appeared in a hostile manner, to the terror and fright of his majesty's subjects, and had levied war against the king and kingdom. Petitions from all quarters loudly demanded of the Parliament to put the nation in a posture of defense; and the county of Stafford in particular expressed such dread of an insurrection among the papists that every man, they said, was constrained to stand upon his guard, not even daring to go to church unarmed.

King arrives at York

That the same violence by which he had so long been oppressed might not still reach him and extort his consent to the militia bill, Charles had resolved to remove farther from London. And accordingly, taking the Prince of Wales and the Duke of York along with him, he arrived by slow journeys at York, which he determined to make the place of his residence for some time. The distant parts of the kingdom, being removed from that furious vortex of new principles and opinions which had transported the capital, still retained a sincere regard for the church and monarchy; and the king here found marks of attachment beyond what he had before expected. From all quarters of England, the prime nobility and gentry, either personally or by messages and letters, expressed their duty towards him and exhorted him to save himself and them from that ignominious slavery with which they were threatened. The small interval of time which had passed since the fatal accusation of the members had been sufficient to open the eyes of many and to recover them from the astonishment with which at first they had been seized. One rash and passionate attempt of the king's seemed but a small counterbalance to so many acts of deliberate violence which had been offered to him and every branch of the legislature. And however sweet the sound of liberty, many resolved to adhere to that moderate freedom transmitted to them from their ancestors, and now better secured by such important concessions, rather than, by engaging in a giddy search after more independence, run a manifest risk either of incurring a cruel subjection or abandoning all law and order.

Charles, finding himself supported by a considerable party in the kingdom, began to speak in a firmer tone and to retort the accusations of the Commons with a vigor which he had not before exerted. Notwithstanding their remonstrances and menaces and insults, he still persisted in refusing their bill. They proceeded to frame an ordinance in which—by the authority of the two houses only, without the king's consent—they named lieutenants for all the counties and conferred on them the command of the whole military force, of all the guards, garrisons, and forts of the kingdom. Charles issued proclamations against this manifest usurpation; and as he professed a resolution strictly to observe the law himself, so was he determined, he said, to oblige every other person to pay it a like obedience. The name of the king was so essential to all laws and so familiar in all acts of executive authority that the Parliament was afraid, had they totally omitted it, that the innovation would be too easily perceived by the people. In all commands, therefore, which they conferred, they bound the persons to obey the orders of his majesty, signified by both houses of Parliament. And inventing a previously unheard of distinction between the office and the person of the king, those very forces which they employed against him they levied in his name and by his authority.

It is remarkable how much the topics of argument were now reversed between the parties. The king, while he acknowledged his former error of employing a plea of necessity in order to infringe the laws and constitution, warned the Parliament not to imitate an example on which they threw such violent blame; and the Parliament, clothing their personal fears or ambition under the appearance of national and imminent danger, made unknowingly an apology of the most exceptionable part of the king's conduct. That the liberties of the people were no longer exposed to any peril from royal authority so narrowly circumscribed, so exactly defined, so much unsupported by revenue and by military power, might be maintained very plausibly. But that the danger, allowing it to have any existence, was not of that kind—great, urgent, inevitable—which dissolves all law and levels all limitations seems apparent from the simplest view of these transactions. So obvious, indeed, was the king's present inability to invade the constitution that the fears and jealousies which operated on the people and pushed them so furiously to arms were undoubtedly not of a civil nature but of a religious one. The distempered imaginations of men were agitated with a continual dread of popery, with a horror against prelacy, with an antipathy to ceremonies and the liturgy, and with a violent affection for whatever was most opposite to these objects of aversion. The fanatical spirit, let loose, confounded all regard to ease, safety, and interest and dissolved every moral and civil obligation.

The great courage and conduct displayed by many of the popular leaders have commonly inclined men to do them, in one respect, more honor than they deserve: to suppose that, like able politicians, they employed pretenses which they secretly despised to serve their selfish purposes. It is, however, probable, if not certain, that they were, generally speaking, the dupes of their own zeal. Hypocrisy quite pure and free from fanaticism is perhaps (except among men fixed in a determined philosophical skepticism, then unknown) as rare as fanaticism entirely purged from all mixture of hypocrisy. So congenial to the human mind are religions sentiments that it is impossible to counterfeit long these holy fervors without feeling some share of the assumed warmth. And on the other hand, the operation of these spiritual visions is, from the frailty of human nature, so precarious and temporary that the religious ecstasies, if constantly employed, must often be counterfeit and must be warped by those more familiar motives of interest and ambition, which imperceptibly gain upon the mind. This, indeed, seems the key to most of the celebrated characters of that age. Equally full of fraud and of ardor, these pious patriots talked perpetually of seeking the Lord, yet still pursued their own purposes. They have left a memorable lesson to posterity: how delusive, how destructive is that principle by which they were animated.

With regard to the people they led, we can entertain no doubt that the controversy was, on their part, entirely theological. The greatest part of the nation could never have flown out into such fury in order to obtain new privileges and acquire greater liberty than they and their ancestors had ever been acquainted with. Their fathers had been entirely satisfied with the government of Elizabeth; why would they have been thrown into such extreme rage against Charles, who from the beginning of his reign wished only to maintain such a government? And why not at least compound matters with him when it appeared by all his laws that he had agreed to depart from his previous questionable measures? Especially as he had put it entirely out of his power to retract that resolution. It is in vain, therefore, to dignify this civil war, and the parliamentary authors of it, by supposing it to have any other considerable foundation than theological zeal, that great source of animosity among men. The Royalists also were very commonly zealots; but as they were at the same time maintaining the established constitution in state as well as church, they had an object which was natural and which might produce the greatest passion even without any considerable mixture of theological fervor.

Preparations for civil war

Each party was now willing to throw on its antagonist the odium of commencing a civil war; but both of them prepared for an event which they deemed inevitable. To gain the people's favor and good opinion was the chief point on both sides. Never was there a people less corrupted by vice and more actuated by principle than the English during that period; never were there individuals who possessed more capacity, more courage, more public spirit, more disinterested zeal. The infusion of one ingredient in too large a proportion had corrupted all these noble principles and converted them into the most virulent poison. To determine his choice in the approaching contests, every man hearkened with avidity to the reasons proposed on both sides. The war of the pen preceded that of the sword and daily sharpened the humors of the opposite parties. Besides private adventurers without number, the king and Parliament themselves, by messages, remonstrances, and declarations, carried on the controversy, in which the nation was really the party to whom all arguments were addressed. Charles had here a double advantage. Not only was his cause more favorable, as supporting the ancient government in church and state against the most illegal pretensions; it was also defended with more art and eloquence. Lord Falkland, a man who adorned the purest virtue with the richest gifts of nature and the most valuable acquisitions of learning, had accepted the office of secretary. By him, assisted by the king himself, were the statements of the royal party chiefly composed. Charles was so aware of his superiority in this particular that he took care to disperse everywhere the papers of the Parliament together with his own, so that the people might be more enabled by comparison to form a judgment between them. As the Parliament distributed copies of their own, they were anxious to suppress all the king's compositions.

To clear up the principles of the constitution, to mark the boundaries of the powers entrusted by law to the several parts, to show what great improvements the whole political system had received from the king's late concessions, to demonstrate his entire confidence in his people and his reliance on their affections, to point out the ungrateful returns which had been made to him and the enormous encroachments, insults, and indignities to which he had been exposed: these were the topics which, with so much justness of reasoning and propriety of expression, were insisted on in the king's declarations and remonstrances.

Though these writings were of consequence and tended much to reconcile the nation to Charles, it was evident that they would not be decisive and that keener weapons must determine the controversy. To the ordinance of the Parliament concerning the militia, the king opposed his commissions of array. The counties obeyed the one or the other according to their inclinations. And in many counties where the people were divided, mobbish combats and skirmishes ensued. The Parliament on this occasion went so far as to vote, "That when the Lords and Commons in Parliament, which is the supreme court of judicature, shall declare what the law of the land is, to have this not only questioned, but contradicted, is a high breach of their privileges." This was a plain assuming of the whole legislative authority and exerting it in the most material article, the government of the militia. Upon the same principles, they attempted by a verbal criticism on the tense of a Latin verb to ravish from the king his negative voice in the legislature. The king, by his coronation oath, promises that he will maintain the laws and customs which the people had chosen: "quas vulgus elegerit"; the Parliament claimed that "elegerit" meant "shall choose," and consequently, that the king had no right to refuse any bills which would be presented to him.

The magazine of Hull contained the arms of all the forces levied against the Scots; and Sir John Hotham, the governor, though he had accepted a commission from the Parliament, was not thought to be much disaffected to the church and monarchy. Charles, therefore, entertained hopes that if he presented himself at Hull before the commencement of hostilities, Hotham, overawed by his presence, would admit him with his retinue, after which he might easily render himself master of the place. But the governor was on his guard. He shut the gates and refused to receive the king, who desired leave to enter with twenty persons only. Charles immediately proclaimed him traitor and complained to the Parliament of his disobedience. The Parliament avowed and justified the action.

The county of York levied a guard for the king of six hundred men; for the kings of England had till then lived among their subjects like fathers among their children and had derived all their security from the dignity of their character and the protection of the laws. The two houses, though they had already levied a guard for themselves, had attempted to seize all the military power, all the navy, all the forts of the kingdom, and had openly employed their authority in every kind of warlike preparations, yet immediately voted, "That the king, seduced by wicked counsel, intended to make war against his Parliament, who, in all their consultations and actions, had proposed no other end, but the care of his kingdoms, and the performance of all duty and loyalty to his person; that this attempt was a breach of the trust reposed in him by his people, contrary to his oath, and tending to a dissolution of the government; and that whoever should assist him in such a war, were traitors by the fundamental laws of the kingdom."

The armies which had been everywhere raised on pretense of the service in Ireland were now more openly enlisted by the Parliament for their own purposes, and the command of them was given to the Earl of Essex. In London, no less than four thousand men enlisted in one day. And the Parliament voted a declaration, which they required every member to subscribe, that they would live and die with their general.

They issued orders on June 10 for bringing in loans of money and plate in order to maintain forces which would defend the king and both houses of Parliament; for this style they still preserved. Within ten days, vast quantities of plate were brought to their treasurers. Hardly were there men enough to receive it or room sufficient to stow it; and many, with regret, were obliged to carry back their offerings and wait till the treasurers could find leisure to receive them. Such zeal animated the pious partisans of the Parliament, especially in the city! The women gave up all the plate and ornaments of their houses, and even their silver thimbles and bodkins, in order to support the "good cause" against the malignants.

Meanwhile, the splendor of the nobility with which the king was environed much eclipsed the appearance at Westminster. Lord Keeper Littleton, after sending the great seal before him, had fled to York. More than forty peers of the first rank attended the king, while the House of Lords seldom consisted of more than sixteen members. Nearly half of the lower house too absented themselves from counsels which they deemed so full of danger. The Commons sent up an impeachment against nine peers for deserting their duty in Parliament. They voted also not to admit their own members who would return to them till satisfied concerning the reason of their absence.

Charles made a declaration to the peers who attended him that he expected from them no obedience to any commands which were not warranted by the laws of the land. The peers answered this declaration by a protest in which they declared their resolution to obey no commands but such as were warranted by that authority. By these deliberate engagements, so worthy of an English prince and English nobility, they meant to confound the furious and tumultuous resolutions taken by the Parliament.

The queen, disposing of the crown jewels in Holland, had been enabled to purchase a cargo of arms and ammunition. Part of these, after escaping many perils, arrived safely to the king. His preparations were not nearly so forward as those of the Parliament. In order to remove all jealousy, he had resolved that their usurpations and illegal pretensions would be apparent to the whole world; he had thought that to recover the confidence of the people was a point much more material to his interest than the collecting of any magazines, stores, or armies, which might breed apprehensions of violent or illegal counsels. But the urgent necessity of his situation no longer admitted of delay. He now prepared himself for defense. With a spirit, activity, and skill which neither the one party feared nor the other expected, he employed all the advantages which remained to him and roused up his adherents to arms. The resources of this prince's genius increased in proportion to his difficulties; and he never appeared greater than when plunged into the deepest perils and distresses. From the mixed character, indeed, of Charles arose in part the misfortunes in which England was at this time involved. His political errors, or rather weaknesses, had raised him inveterate enemies; his eminent moral virtues had procured him zealous partisans. And between the hatred of the one and the affections of the other, the nation was agitated with the most violent convulsions.

That the king might despair of all composition, the Parliament sent him the conditions on which they were willing to come to an agreement. Their demands, contained in nineteen propositions, amounted to a total abolition of monarchical authority. They required that no man would remain in the Council who was not agreeable to Parliament; that no deed of the king's would have validity unless it passed the Council and was attested under their hand; that all the officers of state and principal judges would be chosen with consent of Parliament and enjoy their offices for life; that none of the royal family would marry without consent of Parliament or Council; that the laws would be executed against Catholics; that the votes of popish lords would be excluded; that the reformation of the liturgy and church government would have place, complying with advice of Parliament; that the ordinance with regard to the militia be submitted to; that the justice of Parliament pass upon all delinquents; that a general pardon be granted, with such exceptions as would be advised by Parliament; that the forts and castles be disposed of by consent of Parliament; and that no peer be made but with consent of both houses.

"Should I grant these demands," said the king in reply, "I may be waited on bareheaded; I may have my hand kissed; the title of Majesty may be continued to me; and 'the king's authority, signified by both houses' may still be the style of your commands; I may have swords and maces carried before me, and please myself with the sight of a crown and sceptre (though even these twigs would not long flourish, when the stock upon which they grew was dead). But as to true and real power, I should remain but the outside, but the picture, but the sign of a king." War on any terms was esteemed by the king and all the counselors preferable to so ignominious a peace. Charles, accordingly, resolved to support his authority by arms. "His towns," he said, "were taken from him, his ships, his arms, his money; but there still remained to him a good cause, and the hearts of his loyal subjects, which, with God's blessing, he doubted not would recover all the rest." Collecting, therefore, some forces, he advanced southwards; and on August 25, at Nottingham, he erected his royal standard, the open signal of discord and civil war throughout the kingdom.

CHAPTER 56
1642 – 1643

Commencement of the civil war – State of parties – Battle of Edgehill – Negotiation at Oxford – Victories of the Royalists in the west – Battle of Stratton – Battles of Lansdown and Roundway Down – Death of Hampden – Bristol taken – Siege of Gloucester – Battle of Newbury – Actions in the north of England – Solemn League and Covenant – Arming of the Scots – State of Ireland

Commencement of the civil war

WHEN two names so sacred in the English constitution as those of king and Parliament were placed in opposition, it is no wonder that the people were divided in their choice and were agitated with the most violent animosities and factions.

State of parties

The nobility and more considerable gentry, dreading a total overthrow of rank from the fury of the populace, enlisted themselves in defense of the monarch, from whom they received, and to whom they communicated, their luster. Animated with the spirit of loyalty derived from their ancestors, they adhered to the ancient principles of the constitution; they valued themselves on exerting the maxims as well as inheriting the possessions of the old English families. And while they passed their time mostly at their country seats, they were surprised to hear of opinions prevailing with which they had never been acquainted and which implied not a limitation but an abolition almost total of monarchical authority.

The city of London, on the other hand, and most of its great corporation took part with the Parliament and adopted with zeal those democratic principles on which the pretensions of that assembly were founded. The government of cities, which even under absolute monarchies is commonly republican, inclined them to this party. The small hereditary influence which can be retained over the industrious inhabitants of towns; the natural independence of citizens; the force of popular currents over those more numerous associations of mankind: all these causes there gave authority to the new principles propagated throughout the nation. Many families which had lately been enriched by commerce saw too with indignation that notwithstanding their opulence, they could not raise themselves to a level with the ancient gentry; they, therefore, adhered to a power by whose success they hoped to acquire rank and consideration. And the new splendor and glory of the Dutch commonwealth, where liberty so happily supported industry, made the commercial part of the nation desire to see a like form of government established in England.

The genius of the two religions, so closely at this time interwoven with politics, corresponded exactly to these divisions. The Presbyterian religion was new, republican, and suited to the spirit of the populace; the Church of England had an air of greater show and ornament, was established on ancient authority, and bore an affinity to the kingly and aristocratic parts of the constitution. The devotees of presbytery became of course zealous partisans of the Parliament; the friends of the episcopal church valued themselves on defending the rights of monarchy.

There were some men also of liberal education who, being either careless or ignorant of those disputes bandied about by the clergy of both sides, aspired to nothing but an easy enjoyment of life amidst the jovial entertainment and social intercourse of their companions. All these flocked to the king's standard, where they breathed a freer air and were exempted from that rigid preciseness and melancholy austerity which reigned among the parliamentary party.

Never was a quarrel more unequal, it seemed at first, than that between the contending parties: almost every advantage lay against the royal cause. The king's revenue had been seized from the beginning by the Parliament, who issued out to him from time to time small sums for his present subsistence; and as soon as he withdrew to York, they totally stopped all payments. London and all the seaports except Newcastle being in their hands, the customs yielded them a certain and considerable supply of money. And all contributions, loans, and impositions were more easily raised from the cities, which possessed the ready money and where men lived under their inspection, than they could be levied by the king in those open countries which later declared for him.

The seamen naturally followed the disposition of the seaports to which they belonged. And the Earl of Northumberland, lord admiral, having embraced the party of the Parliament, at their desire had appointed as his lieutenant the Earl of Warwick, who at once established his authority in the fleet and kept the entire dominion of the sea in the hands of that assembly.

All the magazines of arms and ammunition were from the first seized by the Parliament, and their fleet intercepted the greater part of those which were sent by the queen from Holland. The king was obliged, in order to arm his followers, to borrow the weapons of the trainbands [companies of militia] under promise of restoring them as soon as peace would be settled in the kingdom.

The veneration for Parliaments was at this time extreme throughout the nation. The present custom of reviling those assemblies for corruption was unknown during all former ages, as that corruption had not yet appeared. Few or no instances of their encroaching ambition or selfish claims had previously been observed. Men considered the House of Commons in no other light than as the representatives of the nation, whose interest was the same as that of the public, who were the eternal guardians of law and liberty, and whom no motive but the necessary defense of the people could ever engage in an opposition to the Crown. The torrent, therefore, of general affection ran to the Parliament. The privilege of affixing epithets—the great advantage of popularity—fell of course to that party. The king's adherents were the "wicked" and the "malignant"; their adversaries were the "godly" and the "well-affected." And as the force of the cities was more united than that of the country and gave both shelter and protection to the parliamentary party, who could easily suppress the Royalists in their neighborhood, almost the whole kingdom seemed to be in the hands of the Parliament at the commencement of the war.

What alone gave the king some compensation for all the advantages possessed by his adversaries was the nature and qualities of his adherents. More bravery and activity were hoped for from the generous spirit of the nobles and gentry than from the base disposition of the multitude. And as the men of estates levied and armed their tenants at their own expense, it was expected that besides an attachment to their masters, greater force and courage were to be expected in these rustic troops than in the vicious and enervated populace of cities.

The neighboring states of Europe, being engaged in violent wars, little interested themselves in these civil commotions; and Britain enjoyed the singular advantage (for such it surely was) of fighting out its own quarrels without the interposition of foreigners. France, from policy, had fomented the first disorders in Scotland, had sent over arms to the Irish rebels, and continued to give favor to the English Parliament; Spain, from bigotry, furnished the Irish with some supplies of money and arms. The prince of Orange, closely allied to the Crown, encouraged English officers who served in the Low Countries to enlist in the king's army. The Scottish officers, who had been trained in Germany and in the late commotions, chiefly took part with the Parliament.

The contempt entertained by the Parliament for the king's party was so great that it was the chief cause of pushing matters to such extremities against him; and many believed that he never would attempt resistance but must soon yield to the pretensions, however enormous, of the two houses. Even after his standard was erected, men could not be brought to apprehend the danger of a civil war; nor was it imagined that he would have the imprudence to enrage his implacable enemies and render his own condition more desperate by opposing a force which was so much superior. The low condition in which he appeared at Nottingham confirmed all these hopes. His artillery, though far from numerous, had been left at York for lack of horses to transport it. Besides the trainbands of the county raised by Sir John Digby, the sheriff, he had not gotten together more than three hundred infantry. His cavalry, in which consisted his chief strength, exceeded not eight hundred and were very ill provided with arms. The forces of the Parliament lay at Northampton, within a few days march of him, and consisted of more than six thousand men, well armed and well appointed. Had these troops advanced upon him, they must soon have dissipated the small force which he had assembled. By pursuing him in his retreat, they would have so discredited his cause and discouraged his adherents as to have forever prevented his collecting an army able to make headway against them. But the Earl of Essex, the parliamentary general, had not yet received any orders from his masters. What rendered them so backward, after such precipitate steps as they had formerly taken, is not easily explained. It is probable that the present safety of the king lay in the extreme distress of his party. The Parliament hoped that the Royalists, aware of their feeble condition and convinced of their slender resources, would disperse of their own accord and leave their adversaries a victory so much the more complete and secure as it would be gained without the appearance of force and without bloodshed. Perhaps too, when it became necessary to make the concluding step and offer barefaced violence to their sovereign, their scruples and apprehensions, though not sufficient to overcome their resolutions, were able to retard the execution of them.

Sir Jacob Astley, whom the king had appointed major general of his intended army, told him that he could not give him assurance that he would not be taken out of his bed if the rebels made a brisk attempt to that purpose. All the king's attendants were full of well-grounded apprehensions. Some of the lords having desired that a message be sent to the Parliament with overtures to a treaty, Charles, who well knew that an accommodation in his present condition meant nothing but a total submission, hastily broke up the Council lest this proposal be further insisted on. But next day, the Earl of Southampton, whom no one could suspect of base or timid sentiments, offered the same advice in Council, and it was hearkened to with more coolness and deliberation. He urged that though such a step would probably increase the insolence of the Parliament, this was far from being an objection, for such dispositions must necessarily turn to the advantage of the royal cause. That if they refused to treat, which was more probable, the very sound of peace was so popular that nothing could more disgust the nation than such haughty severity. That if they admitted of a treaty [agreed to negotiate], their proposals, considering their present situation, would be so exorbitant as to open the eyes of their most partial adherents and turn the general favor to the king's party. And that at worst, time might be gained by this expedient, and a delay of the imminent danger with which the king was at present threatened.

Charles, on assembling the Council, had declared against all advances towards an accommodation and had said that, having now nothing left him but his honor, this last possession he was resolved steadily to preserve, and rather to perish than yield any further to the pretensions of his enemies. But by the unanimous desire of the counselors, he was prevailed on to embrace Southampton's advice. That nobleman, therefore, with Sir John Culpepper and Sir William Uvedale, was dispatched to London with offers of a treaty. The manner in which they were received gave little hopes of success. Southampton was not allowed by the Peers to take his seat; he was ordered to deliver his message to the usher and immediately to depart the city. The Commons showed little better disposition towards Culpepper and Uvedale. Both houses replied that they could admit of no treaty with the king till he took down his standard and recalled his proclamations, in which the Parliament supposed themselves to be declared traitors. The king, by a second message, denied any such intention against the two houses but offered to recall these proclamations provided the Parliament agreed to recall theirs, in which his adherents were declared traitors. They desired him in return to dismiss his forces, to reside with his Parliament, and to give up delinquents to their justice; that is, abandon himself and his friends to the mercy of his enemies. Both parties flattered themselves that by these messages and replies, they had gained the ends which they proposed. The king believed that the people were made sufficiently aware of the Parliament's insolence and aversion to peace; the Parliament intended by this vigor in their resolutions to support the vigor of their military operations.

The courage of the Parliament was increased not only by their great superiority of force but by two recent events which had happened in their favor. Goring was governor of Portsmouth, the best fortified town in the kingdom and of great importance from its location. This man seemed to have rendered himself an implacable enemy to the king by betraying, probably magnifying, the secret cabals of the army; and the Parliament thought that his fidelity to them might on that account be entirely depended on. But the same levity of mind and the same disregard to engagements and professions still attended him. He secretly made preparations with the court and declared against the Parliament. But though he had been sufficiently supplied with money and had long known his danger, so small was his foresight that he had left the place entirely destitute of provisions; and in a few days, he was obliged to surrender to the parliamentary forces.

The Marquess of Hertford was a nobleman of the greatest quality and character in the kingdom, and equally with the king, descended by a female from Henry VII. During the reign of James, he had attempted, without having obtained the consent of that monarch, to marry Arabella Stuart, a lady closely related to the Crown; and upon discovery of his intentions, he had been obliged to fly the kingdom and remain abroad for some time. Ever after, he was looked on with an evil eye at court, from which in great measure he withdrew; and living in an independent manner, he addicted himself entirely to literary occupations and amusements. In proportion as the king declined in popularity, Hertford's reputation flourished with the people; and when this Parliament assembled, no nobleman possessed more general favor and authority. By his sagacity, he soon perceived that the Commons, not content with correcting the abuses of government, were carried by the natural current of power and popularity into the opposite extreme and were committing violations no less dangerous than the former upon the English constitution. Immediately, he devoted himself to the support of the king's falling authority and was prevailed with to be governor to the young prince and reside at court, to which, in the eyes of all men, he gave by his presence a new luster and authority. So high was his reputation for mildness and humanity that he still preserved the public favor by means of these popular virtues; and everyone was aware of the true motive of his change. Notwithstanding his habits of ease and study, he now exerted himself in raising an army for the king; and being named general of the western counties, where his influence chiefly lay, he began to assemble forces in Somersetshire. By the assistance of Lord Seymour, Lord Paulet, John Digby (son of the Earl of Bristol), Sir Francis Hawley, and others, he had drawn together some appearance of an army; then the Parliament, apprehensive of the danger, sent the Earl of Bedford with a considerable force against him. On his approach, Hertford was obliged to retire into Sherborne Castle; finding that place untenable, he himself passed over into Wales, leaving Sir Ralph Hopton, Sir John Berkeley, Digby, and other officers, consisting of about one hundred twenty with their cavalry, to march into Cornwall in hopes of finding that county better prepared for their reception.

All the dispersed bodies of the parliamentary army were now ordered to march to Northampton; and the Earl of Essex, who had joined them, found the whole amounted to fifteen thousand men. The king, though his camp had been gradually reinforced from all quarters, was aware that he had no army which could cope with so formidable a force; and he thought it prudent to retire by slow marches to Derby, and from there to Shrewsbury in order to support the levies which his friends were making in those parts. At Wellington, a day's march from Shrewsbury, he made a rendezvous of all his forces and caused his military orders to be read at the head of every regiment. That he might bind himself by reciprocal ties, he solemnly made the following declaration before his whole army:

"I do promise, in the presence of Almighty God, and as I hope for his blessing and protection, that I will, to the utmost of my power, defend and maintain the true reformed Protestant religion, established in the Church of England, and, by the grace of God, in the same will live and die.

"I desire that the laws may ever be the measure of my government, and that the liberty and property of the subject may be preserved by them with the same care as my own just rights. And if it please God, by his blessing on this army, raised for my necessary defense, to preserve me from the present rebellion; I do solemnly and faithfully promise, in the sight of God, to maintain the just privileges and freedom of Parliament, and to govern to the utmost of my power by the known statutes and customs of the kingdom, and particularly, to observe inviolably the laws to which I have given my consent this Parliament. Meanwhile, if this emergence [emergency], and the great necessity to which I am driven, beget any violation of law, I hope it shall be imputed by God and man to the authors of this war; not to me, who have so earnestly labored to preserve the peace of the kingdom.

"When I willingly fail in these particulars, I shall expect no aid or relief from man, nor any protection from above. But in this resolution, I hope for the cheerful assistance of all good men, and am confident of the blessing of heaven."

Though the concurrence of the church undoubtedly increased the king's adherents, it may safely be affirmed that the high monarchical doctrines so much inculcated by the clergy had never done him any real service. The bulk of that generous train of nobility and gentry who now attended the king in his distresses breathed the spirit of liberty as well as of loyalty. And only in the hopes of his submitting to a legal and limited government were they willing in his defense to sacrifice their lives and fortunes.

While the king's army lay at Shrewsbury, and as he was employing himself in collecting money—which he received, though in no great quantities, by voluntary contributions and by the plate of the universities which was sent to him—the news arrived of the first action in these wars where he was successful.

On the appearance of commotions in England, the princes Rupert and Maurice, sons of the unfortunate palatine, had offered their service to the king; and the former now commanded a body of cavalry which had been sent to Worcester in order to watch the motions of Essex, who was marching towards that city. No sooner had the prince arrived than he saw some cavalry of the enemy approaching the gates. Without delay, he briskly attacked them as they were defiling from a lane and forming themselves. Colonel Sandys, who led them and who fought with valor, fell from his horse mortally wounded. The whole party was routed and was pursued more than a mile. The prince, hearing of Essex's approach, retired to the main body. This encounter, though in itself of small importance, mightily raised the reputation of the Royalists and acquired to Prince Rupert the reputation of promptitude and courage, qualities which he eminently displayed during the whole course of the war.

The king, on mustering his army, found that it amounted to ten thousand men. The Earl of Lindsey, who in his youth had sought experience of military service in the Low Countries, was general; Prince Rupert commanded the horse; Sir Jacob Astley, the foot; Sir Arthur Aston, the dragoons; Sir John Heydon, the artillery. Lord Bernard Stewart was at the head of a troop of guards. The estates and revenue of this single troop, according to Lord Clarendon's computation, were at least equal to those of all the members who at the commencement of war voted in both houses. Their servants, under the command of Sir William Killigrew, made another troop and always marched with their masters.

With this army the king left Shrewsbury on October 15, resolving to give battle as soon as possible to the army of the Parliament, which he heard was continually augmenting by supplies from London. In order to bring on an action, he directed his march towards the capital, which he knew the enemy would not abandon to him. Essex had now received his instructions. The import of them was to present a most humble petition to the king and to rescue him and the royal family from those desperate malignants who had seized their persons. Two days after the departure of the Royalists from Shrewsbury, he left Worcester. Though it is commonly easy in civil wars to get intelligence, the armies were within six miles of each other before either of the generals was acquainted with the approach of his enemy. Shrewsbury and Worcester, the places from which they set out, are not more than twenty miles distant; yet the two armies had marched ten days in this mutual ignorance. So much had military skill decayed in England during a long peace.

Battle of Edgehill

On October 23, the royal army lay near Banbury; that of the Parliament, at Kineton, in the county of Warwick. Prince Rupert sent intelligence of the enemy's approach. Though the day was far advanced, the king resolved upon the attack; Essex drew up his men to receive him. Sir Faithful Fortescue, who had levied a troop for the Irish wars, had been obliged to serve in the parliamentary army and was now posted on the left wing, commanded by Ramsay, a Scotsman. No sooner did the king's army approach than Fortescue, ordering his troop to discharge their pistols in the ground, put himself under the command of Prince Rupert. Partly from this incident, partly from the furious shock made upon them by the prince, that whole wing of cavalry immediately fled and were pursued for two miles. The right wing of the Parliament's army had no better success. Chased from their ground by Sir Henry Wilmot and Sir Arthur Aston, they also took to flight. The king's body of reserve, commanded by Sir John Byron, judging like raw soldiers that all was over and impatient to have some share in the action, heedlessly followed the chase which their left wing had precipitately led them. Sir William Balfour, who commanded Essex's reserve, perceived the advantage. He wheeled about upon the king's infantry, now quite unfurnished of cavalry; and he made great havoc among them. Lindsey, the general, was mortally wounded and taken prisoner. His son, endeavoring his rescue, fell likewise into the enemy's hands. Sir Edmund Verney, who carried the king's standard, was killed, and the standard taken; but it was afterwards recovered. Prince Rupert found affairs in this situation on his return. Everything bore the appearance of a defeat instead of a victory, with which he had hastily flattered himself. Some advised the king to leave the field; but that prince rejected such pusillanimous counsel. The two armies faced each other for some time, and neither of them retained courage sufficient for a new attack. All night they lay under arms; and next morning found themselves in sight of each other. General as well as soldier on both sides seemed averse to renew the battle. Essex drew off first and retired to Warwick. The king returned to his former quarters. Five thousand men are said to have been found dead on the field of battle; and the loss of the two armies, as far as we can judge by the opposite accounts, was nearly equal. Such was the result of this first battle, fought at Kineton, or Edgehill.

Some of Essex's cavalymen, who had been driven off the field in the beginning of the action and continued flying to a great distance, carried news of a total defeat and struck a mighty terror into the city and Parliament. A more just account arrived after a few days; and then the Parliament claimed a complete victory. The king also, on his part, did not fail to display his advantages; though except for the taking of Banbury a few days later, he had few marks of victory to boast of. He continued his march and took possession of Oxford, the only town in his dominions which was altogether at his devotion.

As the weather still continued favorable, the royal army, after it was recruited and refreshed, was again put in motion. A party of cavalry approached to Reading, of which Henry Marten was appointed governor by the Parliament. Both governor and garrison were seized with a panic and fled with precipitation to London. The king, hoping that everything would yield before him, advanced with his whole army to Reading. The Parliament, who, instead of their fond expectations that Charles would never be able to collect an army, had now the prospect of a civil war, bloody and of uncertain result, were further alarmed at the near approach of the royal army while their own forces lay at a distance. They voted an address for a treaty [conference]. The king's nearer approach to Colnbrook quickened their advances for peace. Northumberland and Pembroke with three commoners presented the address of both houses, in which they besought his majesty to appoint some convenient place where he might reside till committees could attend him with proposals. The king named Windsor and desired that their garrison might be removed and his own troops admitted into that castle.

Meanwhile, on November 30, Essex, advancing by hasty marches, had arrived at London. But neither the presence of his army nor the precarious hopes of a treaty retarded the king's approaches. At Brentford, Charles attacked two regiments quartered there; and after a sharp action, he beat them from that village and took about five hundred prisoners. The Parliament had sent orders to forbear all hostilities and had expected the same from the king, though no stipulations to that purpose had been mentioned by their commissioners. Loud complaints were raised against this attack as if it had been the most apparent perfidy and breach of treaty. Inflamed with resentment as well as anxious for its own safety, the city marched its trainbands in excellent order and joined the army under Essex. The parliamentary army now amounted to more than twenty-four thousand men and was much superior to that of the king. After both armies had faced each other for some time, Charles drew off and retired to Reading, and from there to Oxford.

While the principal armies on both sides were kept in inaction by the winter season, the king and Parliament were employed in real preparations for war and in seeming advances towards peace. By means of contributions or assessments levied by the horse, Charles maintained his cavalry; by loans and voluntary presents sent to him from all parts of the kingdom, he supported his infantry. But the supplies were still very unequal to the necessities under which he labored. The Parliament had much greater resources for money; and they had, by consequence, every military preparation in much greater order and abundance. Besides an imposition levied in London amounting to the twenty-fifth part of every person's substance, they established on that city a weekly assessment of £10,000 and another of £23,518 on the rest of the kingdom. And as their authority was at present established in most counties, they levied these taxes with regularity, though they amounted to sums much greater than the nation had formerly paid to the public.

Negotiation at Oxford

The king and Parliament sent reciprocally their demands; and a treaty [conference] commenced, but without any

1643

cessation of hostilities as had at first been proposed. The Earl of Northumberland and four members of the lower house came to Oxford as commissioners. In this treaty, the king perpetually insisted on the reestablishment of the Crown in its legal powers and on the restoration of his constitutional prerogative; the Parliament still required new concessions and a further abridgment of regal authority as a more effectual remedy to their fears and jealousies. Finding the king supported by more forces and a greater party than they had ever looked for, they seemingly abated somewhat of those extravagant conditions which they had formerly claimed; but their demands were still too high for an equal treaty. Besides other articles to which a complete victory alone could entitle them, they required the king, in express terms, utterly to abolish episcopacy, a demand which before they had only insinuated. And they required that all other ecclesiastical controversies would be determined by *their* assembly of divines—that is, in the manner most repugnant to the inclinations of the king and all his partisans. They insisted that he would submit to the punishment of his most faithful adherents. And they desired him to acquiesce in their settlement of the militia and to confer on their adherents the entire power of the sword. In answer to the king's proposal that his magazines, towns, forts, and ships would be restored to him, the Parliament required that they would be put into such hands as they could confide in. The nineteen propositions which they formerly sent to the king showed their *inclination* to abolish monarchy; they only asked at present the *power* of doing it. And having now, in the eye of the law, been guilty of treason by levying war against their sovereign, it is evident that their fears and jealousies must on that account have multiplied extremely and have rendered their personal safety, which they interwove with the safety of the nation, still more incompatible with the authority of the monarch. Though the gentleness and lenity of the king's temper might have ensured them against schemes of future vengeance, they preferred—as is no doubt natural—an independent security, and one accompanied with sovereign power, to the station of subjects, and that not entirely guarded from all apprehensions of danger.

The conferences went no further than the first demand on each side. The Parliament, finding that there was no likelihood of coming to any agreement, suddenly recalled their commissioners.

A military enterprise which they had planned early in the spring was immediately undertaken. Reading, the garrison of the king's which lay nearest to London, was deemed a place of considerable strength in that age, when the art of attacking towns was not well understood in Europe and was totally unknown in England. The Earl of Essex encamped outside this place with an army of eighteen thousand men on April 15 and carried on a siege by regular approaches. Sir Arthur Aston, the governor, was wounded, and Colonel Fielding succeeded to the command. In a little time, the town was found to be no longer in a condition of defense; and though the king approached with an intention of obliging Essex to raise the siege, the disposition of the parliamentary army was strong enough to render that design impracticable. Fielding, therefore, on April 27, was contented to yield the town, on condition that he would bring off all the garrison with the honors of war and deliver up deserters. This last article was thought so ignominious and so prejudicial to the king's interests that the governor was tried by a council of war and condemned to lose his life for consenting to it. His sentence was afterwards abated by the king.

Essex's army had been fully supplied with all necessaries from London; even many superfluities and luxuries were sent them by the care of the zealous citizens. Yet the hardships which they suffered from the siege during so early a season had weakened them to such a degree that they were no longer fit for any new enterprise. And the two armies for some time encamped nearby each other without attempting on either side any action of moment.

Besides the military operations between the principal armies, which lay in the center of England, each county, each town, almost each family was divided within itself; and the most violent convulsions shook the whole kingdom. Throughout the winter, continual efforts had everywhere been made by each party to surmount its antagonist; and the English, roused from the lethargy of peace, employed their long-neglected weapons with eager though unskillful hands against their fellow citizens. The furious zeal for liberty and Presbyterian discipline, which had till then run uncontrolled throughout the nation, now at last excited an equal ardor for monarchy and episcopacy when the intention of abolishing these ancient modes of government was openly avowed by the Parliament. In several counties, conventions for neutrality had been entered into and confirmed by the most solemn oaths, but they were immediately broken when the two houses voted them illegal; and the fire of discord was spread into every quarter. The altercation of discourse, the controversies of the pen, but above all, the declamations of the pulpit, indisposed the minds of men towards each other and propagated the blind rage of party. As fierce and inflamed, however, as were the dispositions of the English by a war both civil and religious—that great destroyer of humanity—all the events of this period are less distinguished by atrocious deeds, either of treachery or cruelty, than were ever any internal discords which had so long a continuance; a circumstance which will be found to reflect great praise on the national character of that people, now so unhappily roused to arms.

In the north, Lord Fairfax commanded for the Parliament, the Earl of Newcastle for the king. The latter nobleman began those associations which later were so much practiced in other parts of the kingdom. He united in a league for the king the counties of Northumberland, Cumberland, Westmorland, and the bishopric; some time later, he engaged other counties in the same association. Finding that Fairfax, assisted by Hotham and the garrison of Hull, was making progress in the southern parts of Yorkshire, he advanced with a body of four thousand men and took possession of York. At Tadcaster, he attacked the forces of the Parliament and dislodged them; but his victory was not decisive. In other encounters, he obtained some inconsiderable advantages. But the chief benefit which resulted from his enterprises was the establishing of the king's authority in all the northern provinces.

In another part of the kingdom, Lord Brooke was killed by a shot while he was taking possession of Lichfield for the Parliament. He was viewing from a window St. Chad's Cathedral, in which a party of Royalists had fortified themselves. He was cased in complete armor but was shot through the eye by a random ball. Lord Brooke was a zealous Puritan and had formerly said that he hoped to see with his eyes the ruin of all the cathedrals of England. It was a superstitious remark of the Royalists that he was killed on St. Chad's Day, by a shot from St. Chad's Cathedral, which pierced the very eye by which he hoped to see the ruin of all cathedrals.

After a sharp combat near Stafford between the Earl of Northampton and Sir John Gell, the former, who commanded the king's forces, was killed while he fought with great valor; and his forces, discouraged by his death though they had obtained the advantage in the action, retreated into the town of Stafford.

Sir William Waller began to distinguish himself among the generals of the Parliament. Active and indefatigable in his operations, rapid and enterprising, he was fitted by his genius to the nature of the war, which, being manned by raw troops and conducted by inexperienced commanders, afforded success to every bold and sudden undertaking. After taking Winchester and Chichester, he advanced towards Gloucester, which was to some degree blockaded by Lord Herbert, who had levied considerable forces in Wales for the royal party. While he attacked the Welsh on one side, a sally from Gloucester made impression on the other. Herbert was defeated, five hundred of his men killed on the spot, a thousand taken prisoners, and he himself escaped with some difficulty to Oxford. Hereford, deemed a strong town, defended by a considerable garrison, was surrendered to Waller from the cowardice of Colonel Price, the governor. Tewkesbury underwent the same fate. Worcester refused him admittance; and Waller, without placing any garrisons in his new conquests, retired to Gloucester, and from there he joined the army under the Earl of Essex.

Victories of the Royalists in the west
But the most memorable actions of valor during this winter season were performed in the west. When Sir Ralph Hopton with his small troop retired into Cornwall before the Earl of Bedford, that nobleman, despising so inconsiderable a force, abandoned the pursuit and

committed the care of suppressing the royal party to the sheriffs of the county. But the affections of Cornwall were much inclined to the king's service. While Sir Richard Buller and Sir Alexander Carew lay at Launceston and employed themselves in executing the Parliament's ordinance for the militia, a meeting of the county was assembled at Truro; and after Hopton produced his commission from the Earl of Hertford, the king's general, it was agreed to execute the laws and to expel these invaders of the county. Accordingly, the trainbands were levied, Launceston taken, and all Cornwall reduced to peace and to obedience under the king.

It had been usual for the royal party, on the commencement of these disorders, to claim on all occasions the strict execution of the laws, which, they knew, were favorable to them; and the Parliament, rather than have recourse to the plea of necessity and avow the transgression of any statute, had also been accustomed to warp the laws and by forced constructions to interpret them in their own favor. But though the king was naturally the gainer by such a method of conducting war, and it was by favor of law that the trainbands were raised in Cornwall, it appeared that those maxims were now prejudicial to the royal party. These troops could not legally be carried out of the county without their own consent; and consequently, it was impossible to push into Devonshire the advantage which they had obtained. The Cornish Royalists, therefore, resolved to levy a force which might be more serviceable. Sir Bevil Grenville, the most beloved man of that country, Sir Ralph Hopton, Sir Nicholas Slanning, John Arundel, and John Trevanion undertook on their own responsibility to raise an army for the king; and their great influence in Cornwall soon enabled them to effect their purpose. The Parliament, alarmed at this appearance of the Royalists, gave a commission to William Ruthven, a Scotsman, governor of Plymouth, to march with all the forces of Dorset, Somerset, and Devon and make an entire conquest of Cornwall. The Earl of Stamford followed him at some distance with a considerable supply. Ruthven, having entered Cornwall by bridges thrown over the Tamar, hastened to an action lest Stamford join him and obtain the honor of that victory which he looked for with assurance. The Royalists in like manner were impatient to bring the affair to a decision before Ruthven's army received so considerable a reinforcement. The battle was fought on Braddock Down; and the king's forces, though inferior in number, gave a total defeat to their enemies. Ruthven fled to Saltash with a few broken troops; and when that town was taken, he escaped with some difficulty, and almost alone, into Plymouth. Stamford retired and distributed his forces into Plymouth and Exeter.

Battle of Stratton

Notwithstanding these advantages, the extreme lack both of money and ammunition under which the Cornish Royalists labored obliged them to enter into a convention of neutrality with the parliamentary party in Devonshire, and this neutrality held all the winter season. In the spring, it was broken by the authority of the two houses; and war recommenced with great appearance of disadvantage to the king's party. Stamford, having assembled a strong body of nearly seven thousand men well supplied with money, provisions, and ammunition, advanced upon the Royalists, who were not half his number and were oppressed by every kind of necessity. Despair, joined to the natural gallantry of these troops, commanded by the prime gentry of the county, made them resolve by one vigorous effort to overcome all these disadvantages. Stamford being encamped on the top of a high hill near Stratton, they attacked him in four divisions at five in the morning on May 16, having lain all night under arms. One division was commanded by Lord Mohun and Sir Ralph Hopton, another by Sir Bevil Grenville and Sir John Berkeley, a third by Slanning and Trevanion, a fourth by Basset and Godolphin. The action began with the king's forces pressing with vigor those four ways up the hill, and their enemies obstinately defending themselves. The fight continued with doubtful success till word was brought to the chief officers of the Cornish that their ammunition was spent to less than four barrels of powder. This defect, which they concealed from the soldiers, they resolved to supply by their valor. They agreed to advance without firing till they reached the top of the hill, where they would be on equal ground with the enemy. The courage of the officers was so well seconded by the soldiers that the Royalists began on all sides to gain ground. Major General Chudleigh, who commanded the parliamentary army (for Stamford kept at a distance), failed not in his duty; and when he saw his men recoil, he himself advanced with a good stand of pikes, and piercing into the thickest of the enemy, was at last overpowered by numbers and taken prisoner. Upon this disaster, his army gave ground apace; with the result that the four parties of the Royalists, growing nearer and nearer as they ascended, at length met together upon the plain at the top, where they embraced with great joy and signalized their victory with loud shouts and mutual congratulations.

Battles of Lansdown and Roundway Down

After this success, the attention both of king and Parliament was turned towards the west as to a very important scene of action. The king sent there the Marquess of Hertford and Prince Maurice with a reinforcement of cavalry; having joined the Cornish army, they soon overran the county of Devon; and advancing into that of Somerset, began to reduce it to obedience. On the other hand, the Parliament, having supplied Sir William Waller, in whom they much trusted, with a complete army, dispatched him westwards in order to check the progress of the Royalists. After some skirmishes, the two armies met on July 5 at Lansdown, near Bath, and fought a pitched battle with great loss on both sides but without any decisive result. The gallant Grenville was there killed, and Hopton was dangerously hurt by the blowing up of some powder. The Royalists next attempted to march eastwards and to join their forces to the king's at Oxford; but Waller hung on their rear and infested their march till they reached Devizes. Reinforced by additional troops, which flocked to him from all quarters, he so much surpassed the Royalists in number that they dared no longer continue their march or expose themselves to the hazard of an action. It was resolved that Hertford and Prince Maurice would proceed with the cavalry, and after procuring a reinforcement from the king, would hasten back to the relief of their friends. Waller was so confident of taking this body of infantry, now abandoned by the horse, that he wrote to the Parliament that their work was done, and that by the next post he would inform them of the number and quality of the prisoners. But the king, even before Hertford's arrival, hearing of the great difficulties to which his western army was reduced, had prepared a considerable body of cavalry, which he immediately dispatched to their succor under the command of Lord Wilmot. Waller drew up on Roundway Down, about two miles from Devizes, on July 13; and advancing with his cavalry to fight Wilmot and prevent his conjunction with the Cornish infantry, he was received with equal valor by the Royalists. After a sharp action, he was totally routed, and flying with a few horse, escaped to Bristol. Wilmot, seizing the enemy's cannon and having joined his friends whom he came to relieve, attacked Waller's infantry with redoubled courage, drove them off the field, and routed and dispersed the whole army.

This important victory, following so quickly after many other successes, struck great dismay into the Parliament and gave an alarm to their principal army, commanded by Essex. Waller exclaimed loudly against that general for allowing Wilmot to pass him and proceed without any interruption to the succor of the distressed infantry at Devizes. But Essex, finding that his army fell continually to decay after the siege of Reading, was resolved to remain upon the defensive; and the weakness of the king and his lack of all military stores had also restrained the activity of the royal army. No action had happened in that part of England except one skirmish, which by itself was of no great consequence and was rendered memorable only by the death of the famous Hampden.

Death of Hampden

Colonel John Hurry, a Scotsman, first served in the parliamentary army; having received some disgust there, he came to Oxford and offered his services to the king. In order to prove the sincerity of his conversion, he informed Prince Rupert of the loose disposition of the enemy's quarters and exhorted him to form some attempt upon them. The prince, who was entirely fitted for that kind of service, fell suddenly upon the dispersed bodies of Essex's army, routed two regiments of cavalry and one of infantry, and carried his ravages within two miles of the general's quarters. The alarm being given there, everyone mounted on horseback in order to pursue the prince, to recover the prisoners, and to repair the disgrace which the army had sustained. Among the rest, Hampden, who had a regiment of infantry that lay at a distance, joined the horse as a volunteer; and overtaking the Royalists on Chalgrove Field, he entered into the thickest of the battle. By the bravery and activity of Rupert, the king's troops were victorious; and a great booty, together with two hundred prisoners, was conveyed to Oxford. But what most pleased the Royalists was the expectation that some disaster had happened to Hampden, their capital and much-dreaded enemy. One of the prisoners taken in the action said that he was confident Mr. Hampden was hurt, for he saw him, contrary to his usual custom, ride off the field before the action was finished, his head hanging down and his hands leaning upon his horse's neck. The news arrived the next day that he had been shot in the shoulder with a brace of bullets, and the bone broken. After some days in exquisite pain, he died of his wound; his whole party could not have been thrown into greater consternation had their army met with a total overthrow. The king himself so highly valued him that either from generosity or policy, he intended to have sent him his own surgeon to assist at his cure.

Many were the virtues and talents of this eminent personage; and his valor during the war had shone out with a luster equal to that of the other accomplishments by which he had always been distinguished. Affability in conversation; temper, art, and eloquence in debate; penetration and discernment in counsel; industry, vigilance, and enterprise in action: all these praises are unanimously ascribed to him by historians of the most opposite parties. In all the duties of private life, his virtue and integrity too are allowed to have been beyond exception. We must only be cautious, notwithstanding his generous zeal for liberty, not hastily to ascribe to him the praises of a good citizen. Through all the horrors of civil war, he sought the abolition of monarchy and subversion of the constitution; an end which, even if it had been attainable by peaceful measures, ought carefully to have been avoided by every lover of his country. But whether, in the pursuit of this violent enterprise, he was actuated by private ambition or by honest prejudices derived from the former exorbitant powers of royalty, it belongs not to a historian of this age—scarcely even to an intimate friend—positively to determine.

Bristol taken

Essex, discouraged by this event, dismayed by the total rout of Waller, was further informed that the queen, after landing at Bridlington Bay, had arrived at Oxford and had brought from the north a reinforcement of three thousand foot and fifteen hundred horse. Dislodging from Thame and Aylesbury, where he had till then lain, he thought proper to retreat nearer to London; and he showed to his friends his broken and disheartened forces, which a few months before he had led into the field in so flourishing a condition. The king, freed from this enemy, sent his army westwards under Prince Rupert; and by their conjunction with the Cornish troops, a formidable force, in numbers as well as reputation and valor, was composed. That an enterprise correspondent to men's expectations might be undertaken, the prince resolved to lay siege to Bristol, the second town for riches and greatness in the kingdom. Nathaniel Fiennes—like his father, Lord Saye and Sele, a great parliamentary leader—was governor there and commanded a garrison of two thousand five hundred foot and two regiments, one of horse, another of dragoons. The fortifications not being complete or regular, it was resolved by Prince Rupert to storm the city; and next morning, with few provisions suitable to such work besides the courage of the troops, the assault began. The Cornish in three divisions attacked the west side, with a resolution which nothing could control; but though the middle division had already mounted the wall, so great was the disadvantage of the ground, and so brave the defense of the garrison, that in the end, the assailants were repulsed, with a considerable loss both of officers and soldiers. On the prince's side, the assault was conducted with equal courage, and almost with equal loss, but with better success. One party, led by Lord Grandison, was indeed beaten off, and the commander himself mortally wounded; another, conducted by Colonel Belasyse, met with a like fate; but Washington, with a smaller party, finding a place in the curtain weaker than the rest, broke in and quickly made room for the horse to follow. By this irruption, however, nothing but the suburbs was yet gained; the entrance into the town was still more difficult. Everyone was extremely discouraged by the loss already sustained as well as by the prospect of further danger when, to the great joy of the army, the city surrendered on July 25. The garrison was allowed to march out with their arms and baggage, leaving their cannon, ammunition, and colors. For this instance of cowardice, Fiennes was afterwards tried by a court martial and condemned to lose his head; but the sentence was abated by Essex.

Great complaints were made of violences exercised on the garrison contrary to the capitulation. An apology was made by the Royalists, claiming that these were a retaliation for some violences committed on their friends at the surrender of Reading. And under pretense of like retaliations, but really from the extreme animosity of the parties, such irregularities were continued during the whole course of the war.

The losses sustained by the Royalists in the assault of Bristol were considerable. Five hundred excellent soldiers perished. Among those of condition were Grandison, Slanning, Trevanion, and Moyle; Belasyse, Ashley, and Sir John Owen were wounded. Yet upon the whole, the success was so considerable that it mightily raised the courage of the one party and depressed that of the other. The king, to show that he was not intoxicated with good fortune nor aspired to a total victory over the Parliament, published a manifesto; in it, he renewed the protestation formerly taken with great solemnity at the head of his army and expressed his firm intention of making peace upon the reestablishment of the constitution. Having joined the camp at Bristol and sent Prince Maurice with a detachment into Devonshire, he deliberated how to employ the remaining forces in an enterprise of moment. Some proposed, and seemingly with reason, to march directly to London, where everything was in confusion, where the army of the Parliament was baffled, weakened, and dismayed, and where, it was hoped—perhaps by an insurrection of the citizens, or by victory, or by treaty—a speedy end might be put to the civil disorders. But this undertaking, by reason of the great number and force of the London militia, was thought by many to be attended with considerable difficulties. Gloucester, lying within twenty miles, presented an easier, yet a very important, conquest. It was the only remaining garrison possessed by the Parliament in those parts. Could that city be reduced, the king would hold the whole course of the Severn under his command; the rich and malcontent counties of the west, having lost all protection from their friends, might be forced to pay high contributions as an atonement for their disaffection; an open communication could be preserved between Wales and these new conquests; and half of the kingdom, being entirely freed from the enemy and thus united into one firm body, might be employed in reestablishing the king's authority throughout the remainder. These were the reasons for embracing that resolution, fatal though it was later deemed to the royal party.

Siege of Gloucester

The governor of Gloucester was one Massey, a soldier of fortune who had offered his service to the king before he engaged with the Parliament; and as he was free from the fumes of enthusiasm by which most of the officers on that side were intoxicated, he would lend an ear, it was presumed, to proposals for accommodation. But Massey was resolute to preserve an entire fidelity to his masters; and though no enthusiast himself, he well knew how to employ to advantage that enthusiastic spirit so prevalent in his city and garrison. The summons to surrender was issued on August 10 and allowed two hours for an answer. But before that time expired, there appeared before the king two citizens with lean, pale, sharp, and dismal visages; faces so strange and uncouth, according to Lord Clarendon, figures so clothed and equipped, that they at once moved the most severe countenance to mirth and the most cheerful heart to sadness. It seemed impossible that such messengers could bring less than a defiance. The men, without any circumstance of duty or good manners, in a pert, shrill, undismayed accent, said that they brought an answer from the godly city of Gloucester; and extremely ready they were, according to the historian, to give insolent and seditious replies to any question, as if their business were chiefly, by provoking the king, to make him violate his own safe conduct. The answer from the city was in these words: "We, the inhabitants, magistrates, officers, and soldiers within the garrison of Gloucester, unto his majesty's gracious message, return this humble answer: That we do keep this city, according to our oaths and allegiance, to and for the use of his majesty and his royal posterity; and do, accordingly, conceive ourselves wholly bound to obey the commands of his majesty, signified by both houses of Parliament; and are resolved, by God's help, to keep this city accordingly." After these preliminaries, the siege was resolutely undertaken by the army, and as resolutely sustained by the citizens and garrison.

When intelligence of the siege of Gloucester arrived in London, the consternation among the inhabitants was as great as if the enemy were already at their gates. The rapid progress of the Royalists threatened the Parliament with immediate subjection; the factions and discontents among themselves in the city and throughout the neighboring counties prognosticated some dangerous division or insurrection. Those parliamentary leaders, it must be allowed, who had introduced such mighty innovations into the English constitution, and who had projected so much greater, had not engaged in an enterprise which exceeded their courage and capacity. They had displayed great vigor as well as wisdom from the beginning in all their counsels; and a furious, headstrong body, broken loose from the restraint of law, had till then been retained in subjection under their authority and united by zeal and passion as firmly as by the most legal and established government. A small committee on whom the two houses devolved their power had directed all their military operations and had preserved a secrecy in deliberation and a promptitude in execution beyond what the king, notwithstanding the advantages possessed by a single leader, had ever been able to attain. Aware that no jealousy was entertained against them by their partisans, they had on all occasions exerted an authority much more despotic than the Royalists, even during the pressing exigencies of war, could with patience endure in their sovereign. Whoever incurred their displeasure or was exposed to their suspicions was committed to prison and prosecuted under the notion of delinquency. After all the old jails were full, many new ones were erected; and even the ships were crowded with the Royalists, both gentry and clergy, who languished below decks and perished in those unhealthy confinements. They imposed the heaviest and most unusual taxes by an ordinance of the two houses; they voted a commission for sequestrations; and they seized, wherever they had power, the revenues of all the king's party. (The king afterwards copied from this example; but as the far greater part of the nobility and landed gentry were his friends, he reaped much less profit from this measure.) And knowing that they and all their adherents were, by resisting the prince, exposed to the penalties of law, they resolved to overcome those terrors by a severe administration and to retain the people in obedience by penalties of a more immediate execution. In the beginning of this summer, a combination formed against them in London had obliged them to exert the plenitude of their authority.

Edmund Waller, the first refiner of English versification, was a member of the lower house, a man of considerable fortune, and not more distinguished by his poetical genius than by his parliamentary talents and by the politeness and elegance of his manners. As full of keen satire and invective in his eloquence as of tenderness and panegyric in his poetry, he caught the attention of his hearers and exerted the utmost boldness in blaming those violent counsels by which the Commons were governed. Finding all opposition within doors to be fruitless, he endeavored to form a party without, which might oblige the Parliament to accept reasonable conditions and restore peace to the nation. The charms of his conversation joined to his character of courage and integrity had procured him the entire confidence of Northumberland, Conway, and every eminent person of either sex who resided in London. They opened their breasts to him without reserve and expressed their disapprobation of the furious measures pursued by the Commons and their wishes that some expedient could be found for stopping so impetuous a career. Tomkins, Waller's brother-in-law, and Chaloner, the intimate friend of Tomkins, had entertained like sentiments; and as the connections of these two gentlemen lay chiefly in the city, they informed Waller that the same abhorrence of war prevailed there among all men of reason and moderation. Upon reflection, it seemed not impracticable that a combination between the Lords and citizens might be formed to refuse by mutual concert the illegal taxes which the Parliament imposed on the people without the royal assent. While this affair was in agitation and lists were being made of those who they conceived to be well affected to their design, a servant of Tomkins who had overheard their discourse immediately carried intelligence to Pym. Waller, Tomkins, and Chaloner were seized and tried by a court martial. They were all three condemned, and the two latter executed on gibbets erected before their own doors. A covenant, as a test, was taken by the Lords and Commons, and imposed on their army and on all who lived within their quarters. Besides resolving to amend and reform their lives, the covenanters there vowed that they would never lay down their arms so long as the papists, now in open war against the Parliament, were by force of arms protected from justice; they expressed their abhorrence of the late conspiracy; and they promised to assist to the utmost the forces raised by both houses against the forces levied by the king.

Waller, as soon as he was imprisoned, aware of the great danger into which he had fallen, was so seized with the dread of death that all his former spirit deserted him; and he confessed whatever he knew, without sparing his most intimate friends, without regard to the confidence reposed in him, without distinguishing between the negligence of familiar conversation and the schemes of a regular conspiracy. With the most profound dissimulation, he counterfeited such remorse of conscience that his execution was put off, out of mere Christian compassion, till he might recover the use of his understanding. He invited visits from the ruling clergy of all sects; and while he expressed his own penitence, he received their devout exhortations with humility and reverence, as conveying clearer conviction and information than in his life he had ever before attained. Presents too—to which, along with flattery, these holy men were not indifferent—were distributed among them as a small recompense for their prayers and ghostly counsel. And by all these artifices more than from any regard to the beauty of his genius, of which small account would have been made during that time of furious cant and faction, he prevailed so far as to have his life spared and a fine of £10,000 accepted in lieu of it.

The severity exercised against the conspiracy, or rather the project, of Waller increased the authority of the Parliament and seemed to ensure them against like attempts for the future. But by the progress of the king's arms—the defeat of Sir William Waller, the taking of Bristol, the siege of Gloucester—a cry for peace was renewed, and with more violence than ever. Crowds of women with a petition for that purpose flocked about the House of Commons and were so clamorous and importunate that orders were given for dispersing them; and some of the females were killed in the fray. Bedford, Holland, and Conway had deserted the Parliament and had gone to Oxford; Clare and Lovelace had followed them. Northumberland had retired to his country seat; Essex himself showed extreme dissatisfaction and exhorted the Parliament to make peace. The upper house sent down terms of accommodation, more moderate than had previously been insisted on. It even passed by a majority among the Commons that these proposals should be transmitted to the king. The zealots took the alarm. A petition against peace was framed in the city and presented by Pennington, the factious mayor. Multitudes attended him and renewed all the former menaces against the moderate party. The pulpits thundered, and rumors were spread of twenty thousand Irish who had landed and were to cut the throat of every Protestant. The majority was again turned to the other side; and all thoughts of pacification being dropped, every preparation was made for resistance and for the immediate relief of Gloucester, on which, the Parliament was aware, all their hopes of success in the war so much depended.

Massey, resolute to make a vigorous defense and having under his command a city and garrison ambitious of the crown of martyrdom, had till now maintained against the siege with courage and abilities and had much retarded the advances of the king's army. By continual sallies, he infested them in their trenches and gained sudden advantages over them; by disputing every inch of ground, he repressed the vigor and alacrity of their courage, elated by former successes. His garrison, however, was reduced to the last extremity; and he repeatedly informed the Parliament that unless speedily relieved, he would be necessitated from the extreme lack of provisions and ammunition to open his gates to the enemy.

The Parliament, in order to repair their broken condition and put themselves in a posture of defense, now exerted to the utmost their power and authority. They voted to levy an army under Sir William Waller, in whom, notwithstanding his misfortunes, they lodged every confidence. Having associated in their cause the counties of Hertford, Essex, Cambridge, Norfolk, Suffolk, Lincoln, and Huntingdon, they gave the Earl of Manchester a commission to be general of that association and appointed an army to be levied under his command. But above all, they were intent that Essex's army, on which their whole fortune depended, be put in a condition of marching against the king. They excited afresh their preachers to furious declamations against the royal cause. They even employed the expedient of pressing into forced service, though such had been abolished by a law for which they had strenuously contended. And they engaged the city of London to send four regiments of its militia to the relief of Gloucester. All shops, meanwhile, were ordered to be shut, and every man anticipated with the utmost anxiety the result of that important enterprise.

Essex, carrying with him a well-appointed army of fourteen thousand men, took the road to Bedford and Leicester; and though inferior in cavalry, yet by the mere force of conduct and discipline, he passed over that open countryside and defended himself from the enemy's horse, who had advanced to meet him and who infested him during his whole march. As he approached to Gloucester, the king was obliged to raise the siege and open the way for Essex to enter that city. The necessities of the garrison were extreme. One barrel of powder was their whole stock of ammunition remaining, and their other provisions were in the same proportion. Essex had brought with him military stores, and the neighboring country abundantly supplied him with victuals of every kind. The inhabitants had carefully concealed all provisions from the king's army, and pretending to be quite exhausted, had reserved their stores for that cause which they so much favored.

The chief difficulty still remained. Essex dreaded a battle with the king's army on account of its great superiority in cavalry; and he resolved to return, if possible, without running that hazard. He lay five days at Tewkesbury, which was his first stage after leaving Gloucester; and he feigned by some preparations to point towards Worcester. By a forced march during the night, he reached Cirencester and obtained the double advantage of passing unmolested an open country and of surprising a convoy of provisions which lay in that town. Without delay, he proceeded towards London; but when he reached Newbury, he was surprised to find that the king, by hasty marches, had arrived before him and was already possessed of the place.

Battle of Newbury

An action was now unavoidable; and Essex prepared for it with presence of mind and not without military conduct. The battle, on September 20, was fought with desperate valor and a steady bravery on both sides. Essex's cavalry were several times broken by the king's, but his infantry maintained themselves in firm array; besides giving a continued fire, they presented an invincible rampart of pikes against the furious shock of Prince Rupert and those gallant troops of gentry of which the royal cavalry was chiefly composed. The militia of London especially—though utterly unacquainted with action, though drawn but a few days before from their ordinary occupations, yet having learned all military exercises and being animated with unconquerable zeal for the cause in which they were engaged—equaled on this occasion what could be expected from the most veteran forces. While the armies were engaged with the utmost ardor, night put an end to the action and left the victory undecided. Next morning, Essex proceeded on his march; and though his rear was once put in some disorder by an incursion of the king's horse, he reached London in safety and received applause for his conduct and success in the whole enterprise. The king followed him on his march; and having taken possession of Reading after the earl left it, he there established a garrison and straitened by that means London and the quarters of the enemy.

Unfortunately slain in the Battle of Newbury on the part of the king—besides the Earls of Sunderland and Carnarvon, two noblemen of promising hopes—was, to the regret of every lover of ingenuity and virtue throughout the kingdom, Lucius Cary, Viscount Falkland, secretary of state. Before the present Parliament assembled, this man, devoted to the pursuits of learning and to the society of all the polite and elegant, had enjoyed himself in every pleasure which a fine genius, a generous disposition, and an opulent fortune could afford. Called into public life, he stood foremost in all attacks on the high prerogatives of the Crown and displayed that masculine eloquence and undaunted love of liberty which, from his intimate acquaintance with the sublime spirits of antiquity, he had greedily imbibed. When civil convulsions proceeded to extremities and it became requisite for him to choose his side, he tempered the ardor of his zeal and embraced the defense of those limited powers which remained to monarchy and which he deemed necessary for the support of the English constitution. Still anxious, however, for his country, he seems to have dreaded the too prosperous success of his own party as much as of the enemy; and among his intimate friends, often after a deep silence and frequent sighs, he would reiterate with a sad accent the word, "Peace." In excuse for the too free exposing of his person, which seemed unsuitable in a secretary of state, he alleged that it became him to be more active than other men in all hazardous enterprises, lest his impatience for peace might bear the imputation of cowardice or pusillanimity. From the commencement of the war, his natural cheerfulness and vivacity became clouded; and even his usual attention to dress, required by his birth and station, gave way to a negligence which was easily observable. On the morning of the battle in which he fell, he had shown some care of adorning his person; and he gave for a reason that the enemy should not find his body in any slovenly, indecent condition. "I am weary," he added, "of the times, and foresee much misery to my country; but believe that I shall be out of it ere night." This excellent person was but thirty-four years of age when an end was thus put to his life.

The losses sustained on both sides in the Battle of Newbury and the advanced season obliged the armies to retire into winter quarters.

Actions in the north of England

In the north during this summer, the great influence and popularity of the Earl—now created Marquess—of Newcastle upon Tyne had raised a considerable force for the king; and great hopes of success were entertained from that quarter. There appeared, however, in opposition to him two men on whom the result of the war finally depended, and who began about this time to be remarked for their valor and military conduct. These were Sir Thomas Fairfax, son of the lord of that name, and Oliver Cromwell. The former gained a considerable advantage at Wakefield over a detachment of Royalists and took General Goring prisoner; the latter obtained a victory at Gainsborough over a party commanded by the gallant Charles Cavendish, who perished in the action. But both these defeats of the Royalists were more than sufficiently compensated by the total rout of Lord Fairfax at Adwalton Moor and the dispersion of his army. After this victory, Newcastle, with an army of fifteen thousand men, encamped before Hull in order to besiege it. Hotham was no longer governor of this place. That gentleman and his son—partly from a jealousy entertained of Lord Fairfax, partly repenting of their engagements against the king— had entered into a correspondence with Newcastle and had expressed an intention of delivering Hull into his hands. But their conspiracy being detected, they were arrested and sent as prisoners to London; there, without any regard to their former services, they fell, both of them, victims to the severity of the Parliament.

Newcastle, having carried on the attack of Hull for some time, was beaten off by a sally of the garrison and suffered so much that he thought it proper to raise the siege. About the same time, Manchester, who advanced from the counties of the Eastern Association, having joined Cromwell and young Fairfax, obtained a considerable victory over the Royalists at Winceby, near Horncastle, where the two officers last mentioned gained renown by their conduct and gallantry. And though fortune had thus balanced her favors, the king's party still remained much superior in those parts of England; and had it not been for the garrison of Hull, which kept Yorkshire in awe, a conjunction of the northern forces with the army in the south might have been made, which probably would have enabled the king, instead of entering on the unfortunate, perhaps imprudent, enterprise of Gloucester, to march directly to London and put an end to the war.

While the military enterprises were carried on with vigor in England and the result became every day more doubtful, both parties cast their eye towards the neighboring kingdoms and sought assistance for the finishing of that enterprise in which their own forces experienced such furious opposition. The Parliament had recourse to Scotland; the king, to Ireland.

State of Scotland

When the Scottish Covenanters obtained that end for which they so warmly contended—the establishment of Presbyterian discipline in their own country—they were not satisfied, but indulged still in an ardent passion for propagating by all methods that mode of religion in the neighboring kingdoms. Having flattered themselves, in the fervor of their zeal, that they would be enabled by supernatural assistances to carry their triumphant Covenant to the gates of Rome itself, it behooved them first to render it prevalent in England, which already showed so great a disposition to receive it. Even in the articles of pacification, they expressed a desire of uniformity in worship with England; and the king, employing general expressions, had approved of this inclination as pious and laudable. No sooner was there an appearance of a rupture than the English Parliament, in order to allure that nation into a close confederacy, openly declared their wishes of ecclesiastical reformation and of imitating the example of their northern brethren. When war was actually commenced, the same artifices were used; and the Scots beheld with the utmost impatience a scene of action of which they could not deem themselves indifferent spectators. Should the king, they said, be able by force of arms to prevail over the Parliament of England and reestablish his authority in that powerful kingdom, he will undoubtedly retract all those concessions which, with so many circumstances of violence and indignity, the Scots have extorted from him. Besides a sense of his own interests and a regard to royal power, which has been entirely annihilated in Scotland, his very passion for prelacy and for religious ceremonies must lead him to invade a church which he has always been taught to regard as anti-Christian and unlawful. Let us but consider who the persons are that compose the factions now so furiously engaged in arms. Does not the Parliament consist of those very men who have always opposed all war with Scotland, who have punished the authors of our oppressions, who have obtained us the redress of every grievance, and who, with many honorable expressions, have conferred on us an ample reward for our brotherly assistance? And is not the court full of papists, prel-ates, malignants—all of them zealous enemies to our religious model and resolute to sacrifice their lives for their idolatrous establishments? Not to mention our own necessary security, can we better express our gratitude to heaven for that pure light with which we are, above all na-tions, so eminently distinguished than by conveying the same divine knowledge to our unhappy neighbors, who are wading through a sea of blood in order to attain it? These were in Scotland the topics of every conversation; with these doctrines the pulpits echoed; and the famous curse of Meroz ("Curse ye Meroz, said the angel of the Lord, curse ye bitterly the inhabitants thereof; because they came not to the help of the Lord, to the help of the Lord against the mighty." Judges 5:23), that curse so solemnly denounced and reiterated against neu-trality and moderation, resounded from all quarters.

The Parliament of England had always invited the Scots, from the commencement of the civil dissensions, to interpose their mediation, which they knew would be so little favorable to the king; and the king, for that very reason, had always endeavored, with the least offensive expressions, to decline it. Early this spring, the Earl of Loudoun, the chancellor, with other commissioners and attended by Henderson, a popular and intriguing preacher, was sent to the king at Oxford and renewed the offer of mediation; but with the same success as before. The commissioners were also empowered to press the king on the ar-ticle of religion and to recommend to him the Scottish model of eccle-siastic worship and discipline. This was touching Charles in a very tender point: he believed his honor and his conscience as well as his interest to be intimately concerned in supporting prelacy and the lit-urgy. He begged the commissioners, therefore, to remain satisfied with the concessions which he had made to Scotland; and having modeled their own church in accord with their own principles, to leave their neighbors in the same liberty and not to intermeddle with affairs of which they could not be supposed competent judges.

The divines of Oxford—secure of a victory, as they imagined, by means of their authorities from church history, their quotations from the fathers, and their spiritual arguments—desired a conference with Henderson; and they undertook by dint of reasoning to convert that great apostle of the north. But Henderson, who had always regarded as impious the least doubt with regard to his own principles and who knew of a much better way to reduce opponents than by employing any theological topics, absolutely refused all disputation or controversy. The English divines went away full of admiration at the blind assurance and bigoted prejudices of the man; he on his part was moved with equal wonder at their obstinate attachment to such palpable errors and delusions.

By the concessions which the king had granted to Scotland, it became necessary for him to summon a Parliament once in three years; and the date for the meeting of that assembly was fixed in June of the subsequent year. Charles flattered himself that he would be able by some decisive victory to reduce the English Parliament to a reasonable submission before that time elapsed, and that he might then expect with security the meeting of a Scottish Parliament. Though earnestly solicited by Loudoun to summon presently that great council of the nation, he absolutely refused to give authority to men who had already excited such dangerous commotions and who showed still the same disposition to resist and invade his authority. The commissioners, therefore, not being able to prevail in any of their demands, desired the king's passport for London, where they purposed to confer with the English Parliament; and being likewise denied this request, they returned with extreme dissatisfaction to Edinburgh.

The office of conservators of the peace was newly erected in Scotland in order to maintain the confederacy between the two kingdoms; and these, instigated by the clergy, were resolved, since they could not obtain the king's consent, to summon a Convention of Estates in his name but by their own authority; thus, they would bereave their sovereign of this article, the only one which remained of his prerogative. Under color of providing for national peace, endangered by the nearness of English armies, a Convention was called—an assembly which, though it meets with less solemnity, has the same authority as a Parliament in raising money and levying forces. Hamilton and his brother, the Earl of Lanark, who had been sent into Scotland in order to oppose these measures, lacked either authority or sincerity; and they passively yielded to the torrent. The General Assembly of the church met at the same time with the Convention; and exercising an authority almost absolute over the whole civil power, they made every politi-cal consideration yield to their theological zeal and prejudices.

Solemn League and Covenant

The English Parliament was at that time fallen into great distress by the progress of the royal arms; and they gladly sent to Edinburgh commissioners with ample powers to negotiate a nearer union and confederacy with the Scottish nation. The persons employed were the Earl of Rutland, Sir William Airmine, Sir Henry Vane the younger, Thomas Hatcher, and Henry Darley, attended by Marshall and Nye, two clergymen of signal authority. In this negotiation, the man chiefly trusted was Vane, who in eloquence, skill, and capacity, as well as in art and dissimulation, was not surpassed by anyone even during that age so famous for active talents. By his persuasion was framed at Ed-inburgh that Solemn League and Covenant which effaced all former protestations and vows taken in both kingdoms and long maintained its credit and authority. In this Covenant, the subscribers, besides en-gaging mutually to defend each other against all opponents, bound themselves to endeavor, without respect of persons, the extirpation of popery and prelacy, superstition, heresy, schism, and profaneness, to maintain the rights and privileges of Parliaments together with the king's authority, and to discover and bring to justice all incendiaries and malignants.

The subscribers of the Covenant vowed also to preserve the re-formed religion established in the Church of Scotland; but by the arti-fice of Vane, no declaration more explicit was made with regard to England and Ireland than that these kingdoms would be reformed in accord with the word of God and the example of the purest churches. The Scottish zealots deemed this expression quite free from ambiguity; they regarded their own model, when prelacy was abjured, as the only one which corresponded in any degree to such a description. But Vane, that able politician, had other views; and while he employed his great talents in outwitting the Presbyterians and secretly laughed at their simplicity, he had blindly devoted himself to the maintenance of systems still more absurd and more dangerous.

In the English Parliament there remained some members who, though they had been induced either by private ambition or by zeal for civil liberty to concur with the majority, still retained an attach-ment to the hierarchy and to the ancient modes of worship. But in the present danger which threatened their cause, all scruples were laid aside; and the Covenant, by whose means alone they could expect to obtain so considerable a reinforcement as the accession of the Scottish nation, was received without opposition. The Parliament, therefore, on September 17, having first subscribed it themselves, ordered it to be received by all who lived under their authority.

Arming of the Scots

Great were the rejoicings among the Scots that they would be the happy instruments of extending their mode of religion and dissipating that profound darkness in which the neighboring nations were involved. The General Assembly applauded this glorious imitation of the piety displayed by their ancestors, who, they said, in three different applications during the reign of Elizabeth had endeavored by persuasion to engage the English to lay aside the use of the surplice, tippet, and corner-cap. The Convention too, in the height of their zeal, ordered everyone to swear to this Covenant under the penalty of confiscation, besides what further punishment it would please the ensuing Parliament to inflict on the refusers as enemies to God, to the king, and to the kingdom. And being determined that the sword would carry conviction to all refractory minds, they prepared themselves with great vigilance and activity for their military enterprises. By means of £100,000 which they received from England, by the hopes of good pay and warm quarters, not to mention men's favorable disposition towards the cause, they soon completed their levies. And at about the end of the year, having added to their other forces the troops which they had recalled from Ireland, they were ready to enter England with an army of more than twenty thousand men under the command of their old general, the Earl of Leven.

The king, foreseeing this tempest which was gathering upon him, endeavored to secure himself by every expedient; and he cast his eye towards Ireland, in hopes that this kingdom, from which his cause had already received so much prejudice, might at length contribute somewhat towards his protection and security.

State of Ireland

After the commencement of the Irish insurrection, the English Parliament, though they undertook the suppression of it, had always been too much engaged either in military projects or expeditions at home to take any effectual step towards finishing that enterprise. They had entered, indeed, into a contract with the Scots for sending over an army of ten thousand men into Ireland; and in order to engage that nation in this undertaking, besides giving a promise of pay, they agreed to put Carrickfergus into their hands and to invest their general with an authority quite independent of the English government. These troops, so long as they were allowed to remain, were useful by diverting the force of the Irish rebels and protecting in the north the small remnants of the British planters. But except this contract with the Scottish nation, all the other measures of the Parliament either were absolutely insignificant or tended rather to the prejudice of the Protestant cause in Ireland. By continuing their violent persecution, and still more violent menaces, against priests and papists, they confirmed the Irish Catholics in their rebellion and cut off all hopes of indulgence and toleration. By disposing beforehand of all the Irish forfeitures to subscribers or adventurers, they rendered all men of property desperate and seemed to threaten a total extirpation of the natives. And while they thus infused zeal and animosity into the enemy, no measure was pursued which could tend to support or encourage the Protestants, now reduced to the last extremities.

From a long course of successes, the English nation has acquired an ascendancy so great over the Irish one that though the Irish are not surpassed by any troops when they receive military discipline among foreigners, they have never in their own country been able to make any vigorous effort for the defense or recovery of their liberties. In many encounters, the English, under Lord Moore, Sir William St. Leger, Sir Frederick Hamilton, and others, had, though under great disadvantages of situation and numbers, put the Irish to rout and returned in triumph to Dublin. The rebels raised the siege of Drogheda after an obstinate defense made by the garrison. Ormonde had obtained two complete victories at Kilrush and New Ross and had brought relief to all the forts which were besieged or blockaded in different parts of the kingdom. But notwithstanding these successes, even the most common necessaries of life were lacking to the victorious armies. The Irish had laid waste the whole kingdom in their wild rage against the British planters; and from their habitual sloth and ignorance, they were themselves totally unfit to raise any convenience of human life. During the course of six months, no supplies had come from England, except the fourth part of one small vessel's lading. Dublin, to save itself from starving, had been obliged to send the greater part of its inhabitants to England. The army had little ammunition, scarcely exceeding forty barrels of gunpowder, nor even shoes or clothes; and for lack of food, the soldiers had been obliged to eat their own horses. The distress of the Irish was not much inferior; and though they were more hardened against such extremities, it was but a melancholy reflection that the two nations, while they continued their furious animosities, would make desolate that fertile island which might serve to the subsistence and happiness of both.

The justices and Council of Ireland had been engaged, chiefly by the influence and authority of Ormonde, to fall into an entire dependence on the king. Parsons, Temple, Loftus, and Meredith, who favored the opposite party, had been removed; and Charles had filled their places with others, more inclined to his service. A committee of the English House of Commons which had been sent over to Ireland in order to conduct the affairs of that kingdom had been excluded from the Council in obedience to orders transmitted from the king. And these were reasons sufficient, besides the great difficulties under which they themselves labored, why the Parliament was unwilling to send supplies to an army which, though engaged in a cause much favored by them, was commanded by their declared enemies. They even intercepted some small succors sent there by the king.

The king, as he had neither money, arms, ammunition, nor provisions to spare from his own urgent wants, resolved to embrace an expedient which might at the same time relieve the necessities of the Irish Protestants and contribute to the advancement of his affairs in England. A truce with the rebels, he thought, would enable his subjects in Ireland to provide for their own support and would procure him the assistance of the army against the English Parliament. But as a treaty with a people so odious for their barbarities, and still more for their religion, might be represented in invidious colors and renew all those calumnies with which he had been loaded, it was necessary to proceed with great caution in conducting that measure. A remonstrance from the army was made to the Irish Council, representing their intolerable necessities and craving permission to leave the kingdom. And if that were refused, "We must have recourse," they said, "to that first and primary law, with which God has endowed all men; we mean the law of nature, which teaches every creature to preserve itself." Memorials both to the king and Parliament were transmitted by the justices and Council, in which their wants and dangers were strongly set forth. And though the general expressions in these memorials might perhaps be suspected of exaggeration, yet from the particular facts mentioned, from the confession of the English Parliament itself, and from the very nature of things, it is apparent that the Irish Protestants were reduced to great extremities; and it became prudent in the king, if not absolutely necessary, to embrace some expedient which might secure them for a time from the ruin and misery with which they were threatened.

Accordingly, the king gave orders to Ormonde and the justices to conclude a cessation of arms for a year with the Council of Kilkenny, by whom the Irish were governed, and to leave both sides in possession of their present advantages. The Parliament, whose business it was to find fault with every measure adopted by the opposite party, and who would not lose so fair an opportunity of reproaching the king with his favor to the Irish papists, exclaimed loudly against this cessation. Among other reasons, they insisted upon the divine vengeance which England might justly dread for tolerating anti-Christian idolatry on pretense of civil contracts and political agreements. Religion, though every day employed as the engine of their own ambitious purposes, was supposed too sacred to be yielded up to the temporal interests or safety of kingdoms.

After the cessation, there was little necessity as well as no means of maintaining the army in Ireland. The king ordered Ormonde, who was entirely devoted to him, to send over considerable bodies of it to England. Most of them continued in his service; but a small part, having imbibed in Ireland a strong animosity against the Catholics and hearing the king's party universally reproached with popery, soon after deserted to the Parliament.

Some Irish Catholics came over with these troops and joined the royal army, where they continued the same cruelties and disorders to which they had been accustomed. The Parliament voted that no quarter in any action should ever be given them; but Prince Rupert, by making some reprisals, soon repressed this inhumanity.

CHAPTER 57

1644 – 1645

*Invasion of the Scots – Battle of Marston Moor – Battle of
Cropredy Bridge – Essex's forces disarmed – Second Battle
of Newbury – Rise and character of the Independents –
Self-Denying Ordinance – Fairfax – Cromwell –
Treaty of Uxbridge – Execution of Laud*

T HE king had till now obtained many advantages over
the Parliament during the course of the war and had
| 1644 |

raised himself from that low condition into which he had at first fall-
en to be nearly upon an equal footing with his adversaries. Yorkshire
and all the northern counties were reduced by the Marquess of Newcastle; and excepting Hull, the Parliament was master of no garrison in
these quarters. In the west, Plymouth alone, having been in vain besieged by Prince Maurice, resisted the king's authority. And had it not
been for the disappointment in the enterprise of Gloucester, the royal
garrisons would have reached without interruption from one end of
the kingdom to the other and would have occupied a greater extent of
ground than those of the Parliament. Many of the Royalists flattered
themselves that the same vigorous spirit which had elevated them to
the present height of power would continue to favor their progress
and obtain them a final victory over their enemies. But those who
judged more soundly observed that besides the accession of the whole
Scottish nation to the side of the Parliament, the very principle on
which the royal successes had been founded was every day acquired
more and more by the opposite party. The king's troops, full of gentry
and nobility, had exerted a valor superior to their enemies and had till
now been successful in almost every encounter. But in proportion as

the whole nation became warlike by the continuance of civil discords, this advantage was more equally shared; and superior numbers, it was expected, must at length obtain the victory. The king's troops, ill paid and destitute of every necessity, also could not possibly be retained in equal discipline with the parliamentary forces, to whom all supplies were furnished from unexhausted stores and treasures. The severity of manners so much affected by these zealous religionists assisted their military institutions; and the rigid inflexibility of character by which the austere reformers of church and state were distinguished enabled the parliamentary chiefs to restrain their soldiers within stricter rules and more exact order. And as the king's officers indulged themselves in even greater licenses than those to which they had been accustomed during times of peace, they were apt both to neglect their military duty and to set a pernicious example of disorder to the soldiers under their command.

At the commencement of the civil war, all Englishmen who served abroad were invited over and treated with extraordinary respect; and most of them, being descended of good families, and by reason of their absence, unacquainted with the new principles which depressed the dignity of the Crown, had enlisted under the royal standard. But it is observable that though the military profession requires great genius and long experience in the principal commanders, all its subordinate duties may be discharged by ordinary talents and from superficial practice. Citizens and country gentlemen soon became excellent officers; and the generals of greatest fame and capacity happened, all of them, to spring up on the side of the Parliament. The courtiers and great nobility in the other party checked the growth of any extraordinary genius among the subordinate officers; and every man there, as in a regular established government, was confined to the station in which his birth had placed him.

The king, that he might make preparations during winter for the ensuing campaign, summoned to Oxford all the members of either house who adhered to his interests and endeavored to avail himself of the name of Parliament, so passionately cherished by the English nation. The House of Peers was pretty full; besides the nobility employed in different parts of the kingdom, it contained twice as many members as commonly voted at Westminster. The House of Commons consisted of about one hundred forty, no more than half of the other House of Commons.

So extremely light had government previously lain upon the people that the very name of "excise" was unknown to them; and among the other evils arising from these domestic wars was the introduction of that impost into England. The Parliament at Westminster having voted an excise on beer, wine, and other commodities, those at Oxford imitated the example and conferred that revenue on the king. And in order to enable him the better to recruit his army, they granted him the sum of £100,000, to be levied by way of loan upon the subject. The king circulated privy seals, countersigned by the speakers of both houses, requiring the loan of particular sums from such persons as lived within his quarters. Neither party had as yet got above the pedantry of reproaching their antagonists with these illegal measures.

The Westminster Parliament passed a whimsical ordinance commanding all the inhabitants of London and the neighborhood to retrench a meal a week and to pay the value of it for the support of the public cause. It is easily imagined that provided the money were paid, they troubled themselves but little about the execution of their ordinance.

Such was the king's situation that in order to restore peace to the nation, he had no occasion to demand any other terms than the restoring of the laws and constitution, the reinstating him in the same rights which had always been enjoyed by his predecessors, and the reestablishing on its ancient basis the whole frame of government, civil as well as ecclesiastical. And that he might facilitate an end seemingly so desirable, he offered to employ means equally popular: a universal act of oblivion and a toleration or indulgence to tender consciences. Nothing, therefore, could contribute more to his interests than every discourse of peace and every discussion of the conditions upon which that blessing could be obtained. For this reason, he solicited a treaty on all occasions and desired a conference and mutual examination of pretensions even when he entertained no hopes that any conclusion could possibly result from it.

For like reasons, the leaders of the Parliament prudently avoided, as much as possible, all advances towards negotiation; and they were cautious not to expose too easily to censure those high terms which their apprehensions or their ambition made them previously demand of the king. Though their partisans were blinded with the thickest veil of religious prejudices, they dreaded to bring their pretensions to the test or lay them open before the whole nation. In opposition to the sacred authority of the laws, to the venerable precedents of many ages, the popular leaders were ashamed to plead nothing but fears and jealousies which were not avowed by the constitution and for which neither the personal character of Charles, so full of virtue, nor his situation, so deprived of all independent authority, seemed to afford any reasonable foundation. Grievances which had been fully redressed; powers, either legal or illegal, which had been entirely renounced: it seemed unpopular and invidious and ungrateful to insist any further on these.

The king, that he might abate the universal veneration paid to the name of Parliament, had issued a declaration in which he set forth all the tumults by which he and his partisans in both houses had been driven from London; and he inferred from these that the assembly at Westminster was no longer a free Parliament and was entitled to no authority till its liberty was restored. As this declaration was an obstacle to all treaty, some contrivance seemed requisite in order to elude it.

A letter was written in the foregoing spring to the Earl of Essex and subscribed by the prince, the Duke of York, and forty-three noblemen. They there exhorted him to be an instrument of restoring peace and to promote that happy end with those by whom he was employed. Essex, though much disgusted with the Parliament, though apprehensive of the extremities to which they were driving, though desirous of any reasonable accommodation, yet was still more resolute to preserve an honorable fidelity to the trust reposed in him. He replied that as the paper sent him neither contained any address to the two houses of Parliament nor any acknowledgment of their authority, he could not communicate it to them. Like proposals had been reiterated by the king during the ensuing campaign and still met with a like answer from Essex.

In order to make a new attempt for a treaty, the king this spring sent another letter, directed to the Lords and Commons of Parliament assembled at Westminster. But as he also mentioned in the letter the Lords and Commons of Parliament assembled at Oxford, and declared that his aim and intention was to make provision that all the members of both houses might securely meet in a full and free assembly, the Parliament, perceiving the conclusion implied, refused all treaty upon such terms. And the king, who knew what small hopes there were of accommodation, would not abandon the pretensions which he had assumed nor acknowledge the two houses more expressly for a free Parliament.

This winter the famous Pym died, a man as much hated by one

party as respected by the other. At London, he was considered as a martyr to national liberty who had abridged his life by incessant labors for the interests of his country. At Oxford, he was believed to have been struck with an uncommon disease and to have been consumed with vermin as a mark of divine vengeance for his multiplied crimes and treasons. He had given so little attention to improving his private fortune in those civil wars of which he had been one principal author that the Parliament thought themselves obliged from gratitude to pay the debts which he had contracted.

We now return to the military operations which during the winter were carried on with vigor in several places, notwithstanding the severity of the season.

The forces brought from Ireland were landed at Mostyn, in North Wales; being put under the command of Lord Byron, they besieged and took the Castles of Hawarden, Beeston, Acton, and Deddington House. No place in Cheshire or the neighborhood now adhered to the Parliament except Nantwich, and to this town Byron laid siege during the depth of winter. Sir Thomas Fairfax, alarmed at so considerable a progress of the Royalists, assembled an army of four thousand men in Yorkshire, and having joined Sir William Brereton, was approaching to the camp of the enemy. Byron and his soldiers, elated with successes obtained in Ireland, had entertained the most profound contempt for the parliamentary forces—a disposition which may be regarded as a good presage of victory if confined to the army but is the most probable forerunner of a defeat if it extend to the general. On January 25, Fairfax suddenly attacked the camp of the Royalists. The swelling of the river by a thaw divided one part of the king's army from the other. That part exposed to Fairfax, being beaten from their post, retired into the church of Acton and were all taken prisoners; the other retreated with precipitation. And thus was dissipated or rendered useless that body of forces which had been drawn from Ireland; and the parliamentary party revived in those northwest counties of England.

Invasion of the Scots

The invasion from Scotland was attended with consequences of much greater importance. The Scots, having demanded in vain the surrender of the town of Newcastle, which was fortified by the vigilance of Sir Thomas Glemham, passed the Tyne on February 22 and faced the Marquess of Newcastle, who lay at Durham with an army of fourteen thousand men. After some military operations in which that noble-man reduced the enemy to difficulties for forage and provisions, he received intelligence of a great disaster which had befallen his forces in Yorkshire. Colonel Belasyse, whom he had left with a considerable body of troops, was totally routed at Selby on April 11 by Sir Thomas Fairfax, who had returned from Cheshire with his victorious forces. Afraid of being enclosed between two armies, Newcastle retreated and retired to York. Fairfax having been joined by Leven, they encamped outside of that place, intending to besiege it. But as the parliamentary and Scottish forces were not numerous enough to invest so large a town divided by a river, they contented themselves with incommoding it by a loose blockade; and affairs remained for some time in suspense between these opposite armies.

During this winter and spring, other parts of the kingdom had also been infested with war. Hopton, having assembled an army of four-teen thousand men, endeavored to break into Sussex, Kent, and the Southern Association, which seemed well disposed to receive him. Waller fell upon him at Cheriton and gave him a defeat of considera-ble importance. In another quarter, siege being laid to Newark by the parliamentary forces, Prince Rupert prepared himself for relieving a town of such consequence, which alone preserved the communication open between the king's southern and northern quarters. With a small force, but that animated by his active courage, he broke through the enemy, relieved the town, and totally dissipated that army of the Parliament.

But though fortune seemed to have divided her favors between the parties, the king found himself in the main a considerable loser by this winter campaign; and he prognosticated a still worse result from the ensuing summer. The preparations of the Parliament were great, and much exceeded the slender resources of which he was possessed. In the Eastern Association, they levied fourteen thousand men under the Earl of Manchester, seconded by Cromwell. An army of ten thousand men under Essex and another of nearly the same force under Waller were assembled in the neighborhood of London. The former was des-tined to oppose the king; the latter was appointed to march into the west, where Prince Maurice, with a small army which went continually to decay, was spending his time in vain before Lyme Regis, an incon-siderable town upon the seacoast. The utmost efforts of the king could not raise more than ten thousand men at Oxford, and these were to depend for subsistence during the campaign chiefly on their sword.

The queen, terrified with the dangers which every way environed her and afraid of being enclosed in Oxford in the middle of the kingdom, fled to Exeter, where she hoped to be delivered unmolested of the child with which she was now pregnant and from where she had the means of an easy escape into France if pressed by the forces of the enemy. She knew the implacable hatred which the Parliament, on account of her religion and her credit with the king, had all along borne her. Last summer, the Commons had sent up to the Peers an impeachment of high treason against her because she had assisted her husband in his utmost distresses with arms and ammunition which she had bought in Holland. And had she fallen into their hands, neither her sex, she knew, nor high station could protect her against insults at least, if not danger, from those haughty republicans who so little affected to conduct themselves by the maxims of gallantry and politeness.

It is remarkable that the Parliament, from the beginning of these dissensions, had in all things assumed an extreme ascendant over their sovereign and had displayed a violence and arrogated an authority which on his side would not have been compatible either with his temper or his situation. While he spoke perpetually of pardoning all "rebels," they talked of nothing but the punishment of "delinquents" and "malignants." While he offered a toleration and indulgence to tender consciences, they threatened the utter extirpation of prelacy. To his professions of lenity, they opposed declarations of rigor. And the more the ancient tenor of the laws inculcated a respectful subordination to the Crown, the more careful were they to cover by their lofty pretensions that defect under which they labored.

Battle of Marston Moor

Their great advantages in the north seemed to second their ambition and finally to promise them success in their unwarrantable enterprises. Manchester, having taken Lincoln, had united his army to that of Leven and Fairfax, and York was now closely besieged by their combined forces. That town, though vigorously defended by Newcastle, was reduced to extremity; and the parliamentary generals, after enduring great losses and fatigues, flattered themselves that all their labors would at last be crowned by this important conquest. Suddenly, they were alarmed by the approach of Prince Rupert. This gallant commander, having vigorously exerted himself in Lancashire and Cheshire, had collected a considerable army; and joining Sir Charles Lucas, who commanded Newcastle's cavalry, he hastened to the relief of York with an army of twenty thousand men. The Scottish and parliamentary generals raised the siege, and drawing up on Marston Moor, purposed to give battle to the Royalists. Prince Rupert approached the town by another quarter, and interposing the River Ouse between him and the enemy, safely joined his forces to those of Newcastle. The marquess endeavored to persuade him that having so successfully effected his purpose, he ought to be content with the present advantages and leave the enemy, now much diminished by their losses and discouraged by their ill success, to dissolve by those mutual dissensions which had begun to take place among them. The prince, whose martial disposition was not sufficiently tempered with prudence nor softened by complaisance, pretending to have positive orders from the king, without deigning to consult with Newcastle, whose merits and services deserved better treatment, immediately issued orders for battle and led out the army to Marston Moor. This action was obstinately disputed on July 2 between the most numerous armies that were engaged during the course of these wars; nor were the forces on each side much different in number. Fifty thousand British troops were led to mutual slaughter; and the victory seemed long undecided between them. Prince Rupert, who commanded the right wing of the Royalists, was opposed to Cromwell, who conducted the choice troops of the Parliament, inured to danger under that determined leader, animated by zeal, and confirmed by the most rigid discipline. After a short combat, the cavalry of the Royalists gave way, and such of the infantry as stood next to them were likewise borne down and put to flight. Newcastle's regiment alone, resolute to conquer or to perish, obstinately kept their ground; and they maintained by their dead bodies the same order in which they had at first been ranged. In the other wing, Sir Thomas Fairfax and Colonel Lambert with some troops broke through the Royalists, and transported by the ardor of pursuit, soon reached their victorious friends, engaged also in pursuit of the enemy. But after that tempest was past, Lucas, who commanded the Royalists in this wing, restoring order to his broken forces, made a furious attack on the parliamentary cavalry, threw them into disorder, pushed them upon their own infantry, and put that whole wing to rout. When ready to seize on their carriages and baggage, he perceived Cromwell, who was now returned from pursuit of the other wing. Both sides were not a little surprised to find that they must again renew the combat for that victory which each of them thought they had already obtained. The front of the battle was now exactly counter-changed, and each army occupied the ground which had been possessed by the enemy at the beginning of the day. This second battle was equally furious and desperate with the first. But after the utmost efforts of courage by both parties, victory wholly turned to the side of the Parliament. The prince's train of artillery was taken, and his whole army pushed off the field of battle.

This event was in itself a mighty blow to the king; but its consequences proved more fatal. The Marquess of Newcastle was entirely lost to the royal cause. That nobleman, the ornament of the court and of his order, had been engaged, contrary to the natural bent of his disposition, into these military operations merely by a high sense of honor and a personal regard to his master. The dangers of war were disregarded by his valor, but its fatigues were oppressive to his natural indolence. Munificent and generous in his expense, polite and elegant in his taste, courteous and humane in his behavior, he brought a great accession of friends and of credit to the party which he embraced. But amidst all the hurry of action, his inclinations were secretly drawn to the soft arts of peace, in which he took delight; and the charms of poetry, music, and conversation often stole him from his rougher occupations. He chose Sir William Davenant, an ingenious poet, for his lieutenant general. The other persons in whom he placed confidence were more the instruments of his refined pleasures than qualified for the business which they undertook; and the severity and application requisite to the support of discipline were qualities in which he was entirely lacking.

When Prince Rupert, contrary to his advice, resolved on this battle and issued all orders without communicating his intentions to him, he took the field, but, he said, merely as a volunteer; and except by his personal courage, which shone out with luster, he had no share in the action. Enraged to find that all his successful labors were rendered abortive by one act of fatal temerity, terrified with the prospect of renewing his pains and fatigue, he resolved no longer to maintain the few resources which remained to a desperate cause; and he thought that the same regard to honor which had at first called him to arms now required him to abandon a party where he met with such unworthy treatment. Next morning early, he sent word to the prince that he was leaving the kingdom instantly; and without delay, he went to Scarborough, where he found a vessel which carried him overseas. During the ensuing years till the Restoration, he lived abroad in great necessity and saw with indifference his opulent fortune sequestered by those who assumed the government of England. He disdained to show obeisance to their usurped authority by submission or composition; and the least favorable censors of his merit allowed that the fidelity and services of a whole life had sufficiently atoned for one rash action into which his passion had betrayed him.

Prince Rupert, with equal precipitation, drew off the remains of his army and retired into Lancashire. In a few days, on July 16, Glemham was obliged to surrender York; and he marched out his garrison with all the honors of war. Lord Fairfax, remaining in the city, established his government in that whole county and sent a thousand cavalrymen into Lancashire to join with the parliamentary forces in that quarter and attend the motions of Prince Rupert. The Scottish army marched northwards in order to join the Earl of Callendar, who was advancing with ten thousand additional forces, and to reduce the town of Newcastle, which they took by storm. The Earl of Manchester—with Cromwell, to whom the fame of this great victory was chiefly ascribed and who was wounded in the action—returned to the Eastern Association in order to recruit his army.

While these events passed in the north, the king's affairs in the south were conducted with more success and greater abilities. Patrick Ruthven, a Scotsman who had been created Earl of Brentford, acted under the king as general.

Battle of Cropredy Bridge

The Parliament soon completed their two armies commanded by Essex and Waller. The great zeal of London facilitated this undertaking. Many speeches were made to the citizens by the parliamentary leaders in order to excite their ardor. Holles in particular exhorted them not to spare, on this important occasion, their purses, their persons, or their prayers; and in general, it must be confessed, they were sufficiently liberal in all these contributions. The two generals had orders to march with their combined armies towards Oxford, and if the king retired into that city, to lay siege to it, thus putting an end to the war by one enterprise. The king, leaving a numerous garrison in Oxford, passed with dexterity between the two armies, which had taken Abingdon and had enclosed him on both sides. He marched towards Worcester; and Waller received orders from Essex to follow him and watch his motions while Essex himself marched into the west in quest of Prince Maurice. Waller had approached within two miles of the royal camp and was only separated from it by the Severn when he received intelligence that the king was advanced to Bewdley and had directed his course towards Shrewsbury. In order to prevent him, Waller presently dislodged and hastened by quick marches to that town, while the king, suddenly returning upon his own footsteps, reached Oxford, and having reinforced his army from that garrison, now in his turn marched out in quest of Waller. The two armies faced each other at Cropredy Bridge, near Banbury, but the River Cherwell ran between them. Next day, June 29, the king decamped and marched towards Daventry. Waller, intending to fall on the rear of the Royalists, ordered a considerable detachment to pass the bridge. He was repulsed, routed, and pursued with considerable loss. Stunned and disheartened by this blow, his army decayed and melted away by desertion; and the king thought he might safely leave it and march westwards against Essex.

Essex's forces disarmed

That general, having obliged Prince Maurice to raise the siege of Lyme Regis, having taken Weymouth and Taunton, advanced still in his conquests and met with no equal opposition. The king followed him, and having reinforced his army from all quarters, appeared in the field with an army superior to the enemy. Essex, retreating into Cornwall, informed the Parliament of his danger and desired them to send an army which might fall on the king's rear. General Middleton received a commission to execute that service; but he came too late. Essex's army, cooped up in a narrow corner at Lostwithiel, deprived of all forage and provisions, and seeing no prospect of succor, was reduced to the last extremity. The king pressed them on one side, Prince Maurice on another, Sir Richard Grenville on a third. Essex, Robartes, and some of the principal officers escaped in a boat to Plymouth; Balfour with his cavalry passed the king's outposts in a thick mist and got safely to the garrisons of his own party. On September 1, the infantry under Skippon were obliged to surrender their arms, artillery, baggage, and ammunition; and being conducted to the Parliament's quarters, they were dismissed. By this victory, which was much boasted of, the king, besides the honor of the enterprise, obtained what he stood extremely in need of; the Parliament, having preserved the men, lost what they could easily repair.

No sooner did this intelligence reach London than the Committee of the Two Kingdoms voted thanks to Essex for his fidelity, courage, and conduct; and this method of proceeding, no less politic than magnanimous, was preserved by the Parliament throughout the whole course of the war. Equally indulgent to their friends and rigorous to their enemies, they employed with success these two powerful engines of reward and punishment in confirmation of their authority.

Second Battle of Newbury

That the king might have less reason to exult in the advantages which he had obtained in the west, the Parliament opposed to him very numerous forces. Having armed anew Essex's subdued but not disheartened troops, they ordered Manchester and Cromwell to march with their recruited forces from the Eastern Association, and joining their armies to those of Waller and Middleton as well as of Essex, offer battle to the king. Charles chose his post at Newbury, where the parliamentary armies under the Earl of Manchester attacked him with great vigor on October 27; and that town was a second time the scene of the bloody animosities of the English. Essex's soldiers, exhorting one another to repair their broken honor and revenge the disgrace of Lostwithiel, made an impetuous assault on the Royalists; and when they recovered some of their cannon lost in Cornwall, they could not forbear embracing them with tears of joy. Though the king's troops defended themselves with valor, they were overpowered by numbers; the night came very seasonably to their relief and prevented a total overthrow. Charles, leaving his baggage and cannon in Donnington Castle, near Newbury, forthwith retreated to Wallingford, and from there to Oxford. Prince Rupert and the Earl of Northampton joined him there with considerable bodies of cavalry. Strengthened by this reinforcement, he ventured to advance towards the enemy, now employed before Donnington Castle. Essex, detained by sickness, had not joined the army since his misfortune in Cornwall. Manchester was in command; and though his forces were much superior to those of the king, he declined an engagement and rejected the advice of Cromwell, who zealously pressed him not to neglect so favorable an opportunity of finishing the war. The king's army, by bringing off their cannon from Donnington Castle in the face of the enemy on November 9, seemed to have sufficiently repaired the honor which they had lost at Newbury; and Charles, having the satisfaction to excite between Manchester and Cromwell animosities equal with those which formerly took place between Essex and Waller, distributed his army into winter quarters on November 23.

Those contests among the parliamentary generals which had disturbed their military operations were renewed in London during the winter season; and each being supported by his own faction, their mutual reproaches and accusations agitated the whole city and Parliament. There had long prevailed in that party a secret distinction which, though the dread of the king's power had previously suppressed it, began to reveal itself with high contest and animosity in proportion as the hopes of success became nearer and more immediate. The Independents, who had at first taken shelter and concealed themselves under the wings of the Presbyterians, now clearly appeared a distinct party and betrayed very different views and pretensions. We must here endeavor to explain the nature of this party and of its leaders, who from now on occupy the scene of action.

Rise and character of the Independents

During those times, when the enthusiastic spirit met with such honor and encouragement and was the immediate means of distinction and preferment, it was impossible to set bounds to these holy fervors or confine within any natural limits what was directed towards an infinite and a supernatural object. Every man, as prompted by the warmth of his temper, excited by emulation, or supported by his habits of hypocrisy, endeavored to distinguish himself beyond his fellows and to arrive at a higher pitch of saintship and perfection. In proportion to its degree of fanaticism, each sect became dangerous and destructive; and as the Independents went a note higher than the Presbyterians, they could less be restrained within any bounds of temper and moderation. From this distinction, as from a first principle, were derived by a necessary consequence all the other differences of these two sects.

The Independents rejected all ecclesiastical establishments and would admit of no spiritual courts, no government among pastors, no interposition of the magistrate in religious concerns, no fixed encouragement annexed to any system of doctrines or opinions. In accord with their principles, each congregation, united voluntarily and by spiritual ties, composed within itself a separate church and exercised a jurisdiction, but one destitute of temporal sanctions, over its own pastor and its own members. The election alone of the congregation was sufficient to bestow the priestly rank; and as all essential distinction was denied between the laity and the clergy, no ceremony, no institution, no vocation, no imposition of hands was, as in all other churches, supposed requisite to convey a right to holy orders. The enthusiasm of the Presbyterians led them to reject the authority of prelates, to throw off the restraint of liturgies, to retrench ceremonies, to limit the riches and authority of the priestly office. The fanaticism of the Independents, exalted to a higher pitch, abolished ecclesiastical government, disdained creeds and systems, neglected every ceremony, and confounded all ranks and orders. The soldier, the merchant, the mechanic, indulging the fervors of zeal and guided by the sliding in of the spirit, resigned himself to an inward and superior direction and was consecrated, in a sense, by an immediate intercourse and communication with heaven.

The Catholics, laying claim to an infallible guide, had justified upon that principle their doctrine and practice of persecution. The Presbyterians, imagining that such clear and certain tenets as they themselves adopted could be rejected only from a criminal and pertinacious obstinacy, had till this time gratified to the full their bigoted zeal in a like doctrine and practice. The Independents, from the extremity of the same zeal, were led into the milder principles of toleration. Their minds, set afloat in the wide sea of inspiration, could confine themselves within no certain limits; and an enthusiast was apt, by a natural train of thinking, to permit in others the same variations in which he indulged himself. Of all Christian sects, this was the first which, during its prosperity as well as its adversity, always adopted the principle of toleration; and it is remarkable that so reasonable a doctrine owed its origin not to reasoning but to the height of extravagance and fanaticism.

Only popery and prelacy, whose spirit seemed to tend towards superstition, were treated by the Independents with rigor. The doctrines too of fate or destiny were deemed by them essential to all religion. All the sectaries, amidst all their other differences, unanimously concurred in these rigid opinions.

The political system of the Independents kept pace with their religious one. Not content with confining to very narrow limits the power of the Crown and reducing the king to the rank of first magistrate, which was the project of the Presbyterians, this sect, more ardent in the pursuit of liberty, aspired to a total abolition of the monarchy, and even of the aristocracy, and projected an entire equality of rank and order in a republic quite free and independent. In consequence of this scheme, they were declared enemies to all proposals of peace except on such terms as they knew it was impossible to obtain; and they adhered to that maxim, which is in the main prudent and politic, that whoever draws the sword against his sovereign should throw away the scabbard. By terrifying others with the fear of vengeance from the offended prince, they had engaged greater numbers into the opposition against peace than had adopted their other principles with regard to government and religion. And the great success which had already attended the arms of the Parliament, and the greater which was soon expected, confirmed them still further in this obstinacy.

Sir Henry Vane, Oliver Cromwell, Nathaniel Fiennes, and Oliver St. John, the solicitor general, were regarded as the leaders of the Independents. The Earl of Essex, disgusted with a war of which he began to foresee the pernicious consequences, adhered to the Presbyterians and promoted every reasonable plan of accommodation. The Earl of Northumberland, fond of his rank and dignity, regarded with horror a scheme which, if it took place, would confound him and his family with the lowest in the kingdom. The Earls of Warwick and Denbigh, Sir Philip Stapleton, Sir William Waller, Holles, Massey, Whitelocke, Maynard, and Glynn had embraced the same sentiments. A considerable majority in the Parliament, and a much greater one in the nation, were attached to the Presbyterian party; and it was only by cunning and deceit at first, and by military violence afterwards, that the Independents could entertain any hopes of success.

The Earl of Manchester, provoked at the impeachment which the king had lodged against him, had long forwarded the war with alacrity; but being a man of humanity and good principles, the view of public calamities and the prospect of a total subversion of government began to moderate his ardor and inclined him to promote peace on any safe or honorable terms. He was even suspected, in the field, of not having pushed to the utmost against the king the advantages obtained by the arms of the Parliament. In the public debates, Cromwell revived the accusation that this nobleman had willfully neglected at Donnington Castle a favorable opportunity of finishing the war by a total defeat of the Royalists. "I showed him evidently [clearly]," said Cromwell, "how this success might be obtained, and only desired leave, with my own brigade of horse, to charge the king's army in their retreat, leaving it in the earl's choice, if he thought proper, to remain neuter [neutral] with the rest of his forces. But, notwithstanding my importunity, he positively refused his consent, and gave no other reason but that, if we met with a defeat, there was an end of our pretensions: we should all be rebels and traitors, and be executed and forfeited by law."

Manchester, by way of recrimination, informed the Parliament that at another time, Cromwell, having proposed some scheme to which it seemed improbable the Parliament would agree, insisted; he said, "My lord, if you will stick firm to honest men, you shall find yourself at the head of an army which shall give law both to king and Parliament." "This discourse," continued Manchester, "made the greater impression on me because I knew the lieutenant general to be a man of very deep designs; and he has even ventured to tell me that it never would be well with England till I were Mr. Montague, and there were ne'er a lord or peer in the kingdom." So full was Cromwell of these republican projects that notwithstanding his habits of profound dissimulation, he could not so carefully guard his expressions but that sometimes his favorite notions would escape him.

These violent dissensions brought matters to extremity and pushed the Independents to the execution of their designs. The present generals, they thought, were more desirous of protracting than finishing the war; having entertained a scheme for preserving still some balance in the constitution, they were afraid of entirely subduing the king and reducing him to a condition where he would not be entitled to ask any concessions. Only a new model of the army could bring complete victory to the Parliament and free the nation from those calamities under which it labored. But how to effect this project was the difficulty. The authority as well as the merits of Essex was very great with the Parliament. Not only had he served them all along with the most exact and scrupulous honor; it was in some measure owing to his popularity that they had ever been enabled to levy an army or make headway against the royal cause. Manchester, Warwick, and the other commanders had likewise great credit with the public; there were no hopes of prevailing over them but by laying the plan of an oblique and artificial attack which would conceal the real purposes of their antagonists. The Scots and the Scottish commissioners, jealous of the progress of the Independents, were a new obstacle which would be difficult to surmount without the utmost art and subtlety. The methods by which this intrigue was conducted are so singular and show so fully the spirit of the age that we shall give a detail of them, as delivered by Lord Clarendon.

A fast on the last Wednesday of every month had been ordered by the Parliament at the beginning of these commotions; and their preachers on that day were careful to keep alive, by their vehement declamations, the popular prejudices entertained against the king, against prelacy, and against popery. The king, that he might combat the Parliament with their own weapons, appointed likewise a monthly fast, when the people would be instructed in the duties of loyalty and of submission to the higher powers; and he chose the second Friday of every month for the devotion of the Royalists. It was now proposed and carried in Parliament by the Independents that a new and more solemn fast be held, when the people would implore the divine assistance for extricating them from those perplexities in which they were at present involved. On that day, the preachers, after many political prayers, took care to treat of the reigning divisions in the Parliament, which were ascribed entirely to the selfish ends pursued by the members. In the hands of those members, they said, are lodged all the considerable commands of the army, all the lucrative offices in the civil administration; and while the nation is falling every day into poverty and groans under an insupportable load of taxes, these men multiply possession on possession, and soon will be masters of all the wealth of the kingdom. That such persons, who fatten on the calamities of their country, will ever embrace any effectual measure for bringing them to an end or insuring final success to the war cannot reasonably be expected. Lingering expedients alone will be pursued; and operations in the field concurring in the same pernicious end with deliberations in the cabinet, civil commotions will forever be perpetuated in the nation. After exaggerating these disorders, the ministers returned to their prayers and besought the Lord that he would take his own work into his own hand; and if the instruments whom he had till then employed were not worthy to bring to a conclusion so glorious a design, that he would inspire others more fit, who might perfect what was begun, and by establishing true religion, put a speedy end to the public miseries.

When the Parliament met on the day subsequent to these devout animadversions, a new spirit appeared in the looks of many. Sir Henry Vane told the Commons that if ever God appeared to them, it was in the ordinances of yesterday. That, as he was credibly informed by many who had been present in different congregations, the same lamentations and discourses which the godly preachers had made before them had been heard in other churches. That so remarkable a concurrence could proceed only from the immediate operation of the Holy Spirit. That he, therefore, entreated them, in vindication of their own honor, in consideration of their duty to God and their country, to lay aside all private ends and renounce every office attended with profit or advantage. That the absence of so many members occupied in different employments had rendered the house extremely thin and diminished the authority of their determinations. And that for his own part, he could not forbear accusing himself as one who enjoyed a gainful office, that of treasurer of the navy; and though he was possessed of it before the civil commotions and owed it not to the favor of the Parliament, yet was he ready to resign it and to sacrifice to the welfare of his country every consideration of private interest and advantage.

Cromwell next acted his part. He commended the preachers for having dealt with them plainly and impartially in telling them of their errors, of which they were so unwilling to be informed. Though they dwelt on many things, he said, on which he had never before reflected, yet upon considering all aspects of them, he could not but confess that till there were a perfect reformation in these particulars, nothing which they undertook could possibly prosper. The Parliament, he continued, had no doubt done wisely, on the commencement of the war, in engaging several of its members in the most dangerous parts of it, and thereby satisfying the nation that they intended to share all hazards with the meanest of the people. But affairs were now changed. During the progress of military operations, there had arisen in the parliamentary armies many excellent officers who were qualified for higher commands than they were now possessed of. And though it did not become men engaged in such a cause "to put trust in the arm of flesh," yet he could assure them that their troops contained generals fit to command in any enterprise in Christendom. The army, indeed, he was sorry to say it, did not correspond by its discipline to the merit of the officers; nor were there any hopes, till the present vices and disorders which prevailed among the soldiers were repressed by a new model, that their forces would ever be attended with signal success in any undertaking.

In opposition to this reasoning of the Independents, many of the Presbyterians pointed out the inconvenience and danger of the projected alteration. In particular, Whitelocke—a man of honor who loved his country, though in every change of government he always adhered to the ruling power—said that besides the ingratitude of discarding, and that by fraud and artifice, so many noble persons to whom the Parliament had till now owed its chief support, they would find it extremely difficult to supply the place of men now formed by experience to command and authority. That only the rank possessed by such as were members of either house prevented envy, retained the army in obedience, and gave weight to military orders. That greater confidence might safely be reposed in men of family and fortune than in mere adventurers, who would be apt to entertain separate views from those which were embraced by the persons who employed them. That no maxim of policy was more undisputed than the necessity of preserving an inseparable connection between the civil and military powers and of retaining the latter in strict subordination to the former. That the Greeks and Romans, the wisest and most passionate lovers of liberty, had always entrusted to their senators the command of armies and had maintained an unconquerable jealousy of all mercenary forces. And that only such men whose interests were involved in those of the public and who possessed a vote in the civil deliberations would sufficiently respect the authority of Parliament and never could be tempted to turn the sword against those by whom it was committed to them.

Self-Denying Ordinance

Notwithstanding these reasonings, a committee was chosen to frame what was called the Self-Denying Ordinance, by which the members of both houses were excluded from all civil and military employments, except a few offices which were specified. This ordinance was the subject of great debate; and for a long time, it rent the Parliament and city into factions. But at last, by the prevalence of envy with some, of false modesty with others, of the republican and Independent views with a great many, it passed the House of Commons and was sent to the upper house. The Peers, though the scheme was in part leveled against their order, though all of them were at bottom extremely averse to it, though they even ventured once to reject it, yet possessed so little authority that they dared not persevere in opposing the resolution of the Commons; and they thought an unlimited compliance to be better policy to ward off that ruin which they saw approaching. The ordinance, therefore, having passed both houses, Essex, Warwick, Manchester, Denbigh, Waller, Brereton, and many others resigned their commands and received the thanks of Parliament for their good services. A pension of £10,000 a year was settled on Essex.

It was agreed to recruit the army to twenty-two thousand men; and Sir Thomas Fairfax was appointed general. | 1645 |
It is remarkable that his commission did not run, like that of Essex, in the name of the king and Parliament, but in that of the Parliament

alone; and the article concerning the safety of the king's person was omitted. So much had animosities increased between the parties. Cromwell, being a member of the lower house, should have been discarded with the others; but this impartiality would have disappointed all the purposes of those who had introduced the Self-Denying Ordinance. He was saved by a subtlety, and by that political craft in which he was so eminent. At the time when the other officers resigned their commissions, care was taken that Cromwell be sent with a body of cavalry to relieve Taunton, besieged by the Royalists. His absence being remarked, orders were dispatched for his immediate attendance in Parliament; and Fairfax was directed to employ some other officer in that service. A ready compliance was feigned; and the very day was named on which, it was averred, he would take his place in the house. But Fairfax, having appointed a rendezvous of the army, wrote to the Parliament and desired leave to retain for some days Lieutenant General Cromwell, whose advice, he said, would be useful in supplying the place of those officers who had resigned. Shortly after, he begged with much warmth that Parliament allow Cromwell to serve that campaign. And thus, the Independents, though the minority, prevailed by art and cunning over the Presbyterians and bestowed the whole military authority, in appearance, upon Fairfax; in reality, upon Cromwell.

Fairfax

Fairfax was a person equally eminent for courage and for humanity; and though strongly infected with prejudices, or principles, derived from religious and party zeal, he seems never in the course of his public conduct to have been diverted by private interest or ambition from adhering strictly to these principles. Sincere in his professions, disinterested in his views, open in his conduct, he would have formed one of the most shining characters of the age had not the extreme narrowness of his genius in everything but in war and his embarrassed and confused elocution on every occasion but when he gave orders diminished the luster of his merit and rendered the part which he acted, even when vested with the supreme command, but secondary and subordinate.

Cromwell

Cromwell, by whose sagacity and insinuation Fairfax was entirely governed, is one of the most eminent and most singular personages that occurs in history. The strokes of his character are as open and strongly marked as the schemes of his conduct were, at the time, dark and impenetrable. His extensive capacity enabled him to form the most enlarged projects; his enterprising genius was not dismayed with the boldest and most dangerous. Carried by his natural temper to magnanimity, to grandeur, and to an imperious and domineering policy, he yet knew to employ when necessary the most profound dissimulation, the most oblique and refined artifice, the semblance of the greatest moderation and simplicity. A friend to justice, though his public conduct was one continued violation of it; devoted to religion, though he perpetually employed it as the instrument of his ambition; he was engaged in crimes from the prospect of sovereign power, a temptation which is in general irresistible to human nature. And by using well that authority which he had attained by fraud and violence, he has lessened, if not overpowered, our detestation of his enormities by our admiration of his success and of his genius.

Treaty of Uxbridge

During this important transaction of the Self-Denying Ordinance, the negotiations for peace were likewise carried on, though with small hopes of success. The king having sent two messages—one from Evesham, another from Tavistock—desiring a treaty [conference], the Parliament dispatched commissioners to Oxford with proposals as high as if they had obtained a complete victory. The advantages gained during the campaign and the great distresses of the Royalists had much elevated their hopes; and they were resolved to repose no trust in men inflamed with the highest animosity against them and who, were they possessed of power, were fully authorized by law to punish all their opponents as rebels and traitors.

The king, when he considered the proposals and the disposition of the Parliament, could not expect any accommodation, and had no prospect but of war or of total submission and subjection. Yet in order to satisfy his own party, who were impatient for peace, he agreed to send the Duke of Richmond and Earl of Southampton with an answer to the proposals of the Parliament and at the same time to desire a treaty upon their mutual demands and pretensions. It now became necessary for him to retract his former declaration that the two houses at Westminster were not a free Parliament; and accordingly, he was induced, though with great reluctance, to give them in his answer the appellation of the Parliament of England. But it appeared afterwards, by a letter which he wrote to the queen and of which a copy was taken at Naseby, that he secretly entered an explanatory protest in his council book, and he claimed that though he had "called" them the Parliament, he had not thereby "acknowledged" them for such. This subtlety, for which Charles has been much blamed, is the most noted of those very few instances from which the enemies of this prince have endeavored to load him with the imputation of insincerity and have inferred that the Parliament could repose no confidence in his professions and declarations, not even in his laws and statutes. There is, however, it must be confessed, a difference universally avowed between simply giving to men the appellation which they assume and the formal acknowledgment of their title to it; nor is anything more common and familiar in all public transactions.

The time and place of treaty being settled, sixteen commissioners from the king met at Uxbridge on January 30 with twelve authorized by the Parliament, attended by the Scottish commissioners. It was agreed that the Scottish and parliamentary commissioners would submit their demands with regard to three important articles—religion, the militia, and Ireland—and that these would be successively discussed in conference with the king's commissioners. It was soon found impracticable to come to any agreement with regard to any of these articles.

In the summer of 1643, while the negotiations were carried on with Scotland, the Parliament had summoned an Assembly at Westminster consisting of 121 divines and 30 laymen celebrated in their party for piety and learning. By their advice, alterations were made in the Thirty-Nine Articles, or in the metaphysical doctrines of the church; and what was of greater importance, the liturgy was entirely abolished, and in its stead a new Directory for Worship was established by which, suitably to the spirit of the Puritans, the utmost liberty both in praying and preaching was indulged to the public teachers. By the Solemn League and Covenant, episcopacy was abjured as destructive of all true piety, and a national engagement never to suffer its readmission, attended with every circumstance that could render a promise sacred and obligatory, was entered into with the Scots. All these measures showed little spirit of accommodation in the Parliament; and the king's commissioners were not surprised to find the establishment of Presbytery and the Directory positively demanded, together with the subscription of the Covenant by both the king and kingdom.

Had Charles been of a disposition to neglect all theological controversy, he yet would have been obliged in good policy to adhere to episcopal jurisdiction, not only because it was favorable to monarchy but because all his adherents were passionately devoted to it; to abandon them in what they regarded as so important an article was forever to relinquish their friendship and assistance. But Charles had never attained such enlarged principles. He deemed bishops essential to the very being of a Christian church, and he thought himself bound by more sacred ties than those of policy, or even of honor, to the support of that order. He judged his concessions on this head sufficient, therefore, when he agreed that an indulgence would be given to tender consciences with regard to ceremonies; that the bishops would exercise no act of jurisdiction or ordination without the consent and counsel of such presbyters as would be chosen by the clergy of each diocese; that they would reside constantly in their diocese and be bound to preach every Sunday; that pluralities would be abolished; that abuses in ecclesiastical courts would be redressed; and that £100,000 would be levied on the bishops' estates and the chapter lands for payment of debts contracted by the Parliament. These concessions, though considerable, gave no satisfaction to the parliamentary commissioners; and without abating anything of their rigor on this head, they proceeded to their demands with regard to the militia.

The king's partisans had all along maintained that the fears and jealousies of the Parliament, after the securities so early and easily given to public liberty, were either feigned or groundless, and that no human institution could be better poised and adjusted than was now the government of England. By the abolition of the Star Chamber and Court of High Commission, the prerogative, they said, has lost all that coercive power by which it had formerly suppressed or endangered liberty. By the establishment of triennial Parliaments, it can have no leisure to acquire new powers or guard itself during any time from the inspection of that vigilant assembly. By the slender revenue of the Crown, no king can ever attain such influence as to procure a repeal of these salutary statutes. And while the prince commands no military force, he will in vain by violence attempt an infringement of laws so clearly defined by means of late disputes and so passionately cherished by all his subjects. In this situation, surely the nation, governed by so virtuous a monarch, may for the present remain in tranquility and try whether it be not possible by peaceful arts to elude that danger with which it is pretended its liberties are still threatened.

But though the Royalists insisted on these plausible topics before the commencement of war, they were obliged to concede that the progress of civil commotions had somewhat abated the force and evidence of this reasoning. If the power of the militia, said the opposite party, be entrusted to the king, it would not now be difficult for him to abuse that authority. By the rage of internal discord, his partisans are inflamed into an extreme hatred against their antagonists and doubtless have contracted some prejudices against popular privileges, which in their apprehension have been the source of so much disorder. Were the arms of the state, therefore, put entirely into such hands, what public security, it may be demanded, can be given to liberty, or what private security to those who, in opposition to the letter of the law, have so generously ventured their lives in its defense? In compliance with this apprehension, Charles offered that the arms of the state would be entrusted for three years to twenty commissioners who would be named either by common agreement between him and the Parliament or one half by him, the other by the Parliament. And after the expiration of that term, he insisted that his constitutional authority over the militia would again return to him.

The parliamentary commissioners at first demanded that the power of the sword be forever entrusted to such persons as the Parliament alone would appoint. But later they relaxed so far as to require that authority only for seven years, after which it was not to return to the king but to be settled by bill or by common agreement between him and his Parliament. The king's commissioners asked whether jealousies and fears were all on one side and whether the prince, from such violent attempts and pretensions as he had experienced, had not at least as great reason to entertain apprehensions for his authority as they for their liberty? Whether there were any equity in securing only one party and leaving the other during the space of seven years entirely at the mercy of their enemies? Whether, if unlimited power were entrusted to the Parliament during so long a period, it would not be easy for them to frame the subsequent bill in the manner most agreeable to themselves and keep forever possession of the sword as well as of every article of civil power and jurisdiction?

The truth is that after the commencement of war, it was very difficult, if not impossible, to find security for both parties, especially for that of the Parliament. Amidst such violent animosities, power alone could ensure safety; and the power of one side was necessarily attended with danger to the other. Few or no instances occur in history of an equal, peaceful, and durable accommodation that has been concluded between two factions which had been inflamed into civil war.

With regard to Ireland, there were no greater hopes of agreement between the parties. The Parliament demanded that the truce with the rebels be declared null, that the management of the war be given over entirely to the Parliament, and that after the conquest of Ireland, the nomination of the lord lieutenant and of the judges—or in other words, the sovereignty of that kingdom—likewise remain in their hands.

What rendered an accommodation more desperate was that the demands on these three heads, however exorbitant, were acknowledged by the parliamentary commissioners to be nothing but preliminaries. After all these were granted, it would be necessary to proceed to the discussion of those other demands, still more exorbitant, which a little before had been transmitted to the king at Oxford. The terms there insisted on were so ignominious that worse could scarcely be demanded were Charles totally vanquished, a prisoner, and in chains. The king was required to attaint and except from a general pardon forty of the most considerable of his English subjects and nineteen of his Scottish, together with all popish recusants in both kingdoms who had borne arms for him. It was insisted that forty-eight more—including all the members who had sat in either house at Oxford and all lawyers and divines who had embraced the king's party—be rendered incapable of any office, be forbidden the exercise of their profession, be prohibited from coming within the verge of the court, and forfeit the third of their estates to the Parliament. It was required that whoever had borne arms for the king would forfeit the tenth of their estates—or if that did not suffice, the sixth—for the payment of public debts. As if royal authority were not sufficiently annihilated by such terms, it was demanded that the Court of Wards be abolished, that all the considerable officers of the Crown and all the judges be appointed by Parliament, and that the right of peace and war not be exercised without the consent of that assembly. The Presbyterians, it must be confessed, after insisting on such conditions, differed only in words from the Independents, who required the establishment of a pure republic. When the debates had been carried on to no purpose for twenty days among the commissioners, they separated and returned, those of the king, to Oxford, those of the Parliament, to London.

Execution of Laud

A little before the commencement of this fruitless treaty, a deed was executed by the Parliament which proved their determined resolution to yield nothing, but to proceed in the same violent and imperious manner with which they had at first entered on these dangerous enterprises. Archbishop Laud, the most favored minister of the king, was brought to the scaffold; and in this instance the public might see that popular assemblies, which by their very number are in a great measure exempt from the restraint of shame, so when they also overleap the bounds of law naturally break out into acts of the greatest tyranny and injustice.

From the time that Laud had been committed, the House of Commons, engaged in enterprises of greater moment, had found no leisure to finish his impeachment; and he had patiently endured a long imprisonment without being brought to any trial. After the union with Scotland, the bigoted prejudices of that nation revived the like spirit in England; and the sectaries resolved to gratify their vengeance in the punishment of this prelate, who had so long kept their zealous spirit under confinement by his authority and by the execution of penal laws. He was accused of high treason in endeavoring to subvert the fundamental laws and of other high crimes and misdemeanors. The same illegality of an accumulative crime and a constructive evidence which appeared in the case of Strafford, the same violence and iniquity in conducting the trial, were conspicuous throughout the whole course of this prosecution. The groundless charge of popery, though belied by his whole life and conduct, was continually urged against the prisoner; and every error of his was rendered unpardonable by this imputation, which was supposed to imply the height of all enormities. "This man, my lords," said Serjeant Wilde, concluding his long speech against him, "is like Naaman the Syrian: a great man, but a leper."

We shall not enter into a detail of this matter, which at present seems to admit of little controversy. It suffices to say that after a long trial and the examination of more than one hundred fifty witnesses, the Commons found so little likelihood of obtaining a judicial sentence against Laud that they were obliged to have recourse to their legislative authority and to pass an ordinance for taking away the life of this aged prelate. Notwithstanding the low condition into which the House of Peers had fallen, there appeared some intention of rejecting this ordinance; and the popular leaders were again obliged to apply to the multitude, and to extinguish by threats of new tumults the small remains of liberty possessed by the upper house. Only seven peers voted in this important question. The rest, either from shame or fear, took care to absent themselves.

Laud, who had behaved during his trial with spirit and vigor of genius, sunk not under the horrors of his execution; though he had usually professed himself apprehensive of a violent death, he found all his fears to be dissipated before that superior courage by which he was animated. "No one," said he, "can be more willing to send me out of life than I am desirous to go." Even upon the scaffold and during the intervals of his prayers, he was harassed and molested by Sir John Clotworthy, a zealot of the reigning sect and a great leader in the lower house. This was the time the latter chose for examining the principles of the dying primate and trepanning him into a confession that he trusted for his salvation to the merits of good works, not to the death of the Redeemer. Having extricated himself from these theological toils, the archbishop laid his head on the block; and it was severed from the body at one blow. Those religious opinions for which he suffered doubtless contributed to the courage and constancy of his end. Sincere he undoubtedly was, and however misguided, actuated by pious motives in all his pursuits; and it is to be regretted that a man of such spirit, who conducted his enterprises with so much warmth and industry, had not entertained more enlarged views and embraced principles more favorable to the general happiness of society.

The great and important advantage which the party gained by Strafford's death may in some degree palliate the iniquity of the sentence pronounced against him. But the execution of this old, infirm prelate, who had so long remained an inoffensive prisoner, can be ascribed to nothing but vengeance and bigotry in those severe religionists by whom the Parliament was entirely governed. That he deserved a better fate was not questioned by any reasonable man; the degree of his merit in other respects was disputed. Some accused him of recommending slavish doctrines, of promoting persecution, and of encouraging superstition, while others thought that his conduct in these three particulars would admit of apology and extenuation.

That the *letter* of the law, as much as the most flaming court sermon, inculcates passive obedience is apparent. And though the *spirit* of a limited government seems to require in extraordinary cases some mitigation of so rigorous a doctrine, it must be confessed that the preceding nature of the English constitution had rendered a mistake in this particular very natural and excusable. To inflict nothing less than death on those who depart from the exact line of truth in these nice questions, so far from being favorable to national liberty, savors strongly of the spirit of tyranny and proscription.

Toleration had previously been so little the principle of any Christian sect that even the Catholics, the remnant of the religion professed by their forefathers, could not obtain from the English the least indulgence. This very House of Commons, in their famous Remonstrance, took care to justify themselves, as from the highest imputation, from any intention to relax the golden reins of discipline, as they called them, or to grant any toleration. And the enemies of the Church of England were so fair from the beginning as not to lay claim to liberty of conscience, which they called a toleration for soul murder. They openly claimed the superiority as their due, and even menaced the established church with that persecution which they later exercised against it with such severity. And if the question be considered in the view of policy, though a sect already formed and advanced may with good reason demand a toleration, what title had the Puritans—who were just on the point of separation from the church, and it might have been hoped that some wholesome and legal severities would still retain them in obedience—to this indulgence? It is a principle advanced by Montesquieu that where the magistrate is satisfied with the established religion, he ought to repress the first attempts towards innovation, and only grant a toleration to sects that are diffused and established. According to this principle, Laud's indulgence to the Catholics and severity to the Puritans would admit of defense. I confess, however, that it is very questionable whether persecution can in any case be justified; but at the same time, it would be hard to give that appellation to the conduct of Laud, who only enforced the act of uniformity and expelled the clergymen that accepted of benefices and yet refused to observe the ceremonies which they previously knew to be enjoined by law. He never refused them separate places of worship, because they themselves would have esteemed it impious to demand them and no less impious to allow them.

However ridiculous pious ceremonies may appear to a philosophical mind, it must be confessed that during a very religious age, no institutions can be more advantageous to the rude multitude and tend more to mollify that fierce and gloomy spirit of devotion to which they are subject. Even the English church, though it had retained a share of popish ceremonies, could justly have been thought too naked and unadorned, and to have approached still too near the abstract and spiritual religion of the Puritans. By reviving a few primitive institutions of this nature, Laud and his associates corrected the error of the first reformers and presented to the frightened and astonished mind some perceptible, exterior observances which might occupy it during its religious exercises and abate the violence of its disappointed efforts. The thought, no longer bent on that divine and mysterious essence so superior to the narrow capacities of mankind, was able by means of the new model of devotion to relax itself in the contemplation of pictures, postures, vestments, buildings; and all the fine arts which minister to religion thereby received additional encouragement. The primate, it is true, conducted this scheme not with the enlarged sentiments and cool reflection of a legislator but with the intemperate zeal of a sectary; by overlooking the circumstances of the times, he served rather to inflame that religious fury which he meant to repress. But this blemish is more to be regarded as a general imputation on the whole age than any particular failing of Laud's; and it is sufficient for his vindication to observe that his errors were the most excusable of all those which prevailed during that zealous period.

CHAPTER 58
1645 – 1647

*Montrose's victories – The New Model of the army – Battle of
Naseby – Surrender of Bristol – The west conquered by
Fairfax – Defeat of Montrose – Ecclesiastical affairs – King
goes to the Scots at Newark – End of the war –
King delivered up by the Scots*

WHILE the king's affairs declined in England, some events happened in Scotland which seemed to promise him a more prosperous conclusion of the quarrel.

Montrose's victories
Before the commencement of these civil disorders, the Earl of Montrose, a young nobleman of a distinguished family returning from his
travels, had been introduced to the king and had made an offer of his
services; but by the insinuations of the Marquess, afterwards Duke, of
Hamilton, who possessed much of Charles's confidence, he had not
been received with that distinction to which he thought himself justly
entitled. Disgusted with this treatment, he had forwarded all the violence of the Covenanters; agreeably to the natural ardor of his genius,
he had employed himself during the first Scottish insurrection with
great zeal as well as success in levying and conducting their armies. Being commissioned by the "Tables" to wait upon the king while the
royal army lay at Berwick, he was so gained by the civilities and caresses of that monarch that he from then on devoted himself entirely,
though secretly, to his service and entered into a close correspondence
with him. In the second insurrection, a great military command was
entrusted to him by the Covenanters; he was the first that passed the

Tweed at the head of their troops in the invasion of England. He found means, however, soon after to convey a letter to the king. By the infidelity of some about that prince—Hamilton, as was suspected—a copy of this letter was sent to Leven, the Scottish general. Being accused of treachery and a correspondence with the enemy, Montrose openly avowed the letter and asked the generals if they dared to call their sovereign an enemy; and by this bold and magnanimous behavior, he escaped the danger of an immediate prosecution. As he was now fully known to be of the royal party, he no longer concealed his principles; and he endeavored to draw those who had entertained like sentiments into a bond of association for his master's service. Though thrown into prison for this enterprise and detained some time, he was not discouraged, but still continued by his support and protection to infuse spirit into the distressed Royalists. Among other persons of distinction who united themselves to him was Lord Napier of Merchiston, son of the famous inventor of the logarithms, the person to whom the title of a Great Man is more justly due than to any other whom Scotland ever produced.

There was in Scotland another party who, professing equal attachment to the king's service, claimed only to differ with Montrose about the means of attaining the same end; and of that party, the Duke of Hamilton was the leader. This nobleman had cause to be extremely devoted to the king, not only by reason of the connection of blood which united him to the royal family but on account of the great confidence and favor with which he had always been honored by his master. Though Hamilton was accused by Lord Reay, not without some appearance of probability, of a conspiracy against the king, Charles was so far from harboring suspicion against him that the very first time Hamilton came to court, the king received him into his bedchamber and passed the night with him only. But such was the duke's unhappy fate, or conduct, that he did not escape the imputation of treachery to his friend and sovereign; and though he at last sacrificed his life in the king's service, his integrity and sincerity have not been thought by historians entirely free from blemish. Perhaps (and this is the more probable opinion) the subtleties and refinements of his conduct and his temporizing maxims, though accompanied with good intentions, have been the chief cause of a suspicion which has never yet been either fully proved or refuted. As much as the bold and vivid spirit of Montrose prompted him to enterprising measures, the cautious temper of Hamilton inclined him to such as were moderate and dilatory. While the former foretold that the Scottish Covenanters were secretly forming a union with the English Parliament and inculcated the necessity of preventing them by some vigorous undertaking, the latter still insisted that every such attempt would precipitate them into measures to which otherwise they were not perhaps inclined. After the Scottish Convention was summoned without the king's authority, the former exclaimed that their intentions were now visible, and that if some unexpected blow were not struck to dissipate them, they would arm the whole nation against the king; the latter maintained the possibility of outvoting the disaffected party and securing by peaceful means the allegiance of the kingdom. Unhappily for the royal cause, Hamilton's representations met with more credit from the king and queen than those of Montrose; and the Covenanters were allowed without interruption to proceed in all their hostile measures. Montrose then hastened to Oxford, where his invectives against Hamilton's treachery, concurring with the general prepossession and supported by the unfortunate result of the duke's counsels, were entertained with universal approbation. Influenced by the clamor of his party more than his own suspicions, Charles, as soon as Hamilton appeared, sent him prisoner to Pendennis Castle in Cornwall. His brother, the Earl of Lanark, who was also put under confinement, found means to make his escape and to fly into Scotland.

The king's ears were now open to the counsels of Montrose, who proposed none but the boldest and most daring, agreeably to the desperate state of the royal cause in Scotland. Though the whole nation was subjected by the Covenanters, though great armies were kept on foot by them and every place guarded by a vigilant administration, Montrose undertook by his own credit and that of the few friends who remained to the king to raise such commotions as would soon oblige the malcontents to recall those forces which had so clearly thrown the balance in favor of the Parliament. Not discouraged with the defeat at Marston Moor, which rendered it impossible for him to draw any succor from England, he was content to stipulate with the Earl of Antrim, a nobleman of Ireland, for some supply of men from that country. And he himself, changing his disguises and passing through many dangers, arrived in Scotland, where he lay concealed in the borders of the Highlands and secretly prepared the minds of his partisans for attempting some great enterprise.

As soon as the Irish landed, though they numbered no more than eleven hundred infantry and were very ill armed, Montrose declared himself and entered upon that scene of action which has rendered his name so celebrated. About eight hundred of the men of Atholl flocked to his standard. Five hundred more who had been levied by the Covenanters were persuaded to embrace the royal cause. And with this combined force, he hastened to attack Lord Elcho, who lay at Perth with an army of six thousand men, assembled upon the first news of the Irish invasion. Montrose—inferior in number, totally unprovided with horse, ill supplied with arms and ammunition—had nothing to depend on but the courage which he himself could inspire into his raw soldiers by his own example and the rapidity of his enterprises. Having received the fire of the enemy, which was answered chiefly by a volley of stones, he rushed amidst them with his sword drawn, threw them into confusion, pushed his advantage, and obtained a complete victory, with the slaughter of two thousand of the Covenanters.

This victory, though it augmented the renown of Montrose, failed to increase his power or numbers. The far greater part of the kingdom was extremely attached to the Covenant, and those who bore an affection to the royal cause were terrified by the established authority of the opposite party. Dreading the superior power of Argyll, who, having joined his vassals to a force levied by the public, was approaching with a considerable army, Montrose hastened northwards in order to rouse again the Marquess of Huntly and the Gordons, who, having before hastily taken arms, had been instantly suppressed by the Covenanters. He was joined on his march by the Earl of Airlie, with his two younger sons, Sir Thomas and Sir David Ogilvie; the eldest was at that time a prisoner with the enemy. At Aberdeen, he attacked Lord Burleigh, who commanded a force of two thousand five hundred men. After a sharp combat, by his undaunted courage, which in his situation was true policy and was also not unaccompanied with military skill, he put the enemy to flight and in the pursuit did great execution upon them.

But by this second victory, he failed to obtain the end which he expected. The envious nature of Huntly, jealous of Montrose's glory, rendered him averse to join an army where he himself must be so much eclipsed by the superior merit of the general. Argyll, reinforced by the Earl of Lothian, was behind him with a great army. The militia of the northern counties—Moray, Ross, and Caithness—to the number of five thousand men opposed him in front and guarded the banks of the Spey, a deep and rapid river. In order to elude these numerous armies, he turned aside into the hills and saved his weak but active troops in Badenoch. After some marches and countermarches, Argyll came up with him at Fyvie Castle. This nobleman's character, though celebrated for political courage and conduct, was very low for military prowess; after some skirmishes in which he was worsted, he here allowed Montrose to escape him. By quick marches through these inaccessible mountains, that general freed himself from the superior forces of the Covenanters.

Such was the situation of Montrose that very good or very ill fortune was equally destructive to him and diminished his army. After every victory, his soldiers, greedy of spoil but deeming the smallest acquisition to be unexhausted riches, deserted in great numbers and went home to secure the treasures which they had acquired. Tired too and spent with hasty and long marches in the depth of winter through snowy mountains, unprovided with every necessity, they fell off and left their general almost alone with the Irish, who, having no place to which they could retire, still adhered to him in every fortune.

With these and some reinforcements of the Athollmen and Mac-Donalds, whom he had recalled, Montrose fell suddenly upon Argyll's country and let loose upon it all the rage of war, carrying off the cattle, burning the houses, and putting the inhabitants to the sword. This severity, by which Montrose sullied his victories, was the result of private animosity against the chieftain as much as of zeal for the public cause. Argyll, collecting three thousand men, marched in quest of the enemy, who had retired with their plunder; and he lay at Inverlochy, supposing himself still at a considerable distance from them. The Earl of Seaforth, at the head of the garrison of Inverness, who were veteran soldiers joined to five thousand newly levied troops of the northern counties, pressed the Royalists on the other side and threatened them with inevitable destruction. By a quick and unexpected march, Montrose hastened to Inverlochy, and on February 2, presented himself in order of battle before the surprised but not frightened Covenanters. Argyll alone, seized with a panic, deserted his army, who still maintained their ground and gave battle to the Royalists. After a vigorous resistance, they were defeated and pursued with great slaughter. And the power of the Campbells (that is Argyll's name) being thus broken, the Highlanders, who were in general well affected to the royal cause, began to join Montrose's camp in great numbers. Seaforth's army dispersed by itself at the very terror of his name. And Lord Gordon, eldest son of Huntly, having escaped from his uncle Argyll, who had till then detained him, now joined Montrose with no contemptible number of his followers, attended by his brother, the Earl of Aboyne.

The Council at Edinburgh, alarmed at Montrose's progress, began to think of a more regular plan of defense against an enemy whose repeated victories had rendered him extremely formidable. They sent for Baillie, an officer of reputation, from England; and joining him in command with Hurry, who had again enlisted himself among the king's enemies, they sent them to the field with a considerable army against the Royalists. Montrose, with a detachment of eight hundred men, had attacked Dundee, a town extremely zealous for the Covenant; having carried it by assault, he had delivered it up to be plundered by his soldiers when Baillie and Hurry, with their whole force, were unexpectedly upon him. His conduct and presence of mind in this emergency appeared conspicuous. Instantly he called off his soldiers from plunder, put them in order, secured his retreat by the most skillful measures; and having marched sixty miles in the face of an enemy much superior without stopping or allowing his soldiers the least sleep or refreshment, he at last secured himself in the mountains.

Baillie and Hurry now divided their troops, in order to conduct the war the better against an enemy who surprised them as much by the rapidity of his marches as by the boldness of his enterprises. Hurry, at the head of four thousand men, met him at Auldearn, near Inverness; encouraged by the superiority of number (for the Covenanters were double the Royalists), he attacked him in the post which he had chosen. Montrose, having placed his right wing in strong ground, drew the best of his forces to the other and left no main body between them, a defect which he artfully concealed by showing a few men through the trees and bushes with which that ground was covered. That Hurry might have no leisure to perceive the stratagem, he instantly led his left wing to the charge; and making a furious impression upon the Covenanters, he drove them off the field and gained a complete victory. In this battle, the valor of young Napier, son to the lord of that name, shone out with signal luster.

Baillie now advanced to revenge Hurry's discomfiture; but at Alford, he himself met with a like fate. Montrose, weak in cavalry, here lined his troops of horse with infantry; and after putting the enemy's horse to rout, he fell with united force upon their foot, who were entirely cut in pieces, though with the loss of the gallant Lord Gordon on the part of the Royalists. And having thus prevailed in so many battles, which his vigor always rendered as decisive as they were successful, he summoned together all his friends and partisans and prepared himself for marching into the southern provinces in order to put a final end to the power of the Covenanters and dissipate the Parliament which, with great pomp and solemnity, they had summoned to meet at Perth.

While the fire was thus kindled in the north of the island, it blazed out with no less fury in the south. The parliamentary and royal armies prepared to take the field as soon as the season would permit in hopes of bringing their important quarrel to a quick decision. The passing of the Self-Denying Ordinance had been protracted by so many debates and intrigues that the spring was far advanced before it received the sanction of both houses; and it was thought dangerous by many to introduce, so near the time of action, such great innovations into the army. Had not the punctilious principles of Essex bound him, amidst all the disgusts which he received, to pay implicit obedience to the Parliament, this alteration would not have been effected without some fatal accident; since, notwithstanding his prompt resignation of the command, a mutiny was generally feared. Fairfax—or more properly speaking, Cromwell under his name—introduced at last the New Model into the army and threw the troops into a different shape. From the same men, new regiments and new companies were formed, different officers appointed, and the whole military force put into such hands as the Independents could rely on. Besides members of Parliament who were excluded, many officers, unwilling to serve under the new generals, threw up their commissions and unwarily facilitated the project of putting the army entirely into the hands of that faction.

Though the discipline of the former parliamentary army was not contemptible, a more exact plan was introduced and rigorously executed by these new commanders. Valor was indeed very generally diffused over the one party as much as the other during this period. Discipline also was attained by the forces of the Parliament. But the perfection of the military art in concerting the general plans of action and the operations of the field seems still, on both sides, to have been in a great measure lacking. Historians at least, perhaps from their own ignorance and inexperience, have not remarked anything but a headlong, impetuous conduct: each party hurrying to a battle where valor and fortune chiefly determined the success. The great ornament of history during these reigns are the civil, not the military, transactions.

The New Model of the army

Surely never was a more singular army assembled than that which was now set on foot by the Parliament. To the greater number of the regiments, chaplains were not appointed; the officers assumed the spiritual duty and united it with their military functions. During the intervals of action, they occupied themselves in sermons, prayers, exhortations; and the same emulation there attended them which in the field is so necessary to support the honor of that profession. Rapturous ecstasies supplied the place of study and reflection; and while the zealous devotees poured out their thoughts in unpremeditated harangues, they mistook that eloquence which, to their own surprise as well as that of others, flowed in upon them for divine illuminations and for entries into them of the Holy Spirit. Wherever they were quartered, they excluded the minister from his pulpit, and usurping his place, conveyed their sentiments to the audience with all the authority which followed their power, their valor, and their military exploits, united to their evident zeal and fervor. The private soldiers, seized with the same spirit, employed their vacant hours in prayer, in perusing the Holy Scriptures, in ghostly conferences where they compared the progress of their souls in grace and mutually stimulated each other to further advances in the great work of their salvation. When they were marching to battle, the whole field resounded as much with psalms and spiritual songs adapted to the occasion as with the instruments of military music; and every man endeavored to drown the sense of present danger in the prospect of that crown of glory which was set before him. In so holy a cause, wounds were deemed meritorious; death, martyrdom; and the hurry and dangers of action, instead of banishing their pious visions, rather served to impress their minds more strongly with them.

The Royalists were desirous of throwing ridicule on this fanaticism of the parliamentary armies, without being aware of how much reason they had to fear its dangerous consequences. The forces assembled by the king at Oxford, in the west, and in other places were equal, if not superior, in number to their adversaries, but they were actuated by a very different spirit. That license which had been introduced into the Royalist armies by lack of pay had risen to a great height among them and rendered them more formidable to their friends than to their enemies. Prince Rupert, negligent of the people, fond of the soldiery, had indulged the troops in unwarrantable liberties. Wilmot, a man of dissolute manners, had promoted the same spirit of disorder. And the licentious Goring, Gerard, and Sir Richard Grenville now carried it to a great pitch of enormity. In the west especially, where Goring commanded, universal spoil and havoc were committed; and the whole country was laid waste by the rapine of the army. All distinction of parties being, in a way, dropped, the most devoted friends of the church and monarchy wished there for such success to the parliamentary forces as might put an end to these oppressions. The country people, despoiled of their substance, flocked together in several places armed with clubs and staves; and though they professed an enmity to the soldiers of both parties, their hatred was in most places leveled chiefly against the Royalists, from whom they had met with the worse treatment. Many thousands of these tumultuous peasants were assembled in different parts of England; they destroyed all such straggling soldiers as they met with and much infested the armies.

The disposition of the forces on both sides was as follows: Part of the Scottish army was employed in taking Pontefract and other towns in Yorkshire; part of it besieged Carlisle, valiantly defended by Sir Thomas Glemham. The Royalist stronghold of Chester, where Byron commanded, had long been blockaded by Sir William Brereton and was reduced to great difficulties. The king, being joined by the princes Rupert and Maurice, lay at Oxford with a considerable army, about fifteen thousand men. Fairfax and Cromwell were posted at Windsor with the New Model army, about twenty-two thousand men. The Parliament's enclave of Taunton, in the county of Somerset, defended by Robert Blake, suffered a long siege from Sir Richard Grenville, who commanded an army of about eight thousand men; and though the defense had been obstinate, the garrison was now reduced to the last extremity. Goring commanded in the west an army of nearly the same number.

On opening the campaign, the king formed the project of relieving Chester; Fairfax, that of relieving Taunton. The king was first in motion. When he advanced to Drayton, in Shropshire, Byron met him and brought intelligence that his approach had raised the siege and that the parliamentary army had withdrawn. Fairfax, having reached Salisbury in his road westwards, received orders from the Committee of Both Kingdoms, appointed for the management of the war, to return and lay siege to Oxford, now exposed by the king's absence. He obeyed after sending Colonel Weldon to the west with a detachment of four thousand men. On Weldon's approach, Grenville, who imagined that Fairfax with his whole army was upon him, raised the siege and allowed this very tenacious town, now half taken and half burned, to receive relief. But the Royalists, being reinforced with three thousand horse under Goring, again advanced to Taunton and shut up Weldon with his small army in that ruinous place.

The king, having effected his purpose with regard to Chester, returned southwards; and on his way, he encamped outside of Leicester, a garrison of the Parliament's, in order to besiege it. Having made a breach in the wall, he stormed the town on all sides; after a furious assault, the soldiers entered sword in hand and committed all those disorders to which their natural violence, especially when inflamed by resistance, is so much addicted. A great booty was taken and distributed among them; fifteen hundred prisoners fell into the king's hands. This success, which struck a great terror into the parliamentary army, impelled Fairfax to leave Oxford, which he was beginning to approach; and he marched towards the king with an intention of offering him battle. The king was advancing towards Oxford in order to raise the siege which he feared had now begun; and both armies, before they were aware, had advanced within six miles of each other. A council of war was called by the king in order to deliberate concerning the measures which he should now pursue. On the one hand, it seemed more prudent to delay the combat because Gerard, who lay in Wales with three thousand men, might be enabled in a little time to join the army; and Goring, it was hoped, would soon be master of Taunton, and having put the west in full security, would then unite his forces to those of the king and give him an incontestable superiority over the enemy. On the other hand, Prince Rupert, whose boiling ardor still pushed him on to battle, excited the impatient humor of the nobility and gentry of which the army was full; he urged the many difficulties under which the Royalists labored and from which nothing but a victory could relieve them. The resolution was taken to give battle to Fairfax; and the royal army immediately advanced upon him.

Battle of Naseby

At Naseby was fought, with forces nearly equal, this decisive and well-disputed action between the king and Parliament. The main body of the Royalists was commanded by the king himself; the right wing, by Prince Rupert; the left, by Sir Marmaduke Langdale. Fairfax, seconded by Skippon, placed himself in the main body of the opposite army; Cromwell, in the right wing; Henry Ireton, Cromwell's son-in-law, in the left. The charge was begun, with his usual celerity and usual success, by Prince Rupert. Though Ireton made stout resistance, and even after he was run through the thigh with a pike still maintained the combat till he was taken prisoner, yet that whole wing was broken and pursued with precipitate fury by Rupert. He was even so heedless as to lose time in calling for the surrender of, and then attacking, the artillery of the enemy, which had been left with a good guard of infantry. The king led on his main body and displayed in this action all the conduct of a prudent general and all the valor of a stout soldier. Fairfax and Skippon encountered him and well supported that reputation which they had acquired. Skippon, being dangerously wounded, was desired by Fairfax to leave the field; but he declared that he would remain there as long as one man maintained his ground. The infantry of the Parliament was broken and pressed upon by the king, till Fairfax, with great presence of mind, brought up the reserve and renewed the combat. Meanwhile, Cromwell, having led on his troops to the attack of Langdale, overbore the force of the Royalists. By his prudence, he then improved that advantage which he had gained by his valor. Having pursued the enemy about a quarter of a mile and detached some troops to prevent their rallying, he turned back upon the king's infantry and threw them into the utmost confusion. One regiment alone preserved its order unbroken, though twice desperately assailed by Fairfax; and that general, excited by so steady a resistance, ordered D'Oyley, the captain of his lifeguard, to give them a third charge in front while he himself attacked them in the rear. The regiment was broken. Fairfax killed an ensign with his own hands, and having seized the colors, gave them to a soldier to keep for him. The soldier, afterwards boasting that he had won this trophy, was reproved by D'Oyley, who had seen the action. "Let him retain that honor," said Fairfax. "I have today acquired enough beside."

Prince Rupert, aware too late of his error, left the fruitless attack on the enemy's artillery and joined the king, whose infantry was now totally discomfited. Charles exhorted this body of cavalry not to despair and cried aloud to them, "One charge more, and we recover the day." But the disadvantages under which they labored were too evident, and they could by no means be induced to renew the combat. Charles was obliged to quit the field and leave the victory to the enemy. The slain on the side of the Parliament exceeded those on the side of the king; they lost a thousand men, he not more than eight hundred. But Fairfax made five hundred officers and four thousand private men prisoners, took all the king's artillery and ammunition, and totally dissipated his infantry, so that scarcely any victory could be more complete than that which he obtained.

Among the other spoils, the king's cabinet was seized with the copies of his letters to the queen, which the Parliament afterwards ordered to be published. They chose, no doubt, such of them as they thought would reflect dishonor on him. Yet upon the whole, the letters are written with delicacy and tenderness, and they give an advantageous idea both of the king's genius and morals. A mighty fondness, it is true, and attachment he expresses to his consort, and often professes that he never would embrace any measures which she disapproved. But such declarations of civility and confidence are not always to be taken in a full, literal sense. And so legitimate an affection, avowed by the laws of God and man, may perhaps be excusable towards a woman of beauty and spirit, even though she was a papist.

When the Athenians intercepted a letter written by their enemy Philip of Macedon to his wife, Olympia, they immediately sent the letter to the queen unopened, so far were they from being moved by a curiosity of prying into the secrets of that relation. Philip was not their sovereign, nor were they inflamed with that violent animosity against him which attends all civil commotions.

After the battle, the king retreated with that body of horse which remained entire, first to Hereford, then to Abergavenny; and he remained some time in Wales in the vain hope of raising a body of infantry in those harassed and exhausted quarters. Fairfax, having on June 17 first retaken Leicester, which was surrendered upon articles, began to deliberate concerning his future enterprises. He received a letter written by Goring to the king and unfortunately entrusted to a spy of Fairfax's. Goring there informed the king that he hoped to be master of Taunton in three weeks, after which he would join his majesty with all the forces in the west, and entreated him to avoid coming to any general action meanwhile. This letter, which, had it been safely delivered, probably would have prevented the Battle of Naseby, served now to direct the operations of Fairfax. After leaving a body of three thousand men to Poyntz and Rossiter with orders to attend the king's motions, he marched immediately to the west with a view of saving Taunton and suppressing the only considerable force which now remained to the Royalists.

In the beginning of the campaign, Charles, apprehensive of the result, had sent the Prince of Wales, then fifteen years of age, to the west with the title of general and had given orders that if the prince were pressed by the enemy, he should make his escape into a foreign country and save one part of the royal family from the violence of the Parliament. Prince Rupert had thrown himself into Bristol with an intention of defending that important city. Goring commanded the army before Taunton.

On Fairfax's approach, the siege of Taunton was raised, and the Royalists retired to Langport, an open town in the county of Somerset. Fairfax attacked them in that post, beat them from it, killed about three hundred men, and took one thousand four hundred prisoners. After this gain, he encamped outside of Bridgwater, a town deemed strong and of great consequence in that country, on July 20 and began to besiege it. When he had entered the outer town by storm, Wyndham, the governor, who had retired into the inner, immediately capitulated and delivered up the place to Fairfax on July 23. The garrison, to the number of two thousand six hundred men, were made prisoners of war.

Surrender of Bristol

Fairfax, having next taken Bath and Sherborne, resolved to lay siege to Bristol and made great preparations for an enterprise which, from the strength of the garrison and the reputation of Prince Rupert, the governor, was deemed of the ultimate importance. But so precarious in most men is the quality of military courage that a poorer defense was not made by any town during the whole war, and the general expectations were here extremely disappointed. No sooner had the parliamentary forces entered the lines by storm on September 11 than the prince capitulated and surrendered the city to Fairfax. A few days before, the prince had written a letter to the king in which he undertook to defend the place for four months if no mutiny obliged him to surrender it. Charles, who was forming schemes and collecting forces for the relief of Bristol, was astonished at so unexpected an event, which was little less fatal to his cause than the defeat at Naseby. Full of indignation, he instantly recalled all Prince Rupert's commissions and sent him a pass to go overseas.

The king's affairs now went fast to ruin in all quarters. The Scots, having made themselves masters of Carlisle after an obstinate siege, marched southwards and laid siege to Hereford; but they were obliged to raise it on the king's approach. And this was the last glimpse of success which attended his arms. Having marched to the relief of Chester, which was anew besieged by the parliamentary forces under Colonel Jones, Poyntz attacked his rear and forced him to give battle on September 24. While the fight was continued with great obstinacy and victory seemed to incline to the Royalists, Jones fell upon them from the other side and put them to rout with the loss of six hundred slain and one thousand prisoners. The king, with the remains of his broken army, fled to Newark, and from there escaped to Oxford, where he shut himself up during the winter season.

The reports which he received from every quarter were no less fatal than those events which passed where he himself was present. After the surrender of Bristol, Fairfax and Cromwell divided their forces: the former marched westwards in order to complete the conquest of Devonshire and Cornwall; the latter attacked the king's garrisons which lay to the east of Bristol. Devizes was surrendered to Cromwell, Berkeley Castle was taken by storm, Winchester capitulated, Basing House was entered sword in hand, and all these middle counties of England were soon reduced to obedience under the Parliament.

The west conquered by Fairfax

The same rapid and uninterrupted success attended Fairfax. The parliamentary forces, elated by past victories,

| 1646 |

governed by the most rigid discipline, met with no equal opposition from troops dismayed by repeated defeats and corrupted by licentious manners. After beating up the quarters of the Royalists at Bovey Tracey, Fairfax encamped outside of Dartmouth and began to besiege it; and in a few days, on January 18, he entered it by storm. Powderham Castle was taken by him, and Exeter blockaded on all sides. Hopton, a man of merit who now commanded the Royalists, having advanced to the relief of Exeter with an army of eight thousand men, met with the parliamentary army on February 19 at Torrington; there he was defeated, all his foot dispersed, and he himself with his horse obliged to retire into Cornwall. Fairfax followed him and vigorously pursued the victory. Having enclosed the Royalists at Truro, he forced the whole army, consisting of five thousand men, chiefly cavalry, to surrender upon terms. The soldiers, delivering up their horses and arms, were allowed to disband and received twenty shillings apiece to carry them to their respective abodes. Such of the officers as desired it had passes to retire overseas; the others, having promised nevermore to bear arms, paid compositions to the Parliament and procured their pardon. And thus, Fairfax, after taking Exeter, which completed the conquest of the west, marched with his victorious army to the center of the kingdom and fixed his camp at Newbury. The Prince of Wales, in pursuance of the king's orders, retired to Scilly, from there to Jersey, then to Paris, where he joined the queen, who had fled there from Exeter at the time the Earl of Essex conducted the parliamentary army to the west.

In the other parts of England, Hereford was taken by surprise; Chester surrendered; Lord Digby, who had attempted with one thousand two hundred cavalrymen to break into Scotland and join Montrose, was defeated at Sherburn, in Yorkshire, by Colonel Copley. His whole force was dispersed, and he himself was obliged to fly, first to the Isle of Man, then to Ireland. News too arrived that Montrose himself, after some more successes, was at last routed, and this only remaining hope of the royal party finally extinguished.

When Montrose descended into the southern counties, the Covenanters, assembling their whole force, met him with a numerous army and gave him battle, but without success, at Kilsyth. This was the most complete victory that Montrose ever obtained. The Royalists put to sword six thousand of their enemies and left the Covenanters no remains of any army in Scotland. The whole kingdom was shaken with these repeated successes of Montrose, and many noblemen who secretly favored the royal cause now declared openly for it when they saw a force able to support them. The Marquess of Douglas, the Earls of Annandale and Hartfell, the Lords Fleming, Seton, Maderty, Carnegie, with many others flocked to the royal standard. Edinburgh opened its gates and gave liberty to all the prisoners there detained by the Covenanters. Among the rest was Lord Ogilvie, son of Airlie, whose family had contributed extremely to the victory gained at Kilsyth.

Defeat of Montrose

David Leslie was detached from the army in England and marched to the relief of his distressed party in Scotland. Montrose advanced still farther to the south, allured by vain hopes both of rousing to arms the Earls of Home, Traquair, and Roxburghe, who had promised to join him, and of obtaining from England some supply of cavalry, in which he was deficient. His army—much diminished in numbers from the desertion of the Highlanders, who had retired to the hills, in accord with their custom, in order to secure their plunder—was surprised, owing to the negligence of his scouts, by Leslie at Philiphaugh in the Forest. After a sharp conflict in which Montrose exerted great valor, his forces were routed by Leslie's cavalry; and he himself was obliged to fly with his broken forces into the mountains, where he again prepared himself for new battles and new enterprises.

The Covenanters used the victory with rigor. Their prisoners—Sir Robert Spottiswoode, secretary of state and son to the late primate, Sir Philip Nisbet, Sir William Rollo, Colonel Nathaniel Gordon, Andrew Guthrie, son of the bishop of Moray, and William Murray, son of the Earl of Tullibardine—were condemned and executed. The sole crime imputed to the secretary was his delivering to Montrose the king's commission to be captain general of Scotland. Lord Ogilvie, who was again taken prisoner, would have undergone the same fate had not his sister found means to procure his escape by changing clothes with him. For this instance of courage and dexterity, she met with harsh usage. The clergy solicited the Parliament to execute more Royalists but could not obtain their request.

After all these repeated disasters which everywhere befell the royal party, there remained only one body of troops on which fortune could exercise her rigor. Lord Astley, with a small army of three thousand men, chiefly cavalry, marching to Oxford in order to join the king, was met at Stow on the Wold on March 22 by Colonel Morgan and entirely defeated, himself being taken prisoner. "You have done your work," said Astley to the parliamentary officers, "and may now go to play, unless you choose to fall out among yourselves." It was the same Astley who, before he charged at the Battle of Edgehill, made this short prayer: "O Lord, thou knowest how busy I must be this day. If I forget thee, do not thou forget me," and with that rose up and cried, "March on, boys!" There were certainly much longer prayers said in the parliamentary army, but I doubt if there was so good a one.

The condition of the king during this whole winter was to the last degree disastrous and melancholy. As the dread of ills is commonly more oppressive than their real presence, perhaps in no period of his life was he more justly the object of compassion. His vigor of mind—which, though it sometimes failed him in acting, never deserted him in his sufferings—was what alone supported him. He was determined, as he wrote to Lord Digby, if he could not live as a king, to die like a gentleman; nor should any of his friends, he said, ever have reason to blush for the prince whom they had so unfortunately served. The murmurs of discontented officers, on the one hand, who overrated those services and sufferings which they now saw must forever go unrewarded, harassed their unhappy sovereign. The affectionate duty, on the other hand, of his more generous friends, who respected his mis-fortunes and his virtues as much as his dignity, wrung his heart with a new sorrow when he reflected that such disinterested attachment would so soon be exposed to the rigor of his implacable enemies. Repeated attempts which he made for a peaceful and equitable accommodation with the Parliament served to no purpose but to convince them that the victory was entirely in their hands. They deigned not to make the least reply to several of his messages in which he desired a passport for commissioners. At last, after reproaching him with the blood spilt during the war, they told him that they were preparing bills for him, and that his passing them would be the best pledge of his inclination towards peace; in other words, he must yield at discretion [unconditionally]. He desired a personal treaty [conference] and offered to come to London upon receiving a safe conduct for himself and his attendants. They absolutely refused him admittance and issued orders for the guarding—that is, the seizing—of his person if he attempted to visit them. A new incident which happened in Ireland served to inflame the minds of men and to increase those calumnies with which his enemies had so much loaded him, and which he always regarded as the most grievous part of his misfortunes.

After the cessation with the Irish rebels, the king was desirous of concluding a final peace with them and obtaining their assistance in England. And he gave authority to Ormonde, lord lieutenant, to promise them an abrogation of all the penal laws enacted against Catholics together with the suspension of Poynings's statute with regard to some particular bills which would be agreed on. Lord Herbert—created Earl of Glamorgan (though his patent had not yet passed the seals)—having occasion to go to Ireland for his private affairs, the king considered that this nobleman, being a Catholic and allied to the best Irish families, might be of service. He also foresaw that further concessions with regard to religion might probably be demanded by the bigoted Irish; and that as these concessions, however necessary, would give great scandal to the Protestant zealots in his three kingdoms, it would be requisite both to conceal them for some time and to preserve Ormonde's reputation by giving private orders to Glamorgan to conclude and sign these articles. But as he had a better opinion of Glamorgan's zeal and affection for his service than of his capacity, he enjoined him to communicate all his measures to Ormonde; and though the final conclusion of the treaty would be executed only in Glamorgan's own name, he was required to be directed in the steps towards it by the opinion of the lord lieutenant. Glamorgan, bigoted to his religion and passionate for the king's service but guided in these pursuits by no manner of judgment or discretion, secretly, of his own accord, without any communication with Ormonde, concluded a peace with the Council of Kilkenny and agreed in the king's name that the Irish would enjoy all the churches of which they had ever been in possession since the commencement of their insurrection, on condition that they would assist the king in England with a body of ten thousand men. This transaction was discovered by accident. The titular archbishop of Tuam being killed by a sally of the garrison of Sligo, the articles of the treaty were found among his baggage and were immediately published everywhere, and copies of them were sent over to the English Parliament. The lord lieutenant and Lord Digby, foreseeing the clamor which would be raised against the king, committed Glamorgan to prison, charged him with treason for his temerity, and maintained that he had acted altogether without any authority from his master. The English Parliament, however, did not neglect so favorable an opportunity of reviving the old clamor with regard to the king's favor of popery; they accused him of delivering over, in effect, the whole kingdom of Ireland to that hated sect. The king told them, "That the Earl of Glamorgan, having made an offer to raise forces in the kingdom of Ireland, and to conduct them into England for his majesty's service, had a commission to that purpose, and to that purpose only, and that he had no commission at all to treat of any thing else, without the privity and direction of the lord lieutenant, much less to capitulate any thing concerning religion, or any property belonging either to church or laity." Though this declaration seems agreeable to truth, it gave no satisfaction to the Parliament; and some historians even at present, when the ancient bigotry is somewhat abated, are desirous of representing this very innocent transaction, in which the king was engaged by the most violent necessity, as a stain on the memory of that unfortunate prince.

Having lost all hope of prevailing over the rigor of the Parliament either by arms or by treaty, the only resource which remained to the king was derived from the internal dissensions which ran very high among his enemies. Presbyterians and Independents, even before their victory was fully completed, fell into contests about the division of the spoil; and their religious as well as civil disputes agitated the whole kingdom.

Ecclesiastical affairs

The Parliament, though they had early abolished episcopal authority, had not since that time substituted any other spiritual government in its place; and their committees of religion had since then assumed the whole ecclesiastical jurisdiction. But they now established by an ordinance the Presbyterian model in all its forms of congregational, classical, provincial, and national assemblies. All the inhabitants of each parish were ordered to meet and choose elders, on whom, together with the minister, was bestowed the entire direction of all spiritual concerns within the congregation. A number of neighboring parishes, commonly between twelve and twenty, formed a classis; and the court which governed this division was composed of all the ministers, together with two, three, or four elders chosen from each parish. The provincial assembly retained an inspection over several neighboring classes and was composed entirely of clergymen. The national assembly was constituted in the same manner, and its authority extended over the whole kingdom. It is probable that the tyranny exercised by the Scottish clergy had given warning not to allow laymen a place in the provincial or national assemblies lest the nobility and more considerable gentry, soliciting a seat in these great ecclesiastical courts, would bestow a consideration upon them and render them in the eyes of the multitude a rival to the Parliament. In the inferior courts, the mixture of the laity might serve rather to temper the usual zeal of the clergy.

But though the Presbyterians were gratified by the establishment of parity among the ecclesiastics, they were denied satisfaction in several other points on which they were extremely intent. The Westminster Assembly of Divines had voted Presbytery to be of divine right; the Parliament refused their assent to that decision. Selden, Whitelocke, and other political reasoners, assisted by the Independents, had prevailed in this important deliberation. They thought that had the bigoted religionists been able to get their heavenly charter recognized, the presbyters would soon become more dangerous to the magistrate than the prelatical clergy had ever been. These latter, while they claimed to themselves a divine right, admitted a like origin to civil authority; the former, insisting on a celestial pedigree for their own order, derived the legislative power from a source no more dignified than the voluntary association of the people.

Under color of keeping the sacraments from profanation, the clergy of all Christian sects had assumed what they call the power of the keys, or the right of fulminating excommunication. The example of Scotland was a sufficient lesson for the Parliament to use precaution in guarding against so severe a tyranny. They determined by a general ordinance all the cases in which excommunication could be used. They allowed appeals to Parliament from all ecclesiastical courts. And they appointed commissioners in every province to judge such cases that did not fall within their general ordinance. So much civil authority intermixed with the ecclesiastical gave disgust to all the zealots.

But nothing was attended with more universal scandal than the propensity of many in the Parliament towards a toleration of the Protestant sectaries. The Presbyterians exclaimed that this indulgence made the church of Christ resemble Noah's ark and rendered it a receptacle for all unclean beasts. They insisted that the least of Christ's truths was superior to all political considerations. They maintained the eternal obligation imposed by the Covenant to extirpate heresy and schism. And they menaced all their opponents with the same rigid persecution under which they themselves had groaned when held in subjection by the hierarchy.

So great prudence and reserve in such material points does great honor to the Parliament and proves that notwithstanding the prevalence of bigotry and fanaticism, there were many members who had more enlarged views and paid regard to the civil interests of society. These men, uniting themselves to the enthusiasts, whose spirit is naturally averse to clerical usurpations, exercised so jealous an authority over the Assembly of Divines that they allowed them nothing but the liberty of tendering advice; and they would not entrust them even with the power of electing their own chairman or his substitute or of supplying the vacancies of their own members.

While these disputes were canvassed by theologians who engaged every order of the state in their spiritual contests, the king, though he entertained hopes of reaping advantage from those divisions, was much at a loss which side it would be most for his interest to comply with. The Presbyterians were by their principles the least averse to regal authority but were rigidly bent on the extirpation of prelacy. The Independents were resolute to lay the foundation of a republican government; but as they did not aspire to erect themselves into a national church, it might be hoped that they would admit the reestablishment of the hierarchy if they were gratified with a toleration. So great attachment had the king to episcopal jurisdiction that he was always inclined to put it in balance even with his own power and kingly office.

But whatever advantage he might hope to reap from the divisions in the parliamentary party, he was apprehensive lest it would come too late to save him from the destruction with which he was instantly threatened. Fairfax was approaching with a powerful and victorious army and was taking the proper measures for laying siege to Oxford, which must infallibly fall into his hands. To be taken captive and led in triumph by his insolent enemies was what Charles justly abhorred; and every insult, if not violence, was to be dreaded from that enthusiastic soldiery who hated his person and despised his dignity. In this desperate extremity, he embraced a measure which in any other situation might lie under the imputation of imprudence and indiscretion.

Montreuil, the French minister, interested for the king more by the natural sentiments of humanity than any instructions from his court, which seemed rather to favor the Parliament, had solicited the Scottish generals and commissioners to give protection to their distressed sovereign; and having received many general professions and promises, he had always transmitted these, perhaps with some exaggeration, to the king. From his suggestions, Charles began to entertain thoughts of leaving Oxford and flying to the Scottish army, which at that time lay before Newark. He considered that the Scottish nation had been fully gratified in all their demands; and having already in their own country annihilated both episcopacy and regal authority, they had no further concessions to exact from him. In all disputes which had passed about settling the terms of peace, the Scots, he heard, had continually adhered to the milder side and had endeavored to soften the rigor of the English Parliament. Great disgusts also had taken place between the nations on other accounts; and the Scots found that in proportion as their assistance became less necessary, less value was put upon them. The progress of the Independents gave them great alarm; and they were scandalized to hear their beloved Covenant spoken of every day with less regard and reverence. The refusal of a divine right to Presbytery and the infringing of ecclesiastical discipline from political considerations were to them the subject of much offense. And the king hoped that in their present disposition, the plight of their native prince, flying to them in this extremity of distress, would rouse every spark of generosity in their bosom and procure him their favor and protection.

King goes to the Scots at Newark
That he might better conceal his intentions, orders were given at every

gate in Oxford for allowing three persons to pass; and in the night, the king, accompanied by none but Dr. Hudson and Mr. Ashburnham, went out at that gate which leads to London. He rode before a portmanteau and called himself Ashburnham's servant. He passed through Henley, St. Albans, and came so near to London as Harrow on the Hill. He once entertained thoughts of entering into that city and of throwing himself on the mercy of the Parliament. But at last, after passing through many crossroads, he arrived at the Scottish camp before Newark on May 5. The Parliament, hearing of his escape from Oxford, issued rigorous orders and threatened with instant death whoever would harbor or conceal him.

The Scottish generals and commissioners affected great surprise on the appearance of the king; and though they paid him all the exterior respect due to his dignity, they instantly set a guard upon him under color of protection and made him in reality a prisoner. They informed the English Parliament of this unexpected incident and assured them that they had entered into no private treaty with the king. They applied to him for orders to Belasyse, governor of Newark, to surrender that town, now reduced to extremity; and the orders were instantly obeyed. And hearing that the Parliament laid claim to the entire disposal of the king's person and that the English army was making some motion towards them, they thought proper to retire northwards and to fix their camp at Newcastle.

The king was very grateful for this measure; and he began to entertain hopes of protection from the Scots. He was particularly attentive to the behavior of their preachers, on whom all depended. It was the mode of that age to make the pulpit the scene of news; and on every great event, the whole Scripture was ransacked by the clergy for passages applicable to the present occasion. The first minister who preached before the king chose these words for his text: "And behold, all the men of Israel came to the king, and said unto him, 'Why have our brethren, the men of Judah, stolen thee away, and have brought the king and his household, and all David's men with him, over Jordan?' And all the men of Judah answered the men of Israel, 'Because the king is near of kin to us; wherefore then be ye angry for this matter? Have we eaten at all of the king's cost, or hath he given us any gift?' And the men of Israel answered the men of Judah, and said, 'We have ten parts in the king, and we have also more right in David than ye. Why then did ye despise us, that our advice should not be first had in bringing back our king?' And the words of the men of Judah were fiercer than the words of the men of Israel." But the king soon found that it was chiefly the happiness of the allusion that had tempted the preacher to employ this text, and that the zealous Covenanters were in no way pacified towards him. Another preacher, after reproaching him to his face with his misgovernment, ordered this psalm to be sung:

"Why dost thou, tyrant, boast thyself
Thy wicked deeds to praise?"

The king stood up and called for that psalm which begins with these words:

"Have mercy, Lord, on me, I pray;
For men would me devour."

The good-natured audience, in pity to fallen majesty, showed for once greater deference to the king than to the minister and sung the psalm which the former had called for.

Charles had very little reason to be pleased with his situation. He not only found himself a prisoner, very strictly guarded, but all his friends were kept at a distance; and no intercourse, either by letters or conversation, was allowed him with anyone on whom he could depend or who was suspected of any attachment towards him. The Scottish generals would enter into no confidence with him and still treated him with distant ceremony and feigned respect. And every proposal which they made him tended further to his abasement and to his ruin.

End of the war

They required him to issue orders to Oxford and to all his other garrisons commanding their surrender to the Parliament. And the king, aware that their resistance was to very little purpose, willingly complied. The terms given to most of them were honorable; and Fairfax, as far as it lay in his power, was very exact in observing them. Far from allowing violence, he would not even permit insults or triumph over the unfortunate Royalists; and by his generous humanity, so cruel a civil war was ended, in appearance, very calmly between the parties.

Ormonde, having received like orders, delivered Dublin and other forts into the hands of the parliamentary officers. Montrose also, after having experienced still more variety of good and bad fortune, threw down his arms and retired out of the kingdom.

The Marquess of Worcester, a man past eighty-four, was the last in England that submitted to the authority of the Parliament. He defended Raglan Castle to extremity and did not open its gates till the middle of August. Four years, a few days excepted, were now elapsed since the king first erected his standard at Nottingham. So long had the British nations by civil and religious quarrels been occupied in shedding their own blood and laying waste their native country.

The Parliament and the Scots laid their proposals before the king. They were such as a captive entirely at mercy could expect from the most inexorable victor; yet they were little worse than what were insisted on before the Battle of Naseby. The power of the sword, instead of for ten years, which the king now offered, was demanded for twenty, together with a right to levy whatever money the Parliament would think proper for the support of their armies. The other conditions were in the main the same with those which had formerly been offered to the king.

Charles said that proposals which introduced such important innovations in the constitution demanded time for deliberation; the commissioners replied that he must give his answer in ten days. He desired to reason about the meaning and import of some terms; they informed him that they had no power of debate and peremptorily required his consent or refusal. He requested a personal treaty [conference] with the Parliament; they threatened that if he delayed compliance, the Parliament would by their own authority settle the nation.

What the Parliament was most intent upon was not their treaty with the king, to whom they paid little regard, but that with the Scots. Two important points remained to be settled with that nation: their delivery of the king and the estimation of their arrears.

The Scots might claim that as Charles was king of Scotland as well as of England, they were entitled to an equal vote in the disposal of his person; and that in such a case where the titles are equal and the subject indivisible, the preference was due to the present possessor. The English maintained that the king, being in England, was comprehended [included] within the jurisdiction of that kingdom and could not be disposed of by any foreign nation. A delicate question this, and one which surely could not be decided by precedent, since such a situation is not anywhere to be found in history.

As the Scots concurred with the English in imposing such severe conditions on the king that notwithstanding his unfortunate situation, he still refused to accept them, it is certain that they did not desire his freedom; nor could they ever intend to join lenity and rigor together in so inconsistent a manner. Before the settlement of terms, it was necessary that the administration be possessed entirely by the

Parliaments of both kingdoms; and how incompatible was that scheme with the liberty of the king is easily imagined. To carry him a prisoner into Scotland, where few forces could be supported to guard him, was a measure so full of inconvenience and danger that even if the English had consented to it, it must have appeared to the Scots themselves altogether unworthy of preference. And how could such a plan be supported in opposition to England, possessed of such numerous and victorious armies which were, or at that time at least seemed to be, in entire union with the Parliament? The only expedient, it is obvious, which the Scots could embrace if they scrupled wholly to abandon the king was immediately to return fully and cordially to their allegiance, and uniting themselves with the Royalists in both kingdoms, endeavor by force of arms to reduce the English Parliament to more moderate conditions. But besides that this measure was full of extreme hazard, what was it but instantly to combine with their old enemies against their old friends, and in a fit of romantic generosity, overturn what with so much expense of blood and treasure they had, during the course of so many years, been so carefully erecting?

But though all these reflections occurred to the Scottish commissioners, they resolved to prolong the dispute and to keep the king as a security for those arrears which they claimed from England, and which they were not likely, in the present disposition of that nation, to obtain by any other expedient. The sum, by their account, amounted to nearly two millions, for they had received little regular pay since they had entered England. And though both the contributions which they had levied and the price of their living at free quarters had to be deducted, yet still the sum which they insisted on was very considerable. After many discussions, it was at last agreed that in lieu of all demands, they would accept £400,000, one half to be paid instantly, another in two subsequent payments.

Great pains were taken by the Scots (and the English complied with their pretended delicacy) to make this estimation and payment of arrears appear to be a quite different transaction from that for the delivery of the king's person; but common sense requires that they should be regarded as one and the same. Had the English not been previously assured of receiving the king, it is evident that they would never have parted with so considerable a sum, at the same time weakening themselves and strengthening a people with whom they must afterwards have so material an interest to discuss.

Thus, the Scottish nation underwent, and still undergo (for such grievous stains are not easily wiped off), the reproach of selling their king and betraying their prince for money. In vain did they maintain that this money was, on account of former services, undoubtedly their due; that in their present situation, no other measure could be embraced without the utmost indiscretion or even their apparent ruin; and that though they delivered their king into the hands of his open enemies, they were themselves as much his open enemies as those to whom they surrendered him, and their common hatred against him had long united the two parties in strict alliance with each other. They were still answered that they made use of this scandalous expedient for obtaining their wages; and that after taking arms without any provocation against their sovereign, who had always loved and cherished them, they had deservedly fallen into a situation from which they could not extricate themselves without either infamy or imprudence.

The infamy of this bargain had such an influence on the Scottish Parliament that they once voted that the king should be protected and his liberty insisted on. But the General Assembly interposed and pronounced that as he had refused to take the Covenant, which was pressed on him, it did not become the godly to concern themselves about his fortunes. After this declaration, it behooved the Parliament to retract their vote.

Intelligence concerning the final resolution of the Scottish nation to surrender him was brought to the king; and he happened at that very time to be playing at chess. Such command of temper did he possess that he continued his game without interruption; and none of the bystanders could perceive that the letter which he perused had brought him news of any consequence. The English commissioners who came some days later to take him under their custody were admitted to kiss his hands; and he received them with the same grace and cheerfulness as if they had traveled on no other errand than to pay court to him. He congratulated in particular the old Earl of Pembroke, who was one of them, on his strength and vigor, which still enabled him to perform so long a journey during such a season in company with so many young people.

King delivered up by the Scots

The king, being delivered over by the Scots to the English commissioners, was conducted under a guard to Holdenby House, in the county of Northampton. On his journey, the whole

<table>
<tr><td>1647</td></tr>
</table>

country flocked to behold him, moved partly by curiosity, partly by compassion and affection. If any still retained rancor against him in his present condition, they passed in silence; while his well-wishers, more generous than prudent, accompanied his march with tears, with acclamations, and with prayers for his safety. That ancient superstition likewise of desiring the king's touch in scrofulous distempers seemed to acquire fresh credit among the people, from the general tenderness which began to prevail for this virtuous and unhappy monarch.

The commissioners rendered his confinement at Holdenby very rigorous, dismissing his ancient servants, barring him from visits, and cutting off all communication with his friends or family. The Parliament, though earnestly applied to by the king, refused to allow his chaplains to attend him because they had not taken the Covenant. The king refused to assist at the service exercised in accord with the Directory because he had not as yet given his consent to that mode of worship. Such religious zeal prevailed on both sides, and such was the unhappy and distracted condition to which it had reduced king and people.

During the time that the king remained in the Scottish army at Newcastle, the Earl of Essex, the discarded but still powerful and popular general of the Parliament, died. His death in this conjuncture was a public misfortune. Fully aware of the excesses to which affairs had been carried and of the worse consequences which were still to be feared, he had resolved to conciliate a peace and to remedy as far as possible all those ills to which, from mistake rather than any bad intentions, he had himself so much contributed. The Presbyterian, or the moderate, party among the Commons found themselves considerably weakened by his death; and the small remains of authority which still adhered to the House of Peers were, in effect, wholly extinguished.

CHAPTER 59
1647 – 1649

*Mutiny of the army – The king seized by Joyce – The army
march against the Parliament – The army subdue the
Parliament – The king flies to the Isle of Wight – Second
civil war – Invasion from Scotland – Treaty of Newport –
Civil war and invasion repressed – The king seized again by
the army – The house purged – The king's trial –
And execution – And character*

THE dominion of the Parliament was of short duration. No sooner
had they subdued their sovereign than their own servants rose
against them and tumbled them from their slippery throne. The sacred boundaries of the laws being once violated, nothing remained to
confine the wild projects of zeal and ambition. And every successive
revolution became a precedent for that which followed it.

In proportion as the terror of the king's power diminished, the division between Independent and Presbyterian became every day more
apparent; and the neutrals found it at last requisite to seek shelter in
one or the other faction. Many new writs were issued for elections in
the place of members who had died or were disqualified by adhering
to the king, yet still the Presbyterians retained the superiority among
the Commons. And all the Peers except Lord Say were deemed of that
party. The Independents, to whom the inferior sectaries adhered, predominated in the army; and the troops of the New Model were universally infected with that enthusiastic spirit. To their assistance did
the Independent party among the Commons chiefly trust in their projects for acquiring the ascendant over their antagonists.

Soon after the retreat of the Scots, the Presbyterians, seeing everything reduced to obedience, began to talk of diminishing the army; and on pretense of easing the public burdens, they leveled a deadly blow at the opposite faction. They purposed to embark a strong detachment under Skippon and Massey for the service of Ireland; they openly declared their intention of making a great reduction of the remainder. It was even imagined that another new model of the army was projected in order to regain to the Presbyterians that superiority which they had so imprudently lost by the former.

The army had small inclination to the service of Ireland, a country barbarous, uncultivated, and laid waste by massacres and civil commotions. They had less inclination to disband and to renounce that pay which, having been earned through fatigues and dangers, they now purposed to enjoy in ease and tranquility. And most of the officers, having risen from the dregs of the people, had no other prospect, if deprived of their commission, than that of returning to languish in their native poverty and obscurity.

These motives of interest acquired additional influence and became more dangerous to the Parliament from the religious spirit by which the army was universally actuated. Among the majority of men educated in regular, civilized societies, the sentiments of shame, duty, and honor have considerable authority and serve to counterbalance and direct the motives derived from private advantage. But by the predominance of enthusiasm among the parliamentary forces, these salutary principles lost their credit and were regarded as mere human inventions, indeed, as moral institutions fitter for heathens than for Christians. The saint, resigned over to superior guidance, was at full liberty to gratify all his appetites, disguised under the appearance of pious zeal. And besides the strange corruptions engendered by this spirit, it eluded and loosened all the ties of morality and gave entire scope, and even sanction, to the selfishness and ambition which naturally adhere to the human mind.

The military confessors were further encouraged in disobedience to superiors by that spiritual pride to which a mistaken piety is so subject. They were not, they said, mere janissaries, mercenary troops enlisted for hire and to be disposed of at the will of their paymasters. Religion and liberty were the motives which had excited them to arms, and they had a superior right to see those blessings which they had purchased with their blood ensured to future generations. By the same title that the Presbyterians, in contradistinction to the Royalists, had appropriated to themselves the epithet of "godly and well-affected," the Independents did now, in contradistinction to the Presbyterians, assume this magnificent appellation and arrogate all the ascendant which naturally belongs to it.

The troops, hearing of parties in the House of Commons and being informed that the minority were friends to the army, the majority enemies, naturally interested themselves in that dangerous distinction and were eager to give the superiority to their partisans. Whatever hardships they underwent, though perhaps derived from inevitable necessity, were ascribed to a settled design of oppressing them and resented as an effect of the animosity and malice of their adversaries.

Notwithstanding the great revenue which accrued from taxes, assessments, sequestrations, and compositions, considerable arrears were due to the army; and many of the private men as well as officers had nearly a year's pay still owing them. The army suspected that this deficiency was purposely contrived in order to oblige them to live at free quarters, and by rendering them odious to the country, serve as a pretense for disbanding them. When they saw such members as were employed in committees and civil offices accumulate fortunes, they accused them of rapine and public plunder. And as no plan was pointed out by the Commons for the payment of arrears, the soldiers dreaded that after they were disbanded or embarked for Ireland, their enemies, who predominated in the two houses, would entirely defraud them of their right and oppress them with impunity.

Mutiny of the army

On this ground, or pretense, did the first commotions in the army begin. A petition addressed to Fairfax, the general, was handed about; it craved an indemnity, and that ratified by the king, for any illegal actions of which the soldiers might have been guilty during the course of the war, together with satisfaction in arrears, freedom from pressing, relief of widows and maimed soldiers, and pay till disbanded. The Commons, aware of what combustible materials the army was composed, were alarmed at this intelligence. They knew that such a combination, if not checked in its first appearance, must be attended with the most dangerous consequences and must soon exalt the military above the civil authority. Besides summoning some officers to answer for this attempt, they immediately voted on March 30 that the petition tended to introduce mutiny, to put conditions upon the Parliament, and to obstruct the relief of Ireland; and they threatened to proceed against the promoters of it as enemies to the state and disturbers of public peace. This declaration, which may be deemed violent, especially as the army had some ground for complaint, produced fatal effects. The soldiers lamented that they were deprived of the privileges of Englishmen; that they were not allowed so much as to represent their grievances; that while petitions from Essex and other places were openly encouraged against the army, their mouths were stopped; and that they, who were the authors of liberty to the nation, were reduced by a faction in Parliament to the most grievous servitude.

The army was found in this disposition by Warwick, Dacres, Massey, and other commissioners who were sent to make them proposals for entering into the service of Ireland. Instead of enlisting, most objected to the terms, demanded an indemnity, were clamorous for their arrears; and though they expressed no dissatisfaction against Skippon, who was appointed commander, they revealed much stronger inclination to serve under Fairfax and Cromwell. Some officers who were of the Presbyterian party, having entered into engagements for this service, could prevail on very few of the soldiers to enlist under them. And as these officers all lay under the grievous reproach of deserting the army and betraying the interests of their companions, the rest were further confirmed in that confederacy which they had secretly formed.

To petition and remonstrate being the most cautious method of conducting a confederacy, an application to Parliament was signed by nearly two hundred officers in which they made their apology with a very imperious air, asserted their right of petitioning, and complained of that imputation thrown upon them by the former declaration of the lower house. The private men likewise of some regiments sent a letter to Skippon in which, together with insisting on the same topics, they lamented that designs were formed against them and many of the godly party in the kingdom and declared that they could not engage for Ireland till they were satisfied in their expectations and had their just desires granted. The army, in a word, felt their power and resolved to be masters.

The Parliament too resolved to preserve, if possible, their dominion; but being destitute of power and not retaining much authority, it was not easy for them to employ any expedient which could contribute to their purpose. The expedient which they now made use of was the worst imaginable. They sent Skippon, Cromwell, Ireton, and Fleetwood to the headquarters at Saffron Walden, in Essex, on May 7 and empowered them to make offers to the army and inquire into the cause of its "distempers." These very generals, at least the three last, were secretly the authors of all the discontents; and they failed not to foment those disorders which they pretended to appease. By their suggestion, a measure was embraced which both brought matters to extremity and rendered the mutiny incurable.

In opposition to the Parliament at Westminster, a military parliament was formed. Together with a council of the principal officers, which was appointed after the model of the House of Peers, a freer representative of the army was composed by the election of two private men or inferior officers, under the title of "agitators," from each troop or company. By this means, both the general humor of that time, intent on plans of imaginary republics, was gratified and an easy method contrived for dishonestly conducting and propagating the sedition of the army.

This terrible court, when assembled, having first declared that they found no "distempers" in the army but many "grievances" under which it labored, immediately voted the offers of the Parliament unsatisfactory. Eight weeks' pay only, they said, was promised, a small part of the fifty-six weeks which they claimed as their due; no visible security was given for the remainder; and having been declared public enemies by the Commons, they might hereafter be prosecuted as such unless the declaration were recalled. Before matters came to this height, Cromwell had posted up to London on pretense of laying before the Parliament the rising discontents of the army.

The Parliament made one vigorous effort more to try the force of their authority: they voted that all the troops which did not engage for Ireland would instantly be disbanded in their quarters. At the same time, the council of the army ordered a general rendezvous of all the regiments in order to provide for their common interests. And while they thus prepared themselves for opposition to the Parliament, they struck a blow which at once decided the victory in their favor.

The king seized by Joyce

A party of five hundred cavalrymen appeared on June 3 at Holdenby conducted by one George Joyce, who had once been a tailor by profession but was now advanced to the rank of cornet and was an active agitator in the army. Without being opposed by the guard, whose affections were all on their side, Joyce came into the king's presence armed with pistols and told him that he must immediately go along with him. "Whither?" said the king. "To the army," replied Joyce. "By what warrant?" asked the king. Joyce pointed to the soldiers whom he brought along, tall, handsome, and well equipped. "Your warrant," said Charles, smiling, "is writ in fair characters, legible without spelling." The parliamentary commissioners came into the room. They asked Joyce whether he had any orders from the Parliament. He said, "No." From the general? "No." By what authority came he? He made the same reply as to the king. They would write, they said, to the Parliament to know their pleasure. "You may do so," replied Joyce, "but in the meantime the king must immediately go with me." Resistance was vain. The king, after protracting the time as long as he could, went into his coach; and he was safely conducted to the army, who were hastening to their rendezvous at Thriplow Heath, near Cambridge. The Parliament, informed of this event by their commissioners, were thrown into the utmost consternation.

Fairfax himself was no less surprised at the king's arrival. That bold measure executed by Joyce had never been communicated to the general. The orders were entirely verbal, and nobody avowed them. And while everyone affected astonishment at the enterprise, Cromwell, by whose counsel it had been directed, arrived from London and put an end to their deliberations.

This artful and audacious conspirator had conducted himself in the Parliament with such profound dissimulation, with such refined hypocrisy, that he had long deceived those who, being themselves very dexterous practitioners in the same arts, should naturally have entertained the more suspicion against others. At every intelligence of disorders in the army, he was moved to the highest pitch of grief and of anger. He wept bitterly; he lamented the misfortunes of his country; he advised every violent measure for suppressing the mutiny; and by these precipitate counsels, he both seemed to evince his own sincerity and inflamed those discontents of which he intended to make advantage. He called on heaven and earth to confirm that his devoted attachment to the Parliament had rendered him so odious in the army that his life, while among them, was in the utmost danger, and that he had very narrowly escaped a conspiracy formed to assassinate him. But information being brought that the most active officers and agitators were entirely his creatures, the parliamentary leaders secretly resolved that next day, when he would come to the house, an accusation would be entered against him, and he would be sent to the Tower. Cromwell, who frequently approached to the very brink of destruction in the conduct of his desperate enterprises, knew how to make the requisite turn with proper dexterity and boldness. Being informed of this design, he hastened to the camp, where he was received with acclamations and was instantly invested with the supreme command both of the council of general officers and of the army.

Fairfax, having neither talents himself for cabal nor penetration to discover the cabals of others, had given his entire confidence to Cromwell, who, by the best colored pretenses and by the appearance of an open sincerity and a scrupulous conscience, imposed on the easy nature of this brave and virtuous man. The council of officers and the agitators were moved altogether by Cromwell's direction and conveyed his will to the whole army. By his profound and artful conduct, he had now attained a situation where he could cover his enterprises from public view, and seeming either to obey the commands of his superior officer or yield to the movements of the soldiers, could secretly pave the way for his future greatness. While the disorders of the army were yet in their infancy, he kept at a distance, lest his counterfeit aversion might throw a damp upon them or his secret encouragement beget suspicion in the Parliament. As soon as they came to maturity, he openly joined the troops; and in the critical moment, he struck that important blow of seizing the king's person and depriving the Parliament of any resource of an accommodation with him. Though one visor fell off, another still remained to cover his natural countenance. Where delay was requisite, he could employ the most indefatigable patience; where celerity was necessary, he flew to a decision. And by thus uniting in his person the most opposite talents, he was enabled to combine the most contrary interests in a subservience to his secret purposes.

The army march against the Parliament

The Parliament, though at present defenseless, was possessed of many resources; and time might easily enable them to resist that violence with which they were threatened. Without further deliberation, therefore, Cromwell advanced the army upon them and arrived in a few days at St. Albans.

Nothing could have been more popular than this hostility which the army commenced against the Parliament. As much as that assembly was once the idol of the nation, so much had it now become the object of general hatred and aversion.

The Self-Denying Ordinance had remained in effect only till Essex, Manchester, Waller, and the other officers of that party had resigned their commissions. Immediately after, it was laid aside by tacit consent; and the members, sharing all offices of power and profit among them, proceeded with impunity in exercising acts of oppression on the helpless nation. Though the necessity of their situation might serve as an apology for many of their measures, the people, not accustomed to such a species of government, were not disposed to make the requisite allowances.

A small supply of £100,000 a year could never be obtained by former kings from the jealous humor of Parliaments; and of all nations in Europe, the English were the least accustomed to taxes. But this Parliament, according to some computations, had levied in the five years since the commencement of the war more than forty millions, yet were loaded with debts and encumbrances which during that age were regarded as prodigious. If these computations should be thought much exaggerated, as they probably are, the taxes and impositions were certainly far higher than in any former state of the English government; and such popular exaggerations are at least a proof of popular discontents.

But the disposal of this money was no less the object of general complaint against the Parliament than the levying of it. The sum of £300,000 they openly took, it is affirmed, and divided among their own members. The committees to whom the management of the different branches of revenue was entrusted never brought in their accounts, and they had unlimited power of secreting whatever sums they pleased from the public treasure. These branches were needlessly multiplied in order to render the revenue more intricate, to share the advantages among greater numbers, and to conceal the frauds of which they were universally suspected.

The method of keeping accounts practiced in the Exchequer was confessedly the most exact, the most ancient, the best known, and the least liable to fraud. The Exchequer was for that reason abolished, and the revenue put under the management of a committee who were subject to no control.

The excise, an odious tax formerly unknown to the nation, was now extended over provisions and the common necessaries of life. Sequestration had been imposed on nearly one-half of the goods and chattels, and at least one-half of the lands, rents, and revenues, of the kingdom. To great numbers of Royalists, all redress from these sequestrations was refused; to the rest, the remedy could be obtained only by paying large compositions and subscribing the Covenant, which they abhorred. Besides pitying the ruin and desolation of so many ancient and honorable families, indifferent spectators could not but blame the hardship of punishing with such severity actions which the law, in its usual and most undisputed interpretation, strictly required of every subject.

The severities exercised against the episcopal clergy also naturally affected the Royalists, and even all men of candor, in a perceptible manner. By the most moderate computation, it appears that more than half of the established clergy had been turned out to beggary and want for no other crime than their adhering to the civil and religious principles in which they had been educated, and for their attachment to those laws under whose sanction they had at first embraced that profession. To renounce episcopacy and the liturgy and to subscribe the Covenant were the only terms which could save them from so rigorous a fate; and if the least mark of malignancy, as it was called, or affection to the king who so entirely loved them had ever escaped their lips, even this hard choice was not permitted. The sacred character which gives the priesthood such authority over mankind became more venerable from the sufferings endured for the sake of principle by these distressed Royalists, intensifying the general indignation against their persecutors.

But what excited the most universal complaint was the unlimited tyranny and despotic rule of the county committees. During the war, the discretionary power of these courts was excused from the plea of necessity; but the nation was reduced to despair when it saw neither end put to their duration nor bounds to their authority. These could sequester, fine, imprison, and corporally punish without law or remedy. They interposed in questions of private property. Under color of malignancy, they exercised vengeance against their private enemies. To the obnoxious, and sometimes to the innocent, they sold their protection. And instead of one Star Chamber, which had been abolished, a great number were anew erected, fortified with better pretenses, and armed with more unlimited authority.

If anything could have increased the indignation against that slavery into which the nation had fallen from the too eager pursuit of liberty, it must have been the reflection on the pretenses by which the people had so long been deluded. The sanctified hypocrites, who called their oppressions the spoiling of the Egyptians and their rigid severity the dominion of the elect, interlarded all their iniquities with long and fervent prayers, saved themselves from blushing by their pious grimaces, and exercised all their cruelty on men in the name of the Lord. An undisguised violence could be forgiven; but such a mockery of the understanding, such an abuse of religion, were objects of particular resentment with men of penetration.

The Parliament, conscious of their decay in popularity, seeing a formidable armed force advance upon them, were reduced to despair and found all their resources much inferior to the present necessity. London still retained a strong attachment to Presbyterianism; and its militia, which was numerous and had acquired reputation in the wars, had by a late ordinance been put into hands in whom the Parliament could entirely confide. This militia was now called out and ordered to guard the lines which had been drawn round the city in order to secure it against the king. A body of cavalry was ordered to be instantly levied. Many officers who had been cashiered by the New Model of the army offered their service to the Parliament. An army of five thousand men lay in the north under the command of General Poyntz, who was of the Presbyterian faction, but these were too distant to be employed in so urgent a necessity. The forces destined for Ireland were quartered in the west; though deemed faithful to the Parliament, they also lay at a distance. Many inland garrisons were commanded by officers of the same party, but their troops, being so much dispersed, could at present be of no manner of service. The Scots were faithful friends and zealous for Presbytery and the Covenant, but a long time was required before they could collect their forces and march to the assistance of the Parliament.

In this situation, it was thought more prudent to submit, and by compliance to stop the fury of the enraged army. The declaration by which the military petitioners had been voted public enemies was recalled and erased from the journal book on June 8. This was the first symptom which the Parliament gave of submission; and the army, hoping by terror alone to effect all their purposes, stopped at St. Albans and entered into negotiation with their masters.

Here commenced the encroachments of the military upon the civil authority. The army, in their usurpations on the Parliament, copied exactly the model which the Parliament itself had set them in their recent usurpations on the Crown.

Every day they rose in their demands. If one claim was granted, they had another ready, still more enormous and exorbitant, and were determined never to be satisfied. At first, they pretended only to petition for what concerned themselves as soldiers; next, they must have a

417

vindication of their character; then, it was necessary that their enemies be punished; at last, they claimed a right of modeling the whole government and settling the nation.

In words, they preserved all deference and respect to the Parliament; but in reality, they insulted them and tyrannized over them. That assembly they pretended not to accuse; it was only evil counselors who seduced and betrayed it.

On June 16, they proceeded so far as to name eleven members whom, in general terms, they charged with high treason as enemies to the army and evil counselors to the Parliament. Their names were Holles, Sir Philip Stapleton, Sir William Lewis, Sir John Clotworthy, Sir William Waller, Sir John Maynard, Massey, Glynn, Long, Harley, and Nichols. These were the very leaders of the Presbyterian party.

They insisted that these members be immediately sequestered from Parliament and thrown into prison. The Commons replied that they could not proceed so far upon a general charge. The army observed to them that the cases of Strafford and Laud were direct precedents for that purpose. At last, the eleven members themselves, not to give occasion for discord, begged leave to retire from the house; and the army seemed satisfied for the present with this mark of submission.

Pretending that the Parliament intended to levy war upon them and to involve the nation again in blood and confusion, they required that all new levies be stopped. The Parliament complied with this demand.

There being no signs of resistance, the army, in order to save appearances, removed to a greater distance from London at the desire of the Parliament and fixed their headquarters at Reading. They carried the king along with them in all their marches.

That prince now found himself in a better situation than at Holdenby and had attained some greater degree of freedom as well as of consideration with both parties. All his friends had access to his presence; his correspondence with the queen was not interrupted; his chaplains were restored to him, and he was allowed the use of the liturgy; his children were once allowed to visit him, and they passed a few days at Caversham, where he then resided. He had not seen the Duke of Gloucester, his youngest son, and the princess Elizabeth since he left London at the commencement of the civil disorders. When the king applied to have his children, the Parliament always told him that they could take as much care of both their bodies and souls at London as could be done at Oxford. Nor had he seen the Duke of York since he went to the Scottish army before Newark. No private man unacquainted with the pleasures of a court and the tumult of a camp more passionately loved his family than did this good prince, and he was extremely grateful for such an instance of indulgence. Cromwell, who was witness to the meeting of the royal family, confessed that he never had been present at so tender a scene, and he extremely applauded the benignity which displayed itself in the whole disposition and behavior of Charles.

That artful politician as well as the leaders of all parties paid court to the king; and fortune, notwithstanding all his calamities, seemed again to smile upon him. The Parliament, afraid of his forming some accommodation with the army, addressed him in a more respectful style than formerly and invited him to reside at Richmond and contribute his assistance to the settlement of the nation. The chief officers treated him with regard and spoke on all occasions of restoring him to his just powers and prerogatives. In the public declarations of the army, the settlement of his revenue and authority was insisted on. The Royalists everywhere entertained hopes of the restoration of monarchy; and the favor which they universally bore to the army contributed very much to discourage the Parliament and to forward their submission.

The king began to feel of what consequence he was. The more the national confusions increased, the more he was confident that all parties would at length have recourse to his lawful authority as the only remedy for the public disorders. "You cannot be without me," he said on several occasions. "You cannot settle the nation but by my assistance." A people without government and without liberty, a Parliament without authority, an army without a legal master, distractions everywhere, terrors, oppressions, convulsions: from this scene of confusion, which could not long continue, all men, he hoped, would be brought to reflect on that ancient government under which they and their ancestors had so long enjoyed happiness and tranquility.

Though Charles kept his ears open to all proposals and expected to hold the balance between the opposite parties, he entertained more hopes of accommodation with the army. He had experienced the extreme rigor of the Parliament: they attempted totally to annihilate his authority; they had confined his person. In both these particulars, the army showed more indulgence. He had a free intercourse with his friends. And in the proposals which the council of officers sent for the settlement of the nation, they insisted neither on the abolition of episcopacy nor on the punishment of the Royalists, the two points to which the king had the most extreme reluctance. And they demanded that an end be put to the present Parliament, the event for which he most ardently longed.

His conjunction too seemed more natural with the generals than with that usurping assembly who had so long assumed the entire sovereignty of the state, and who had declared their resolution still to continue masters. By gratifying a few persons with titles and preferments, he might draw over, he hoped, the whole military power and in an instant reinstate himself in his civil authority. To Ireton, he offered the lieutenancy of Ireland; to Cromwell, the garter, the title of Earl of Essex, and the command of the army. Negotiations to this purpose were secretly conducted. Cromwell pretended to hearken to them; and he was well pleased to keep the door open for an accommodation should the course of events at any time render it necessary. And the king, who had no suspicion that one born a private gentleman could entertain the daring ambition of seizing a scepter transmitted through a long line of monarchs, indulged hopes that Cromwell would at last embrace a measure which seemed to be recommended to him by all the motives of duty, interest, and safety.

While Cromwell allured the king by these expectations, he still continued his scheme of reducing the Parliament to subjection and depriving them of all means of resistance. To gratify the army, the Parliament invested Fairfax with the title of general in chief of all the forces in England and Ireland; and they thus entrusted the whole military authority to a person who, though well inclined to their service, was no longer at his own disposal.

The Parliament also voted that the troops who, in obedience to its own order, had enlisted for Ireland and deserted the rebellious army be disbanded—or in other words, be punished for their fidelity. The forces in the north under Poyntz had already mutinied against their general and had entered into an association with that body of the army which was so successfully employed in exalting the military above the civil authority.

That no resource might remain to the Parliament, it was demanded that the militia of London be changed, the Presbyterian commissioners displaced, and the command restored to those who had constantly exercised it during the course of the war. The Parliament even complied with so violent a demand and passed a vote in obedience to the army.

By this unlimited patience, they purposed to temporize under their present difficulties, and they hoped to find a more favorable opportunity for recovering their authority and influence. But the impatience of the city lost them all the advantage of their cautious measures. On July 20, a petition against the alteration of the militia was carried to Westminster, attended by the apprentices and a seditious multitude, who besieged the door of the House of Commons; and by their clamor, noise, and violence, they obliged the house to reverse that vote which they had passed so lately. When gratified in this pretension, they immediately dispersed and left the Parliament at liberty.

No sooner was intelligence of this tumult conveyed to Reading than the army was put in motion. The two houses being under restraint, they were resolved, they said, to vindicate against the seditious citizens the invaded privileges of Parliament and restore that assembly to its just freedom of debate and counsel. On their way to London, they were drawn up on Hounslow Heath: a formidable body, twenty thousand strong and determined to pursue whatever measures their generals would dictate to them without regard to laws or liberty. Here the most favorable event happened to quicken and encourage their advance. The speakers of the two houses, Manchester and Lenthall, attended by eight peers and about sixty commoners, having secretly retired from the city, presented themselves with their maces and all the ensigns of their dignity; and complaining of the violence put upon them, they applied to the army for defense and protection. They were received with shouts and acclamations; respect was paid to them as to the Parliament of England; and the army, being provided with so plausible a pretense, which in all public transactions is of great consequence, advanced to chastise the rebellious city and to reinstate the violated Parliament.

Neither Lenthall nor Manchester were deemed Independents, and such a step in them was unexpected. But they probably foresaw that the army must in the end prevail, and they were willing to pay court in time to that authority which began to predominate in the nation.

The Parliament, forced from their temporizing measures and obliged to resign at once or combat for their liberty and power, prepared themselves with vigor for defense and resolved to resist the violence of the army. The two houses immediately chose new speakers, Lord Hunsdon and Henry Pelham; they renewed their former orders for enlisting troops; they appointed Massey to be commander; they ordered the trainbands to man the lines; and the whole city was in a ferment and resounded with military preparations.

When any intelligence arrived that the army stopped or retreated, the shout of "One and all!" ran with alacrity from street to street among the citizens. When news came of their advancing, the cry of "Treat and capitulate!" was no less loud and vehement. The terror of a universal pillage, and even massacre, had seized the timid inhabitants.

The army subdue the Parliament

As the army approached, Rainsborough, being sent by the general over the Thames, presented himself before Southwark and was gladly received by some soldiers who were quartered there for its defense, and who were resolved not to separate their interests from those of the army. It behooved then the Parliament to submit. On August 6, the army marched in triumph through the city but preserved the greatest order, decency, and appearance of humility. They conducted to Westminster the two speakers, who took their seats as if nothing had happened. The eleven impeached members, being accused as authors of the tumult, were expelled, and most of them retired overseas; seven peers were impeached; the mayor, one sheriff, and three aldermen were sent to the Tower; several citizens and officers of the militia were committed to prison; every deed of the Parliament from the day of the tumult till the return of the speakers was annulled; the lines about the city were leveled; the militia was restored to the Independents; regiments were quartered in Whitehall and the Mews; and the Parliament being reduced to a regular formed servitude, a day was appointed of solemn thanksgiving for the restoration of its liberty.

The Independent party among the Commons exulted in their victory. The whole authority of the nation, they imagined, was now lodged in their hands; and they had a near prospect of molding the government into that imaginary republic which had long been the object of their wishes. They had secretly concurred in all encroachments of the military upon the civil power; and they expected to impose a more perfect system of liberty on the reluctant nation by the terror of the sword. All parties—the king, the church, the Parliament, the Presbyterians—had been guilty of errors since the commencement of these disorders; but it must be confessed that this delusion of the Independents and republicans was of all others the most contrary to common sense and the established maxims of policy. Yet the leaders of that party—Vane, Fiennes, St. John, Marten—were the men in England the most celebrated for profound thought and deep contrivance; and by their well-colored pretenses and professions, they had outwitted the whole nation. To deceive such men would argue a superlative capacity in Cromwell were it not that besides the great difference there is between dark, crooked counsels and true wisdom, an exorbitant passion for rule and authority will make the most prudent overlook the dangerous consequences of such measures as seem to tend in any degree to their own advancement.

The leaders of the army, having established their dominion over the Parliament and city, ventured to bring the king to Hampton Court; and he lived for some time in that palace with an appearance of dignity and freedom. Such equability of temper did he possess that during all the variety of fortune which he underwent, no difference was perceived in his countenance or behavior; and though a prisoner in the hands of his most inveterate enemies, he supported towards all who approached him the majesty of a monarch, and that with neither less nor greater state than he had been accustomed to maintain. His manner, which was not in itself popular nor gracious, now appeared amiable from its great meekness and equality.

The Parliament renewed their applications to him and presented him with the same conditions which they had offered at Newcastle. The king declined accepting them and desired the Parliament to take the proposals of the army into consideration and make them the foundation of the public sentiment. He still entertained hopes that his negotiations with the generals would be crowned with success, though everything in that particular daily bore a worse aspect. Most historians have thought that Cromwell never was sincere in his professions; and that having by force rendered himself master of the king's person and by fair pretenses acquired the tolerance of the Royalists, he had employed these advantages to the enslaving of the Parliament; and afterwards, he thought of nothing but the establishment of his own unlimited authority, with which he deemed the restoration, and even life, of the king altogether incompatible. This opinion, so much warranted by the boundless ambition and profound dissimulation of his character, meets with ready belief; though it is more agreeable to the narrowness of human vision and the darkness of futurity to suppose that this daring usurper was guided by events and did not as yet foresee with any assurance that unparalleled greatness which he later attained. Many writers of that age have asserted that he really intended to make a private bargain with the king, a measure which carried the most plausible appearance both for his safety and advancement, but that he found insuperable difficulties in reconciling to it the wild humors of the army. The horror and antipathy of these fanatics had for many years been artfully fomented against Charles; though their principles were on all occasions easily warped and eluded by private interest, yet some coloring was requisite, and a flat contradiction to all former professions and tenets could not safely be proposed to them. It is certain at least that Cromwell made use of this reason to explain why he admitted rarely of visits from the king's friends and showed less favor than formerly to the royal cause. The agitators, he said, had rendered him odious to the army and had represented him as a traitor who, for the sake of private interest, was ready to betray the cause of God to the great enemy of piety and religion. Desperate projects too, he asserted, were secretly formed for the murder of the king; and he pretended much to dread lest all his authority and that of the commanding officers would not be able to restrain these enthusiasts from their bloody purposes.

Intelligence being daily brought to the king of menaces thrown out by the agitators, he began to think of retiring from Hampton Court and of putting himself in some place of safety. The guards were doubled upon him, the promiscuous concourse of people restrained, a more jealous care exerted in attending his person, all under color of protecting him from danger but really with a view of making him uneasy in his present situation. These artifices soon produced the intended effect. Charles, who was naturally apt to be swayed by counsel and who had not then access to any good counsel, suddenly decided to withdraw himself, though without any concerted, or at least any rational, scheme for the future disposal of his person. Attended only by Sir John Berkeley, John Ashburnham, and William Legge, he privately left Hampton Court on November 11; his escape was not discovered till nearly an hour later, when those who entered his chamber found on the table some letters directed to the Parliament, to the general, and to the officer who had attended him. All night he traveled through the forest, and he arrived next day at Titchfield, a seat of the Earl of Southampton's where the countess dowager resided, a woman of honor to whom the king knew he might safely entrust his person. Before he arrived at this place, he had gone to the seacoast and expressed great anxiety that a ship which he seemed to look for had not arrived; from that, Berkeley and Legge, who were not privy to the secret, conjectured that his intention was to transport himself overseas.

The king flies to the Isle of Wight

The king could not hope to remain long concealed at Titchfield; what measure should next be embraced was the question. Nearby lay the Isle of Wight, of which Hammond was governor. This man was entirely dependent on Cromwell. At the latter's recommendation, he had married a daughter of the famous Hampden, who during his lifetime had been an intimate friend of Cromwell's and whose memory was always respected by him. These circumstances were very unfavorable; yet because the governor was nephew to Dr. Hammond, the king's favorite chaplain, and had acquired a good reputation in the army, it was thought proper to have recourse to him in the present exigency, when no other rational expedient could be thought of. Ashburnham and Berkeley were dispatched to the island. They had orders not to inform Hammond of the place where the king was concealed till they had first obtained a promise from him not to deliver up his majesty if the Parliament and the army required him to do so, but rather to restore him to his liberty if he could not protect him. This promise, it is evident, would have been a very slender security. Yet even without exacting it, Ashburnham imprudently, if not treacherously, brought Hammond to Titchfield; the king was obliged to put himself in his hands and to attend him to Carisbrooke Castle, in the Isle of Wight, where, though received with great demonstrations of respect and duty, he was in reality a prisoner.

Lord Clarendon is positive that the king, when he fled from Hampton Court, had no intention of going to this island; and indeed, all the circumstances of that historian's narrative, which we have here followed, strongly favor this opinion. But there remains a letter of Charles's to the Earl of Lanark, secretary of Scotland, in which he plainly intimates that that measure was voluntarily embraced, and even insinuates that if he had thought proper, he might have been in Jersey or any other place of safety. Perhaps he still confided in the promises of the generals and flattered himself that if he were removed from the fury of the agitators, by which his life was immediately threatened, they would execute what they had so often promised in his favor.

Whatever may be the truth in this matter—for it is impossible fully to ascertain the truth—Charles never took a weaker step, nor one more agreeable to Cromwell and all his enemies. He was now lodged in a place removed from his partisans, at the disposal of the army, from where it would be very difficult to deliver him either by force or artifice. And though it was always in the power of Cromwell to have sent him there whenever he pleased, yet such a measure without the king's consent would have been very invidious, if not attended with some danger. That the king would voluntarily throw himself into the snare and thereby gratify his implacable persecutors was to them an incident singularly fortunate, and one that proved in the event very fatal to him.

Cromwell, being now entirely master of the Parliament and free from all anxiety with regard to the custody of the king's person, applied himself seriously to quell those disorders in the army which he himself had so artfully raised and so successfully employed against both king and Parliament. In order to engage the troops into a rebellion against their masters, he had encouraged an arrogant spirit among the inferior officers and private men; the camp in many respects carried more the appearance of civil liberty than of military obedience. The troops themselves were formed into a kind of republic; and the plans of imaginary republics for the settlement of the state were every day the topics of conversation among these armed legislators. Royalty it was agreed to abolish, nobility must be set aside, even all ranks of men be leveled, and a universal equality of property as well as of power be introduced among the citizens. The saints, they said, were the salt of the earth; an entire parity had place among the elect; and by the same rule that the apostles were exalted from the most ignoble professions, the meanest sentinel, if enlightened by the Spirit, was entitled to equal regard with the greatest commander. In order to wean the soldiers from these licentious maxims, Cromwell had issued orders for discontinuing the meetings of the agitators; and he pretended to pay entire obedience to the Parliament, whom, being now fully reduced to subjection, he purposed to make for the future the instruments of his authority. But the Levelers—for so that party in the army was called—having experienced the sweets of dominion, would not so easily be deprived of it. They secretly continued their meetings; they asserted that their officers, as much as any part of the church or state, needed reformation; several regiments joined in seditious remonstrances and petitions; separate rendezvous were concerted; and everything tended to anarchy and confusion. But this distemper was soon cured by the rough but dexterous hand of Cromwell. He chose the opportunity of a review, that he might display the greater boldness and spread the terror the wider. He seized the ringleaders before their companions, held in the field a council of war, shot one mutineer instantly, and struck such dread into the rest that they presently threw down the symbols of sedition which they had displayed and from then on returned to their wonted discipline and obedience.

Cromwell had great deference for the counsels of Ireton, a man who, having grafted the soldier on the lawyer, the statesman on the saint, had adopted such principles as were fitted to introduce the severest tyranny, while they seemed to encourage the most unbounded license, in human society. Fierce in his nature, though probably sincere in his intentions, he purposed by arbitrary power to establish liberty; in prosecution of his imagined religious purposes, he thought himself dispensed from all the ordinary rules of morality by which inferior mortals must allow themselves to be governed. From his suggestion, Cromwell secretly called at Windsor a council of the chief officers in order to deliberate concerning the settlement of the nation and the future disposal of the king's person. In this conference—which commenced with devout prayers poured forth by Cromwell himself and other inspired persons (for the officers of this army received inspiration with their commissions)—was first opened the daring and unheard-of counsel of bringing the king to justice and of punishing by a judicial sentence their sovereign for his claimed tyranny and maladministration. They knew that while Charles lived, even though restrained to the closest prison, conspiracies and insurrections would never be lacking in favor of a prince who was so extremely revered and beloved by his own party, and whom the nation in general began to regard with great affection and compassion. To murder him privately was exposed to the imputation of injustice and cruelty, aggravated by the baseness of such a crime; and every odious epithet of "traitor" and "assassin" would be indisputably ascribed by the general voice of mankind to the actors in such a villainy. Some unexpected procedure must be attempted which would astonish the world by its novelty, would bear the semblance of justice, and would cover its barbarity by the audaciousness of the enterprise. Striking in with the fanatical notions of the entire equality of mankind, it would ensure the devoted obedience of the army and serve as a general engagement [attack] against the royal family, whom they would so heinously affront and injure by their open and united deed.

This measure, therefore, being secretly resolved on, it was requisite to make the Parliament adopt it by degrees, to conduct them from violence to violence, till this last act of atrocious iniquity would seem almost wholly inevitable. The king, in order to remove those fears and jealousies which were perpetually pleaded as reasons for every invasion of the constitution, had offered by a message sent from Carisbrooke Castle to resign the power of the militia and the nomination to all the great offices during his own life, provided that these prerogatives would revert to the Crown after his demise. But the Parliament acted entirely as victors and enemies; in all their transactions with him, they no longer paid any regard to equity or reason. At the instigation of the Independents and army, they neglected this offer and framed four proposals which they sent him as preliminaries; before they would deign to treat, they demanded his positive assent to all of them. By one, he was required to invest the Parliament with the military power for twenty years, together with an authority to levy whatever money would be necessary for exercising it; and even after the twenty years elapsed, they reserved a right of resuming the same authority whenever they would declare the safety of the kingdom to require it. By the second, he was to recall all his proclamations and declarations against the Parliament and acknowledge that assembly to have taken arms in their just and necessary defense. By the third, he was to annul all the acts and void all the patents of peerage which had passed the great seal since it had been carried from London by Lord Keeper Littleton, and at the same time, renounce for the future the power of making peers without consent of Parliament. By the fourth, he was to give the two houses power to adjourn as they thought proper; this demand, seemingly of no great importance, was contrived by the Independents so that they might be able to remove the Parliament to places where it would remain in perpetual subjection to the army.

The king regarded as unusual and exorbitant the pretension that he would make such concessions while not

1648

secure of any settlement and would blindly trust his enemies for the conditions which they were afterwards to grant him. He required, therefore, a personal treaty [conference] with the Parliament and desired that all the terms on both sides be adjusted before any concession on either side be insisted on. The republican party in the house pretended to take fire at this answer; and they openly inveighed in violent terms against the person and government of the king, whose name till then had commonly in all debates been mentioned with some degree of reverence. Ireton, seeming to speak the sense of the army in the name of many thousand godly men who had ventured their lives in defense of the Parliament, said that the king had refused safety and protection to his people by denying the four bills; that their obedience to him was but a reciprocal duty for his protection of them; and that as he had failed on his part, they were freed from all obligations to allegiance and must settle the nation without consulting any longer so misguided a prince. Cromwell, after giving an ample testimonial of the valor, good affections, and godliness of the army, appended that it was expected the Parliament would guide and defend the kingdom by their own power and resolutions and not accustom the people any longer to expect safety and government from an obstinate man whose heart God had hardened; and that those who had till then defended the Parliament from so many dangers at the expense of their blood would still continue with fidelity and courage to protect them against all opposition in this vigorous measure. "Teach them not," added he, "by your neglecting your own safety and that of the kingdom (in which theirs too is involved), to imagine themselves betrayed, and their interests abandoned to the rage and malice of an irreconcilable enemy, whom, for your sake, they have dared to provoke. Beware,"—and at these words, he laid his hand on his sword—"beware, lest despair cause them to seek safety by some other means than by adhering to you, who know not how to consult your own safety." Such arguments prevailed, though ninety-one members had still the courage to oppose. It was voted on January 15 that no more addresses be made to the king, nor any letters or messages be received from him, and that it be treason for anyone, without leave of the two houses, to have any intercourse with him. The Lords concurred in the same ordinance.

By this Vote of No Addresses—so it was called—the king was in reality dethroned, and the whole constitution formally overthrown. So violent a measure was supported by a declaration of the Commons no less violent. The blackest calumnies were there thrown upon the king, such as even in their famous Remonstrance they thought proper to omit as incredible and extravagant: the poisoning of his father, the betraying of La Rochelle, the contriving of the Irish massacre. By blasting his fame, had that injury been in their power, they formed a very proper prelude to the executing of violence on his person.

No sooner had the king refused his assent to the four bills than Hammond, by orders from the army, removed all his servants, cut off his correspondence with his friends, and shut him up in close confinement. The king later showed to Sir Philip Warwick a decrepit old man who, he said, was employed to kindle his fire and was the best company he enjoyed during the several months that this rigorous confinement lasted. No amusement was allowed him, nor society which might relieve his anxious thoughts. To be speedily poisoned or assassinated was the only prospect which he had every moment before his eyes; for he entertained no fear of a judicial sentence and execution, an event of which no history before then furnished an example. Meanwhile, the Parliament was very industrious in publishing from time to time the intelligence which they received from Hammond—how cheerful the king was, how pleased with everyone that approached him, how satisfied in his present condition—as if the view of such benignity and constancy would have been more suited to allay than inflame the general compassion of the people. The great source from which the king derived consolation amidst all his calamities was undoubtedly religion, a principle which in him seems to have contained nothing fierce or gloomy, nothing which enraged him against his adversaries or terrified him with the dismal prospect of futurity. While everything around him bore a hostile aspect, while friends, family, and relations whom he passionately loved were placed at a distance and unable to serve him, he reposed himself with confidence in the arms of that Being who penetrates and sustains all nature, and whose severities, if received with piety and resignation, he regarded as the surest pledges of unexhausted favor.

Second civil war

The Parliament and army, meanwhile, enjoyed in turmoil that power which they had obtained with so much violence and injustice. Combinations and conspiracies, they were aware, were everywhere forming around them; and Scotland, from where the king's cause had received the first fatal disaster, seemed now to promise it support and assistance.

Before the surrender of the king's person at Newcastle, and much more since that event, the subjects of discontent had been daily multiplying between the two kingdoms. The Independents, who began to prevail, took all occasions of mortifying the Scots, whom the Presbyterians looked on with the greatest affection and veneration. When the Scottish commissioners who, joined to a committee of English Lords and Commons, had managed the war were ready to depart, it was proposed in Parliament to give them thanks for their civilities and good offices. The Independents insisted that the words "good offices" be struck out; and thus, the whole brotherly friendship and intimate alliance with the Scots resolved itself into an acknowledgment of their being well-bred gentlemen.

The advance of the army to London, the subjection of the Parliament, the seizing of the king at Holdenby and his confinement in Carisbrooke Castle, were so many blows keenly felt by the Scots as threatening the final overthrow of Presbytery, to which they were so passionately devoted. The Covenant was profanely called in the House of Commons an almanac out of date, and that impiety, though complained of, had passed uncensured. Instead of being able to determine and establish orthodoxy by the sword and by penal statutes, they saw the sectarian army, who were absolute masters, claim an unbounded liberty of conscience, which the Presbyterians regarded with the utmost abhorrence. All the violences put on the king they loudly blamed as repugnant to the Covenant, by which they stood pledged to defend his royal person. And those very actions of which they themselves had been guilty they denominated treason and rebellion when executed by an opposite party.

The Earls of Loudoun, Lauderdale, and Lanark, who were sent to London, protested against the four bills as containing too great a diminution of the king's civil power and providing no security for religion. They complained that notwithstanding this protestation, the bills were still insisted on, contrary to the Solemn League and to the treaty between the two nations. And when they accompanied the English commissioners to the Isle of Wight, they secretly formed a treaty with the king for arming Scotland in his favor.

Invasion from Scotland

Three parties at that time prevailed in Scotland: The Royalists, who insisted upon the restoration of the king's authority without any regard to religious sects or tenets; of these, Montrose, though absent, was regarded as the head. The rigid Presbyterians, who hated the king even more than they abhorred toleration and who resolved to give him no assistance till he would subscribe the Covenant; these were governed by Argyll. The moderate Presbyterians, who endeavored to reconcile the interests of religion and of the Crown and who hoped, by supporting the Presbyterian party in England, to suppress the sectarian army and to reinstate the Parliament as well as the king in their just freedom and authority; the two brothers Hamilton and Lanark were leaders of this party.

When Pendennis Castle was surrendered to the parliamentary army, Hamilton, who then obtained his liberty, returned into Scotland; and being generously impelled to remember ancient favors more than recent injuries, he immediately embraced the protection of the royal cause with zeal and success. He obtained a vote from the Scottish Parliament to arm forty thousand men in support of the king's authority and to call over a considerable body under Monro, who commanded the Scottish forces in Ulster. And though he openly protested that the Covenant was the foundation of all his measures, he secretly entered into correspondence with the English Royalists Sir Marmaduke Langdale and Sir Philip Musgrave, who had levied considerable forces in the north of England.

The General Assembly, who sat at the same time and was guided by Argyll, dreaded the consequences of these measures and foresaw that the opposite party, if successful, would effect the restoration of monarchy without the establishment of Presbytery in England. To join the king before he had subscribed the Covenant was, in their eyes, to restore him to his honor before Christ had obtained his; and they thundered out anathemas against everyone who paid obedience to the Parliament. Two supreme independent judicatures were erected in the kingdom, one threatening the people with damnation and eternal torments, the other with imprisonment, banishment, and military execution. The people were distracted in their choice; and the armament of Hamilton's party, though seconded by all the civil power, went on but slowly. The Royalists he would not as yet allow to join him lest he might give offense to the ecclesiastical party, though he secretly promised them trust and preferment as soon as his army advanced into England.

While the Scots were making preparations for the invasion of England, every part of that kingdom was agitated with tumults, insurrections, conspiracies, discontents. It is seldom that the people gain anything by revolutions in government, because the new settlement, jealous and insecure, must commonly be supported with more expense and severity than the old; but on no occasion was the truth of this maxim more keenly felt than in the present situation of England. Complaints against the oppression of ship money and against the tyranny of the Star Chamber had roused the people to arms; and having gained a complete victory over the Crown, they found themselves loaded with a multiplicity of taxes formerly unknown, and scarcely an appearance of law and liberty remained in the administration. The Presbyterians, who had chiefly supported the war, were enraged to find the prize, just when it seemed within their reach, snatched by violence from them. The Royalists, disappointed in their expectations by the cruel treatment which the king now received from the army, were strongly animated to restore him to liberty and to recover the advantages which they had unfortunately lost. All orders of men were inflamed with indignation at seeing the military prevail over the civil power and both king and Parliament reduced to subjection by a mercenary army. Many persons of family and distinction had from the beginning of the war adhered to the Parliament; but all these were deprived of authority by the new party, and every office was entrusted to the most ignoble part of the nation. A base populace exalted above their superiors, hypocrites exercising iniquity under the visor of religion: these circumstances promised not much liberty or lenity to the people, and these were now found united in the same usurped and illegal administration.

Though the whole nation seemed to combine in their hatred of military tyranny, the ends which the several parties pursued were so different that little concert was observed in their insurrections. Laugharne, Poyer, and Powell, Presbyterian officers who commanded bodies of troops in Wales, were the first that declared themselves; and they drew together a considerable army in those parts which were extremely devoted to the royal cause. An insurrection was raised in Kent by young Hales and the Earl of Norwich. Lord Capell, Sir Charles Lucas, and Sir George Lisle excited commotions in Essex. The Earl of Holland, who had several times changed sides since the commencement of the civil wars, endeavored to assemble forces in Surrey. Pontefract Castle, in Yorkshire, was surprised by Morris. Langdale and Musgrave were in arms and masters of Berwick and Carlisle in the north.

In what seemed the most dangerous circumstance, the general spirit of discontent had seized the fleet. Seventeen ships lying in the mouth of the Thames declared for the king; and putting Rainsborough, their admiral, ashore, they sailed over to Holland, where the Prince of Wales took the command of them.

The English Royalists exclaimed loudly against Hamilton's delays, which they attributed to a refined policy in the Scots, as if their intentions were that all the king's party should first be suppressed and the victory remain solely to the Presbyterians. Hamilton, with better reason, complained of the precipitate humor of the English Royalists, who by their ill-timed insurrections forced him to march his army before his levies were completed or his preparations in any forwardness.

No commotions beyond a tumult of the apprentices, which was soon suppressed, were raised in London; the terror of the army kept the citizens in subjection. The Parliament was so overawed that they declared the Scots to be enemies and all who joined them traitors. Ninety members, however, of the lower house had the courage to dissent from this vote.

Cromwell and the military council prepared themselves with vigor and conduct for defense. The establishment of the army was at this time twenty-six thousand men; but the regiments were greatly augmented by enlisting supernumeraries, and they commonly consisted of more than double their stated complement. Colonel Horton first attacked the rebellious troops in Wales and gave them a considerable defeat. The remnants of the vanquished threw themselves into Pembroke; they were there closely besieged and soon after taken by Cromwell. Lambert was opposed to Langdale and Musgrave in the north and gained advantages over them. Sir Michael Livesey defeated the Earl of Holland at Kingston, and pursuing his victory, took him prisoner at St. Neots. Fairfax, having routed the Kentish Royalists at Maidstone, followed the broken army; and when they joined the Royalists of Essex and threw themselves into Colchester, he laid siege to that place, which defended itself to the last extremity. A new fleet was manned and sent out under the command of Warwick to oppose the mutinous ships of which the prince had taken the command.

While the forces were employed in all quarters, the Parliament regained its liberty and began to act with its wonted courage and spirit. The members who had withdrawn from terror of the army returned; and infusing boldness into their companions, they restored to the Presbyterian party the ascendant which it had formerly lost. The eleven impeached members were recalled, and the vote by which they were expelled was reversed. The Vote of No Addresses too was repealed, and commissioners—five peers and ten commoners—were sent to Newport, in the Isle of Wight, in order to treat with the king. He was allowed to summon several of his friends and old counselors so that he might have their advice in this important transaction. The theologians on both sides, armed with their syllogisms and quotations, attended as auxiliaries. By them the flame had first been raised, and their appearance was but a bad omen of its extinction. Any other instruments seemed better adapted for a treaty of pacification.

Treaty of Newport

When the king presented himself to this company on September 18, a great and perceptible alteration was remarked in his aspect from what it appeared the year before, when he resided at Hampton Court. The moment his servants had been removed, he had laid aside all care of his person and had allowed his beard and hair to grow and to hang disheveled and neglected. His hair had become almost entirely gray, either from the decline of years or from that load of sorrows under which he labored and which, though borne with constancy, preyed inwardly on his aware and tender mind. His friends, and perhaps even his enemies, beheld with compassion "that gray and discrowned head," as he himself termed it in a copy of verses, which the truth of the sentiment rather than any elegance of expression renders very pathetic. Having in vain endeavored by courage to defend his throne from his armed adversaries, it now behooved him by reasoning and persuasion to save some fragments of it from these peaceful, and no less implacable, negotiators.

The vigor of the king's mind, notwithstanding the seeming decline of his body, here appeared unbroken and undecayed. The parliamentary commissioners would allow none of his Council to be present and refused to enter into reasoning with any but himself. During the transactions of two months, he alone was obliged to maintain the argument against fifteen men of the greatest talents and capacity in both houses; and no advantage was ever obtained over him. This was the scene above all others in which he was qualified to excel. A quick conception, a cultivated understanding, a chaste conclusion, a dignified manner: by these accomplishments he triumphed in all discussions of cool and temperate reasoning. "The king is much changed," said the Earl of Salisbury to Sir Philip Warwick. "He is extremely improved of late." "No," replied Sir Philip, "he was always so. But you are now at last sensible [aware] of it." Sir Henry Vane, discoursing with his fellow commissioners, drew an argument from the king's uncommon abilities that the terms of pacification must be rendered more strict and rigid. But Charles's capacity shone not equally in action as in reasoning.

The first point insisted on by the parliamentary commissioners was the king's recalling all his proclamations and declarations against the Parliament and the acknowledging that they had taken arms in their own defense. He frankly offered the former concession but long scrupled the latter. The falsehood as well as indignity of that acknowledgment begat in his breast an extreme reluctance against it. The king had in some particulars of moment no doubt invaded, from a seeming necessity, the privileges of his people; but having renounced all claim to these usurped powers, having confessed his errors, and having repaired every breach in the constitution and even erected new ramparts in order to secure it, he could no longer be represented as the aggressor at the commencement of the war. However it might be claimed that the former display of his arbitrary inclinations, or rather his monarchical principles, rendered an offensive or preventive war in the Parliament prudent and reasonable, it could never in any propriety of speech make it be termed a defensive one. But the Parliament, aware that the letter of the law condemned them as rebels and traitors, deemed this point absolutely necessary for their future security; and the king, finding that peace could be obtained on no other terms, at last yielded to it. He only entered a protest, which was admitted, that no concession made by him would be valid unless the whole treaty of pacification were concluded.

He agreed that the Parliament would retain for twenty years the power over the militia and army, and that of levying what money they pleased for their support. He even yielded to them the right of resuming this authority at any time afterwards, whenever they would declare such a resumption necessary for public safety. In effect, the important power of the sword was forever ravished from him and his successors.

He agreed that all the great offices would be filled by both houses of Parliament for twenty years. He relinquished to them the entire government of Ireland and the conduct of the war there. He renounced the power of the wards and accepted £100,000 a year in lieu of it. He acknowledged the validity of their great seal and gave up his own. He abandoned the power of creating peers without consent of Parliament. And he agreed that all the debts contracted in order to support the war against him would be paid by the people.

So great were the alterations made on the English constitution by this treaty that the king said, not without reason, that he would have been more an enemy to his people by these concessions, could he have prevented them, than by any other action of his life.

Of all the demands of the Parliament, Charles refused only two. Though he relinquished almost every power of the Crown, he would neither give up his friends to punishment nor desert what he deemed his religious duty. The severe repentance which he had undergone for abandoning Strafford had no doubt confirmed him in the resolution never again to be guilty of a like error. His long solitude and severe afflictions had contributed to firmly fix him the more in those religious principles which always had a considerable influence over him. His desire, however, of finishing an accommodation induced him to go as far in both these particulars as he thought in any way consistent with his duty.

The estates of the Royalists being at that time almost entirely under sequestration, Charles, who could give them no protection, consented that they would pay such compositions as they and the Parliament would agree on; he only begged that they might be made as moderate as possible. He had not the disposal of offices, so it seemed but a small sacrifice to consent that a certain number of his friends would be rendered incapable of public employments. But when the Parliament demanded a bill of attainder and banishment against seven persons—the Marquess of Newcastle, Lord Digby, Lord Byron, Sir Marmaduke Langdale, Sir Richard Grenville, Sir Francis Doddington, and Judge Jenkins—the king absolutely refused compliance; their banishment for a limited time he was willing to agree to.

Religion was the fatal point about which the differences had arisen; and of all others, it was the least susceptible of composition or moderation between the contending parties. The Parliament insisted on the establishment of Presbytery, the sale of the chapter lands, the abolition of all forms of prayer, and strict laws against Catholics. The king offered to retrench everything which he did not deem of apostolic institution. He was willing to abolish archbishops, deans, prebends, canons. He offered that the chapter lands would be let at low leases for ninety-nine years. He consented that the present church government would continue for three years. After that time, he did not require anything to be restored to bishops but the power of ordination, and even that power to be exercised by advice of the presbyters. If the Parliament, upon the expiration of that period, still insisted on their demand, all other branches of episcopal jurisdiction would be abolished, and a new form of church government established by common consent. He was willing to renounce the Book of Common Prayer but required the liberty of using some other liturgy in his own chapel; a demand which, though seemingly reasonable, was positively refused by the Parliament.

In the dispute on these articles, one is not surprised that two of the parliamentary theologians would tell the king, "That if he did not consent to the utter abolition of episcopacy, he would be damned." But it is not without some indignation that we read the following vote of the Lords and Commons: "The houses, out of their detestation to that abominable idolatry used in the mass, do declare that they cannot admit of, or consent unto, any such indulgence in any law, as is desired by his majesty, for exempting the queen and her family from the penalties to be enacted against the exercise of the mass." The treaty of marriage, the regard to the queen's sex and high station, even common humanity: all considerations were undervalued in comparison with their bigoted prejudices.

It was manifestly the interest both of king and Parliament to finish their treaty with all expedition and endeavor by their combined force to resist, if possible, the usurping fury of the army. It seemed even the interest of the Parliament to leave in the king's hand a considerable share of authority, by which he might be enabled to protect them and himself from so dangerous an enemy. But the terms on which they insisted were so rigorous that the king, fearing no worse from the most implacable enemies, was in no haste to come to a conclusion. And so great was the bigotry on both sides that they were willing to sacrifice the greatest civil interests rather than relinquish the most minute of their theological contentions. From these causes, assisted by the artifice of the Independents, the treaty [conference] was spun out to such a length that the invasions and insurrections were everywhere subdued, and the army had leisure to execute their violent and sanguinary purposes.

Civil war and invasion repressed

Hamilton, having entered England with a numerous though undisciplined army, dared not unite his forces with those of Langdale because the English Royalists had refused to take the Covenant; and the Scottish Presbyterians, though engaged for the king, refused to join them on any other terms. The two armies marched together, though at some distance; nor could even the approach of the parliamentary army under Cromwell oblige the Covenanters to consult their own safety by a close union with the Royalists. When principles are so absurd and so destructive of human society, it may safely be averred that the more sincere and disinterested they are, the more ridiculous and odious they become.

Cromwell feared not to oppose eight thousand men to the numerous armies of twenty thousand commanded by Hamilton and Langdale. He attacked the latter by surprise near Preston, in Lancashire; though the Royalists made a brave resistance, they were not succored in time by their confederates and were almost entirely cut in pieces. Hamilton was next attacked, put to rout, and pursued to Uttoxeter, where he surrendered himself prisoner. Cromwell followed his advantage, and marching into Scotland with a considerable body, joined Argyll, who was also in arms; and having suppressed Lanark, Monro, and other moderate Presbyterians, he placed the power entirely in the hands of the violent party. The ecclesiastical authority, exalted above the civil, exercised the severest vengeance on all who had a share in Hamilton's engagement, as it was called; nor could any of that party recover trust, or even live in safety, but by doing solemn and public penance for taking arms by authority of Parliament in defense of their lawful sovereign.

The chancellor, Loudoun, who had at first supported Hamilton's enterprise, being terrified with the menaces of the clergy, had some time before gone over to the other party; and he now openly in the church—though invested with the highest civil rank in the kingdom—did penance for his obedience to the Parliament, which he termed a "carnal self-seeking." He accompanied his penance with so many tears and such pathetic addresses to the people for their prayers in this, his uttermost sorrow and distress, that a universal weeping and lamentation took place among the deluded audience.

The loan of great sums of money, often to the ruin of families, was exacted from all who lay under any suspicion of favoring the king's party, though their conduct had been ever so inoffensive. This was a device fallen upon by the ruling party in order, as they said, to reach "heart malignants." Never in Britain was known a more severe and arbitrary government than was generally exercised by the patrons of liberty in both kingdoms.

The siege of Colchester terminated in a manner no less unfortunate for the royal cause than had Hamilton's engagement. After suffering the utmost extremities of famine, after feeding on the vilest aliments, the garrison desired at last to capitulate. Fairfax required them to surrender at discretion; and he gave such an explanation to these terms as to reserve to himself power, if he pleased, to put them all instantly to the sword. The officers endeavored, though in vain, to persuade the soldiers to break through by making a vigorous sally, at least to sell their lives as dearly as possible. They were obliged to accept the conditions offered; and Fairfax—instigated by Ireton, to whom Cromwell in his absence had consigned over the government of the passive general—seized Sir Charles Lucas and Sir George Lisle and resolved to make them instant sacrifices to military justice. This unusual severity was loudly exclaimed against by all the prisoners. Lord Capell, fearless of danger, reproached Ireton with it; and he challenged him to exercise the same impartial vengeance on all of them, as they were all engaged in the same honorable cause. Lucas was first shot, and he himself gave orders to fire with the same alacrity as if he had commanded a platoon of his own soldiers. Lisle instantly ran and kissed the dead body, then cheerfully presented himself to a like fate. Thinking that the soldiers destined for his execution stood at too great a distance, he called to them to come nearer. One of them replied, "I'll warrant you, sir, we'll hit you." He answered, smiling, "Friends, I have been nearer you when you have missed me." Thus perished this generous spirit, not less beloved for his modesty and humanity than esteemed for his courage and military conduct.

Soon after, a gentleman appeared in the king's presence clothed in mourning for Sir Charles Lucas. That humane prince, suddenly recollecting the hard fate of his friends, paid them a tribute which none of his own unparalleled misfortunes ever extorted from him: he dissolved into a flood of tears.

The king seized again by the army

By these multiple successes of the army, they had subdued all their enemies; and none remained but the helpless king and Parliament to oppose their violent measures. From Cromwell's suggestion, a remonstrance was drawn by the council of general officers and sent to the Parliament. They there complained of the treaty with the king; demanded his punishment for the blood spilt during the war; required a dissolution of the present Parliament and a more equal representative for the future; and asserted that though servants, they were entitled to represent these important points to their masters, who were themselves no better than servants and trustees of the people. At the same time, they advanced with the army to Windsor and sent Colonel Eyre to seize the king's person at Newport and convey him to Hurst Castle nearby, where he was detained in strict confinement.

This measure being foreseen some time before, the king was exhorted to make his escape, which was conceived to be very easy. But having given his word to the Parliament not to attempt the recovery of his liberty during the treaty and three weeks after, he would not by any persuasion be induced to hazard the reproach of violating that promise. In vain was it urged that a promise given to the Parliament could no longer be binding, since they could no longer afford him protection from violence threatened him by other persons to whom he was bound by no tie or engagement. The king would indulge no refinements of casuistry, however plausible, in such delicate subjects; he was resolved that whatever depredations fortune might commit upon him, she never would bereave him of his honor.

The Parliament did not lose courage, notwithstanding the danger with which they were so nearly menaced. Though without any plan for resisting military usurpations, they resolved to withstand them to the uttermost and to bring on a violent and visible subversion of government rather than lend their authority to those illegal and sanguinary measures which were projected. They set aside the remonstrance of the army without deigning to answer it; they voted the seizing of the king's person to be without their consent and sent a message to the general to know by what authority that enterprise had been executed; and they issued orders that the army not advance any nearer to London.

Holles, the present leader of the Presbyterians, was a man of unconquerable intrepidity; and many others of that party seconded his magnanimous spirit. It was proposed by them that the generals and principal officers be proclaimed traitors by the Parliament for their disobedience and usurpations.

But the Parliament was dealing with men who would not be frightened by words nor retarded by any scrupulous delicacy. The generals, under the name of Fairfax (for he still allowed them to employ his name), marched the army to London, and placing guards in Whitehall, the Mews, St. James's, Durham House, Covent Garden, and Palace Yard, surrounded the Parliament with their hostile armaments.

The Parliament, destitute of all hopes of prevailing, retained, however, courage to resist. They attempted, in the face of the army, to close their treaty with the king; and though they had formerly voted his concessions with regard to the church and delinquents to be unsatisfactory, they now took into consideration the final resolution with regard to the whole. After a violent debate of three days, it was carried in the House of Commons by a majority of 129 against 83 that the king's concessions were a foundation for the houses to proceed upon in the settlement of the kingdom.

The house purged

Next day, December 6, when the Commons were to meet, Colonel Thomas Pride, formerly a drayman, had environed the house with two regiments; directed by Lord Grey of Groby, he seized in the passage forty-one members of the Presbyterian party and sent them to a low room which passed by the appellation of "hell," from where they were afterwards carried to several inns. Over one hundred sixty members more were excluded; none were allowed to enter but the most furious and the most determined of the Independents, and these did not exceed fifty or sixty. This invasion of the Parliament commonly passed under the name of "Colonel Pride's Purge"; so much disposed was the nation to make merry with the dethroning of those members who had violently arrogated the whole authority of government and deprived the king of his legal prerogatives.

The subsequent proceedings of the Parliament—if this diminutive assembly deserves that honorable name—retain not the least appearance of law, equity, or freedom. They instantly reversed the former vote and declared the king's concessions unsatisfactory. They determined that no member absent at this last vote would be received till he subscribed it as agreeable to his judgment. They renewed their former Vote of No Addresses. And they committed to prison Sir William Waller, Sir John Clotworthy, Generals Massey, Brown, and Copley, and other leaders of the Presbyterians. These men, by their credit and authority, which was then very high, had at the commencement of the war supported the Parliament and thereby prepared the way for the greatness of the present leaders, who at that time were of small account in the nation.

The excluded members published a paper containing a narrative of the violence which had been exercised upon them and a protestation that all acts were void which from that time had been transacted in the House of Commons; the remaining members countered it with a declaration in which they pronounced it false, scandalous, seditious, and tending to the destruction of the visible and fundamental government of the kingdom.

These sudden and violent revolutions held the whole nation in terror and astonishment. Every man dreaded to be trampled underfoot in the contention between those mighty powers which disputed for the sovereignty of the state. Many began to withdraw their effects overseas. Foreigners hesitated to give any credit to a people so torn by domestic faction and oppressed by military usurpation. Even the internal commerce of the kingdom began to stagnate. And in order to remedy these growing evils, the generals, in the name of the army, published a declaration in which they expressed their resolution to support law and justice.

The more to quiet the minds of men, the council of officers took into consideration a scheme called "The Agreement of the People," being the plan of a republic to be substituted in the place of that government which they had so violently pulled in pieces. Many parts of this scheme for correcting the inequalities of the representative are plausible, had the nation been disposed to receive it or had the army intended to impose it. Other parts are too perfect for human nature and savor strongly of that fanatical spirit so prevalent throughout the kingdom.

The height of all iniquity and fanatical extravagance yet remained: the public trial and execution of their sovereign. To this end was every measure precipitated by the zealous Independents. The parliamentary leaders of that party had intended that the army themselves should execute that daring enterprise; and they deemed so irregular and lawless a deed best fitted to such irregular and lawless instruments. But the generals were too wise to load themselves singly with the infamy which they knew must attend an action so shocking to the general sentiments of mankind. They were resolved that the Parliament should share with them the reproach of a measure which was thought requisite for the advancement of their common ends of safety and ambition. In the House of Commons, therefore, a committee was appointed to bring in a charge against the king. On their report a vote passed declaring it treason in a king to levy war against his Parliament and appointing a High Court of Justice to try Charles for this newly invented treason. This vote was sent up to the House of Peers.

The House of Peers, during the civil wars, had all along been of small account; but it had lately, since the king's fall, become totally contemptible, and very few members would submit to the mortification of attending it. It happened that day to be fuller than usual, and they were assembled to the number of sixteen. Without one dissenting voice and almost without deliberation, they instantly rejected the vote of the lower house and adjourned themselves for ten days, hoping that this delay would be able to retard the furious career of the Commons.

The Commons were not to be stopped by so small an obstacle. On January 4, having first established, "That the people are the origin of all just power"—a principle which is noble in itself and seems beautiful and attractive but is belied by all history and experience—they next declared that the Commons of England, assembled in Parliament, being chosen by the people and representing them, are the supreme authority of the nation, and that whatever is

1649

enacted and declared to be law by the Commons has the force of law without the consent of king or House of Peers. The ordinance for the trial of Charles Stuart, king of England (so they called him), was again read and unanimously assented to.

Among those regicides, the pretenses of sanctity were augmented in proportion to the enormity of the violences and usurpations. "Should any one have voluntarily proposed," said Cromwell in the house, "to bring the king to punishment, I should have regarded him as the greatest traitor; but since Providence and necessity have cast us upon it, I will pray to God for a blessing on your counsels; though I am not prepared to give you any advice on this important occasion. Even I myself," he added, "when I was lately offering up petitions for his majesty's restoration, felt my tongue cleave to the roof of my mouth, and considered this preternatural movement as the answer which heaven, having rejected the king, had sent to my supplications."

A woman of Hertfordshire, illuminated by prophetical visions, desired admittance into the military council; she communicated to the officers a revelation which assured them that their measures were consecrated from above and ratified by a heavenly sanction. This intelligence gave them great comfort and much confirmed them in their present resolutions.

Colonel Harrison, the son of a butcher and the most furious enthusiast in the army, was sent with a strong party to conduct the king to London. At Windsor, the Duke of Hamilton, who was there detained a prisoner, was admitted into the king's presence; and falling on his knees, he passionately exclaimed, "My dear master!" "I have indeed been so to you," replied Charles, embracing him. No further intercourse was allowed between them. The king was instantly hurried away. Hamilton long followed him with his eyes all suffused in tears; and he prognosticated that in this short salutation, he had given the last adieu to his sovereign and his friend.

Charles himself was sure that the end of his life was now approaching; but notwithstanding all the preparations which were being made and the intelligence which he received, he could not even yet believe that his enemies really meant to conclude their violences by a public trial and execution. A private assassination he every moment looked for; and though Harrison assured him that his apprehensions were entirely groundless, it was by that catastrophe, so frequent with dethroned princes, that he expected to terminate his life. In appearance as well as in reality, the king was now dethroned. All the exterior symbols of sovereignty were withdrawn, and his attendants had orders to serve him without ceremony. At first, he was shocked with instances of rudeness and familiarity, to which he had been so little accustomed. "Nothing so contemptible as a despised prince!" was the reflection which they suggested to him. But he soon reconciled his mind to this, as he had done to his other calamities.

The king's trial

All the circumstances of the trial were now adjusted, and the High Court of Justice fully constituted. It consisted of 133 persons as named by the Commons, but there scarcely ever sat more than 70; so difficult was it, notwithstanding the blindness of prejudice and the allurements of interest, to engage men of any name or quality in that criminal measure. Cromwell, Ireton, Harrison, and the chief officers of the army, most of them of mean birth, were members, together with some of the lower house and some citizens of London. The twelve judges were at first appointed in the number; but as they had affirmed that it was contrary to all the ideas of English law to try for treason the king, by whose authority all accusations for treason must necessarily be conducted, their names were afterwards struck out, as were those of some peers. Bradshaw, a lawyer, was chosen president. Cook was appointed solicitor for the people of England. Dorislaus, Steele, and Aske were named assistants. The court sat in Westminster Hall.

It is remarkable that when the crier, in calling over the court, pronounced the name of Fairfax, which had been inserted in the number, a voice came from one of the spectators and cried, "He has more wit than to be here." When the charge was read against the king, "In the name of the people of England," the same voice exclaimed, "Not a tenth part of them." When Axtell, the officer who guarded the court, gave orders to fire into the box from where these insolent speeches came, it was discovered that Lady Fairfax was there, and that it was she who had had the courage to utter them. She was a person of noble extraction, daughter of Horace, Lord Vere of Tilbury; but being seduced by the violence of the times, she had long seconded her husband's zeal against the royal cause, and was now struck with abhorrence, as was he, at the fatal and unexpected consequence of all his boasted victories.

The pomp, the dignity, the ceremony of this transaction corresponded to the greatest conception that is suggested in the annals of humankind: the delegates of a great people sitting in judgment upon their supreme magistrate and trying him for his misgovernment and breach of trust. The solicitor, in the name of the Commons, represented that Charles Stuart, being admitted king of England and entrusted with a limited power, yet nevertheless, from a wicked design to erect an unlimited and tyrannical government, had traitorously and maliciously levied war against the present Parliament and the people whom they represented, and was therefore impeached as a tyrant, traitor, murderer, and a public and implacable enemy to the commonwealth. After the charge was finished, the president directed his discourse to the king and told him that the court expected his answer.

The king, though long detained a prisoner and now produced as a criminal, sustained by his magnanimous courage the majesty of a monarch. With great temper and dignity, he declined the authority of the court and refused to submit himself to their jurisdiction. He represented that having been engaged in treaty with his two houses of Parliament and having finished almost every article, he had expected to be brought to his capital in another manner and ere this time to have been restored to his power, dignity, revenue, as well as to his personal liberty. That he could not now perceive any appearance of the upper house, so essential a member of the constitution, and had learned that even the Commons, whose authority was pretended [claimed], were subdued by lawless force and were bereaved of their liberty. That he himself was their *native hereditary king*; nor was the whole authority of the state, though free and united, entitled to try him, who derived his dignity from the Supreme Majesty of heaven. That admitting those extravagant principles which leveled all orders of men, the court could plead no power delegated by the people unless the consent of every individual, down to the meanest and most ignorant peasant, had been previously asked and obtained. That he acknowledged without scruple that he had a trust committed to him, and one most sacred and inviolable: he was entrusted with the liberties of his people, and would not now betray them by recognizing a power founded on the most atrocious violence and usurpation. That having taken arms and frequently exposed his life in defense of public liberty, of the constitution, of the fundamental laws of the kingdom, he was willing, in this last and most solemn scene, to seal with his blood those precious rights for which, though in vain, he had so long contended. That those who arrogated a title to sit as his judges were born his subjects, and born subjects to those laws which determined,

"That the king can do no wrong." That he was not reduced to the necessity of sheltering himself under this general maxim—which guards every English monarch, even the least deserving—but was able by the most satisfactory reasons to justify those measures in which he had been engaged. That to the whole world, and even to them, his pretended judges, he was desirous, if called upon in another manner, to prove the integrity of his conduct and assert the justice of those defensive arms to which, unwillingly and unfortunately, he had had recourse. But that in order to preserve a uniformity of conduct, he must at present forgo the apology of his innocence, lest by ratifying an authority no better founded than that of robbers and pirates, he be justly branded as the betrayer, instead of being applauded as the martyr, of the constitution.

The president, in order to support the majesty of the people and maintain the superiority of his court above the prisoner, still inculcated that he must not decline the authority of his judges; that they overruled his objections; that they were delegated by the people, the only source of every lawful power; and that kings themselves acted but in trust from that community, which had invested this High Court of Justice with its jurisdiction. Even according to those principles which in his present situation he was perhaps obliged to adopt, his behavior in general will appear not a little harsh and barbarous; but when we consider him as a subject—and one too of no high rank—addressing himself to his unfortunate sovereign, his style will be deemed to the last degree audacious and insolent.

Three times was Charles produced before the court, and as often declined their jurisdiction. On the fourth, on January 27, the judges having examined some witnesses by whom it was proved that the king had appeared in arms against the forces commissioned by the Parliament, they pronounced sentence against him. He seemed very anxious at this time to be admitted to a conference with the two houses; and it was supposed that he intended to resign the Crown to his son. But the court refused compliance and considered that request as nothing but a delay of justice.

It is confessed that the king's behavior during this last scene of his life does honor to his memory; and that in all appearances before his judges, he never forgot his part, either as a prince or as a man. Firm and intrepid, he maintained in each reply the utmost perspicuity and justness, both of thought and expression. Mild and equable, he rose into no passion at that unusual authority which was assumed over him. His soul, without effort or affectation, seemed only to remain in the situation familiar to it and to look down with contempt on all the efforts of human malice and iniquity. The soldiers, instigated by their superiors, were brought, though with difficulty, to cry aloud for justice. "Poor souls!" said the king to one of his attendants. "For a little money they would do as much against their commanders." Some of them were permitted to go the utmost length of brutal insolence and to spit in his face as he was conducted along the passage to the court. To excite a sentiment of piety was the only effect which this inhuman insult was able to produce upon him.

The people, though under the rod of lawless, unlimited power, could not forbear pouring forth their wishes for his preservation with the most ardent prayers; and by their generous tears, they avowed him in his present distress for their monarch, whom they had before, in their misguided fury, so violently rejected. The king was softened at this moving scene and expressed his gratitude for their dutiful affection. One soldier too, seized by contagious sympathy, demanded from heaven a blessing on oppressed and fallen majesty. His officer, overhearing the prayer, beat him to the ground in the king's presence. "The punishment, methinks, exceeds the offense"; this was the reflection which Charles formed on that occasion.

As soon as the intention of trying the king was known in foreign countries, so enormous an action was exclaimed against by the general voice of reason and humanity; and all men, under whatever form of government they were born, rejected the example as the utmost effort of undisguised usurpation and the most heinous insult on law and justice. The French ambassador, by orders from his court, interposed in the king's behalf; the Dutch employed their good offices; the Scots exclaimed and protested against the violence; the queen and the prince wrote pathetic letters to the Parliament. All solicitations were found fruitless with men whose resolutions were fixed and irrevocable.

Four of Charles's friends—Richmond, Hertford, Southampton, and Lindsey, persons of virtue and dignity—applied to the Commons. They represented that they were the king's counselors and had concurred by their advice in all those measures which were now imputed as crimes to their royal master; that in the eye of the law and according to the dictates of common reason, they alone were guilty and were alone exposed to censure for every blamable action of the prince; and that they now presented themselves in order to save by their own punishment that precious life which it became the Commons themselves and every subject with the utmost hazard to protect and defend. Such a generous effort tended to their honor, but it contributed nothing towards the king's safety.

The people remained in that silence and astonishment which all great passions, when they have not an opportunity of exerting themselves, naturally produce in the human mind. The soldiers, being incessantly plied with prayers, sermons, and exhortations, were wrought up to a degree of fury and imagined that in the acts of the most extreme disloyalty towards their prince consisted their greatest merit in the eye of heaven.

Three days were allowed the king between his sentence and his execution. This interval he passed with great tranquility, chiefly in reading and devotion. All his family that remained in England were allowed access to him. It consisted only of the princess Elizabeth and the Duke of Gloucester, for the Duke of York had made his escape. Gloucester was little more than an infant. The princess, notwithstanding her tender years, showed an advanced judgment; and the calamities of her family had made a deep impression upon her. After many pious consolations and advices, the king gave her in charge to tell the queen that during the whole course of his life, he had never once, even in thought, failed in his fidelity towards her, and that his conjugal tenderness and his life would have an equal duration.

He could not forbear giving some advice to the young duke too, in order to season his mind with early principles of loyalty and obedience towards his brother, who was so soon to be his sovereign. Holding him on his knee, he said, "Now they will cut off thy father's head." At these words, the child looked very steadfastly upon him. "Mark! child, what I say. They will cut off my head! And perhaps make thee a king. But mark what I say. Thou must not be a king as long as thy brothers, Charles and James, are alive. They will cut off thy brothers' heads, when they can catch them! And thy head too they will cut off at last! Therefore I charge thee, do not be made a king by them!" The duke, sighing, replied, "I will be torn in pieces first!" So determined an answer from one of such tender years filled the king's eyes with tears of joy and admiration.

Every night during this interval, the king slept as soundly as usual, though the noise of workmen employed in framing the scaffold and other preparations for his execution continually resounded in his ears. The morning of the fatal day, January 30, he rose early; calling Herbert, one of his attendants, he bade him employ more than usual care in dressing and preparing him for so great and joyful a solemnity. Bishop Juxon, a man endowed with the same mild and steady virtues by which the king himself was so much distinguished, assisted him in his devotions and paid the last melancholy duties to his friend and sovereign.

And execution

The street before Whitehall was the place destined for the execution; for it was intended by choosing that very place, in sight of his own palace, to display more clearly the triumph of popular justice over royal majesty. When the king came upon the scaffold, he found it so surrounded with soldiers that he could not expect to be heard by any of the people. He addressed, therefore, his discourse to the few persons who were about him, particularly Colonel Tomlinson, to whose care he had lately been committed and upon whom, as upon many others, his amiable deportment had wrought an entire conversion. He justified his own innocence in the late fatal wars and observed that he had not taken arms till after the Parliament had enlisted forces; nor had he any other object in his warlike operations than to preserve that authority entire which his predecessors had transmitted to him. He threw not, however, the blame upon the Parliament, but was more inclined to think that ill instruments had interposed and raised in them fears and jealousies with regard to his intentions. Though innocent towards his people, he acknowledged the equity of his execution in the eyes of his Maker and observed that an unjust sentence which he had suffered to take effect was now punished by an unjust sentence upon himself. He forgave all his enemies, even the chief instruments of his death, but exhorted them and the whole nation to return to the ways of peace by paying obedience to their lawful sovereign, his son and successor. When he was preparing himself for the block, Bishop Juxon called to him. "There is, sir, but one stage more, which, though turbulent and troublesome, is yet a very short one. Consider, it will soon carry you a great way; it will carry you from earth to heaven; and there you shall find, to your great joy, the prize to which you hasten, a crown of glory." "I go," replied the king, "from a corruptible to an incorruptible crown, where no disturbance can have place." At one blow was his head severed from his body. A man in a visor performed the office of executioner. Another in a like disguise held up to the spectators the head, streaming with blood, and cried aloud, "This is the head of a traitor!"

It is impossible to describe the grief, indignation, and astonishment which took place, not only among the spectators, who were overwhelmed with a flood of sorrow, but throughout the whole nation, as soon as the report of this fatal execution was conveyed to them. Never monarch in the full triumph of success and victory was more dear to his people than his misfortunes and magnanimity, his patience and piety, had rendered this unhappy prince. The violence of their return to duty and affection was in proportion to that of their former delusions which had animated them against him; and each reproached himself either with active disloyalty towards him or with too indolent defense of his oppressed cause. On weaker minds, the effect of these complicated passions was prodigious. Women are said to have cast forth the untimely fruit of their womb. Others fell into convulsions or sunk into such a melancholy as attended them to their grave. Indeed, some, it is reported, unmindful of themselves as though they could not or would not survive their beloved prince, suddenly fell down dead. The very pulpits which had formerly thundered out the most violent imprecations and anathemas against him were now bedewed with honest tears. And all men united in their detestation of those hypocritical parricides who had so long disguised their treasons by sanctified pretenses, and in this last act of iniquity had thrown an indelible stain upon the nation.

A fresh instance of hypocrisy was displayed the very day of the king's death. The generous Fairfax, not content with being absent from the trial, had used all the influence which he yet retained to prevent the execution of the fatal sentence; he had even employed persuasion with his own regiment, though none else would follow him, to rescue the king from his disloyal murderers. Cromwell and Ireton, informed of this intention, endeavored to convince him that the Lord had rejected the king; and they exhorted him to seek by prayer some direction from heaven on this important occasion. But they concealed from him that they had already signed the warrant for the execution. Harrison was the person appointed to join in prayer with the unwary general. By agreement, he prolonged his doleful cant till intelligence arrived that the fatal blow was struck. He then rose from his knees and insisted with Fairfax that this event was a miraculous and providential answer which heaven had sent to their devout supplications.

It was remarked that the king, the moment before he stretched out his neck to the executioner, had said to Juxon with a very earnest accent the single word, "Remember." Great mysteries were supposed to be concealed under that expression; and the generals vehemently insisted that the prelate inform them of the king's meaning. Juxon told them that the king, having frequently charged him to inculcate on his son the forgiveness of his murderers, had taken this opportunity—in the last moment of his life, when his commands, he supposed, would be regarded as sacred and inviolable—to reiterate that desire; and that his mild spirit thus terminated its present course by an act of benevolence towards his greatest enemies.

And character

The character of this prince, as that of most men, if not of all men, was mixed; but his virtues predominated extremely above his vices—or more properly speaking, his imperfections, for scarcely any of his faults rose to that pitch as to merit the appellation of vices. To consider him in the most favorable light, it may be affirmed that his dignity was free from pride, his humanity from weakness, his bravery from rashness, his temperance from austerity, his frugality from avarice; all these virtues in him maintained their proper bounds and merited unreserved praise. To speak the most harshly of him, we may affirm that many of his good qualities were attended with some latent frailty which, though seemingly inconsiderable, was able, when seconded by the extreme malevolence of his fortune, to disappoint them of all their influence. His beneficent disposition was clouded by a manner not very gracious, his virtue was tinctured with superstition, his good sense was disfigured by a deference to persons of a capacity inferior to his own, and his moderate temper did not exempt him from hasty and precipitate resolutions. He deserves the epithet of a good rather than of a great man; and he was more fitted to rule in a regular established government than either to give way to the encroachments of a popular assembly or finally to subdue their pretensions. He lacked suppleness and dexterity sufficient for the first measure; he was not endowed with the vigor requisite for the second. Had he been born an absolute prince, his humanity and good sense would have rendered his reign happy and his memory precious. Had the limitations on prerogative been in his time quite fixed and certain, his integrity would have made him regard as sacred the boundaries of the constitution. Unhappily, his fate threw him into a period when the precedents of many former reigns savored strongly of arbitrary power and the genius of the people ran violently towards liberty. And if his political prudence was not sufficient to extricate him from so perilous a situation, he may be excused; since even after the event, when it is commonly easy to correct all errors, one is at a loss to determine what conduct in his circumstances could have maintained the authority of the Crown and preserved the peace of the nation. Exposed—without revenue, without arms—to the assault of furious, implacable, and bigoted factions, he was never permitted to commit the smallest mistake without the most fatal consequences, a condition too rigorous to be imposed on the greatest human capacity.

Some historians have rashly questioned the good faith of this prince; but for this reproach, the most malignant scrutiny of his conduct, which in every circumstance is now thoroughly known, affords not any reasonable foundation. On the contrary, if we consider the extreme difficulties to which he was so frequently reduced and compare the sincerity of his professions and declarations, we shall avow that probity and honor ought justly to be numbered among his most shining qualities. In every treaty, those concessions which he thought he could not in conscience maintain, he never could by any motive or persuasion be induced to make. And though some violations of the Petition of Right may perhaps be imputed to him, these are more to be ascribed to the necessity of his situation and to the lofty ideas of royal prerogative which from former established precedents he had imbibed than to any failure in the integrity of his principles.

This prince was of a comely presence, of a sweet but melancholy aspect. His face was regular, handsome, and well complexioned; his body strong, healthy, and justly proportioned; and being of a middle stature, he was capable of enduring the greatest fatigues. He excelled in horsemanship and other exercises; and he possessed all the exterior, as well as many of the essential, qualities which form an accomplished prince.

The tragic death of Charles begat a question whether the people in any case were entitled to judge and to punish their sovereign; and most men, regarding chiefly the atrocious usurpation of the pretended judges and the merit of the virtuous prince who suffered, were inclined to condemn the republican principle as highly seditious and extravagant. But there still were a few who, abstracting from the particular circumstances of this case, were able to consider the question in general and were inclined to moderate, not contradict, the prevailing sentiment. Such might have been their reasoning: If ever on any occasion it were laudable to conceal truth from the populace, it must be confessed that the doctrine of resistance affords such an example; and

that all speculative reasoners ought to observe with regard to this principle the same cautious silence which the laws in every species of government have always prescribed to themselves. Government is instituted in order to restrain the fury and injustice of the people; and being always founded on opinion, not on force, it is dangerous to weak-
en by these speculations the reverence which the multitude owe to authority and to instruct them beforehand that the case can ever happen
when they may be freed from their duty of allegiance. Or should it be
found impossible to restrain the license of human disquisitions, it
must be acknowledged that only the doctrine of obedience ought to
be *inculcated*, and that the exceptions, which are rare, ought seldom or
never to be mentioned in popular reasonings and discourses. Nor is
there any danger that mankind by this prudent reserve would universally degenerate into a state of abject servitude. When the exception
really occurs, even though it be not previously expected and discussed
at length, it must from its very nature be so obvious and undisputed as
to remove all doubt and overpower the restraint, however great, imposed by teaching the general doctrine of obedience. But between resisting a prince and dethroning him there is a wide interval; and the
abuses of power which can warrant the latter violence are greater and
more enormous than those which will justify the former. History,
however, supplies us with examples even of this kind; and the reality
of the supposition, though for the future it ought always to be little
looked for, must by all candid inquirers be acknowledged in the past.
But between dethroning a prince and punishing him there is another
very wide interval; and it would not be strange if even men of the most
enlarged thought would question whether human nature could ever,
in any monarch, reach that height of depravity as to warrant in revolu-
tionary subjects this last act of extraordinary jurisdiction. That illusion—if it be an illusion—which teaches us to pay a sacred regard to the
persona of princes is so salutary that to dissipate it by the formal trial
and punishment of a sovereign will have more pernicious effects upon
the people than the example of justice can be supposed to have a beneficial influence upon princes by checking their career of tyranny. It is
dangerous also by these examples to reduce princes to despair or bring
matters to such extremities against persons endowed with great power
as to leave them no resource but in the most violent and most sanguinary counsels. This general position being established, it must, however, be observed that no reader, almost of any party or principle, was
ever shocked when he read in ancient history that the Roman Senate

voted Nero, their absolute sovereign, to be a public enemy and condemned him, even without trial, to the severest and most ignominious punishment, a punishment from which the meanest Roman citizen was by the laws exempted. The crimes of that bloody tyrant are so enormous that they break through all rules and extort a confession that such a dethroned prince is no longer superior to his people and can no longer plead in his own defense laws which were established for conducting the ordinary course of administration. But when we pass from the case of Nero to that of Charles, the great disproportion, or rather the total contrariety, of character immediately strikes us; and we stand astonished that so much virtue could ever meet with so fatal a catastrophe among a civilized people. History, the great mistress of wisdom, furnishes examples of all kinds; and every prudential as well as moral precept may be authorized by those events which her enlarged mirror is able to present to us. From the memorable revolutions which passed in England during this period, we may naturally deduce the same useful lesson which Charles himself in his later years inferred: that it is dangerous for princes, even from the appearance of necessity, to assume more authority than the laws have allowed them. But it must be confessed that these events furnish us with another instruction no less natural and no less useful concerning the madness of the people, the furies of fanaticism, and the danger of mercenary armies.

In order to close this part of British history, it is also necessary to relate the dissolution of the monarchy in England. That event soon followed upon the death of the monarch. When the Peers met on the day appointed in their adjournment, February 6, they entered upon business and sent down some votes to the Commons, of which the latter deigned not to take the least notice. In a few days, the lower house passed a vote that they would make no more addresses to the House of Peers nor receive any from them, and that that house was useless and dangerous and was therefore to be abolished. A like vote passed with regard to the monarchy; and it is remarkable that Marten, a zealous republican, in the debate on this question confessed that if they desired a king, the last was as proper as any gentleman in England. The Commons ordered a new great seal to be engraved, on which that assembly was represented, with this legend: "On the first year of freedom, by God's blessing, restored, 1648." ["1648" rather than "1649" because at that time the year number changed on March 25.] The forms of all public business were changed from the king's name to that of the keepers of the liberties of England. And it was declared high treason to proclaim or otherwise acknowledge Charles Stuart, commonly called Prince of Wales.

The Commons intended, it is said, to bind the princess Elizabeth apprentice to a button maker; the Duke of Gloucester was to be taught some other mechanical employment. But the former soon died—of grief, as is supposed, for her father's tragic end; the latter was sent overseas by Cromwell.

The king's statue in the Exchange was thrown down, and on the pedestal these words were inscribed: *Exit tyrannus, regum ultimus.* "The tyrant is gone, the last of the kings."

The Duke of Hamilton was tried, as Earl of Cambridge in England, by a new High Court of Justice and condemned for treason. This sentence, which was certainly hard but which ought to save his memory from all imputations of treachery to his master, was executed on a scaffold erected before Westminster Hall. Lord Capell underwent the same fate. Both these noblemen had escaped from prison but were afterwards discovered and taken. To all the solicitations of their friends for pardon, the generals and parliamentary leaders replied that it was certainly the intention of Providence that they should suffer, since it had permitted them to fall into the hands of their enemies after they had once recovered their liberty.

The Earl of Holland lost his life by a like sentence. Though of a polite and courtly behavior, he died lamented by no party. His ingratitude to the king and his frequent changing of sides were regarded as great stains on his memory. The Earl of Norwich and Sir John Owen, being condemned by the same court, were pardoned by the Commons.

It may be expected that we should here mention the *Eikon Basilike*, a work published in the king's name a few days after his execution. In the controverted parts of history, it seems almost impossible to say anything which will satisfy the zealots of both parties; but with regard to the genuineness of that production, it is not easy for a historian to fix any opinion which will be entirely to his own satisfaction. The proofs brought to evince that this work is or is not the king's are so convincing that if an impartial reader peruse any one side apart, he will think it impossible that arguments could be produced sufficient to counterbalance so strong an evidence. And when he compares both sides, he will be some time at a loss to fix any determination. Should an absolute suspense of judgment be found difficult or disagreeable in so interesting a question, I must confess that I much incline to give the preference to the arguments of the Royalists. The testimonies which prove that performance to be the king's are more numerous, certain, and direct than those on the other side. This is the case even if we consider the external evidence; but when we weigh the internal, derived from the style and composition, there is no manner of comparison. These meditations resemble, in elegance, purity, neatness, and simplicity, the genius of those performances which we know with certainty to have flowed from the royal pen; but they are so unlike the bombastic, perplexed, rhetorical, and corrupt style of Dr. Gauden, to whom they are ascribed, that no human testimony seems sufficient to convince us that he was the author. Yet all the evidences which would rob the king of that honor tend to prove that Dr. Gauden had the merit of writing so fine a performance and the infamy of imposing it on the world for the king's.

It is not easy to conceive the general compassion excited towards the king by the publishing at so critical a juncture of a work so full of piety, meekness, and humanity. Many have not hesitated to ascribe to that book the subsequent restoration of the royal family. Milton compared its effects to those which were wrought on the tumultuous Romans by Antony's reading to them the will of Caesar. The *Eikon* passed through fifty editions in a year; and independent of the great interest taken in it by the nation as the supposed production of their murdered sovereign, it must be acknowledged the best prose composition which at the time of its publication was to be found in the English language.

DAVID HUME'S *HISTORY OF ENGLAND*, EDITED FOR THE MODERN READER: VOLUME 5, 1603-1649

The running text is set in Goudy Old Style, a typeface designed by Frederic W. Goudy in 1915; chapter heads, subheads, headers, footers, and date boxes are set in Century Schoolbook, designed by Morris Fuller Benton in 1918; cover and title page are set in Lucida Bright, designed by Charles Bigelow and Kris Holmes in 1985.

Front cover:
John de Critz the Elder, *James I of England*, 1605
Anthony van Dyck, *Charles I, King of England, from Three Angles*, 1636

Back cover, clockwise from top left:
Allan Ramsay, *David Hume*, 1766
Paul Delaroche, *Charles I Insulted by Cromwell's Soldiers*, 1836
Anthony van Dyck, *Thomas Wentworth, 1st Earl of Strafford, with Sir Philip Mainwaring*, 1639-40
Paul Delaroche, *Cromwell and the Corpse of Charles I*, 1831
Anthony van Dyck, *William Laud*, c. 1636
John Barker, *The Battle of Marston Moor, 1644*, 19th century
Samuel Cooper, *Oliver Cromwell*, 1656
Dupuis after Parrocel, *Battle of Naseby*, 1727
Unknown artist, *Prince Rupert of the Rhine*, 17th century

All cover images are in the public domain and were downloaded from Wikimedia Commons.

Cover design by Richard C. Berry.

Made in the USA
Middletown, DE
31 July 2019